THE COMPLETE BOOK OF
Children's Play

THE COMPLETE BOOK OF

Children's Play

By

RUTH E. HARTLEY, Ph.D.

and

ROBERT M. GOLDENSON, Ph.D.

INTRODUCTION BY LAWRENCE K. FRANK
Formerly Director, Caroline Zachry Institute
for Human Development

REVISED EDITION

THOMAS Y. CROWELL COMPANY

NEW YORK

Dedicated to Two Girls
Sue and Wendy Hartley

And Two Boys
Ronald and Danny Goldenson

Copyright © 1963, 1957 by Ruth E. Hartley and Robert M. Goldenson

All rights reserved. No part of this book may be reproduced in any form, except by a reviewer, without the permission of the publisher.

Manufactured in the United States of America

Library of Congress Catalog Card No. 63-18414
ISBN 0-8152-0245-8
Apollo Edition, 1970

to adults, he seeks in his play and creative activities to discover himself—to learn who and what he is, what he can do, and how he can relate himself to things and situations, to persons and groups. Much of the basic orientation to social life is achieved in the preschool years, primarily in the child's play where, day after day, he faces, in miniature or symbolically, all the crucial tasks of human living. What he learns in his play usually becomes the core of his subsequent life just as his feelings toward people in these early years may color and give the dominant tone to his later experiences.

To meet this need for play we have available today an immense store of toys and playthings, games and creative materials, sometimes bewildering in their variety and quality. To choose wisely from this great array for a particular child at his stage of development may be a baffling task for adults. We have long needed a book of this kind to give parents, grandparents, uncles and aunts, friends of the family, and teachers some guides and criteria for selection. And, as the authors point out, in addition to toys and playthings, there are in every home rich resources of potential play materials which may be as appealing and desirable—if not more so, for many kinds of play—as purchased toys.

To recognize how the child matures, playing and enjoying experiences, then outgrowing that stage of play and eagerly entering the next, is the key to understanding children's play. This recognition offers the best guides to appropriate and acceptable play materials. Too often adults underestimate a child's maturity and give him toys that no longer will evoke his interest and capacity for new learning. And then we may also err by giving him toys that are too complicated for his limited understanding and skills. It seems safer and wiser to provide toys that will be just on the margin of his growing capacities, that will challenge and provoke his imagination and stretch his skills so he will enjoy the triumph of mastering them. But every child treasures a few old toys and playthings that serve as secure landmarks and sanctuaries in the bewildering world of adults.

As the child enters the middle years and then goes on into the second decade, his need to play, to use his imagination, does not cease; it is focussed in new directions and calls for new materials and experiences, congruous with his developing interests and capacities. He is fortunate if he can discover at this time interests that will provide play experience for his adult life.

Since this volume spans the years from infancy through adolescence, it can be warmly commended to parents and other adults as a dependable guide to the world of play for all children. Especially important is the use of toys, play, and creative materials for the many handicapped children—the crippled, the blind, the deaf, the mentally retarded, those with cerebral palsy or polio—since through play each of these children can often learn more quickly and happily how to overcome, at least partially, his limitations and can develop his capacities more fully.

The child who plays is engaged upon what to him is most important, and his play should be encouraged and above all respected as this book so clearly emphasizes.

Acknowledgments

I CANNOT ADEQUATELY ACKNOWLEDGE my debt to all the teachers, therapists, and research workers from whom I have borrowed through the years much that is reflected here. A few who were particularly important in my professional development, however, must be mentioned: Caroline Zachry for her inspiration, Anni Weiss-Frankl for patient guidance, and Lois Barclay Murphy for encouragement when it was most needed.

I owe much to Lawrence K. Frank, who invited me in 1947 to conduct, for the Caroline Zachry Institute for Human Development, a study of the function of play and group activities in fostering healthy personality development in children. Without the years of intensive observation, of gathering and analyzing records, of testing toys and play materials with hundreds of children that that invitation made possible, I doubt that this book would have been written.

My thanks also go to others who helped in lesser but still important ways: to Dr. Grace Langdon and Mrs. Sidonie Gruenberg for their interest in this project, to Mary Frank for many helpful suggestions, to the dozens of manufacturers who graciously sent their products to me for testing on request, to the Child Study Association of America, the Playschool Association, and *Parents' Magazine* for making their materials freely available.

My debt to Margaret C. Dawson for her sympathetic and perceptive editorial contribution can never be fully expressed.

Finally my deepest gratitude goes to my unacknowledged partners in this enterprise: my husband, Eugene L. Hartley, whose unfailing patience and fortitude made the completion of my task possible, and my daughters, Sue Ann and Wendy Ellen, whose enthusiastic cooperation taught me much that I am hoping to share here with other parents.

RUTH E. HARTLEY

Long Island University
Brooklyn

GRATEFUL ACKNOWLEDGMENT IS MADE TO *Child Study, Parents' Magazine,* and *National Parent-Teacher* for permission to use material from articles that I contributed.

To my wife, Irene, I owe my gratitude for sustained interest and particularly for her comments on rhythmic and dance activities. The developing play life of my two sons has been a source of many helpful observations, and they have served as willing subjects in testing many ideas.

Dr. Hartley joins me in expressing our warm appreciation to Mr. Robert L. Crowell for his unfailing aid and encouragement in the task of publishing a book of this scope.

ROBERT M. GOLDENSON

New York

The introductory chapter and chapters I through VIII were written by Dr. Hartley, chapters IX through XIX by Dr. Goldenson.

Contents

	About Play and Players	1
I.	The First Year: Play Begins	9
II.	The Second Year: Enter the Runabout	24
III.	The In-Betweeners: From Two to Three	39
IV.	Three: Settling In	68
V.	Four: Age of Expansion	88
VI.	Five: Welcome to Reality	114
VII.	Six: A New Beginning	144
VIII.	Seven: The Socialite	175
IX.	Eight and Nine	213
X.	Play in the Preteens	230
XI.	What Play Can Do for Teen-Agers	256
XII.	We All Need a Hobby	281
XIII.	Ready-Made Play: Television, Radio, Comic Books, Movies, Records	299
XIV.	They All Want Pets	315
XV.	Finding Room for Play	331
XVI.	Play as You Go	340
XVII.	The Doctor Prescribes Play	348
XVIII.	Fun on the Town	362
XIX.	Play That Develops Minds	369
	Appendix	391
	Household Items to Save and Use in Play	393
	Play Materials to Buy for Different Ages	398

Building Play Equipment	405
Records	419
Song Books	427
Some Reproductions of Pictures for Children's Rooms	428
Books for Younger Children	432
Hobby and Informational Books and Pamphlets, and Sources of Information for Older Children	453
Magazines for Creative Play	466
References for Parents and Recreation and Hobby Leaders	468
Organizations Promoting Leisure-Time Interests	471
Guide to Community Service	475
Index	477

About Play and Players

This Thing Called Play

A wise man said once, "Play is the child's response to life," and this remains profoundly true. Almost where life begins, play begins. No harassed housewife is busier than the playing child and no statesman pondering his country's policies must make more momentous decisions. For play is not only the child's response to life; it *is* his life, if he is to be a vital, growing, creative individual.

Consider all the ways in which play serves the child. First, it teaches him (and by *him* we also mean *her* throughout the book) what the world is—how high is up and what is meant by down; what is soft and what is hard, what solid and what hollow, the meaning of inside and outside, wet and dry, and shape and form.

Second, it teaches him about himself. He learns what he can do to the world outside, where he is strong and where weak, and how a series of failures can lead to success. While he is playing he strengthens his muscles, improves his perceptions, learns new skills, lets off excess energy, tries out different solutions to his problems, practices the tasks of life, learns how to deal with other people, and, eventually, comes to know the values and the symbols of his world. With all this to accomplish, the child must play hard—and he often needs help.

Why Talk About Play?

We talk about play more these days than we used to because we know more about it—how it helps the child (and adult) to develop, when certain kinds of activities can best make their contributions, what tools are needed, and what a child's play can tell us about him as a person: his needs, his problems, his satisfactions, and his strengths. Also, the resources for leisure-time activity have multiplied to such an extent that a guidebook is needed so that parents will know what to look for, where to find it, and when it will be most beneficial and enjoyable for their children.

It was only a short time ago that we discovered that play could heal sick minds and bodies. We found out that sometimes only play could preserve sanity, by preventing a dangerous pile-up of too much feeling. We watched limbs that were crippled by palsy or polio grow supple and strong through playful exercise. With these lessons before us, it is time to ask how much, then, play can do for minds and bodies that are whole.

We have found that play also has something to contribute to the education of our children. We know that the best and most lasting learning takes place when the learner is enjoying what he is doing. In play the child does what springs spontaneously from his mind and heart; here he is most nearly whole, self-directed, open, and creative—and in this kind of situation he learns best. That is why teachers are welcoming play to the classroom, cannily planning to capture some of its magic for the serious tasks they must direct. No longer is a sharp line drawn between curricular and extracurricular activities.

Now that we are becoming increasingly freed from drudgery (and often from creativity also) by machines, children and adults have more and more time on their hands. The use of this time will become a real problem in adult life if creative activity does not gain a firm foothold in childhood and become an integral part of life. When we find ourselves with extra time, it is usually too late to start learning how to use it wisely.

Children Are Different

Every child is different from every other child. The "average" four-year-old or seven-year-old is a mythical creature, made of bits and pieces of many fours and sevens. No child on the face of the earth is likely to do everything exactly as we describe it in the following chapters, at exactly the ages we suggest. Many will come close in most respects, but in one way or another will lag behind or spring ahead. Some will seem different in many ways. Fine; the child is what he is; a book is only a book. We truly hope that all parents who read here will look at their offspring first, and if they must judge, use their children as the measure of the book, not the book as the pattern for the child.

There *are* children who differ more from the average than others, of course. We mean those who are not endowed as fortunately as their fellows in some way—the clumsy, the slow, the overly sensitive. These may not delight in all the activities mentioned in the chapters on play for different age levels, or they may not prove proficient at the age described. What of that? The child remains the measure of himself. If his interests, his abilities, his feelings are read correctly, he can still be helped to reach the highest level of which he is capable, and there is no achievement beyond that.

A little ingenuity helps. A child who cannot run well may be a whiz on a horse. A poor ball-player can be a good craftsman. A clumsy jumper may be good on the harmonica. The point is to give the child a chance to find out. Failure at one activity does not necessarily mean there will be no success with another. Not resignation, but high optimism should be the keynote for the unsuccessful in one field. If we demand of any child that he be most fully like himself, not like his fellows, he cannot fail.

One word of caution: parents face a subtle enemy in the word *cannot*. The four-year-old defeated by his tricycle may yet turn into the Twelve who hostels by bicycle. Phrases like "Why can't you" and "I can't" *must* be banished. Instead, "A little more practice," "When you are older," "Keep trying—it will come"—these will frequently lead to success and self-fulfillment if they are used with real belief. And if they do not, we can usually guide the child to at least moderate success in some other activity.

Awareness, patience, acceptance can bring almost any child through the tribulations of mildly disjointed early years to effective and happy functioning in maturity.

Keeping the Fun in Play

We must not merely accept the fact that play is important in the child's life. We must also remember that it is important because it belongs to the child and because he enjoys it. We must be careful not to take it away from him, to manage and manipulate all the fun out of it with good intentions. If we are skillful, we may be able to play *with* a child; we cannot play *for* him.

The most helpful way a parent can contribute to his child's play life, it seems to us, is to provide the materials, space, and opportunities for the kinds of play activities the child needs. This means planning and finding out something about the abilities and interests of children at different developmental levels, and standing by for times of need.

Planning for Play

Aside from providing play space and materials, the kind of planning that prevents trouble usually revolves about safety factors and the mechanics of housekeeping. If, for example, one knows that children of a certain age enjoy climbing, it is easier to provide them with safe climbing opportunities than to prevent them from climbing where there would be danger. Similarly, anticipating that youngsters are going to love messy and drippy kinds of play, it is best to designate a special place where water and finger paints, mud and clay, may be used without damage to the surroundings.

A good deal of friction often centers on keeping toys neat and picking up after the play is over. Suggestions are made in the early chapters for providing low open shelves rather than a toy chest, and of rotating the use of toys.

Clothing is another thing that often takes the fun out of play. Nobody can really play wholeheartedly if he has to worry about getting himself dirty or tearing his clothes. Light-colored play clothes are inappropriate if laundering presents problems or if the parent is concerned about what the neighbors will think of a messy child. Sometimes an apron or plastic poncho will help. But it is the inalienable privilege of childhood to get messy as soon as possible and to remain that way until play is over for the day.

Ruggedness is also a quality to keep in mind when buying or making play clothes for the child. One cannot play with a divided mind. It is impossible to lose oneself in play while trying to remember not to tear one's clothes; it is almost impossible to play at all if one must anticipate a scolding after every play session. Clothing must be considered expendable; hard wear and even rips should be expected. Reinforcing patches of leather at the points of hardest wear will do much to keep the zest in play and peace in the household.

Party clothes are especially delicate subjects for discussion. There are many parents who feel strongly that one should wear one's "best" clothes for parties. There is nothing wrong with that if "best" clothes are also bought with play in mind, but most often they are not. Then we have the situation in which the poor child is sent off to have a good time wearing clothing that he must be careful not to spoil. But being careful of clothing and having a good time just don't go together in childhood. What happens? One or the other has to give, and either the child or the parent is unhappy—probably both are. The first mother who thought up a "blue-jeans" party is unknown, but she deserves our thanks.

Investing the Toy Dollar

When we buy toys, we are investing our money as surely as when we buy stocks, and the commodity we are investing in may be more important than shares in a concern. We should expect a fair return for our dollar in terms of play interest, encouragement, improvement in skills, and length of service . . . and price is often no criterion of the toy's worth. While a cheap toy may be worse than no toy at all, not all expensive toys are good toys.

To know how to buy wisely, we must establish some general rules. Ordinarily, one cannot depend on most salesclerks or toy manufacturers for guidance. Their job is to sell toys, not to give advice. It is the buyer's job to know how to get the most for his money. If he fails, he has no one to blame but himself.

Some clues to wise choices are fairly obvious. If a child will not or cannot play with a toy, it represents a waste. Therefore, to be a good plaything, a toy must fit in with a child's current interest, and it must be within his level of skill to handle. The child must be the master and manipulator—the toy must be the tool. A tool demanding skills which one does not have and cannot acquire at the moment is not a very useful tool.

The toy that can be used for more than one purpose is often a better purchase than one which is limited to one use only. If possible, a good basic toy should lend itself to different kinds of play and maintain its usefulness for several years. The five-year-old may play with it in one way, and the seven-year-old in quite another, but at either age the toy fits in with the child's needs and can be manipulated to suit his ends. Blocks are a good example of flexible toys. The two-year-old piles them, the four-year-old builds with them, and the seven-year-old uses them to make villages for his trains to go through.

It is almost belaboring the obvious to point out that a toy should be sturdy enough to last beyond one play session, and yet —parents spend considerable sums on ephemeral playthings. There are, of course, those fragile bits of nonsense that one buys for special occasions, and that seem to be created to be destroyed, but those are not the things one usually has in mind when one talks about *toys*. In general, we buy toys to be played with over a period of time, and the toy that breaks the first time it is used is not a good one and will disappoint the child to boot.

As with clothing, so with toys. If a toy has to be handled with special delicacy, in general, the child cannot enjoy playing with it. There may be a place for things of special beauty, to be taken out and looked at occasionally; but those are not toys—they are collector's items. A toy is to play with, and without extraordinary cautions. It is well to be suspicious of gaudy items with delicate parts. Plastic is especially suspect as a toy material. There are several kinds of plastic, and some shatter far too easily. Any plastic toy that has moving parts should be tested vigorously before purchase. One turn of a screw in the wrong direction may break an essential part, and the toy will be useless after that, although most of it survives intact.

Playthings also ought to do what they are supposed to do. If a toy has a moving belt, it should move when the proper part is manipulated. If it is supposed to squirt water, it should squirt water. Unfortunately, many toys promise to do many things they do not do. A child should not be subjected to the aggravation of trying to make a fraud operate. Inexpensive toys that promise much are rarely honest. Gears do not mesh, parts break easily, vacuums leak—all sorts of things happen very soon after they are put into use, and the buyer has no redress.

There is a more serious aspect to the purchase of poor toys than the mere loss of money, though that may be serious enough when the budget is tight. A toy which is too difficult or too delicate for the child to handle induces frustration; in the wake of frustration, anger follows naturally, and in the wake of anger, destruction. Play materials which are not appropriate or not honest may teach a child to destroy rather than to construct; they may discourage rather than encourage. There is too much at stake in selecting the tools of play to permit a salesclerk or a store policy to intimidate one. When a toy cannot be thoroughly examined, or tried out in operation, and where no guarantee is forthcoming, it should not be bought.

We have not spoken of safety factors because we shall be discussing them further on. Here we might simply point out that flimsy toys can be dangerous toys. Cheap finishes may be poisonous; poorly cured wood may splinter; metal that is not well tempered will shatter.

And here we come to the crux of the matter—the philosophy by which one buys toys. From what we have already said it should be obvious that purchasing toys is not a matter for the impulse of the moment. It needs to be planned ahead of time, on the basis of careful observation of the individual child, and some knowledge about the general level of skills and interests to be expected at his age level. If one is contemplating the purchase of a basic piece of equipment or a supply of materials which can be expected to hold the child's interest over a period of time, it is better not to compromise with quality. Buy the best possible, and skimp, if necessary, on less important toys.

For occasions like Christmas and birthdays, if more than one gift is expected, "extras" may be contrived very inexpensively, with the use of a little ingenuity and effort. Much will be said throughout this book about the advantages of making simple toys at home. A handy father (or mother or even a child) can put together just as useful, and less complicated, toys as stores offer, that will be less expensive and probably sturdier and better adapted to the child's needs. Specific information will be found at appropriate places.

The best play materials are often those we do not buy at all, but collect. "Beautiful junk" one delightful teacher calls these things—spools, paper rolls, foil paper, things that glitter, odd screws, hooks, pulleys, etc. With a little forethought it is possible to make up many intriguing "kits" for the young of all ages without much cash expenditure, and reserve the money for things that cannot be improvised. We shall be discussing these improvisations as we go along, and we can say with assurance that they are received with as much joy as any "boughten" thing if properly packaged and presented.

Yes, the buyer must beware. The lure of the toy counter is sometimes overwhelming. If we ask ourselves, "What will this toy do for the child?" before buying, we are less likely to make costly mistakes. If, furthermore, we ask, "How long will he be interested in it?" or "Why should he be interested in it for a long time?" we are more likely to make wise choices. If we insist on buying impulsively, we must be ready to take disappointment with good grace. We have no right, however, to impose disappointment on the child because of our bad judgment.

CHAPTER I

The First Year: Play Begins

WE ADULTS have well-developed apparatus for communication. In our sending equipment we have speech, writing, facial expression, and gesture. In our receiving equipment we have sight, hearing, smell, taste, and touch. We use them all every day. The month-old infant has had hardly any practice with his sending apparatus, other than his vocal cords, and his receiving apparatus is scarcely tuned up. He cannot direct his own hands for touching, and he cannot see very well at all.

However, he can *register* an astonishing number of things. His receiving equipment is miles ahead of his sending equipment. He registers what he hears; he registers what he feels; and in his faltering way he registers what he sees.

As soon as he enjoys sensations, play begins.

The baby's ears, for example, offer one of our earliest means of reaching him. Most infants are startled by loud, sudden noises, but soft, intimate talking and singing seem to soothe them. They learn to stop crying when they hear footsteps. Even the clink of dishes or the recurrent sound patterns of a clock (especially a chiming one or a cuckoo clock) can be interesting.

Going from sound to skin senses, we are on more familiar ground. Everyone knows that a baby, no matter how young, responds to patting and stroking. This kind of skin-play promotes the bond between the child and his elders. Five minutes before or after his bath are sufficient for a miniature "massage." "Exercises" are a form of body play and promote muscle tone. While the baby is lying on his back, his arms may be stretched out to the side, then folded across his chest, and the movement repeated several times. His legs may be raised and revolved in a gentle bicycling motion. After a few experiences, the baby usually smiles or laughs aloud as preparations for exercises begin. Incidentally, if a rhythmic nursery song or nonsense jingle accompanies the motions, everyone's pleasure is doubled.

Light soon comes into the picture. Even before he can focus his eyes, a baby will turn his head toward a window. When he is restless without apparent cause, turning on a light will often soothe him. At about three months, when the baby can follow moving objects with his eyes, a revolving nursery lamp throwing patterns of light and shadow on the ceiling will fascinate him for a time. This kind of eye play may be too strenuous, however, if continued for long periods.

His World Can Be Interesting

People are more interesting than things to a baby. We can make his experiences more meaningful if we try to associate objects with faces and voices. Instead of just putting a toy into the infant's hand, hold it up and move it, talking to him. If the toy makes a noise, so much the better. Then put it in his hand.

The amount of territory the three-month-old can take in with his eyes is still limited to what he can see directly above and at each side as he lies on his back. This means that most of the time he is studying the sides of his crib, the upper walls, and ceiling. It is up to the adult to make these areas as interesting as possible. Large, simple, brightly colored "pictures" will change the monotony of a wall. These may be squares of cloth or paper with bold designs, but you might also experiment with inexpensive prints of striking paintings, for it is not impossible that taste in art begins with the infant's first visual experiences.

Strips of shelf edging, attached to the side of the crib, and a few simple, colorful objects dangling from a cord or ribbon tied across the top give the child something to examine when he is alone. Try a gleaming spoon, bright plastic bracelets, and rattles. If you replace his crib's casters with the spring feet obtainable at any juvenile furniture store, the child's wriggles will make all these objects move. Decorate the head of the crib, too, so that he will have something to look at when he is lying on his stomach. Some stores now sell pretty bird mobiles, but mobiles that are quite as attractive can easily be made from bits of bright foil, paper, colored buttons, and other attractive objects balanced on stiff wire or slender dowels and hung from a string or a hat elastic. A mobile hung above the baby's head will provide fascination where before there was only an empty ceiling. Now, before the grab stage, is the time for these fragile eye entertainers.

The baby appreciates a change of scene. Moving him from one room to another or holding him in a sitting position in your lap widens his horizons and gives him a chance to grow familiar with furniture, windows, doorways. Sitting, he will often study anything bright—a block, spoon, or measuring cup—that is placed on a flat surface before him.

Taking Life in His Own Hands

One day, when he is about three months old, the baby's hands flash into view. He cannot control them enough to keep them in sight very long, but they interest him. He turns his eyes and even his head to follow them. The play of his hands may be frustrating: he gets a glimpse of them and they disappear. If they come together, they are likely to clasp, but this is hardly intentional. However, the baby now *feels* his hands while he sees them—an important advance. At this point he will automatically grasp a rattle if it touches his hand. But since he cannot open his hand to release the toy, except by chance, it will move at random and probably land in his eye. And if the rattle falls, he is unable to recover it. Better wait a few weeks until he has more control of his grip.

At around four months, the child's hands become all important. He used to look hungrily around, exploring one object after another with his eyes. Now he is eager to learn about things with his hands—to touch, to hold, to manipulate. He discovers that things have qualities other than form and color. He can feel their hardness or softness; he experiences their texture. His mouth also helps him find out about the world. When he puts his rattle in his mouth the sensation is different from that of fingers-in-mouth. This is the beginning of finding out that some things are part of himself and some others are not.

At this age the baby can often recover a dropped toy without help, if it falls within his reach. If it goes "out of bounds," better put it on his chest where he can get it himself rather than hand it to him directly.

From simple grasping and groping the child will soon go on to more active reaching. His first efforts are very uncertain. He extends his arm in the general direction of the thing he is trying for, often making a sort of roundhouse swing and missing his target entirely. It may take several tries, but with practice he becomes more efficient. It is the adult's job to provide the practice.

Now the fragile mobiles and all the pretty but sharp or swallowable objects that served so well for early eye exploration must be put away. In their place come sturdy objects with safe surfaces. Shapes should be easy for small fingers to grasp even if they only touch accidentally. Some cradle gyms, with bars and rings, are good, but many homemade toys can serve the same purpose. A pair of smoothly sanded wooden rings or plastic bracelets can be attached to an elastic band fastened across the top of the crib. Small bells sewed securely to the elastic band, so that they tinkle when the rings are pulled, will make the game of reach-and-grasp even more exciting.

Now we can bring out the rattles in force. A supply that varies in color, shape, and sound will help keep the child's interest stimulated. Those that are molded in one piece are best; if there are separate parts, these must be tested to be sure they will not come apart easily. Rubber squeeze toys with feet, ears, snouts, and tails that are easily grasped are also useful. Most inexpensive kinds have metal whistles. These are hazards: they can be poked out or they fall out with use, and they can find their way into a child's windpipe. Toys with the sound mechanism vulcanized permanently into place are safer.

Some babies can sit, with support, in high chair or carriage at about five months. For high-chair play, the soft rubber toy that comes equipped with a vacuum-cup base is excellent. Firmly attached to the baby's tray, slender enough to be grasped easily, and standing free of other things, it offers a fine target for his wavering hands, and he can clamp down on it with his mouth, too, without dislodging it.

He also enjoys a soft cuddle toy that is fairly small, light-weight and yielding, with slender parts here and there. The round, firmly packed variety had better wait till he is older. Limbs on animals should be securely sewed, or cut in one piece with the body. Features should be embroidered. Glass eyes and whiskers are hazards to be avoided, since the child will pull them loose.

Homemade cuddle toys are likely to be the most satisfactory. The washable covering may be old toweling or oilcloth, the stuffing foam rubber, kapok, or your discarded nylon stockings. Although traditional shapes and pastel colors are apt to suggest themselves to the adult, the five-month-old would probably prefer an octopus to a Teddy bear because of its many handles. Doughnuts, starfish, and fat, wriggly snakes make satisfactory shapes, too. If in doubt that the infant prefers a vivid color to a pastel, make two toys. You will doubtless discover that the brighter toy is preferred. A lusty red seems to be one of the first choices.

Rules for Early Toys

Whatever toy is bought or made, it should be checked for the following:
1. The child should be able to grasp it from any angle.
2. It should be easily manageable with one hand.
3. Edges should be rounded and smooth.
4. There should be no detachable parts.
5. There should be no harmful coloring matter.
6. It should be boilable.
7. It should be able to take hard use.

Most of these rules hold for later toys, though shape and weight requirements change as time goes on.

Company Wanted

A baby is a sociable creature. Even the four-month-old usually appreciates the first form of hide-and-seek, played when he is on someone's lap. His mother calls his name, he turns his head toward the sound—and the beloved parent is there!

He also likes to "play" with his father or young sister by watching as they roll a ball across a table or pull a toy in front of him.

From this point on, whether the child will seek pleasure in the company of others or be more at home by himself will depend largely on the parents. There is nothing wrong with liking to be alone—some of the most valuable of the world's work is done by people who are happiest when by themselves—but it is important to realize that the liking of solitude or its opposite can be at least partly determined. Whether or not self-contentment is something parents want for their baby, every child will need times of quiet play; and every mother will welcome the intervals when her child is able to go it alone.

Many babies go into playpens at four months. By five and six months, most young ones squirm about with a good deal of facility, and soft balls, not too big for their grip, offer a pleasant challenge. Made of brightly colored oilcloth, cut in sections and stuffed with kapok, a small bell or two sewed to the outside for added interest, they are an invitation to action. For quiet occupation, a soft, thick cord, knotted at the end and at intervals throughout its length, makes a fascinating toy. It should be tied to the top of the pen, long enough to be handled with ease but too short for the baby to get tangled in it. By now rattles are old stuff, and plastic beach toys are a welcome change. They are good for mouthing, too, if not fully inflated. Investigate pet stores: their hard-rubber crackle bones, doughnuts, and balls with bells inside are as much fun for the baby as the puppy.

Approaching a Landmark

When the baby approaches six months it's time to start tying things down. Picking up is a new skill the baby loves to practice. Put a spoon in front of him, and his eyes brighten as he concentrates on it. Carefully his fingers curl around it, slowly it is raised. Then, heady with success, the child waves it and bangs it until, inevitably, he loses his grip and it flies away. At this stage, tying half a dozen small toys to the side of the high chair or carriage is a help to a busy mother. The baby cannot haul up his own toys yet—in fact, when they fall, he doesn't know what's happened. But tying them saves the toys—and the mother's back!

He needs larger toys now. Plastic and aluminum objects make good sitting-up toys; so do two-inch blocks, especially the kind that make a noise. Small tins and plastic bowls are fun to explore and bang about, and a wooden-handled rattle is a good object for pick-up exercise. Of course *everything* still goes into his mouth.

Be prepared for him to grow bored more quickly now. In many ways, the half-year-old is apt to be at an exasperating stage. He can sit up with a little propping, but cannot get into a sitting position without help. He can propel himself along the floor by wriggling, but cannot creep, and he often scoots back when he wants to go forward. On all fronts he seems to be just on the verge of succeeding; yet everywhere his reach exceeds his grasp, and he is often cross about it.

This is the time for parental ingenuity. If the baby cannot put himself in a new position in relation to the world, we can present the world to him from a new angle. A selection of toys, hung on elastic strips, may be dangled from a pole fastened over one end of the playpen. The child can reach up and secure a toy easily, have the fun of pulling against the elastic, and be entertained by the bounce when he releases it.

Social play is more and more attractive. The child's most exhilarating experiences depend on the presence of another person. For some time he has probably loved being swung up in the air and gently lowered to the ground. Now he is ready to do flip-flops from an adult's lap, with the help of a firm grip on his hands. He likes to slide down a pair of outstretched legs, with ankles held, till his hands touch the floor. He enjoys experimenting with his body and with space. Fun in movement and fun in general become associated with people, and his gentle roughhousing with daddy is a preparation for more strenuous roughhousing with playmates later. In our culture, pleasure in all these activities is a very important part of preparation for living.

Six Months

The baby has had his first half-birthday and he has made tremendous progress. He has gained control of his head, his neck muscles, his arms, and part of his trunk. He is all energy and his hands seem to want to get into everything. Because of his interest in finding out about things he can play happily by himself for twenty to thirty minutes at a time. When he gets restless, a change in position and a new toy may be all he needs, but when he unmistakably lets us know that he wants company, it is time to take him into the room where we are. We need not entertain him, though. Watching us move about at our work can be as absorbing as investigating the possibilities of a new toy.

Common household objects may be more fascinating to the baby than conventional toys. Every time he reaches a new level of development, he regards familiar things with new eyes. A cup that he has played with a thousand times is suddenly something to treat in another way—perhaps to throw. A set of measuring spoons is endlessly amusing, while cup and spoon together offer further joys. A piece of paper to be crumpled, waved, and patted is a good toy at this age. The kind of parchment paper used in cooking has special virtues: it resists tearing, will not melt when sucked, and can be boiled for cleanliness.

One doesn't think of bread crumbs as toys, but they can be just that. Typically, the seven-monther will rivet his eyes on any tiny object and concentrate all his energies on trying to pick it up. If it tastes good (for of course it will go straight into his mouth) he has a double reward for using the fine muscles of his fingers. Fat, round strings, shoelaces with the metal tips removed, and fast-color ribbons are other good pick-up toys. All should be tied firmly to the side of the high chair, to prevent swallowing, and knotted at the end to stop raveling.

Budding Mechanic

The baby's estimates of space are still very inaccurate. Two objects that he means to bring together may cross each other in the air. He reaches out for something too far away to be touched; he thrusts his hand vigorously at something he means to pick up and knocks it out of reach. It does him good to try and try again—unless he shows signs of exasperation. We learn by practice, but we do not learn in a rage.

Part of the baby's vagueness about distance is his initial inability to distinguish between two- and three-dimensional things. He picks constantly at figured materials and printed surfaces. Tablecloths with patterns are not safe when he is near. Yet the experience of trying to pick up what is only pictured is necessary before he can learn to discriminate between flat and solid objects. Patterned playpen pads, pillows with figured covers, and pictures pasted on cardboard backs will give him the necessary practice without producing household crises.

The baby is now a budding mechanic. Those peg boards and carts that were bought or given prematurely can now be brought out. He may not be able to replace the pegs, but he does love pulling them out. (They should be splinter-free, finished with noninjurious substances, and too large to be swallowed, inhaled, or crammed down the throat.)

Everything will go on the floor, so it is best to be prepared. A back-saving scheme is to have a waste basket or shopping bag of small toys nearby, and to hand him one or two at a time. At the end of the play period they can all be picked up at once. A variety of shapes, sizes, textures, weights, and sound qualities will interest him longer than a collection of similar articles.

When Interests Collide

The hand-mindedness of Seven-Months may irritate his mother. Meals can be hectic. His spoon he'll claim as a toy, even if he can't control it. "No, no," is out of order, because he should not be discouraged from doing things for himself. Sometimes it is possible to let him help and still get him fed. If the mother will put her forefinger along the spoon handle, she can direct, even when he makes a lunge. For a time the youngster may insist on "feeding himself" this way, but the novelty soon wears off and he is happy to leave the work to others. Also, it may take diplomacy and dexterity to get the contents of the drinking cup into the baby instead of onto the floor, but the risk is lessened if the cup is only part filled.

The baby's interest in strings can also be troublesome. Bootie and sweater ties are irresistible. If the climate permits, it is a good idea to let the child go barefoot and get acquainted with another set of fascinating objects—his toes. Don't scold him for removing footgear and opening fastenings. Before you know it you'll be asking him to undress himself. The fun he gets out of pulling off socks and slippers at seven months is the basis for continued interest at two years and self-reliance at five.

These instances show how closely play and useful activities are related. From the child's point of view, of course, there is no difference—everything he does is part of his response to living. If the adults around him do not insist on a rigid distinction, the growing child is likely to transfer much of the pleasure of play into the things we call work.

Social Play

What he does with people now becomes more important than ever. He is trying out his vocal apparatus and loves to be clucked at and crooned to. It is fun to be bounced up and down rhythmically and to play "ride a cockhorse" on daddy's knee. Going for a walk, with both hands held, is an adventure. Being passed from one person to another is a game. However, the people he plays with should be the people he knows best, for this is a period of shyness. This feeling becomes more pronounced within the next few months. Then he will be ready again to accept strangers tranquilly, though not as unquestioningly as during the first six months. At six and seven months he will do well to encounter strangers in the safety of his parents' arms.

A daily carriage excursion is also helpful. If strangers stop to talk to him, his mother should be in sight, lending support and reassurance so that he learns that strangeness, whether in people or surroundings, is not threatening. This will help condition him to being left with strangers when that time comes.

Widening Horizons

Between seven and ten months, the baby becomes considerably more of a person, and makes several new discoveries. He is beginning to put things together and to look *inside* them, as well as around them. Round nesting toys (he does not have the co-ordination to cope with square ones yet), a cup into which small cubes can be dropped—these provide the magical lesson that things continue to exist even when they are out of sight. The child will delight in putting one thing inside another and taking it out, over and over again.

The exact age at which they are able to open their hands and release objects at will varies from child to child. Whenever it occurs it means hectic times for mother. Drunk with power, the child spends his time throwing things down or poking them through the bars of his playpen. Since there is nothing you can do about this, you may as well relax, and rejoice with the child that he has finally achieved mastery over his stubborn hands.

The baby's favorite movement, at about the same stage of hand dexterity, changes from a vigorous wave and shake to an equally emphatic hammering. Playthings must be sturdy enough to take incessant banging. Every time two things are taken up at the same time they are clashed together. The faithful metal spoon and cup make a perfect hammer toy. Small pot covers with handles are a delight.

The baby is beginning to notice that the world is made up of more than passing sensations. When he drops an object, he looks after it and tries to get it. Before, he behaved as if it had simply gone out of existence. Now he can be taught to pull up the toys tied to his high chair or carriage—he knows the string leads to something. Now that he sits up most of the time an old rubber toy dangled from an overhead towel rack can be as absorbing to him as though he had never seen it before.

Parents get in on a special kind of fun when the baby begins to imitate them, and shows some understanding of words. This happens most often around the ninth month. He loves to make the sounds he hears others make, for he knows they will respond in kind when they hear him. When he learns to connect words with actions, as in playing pat-a-cake and waving "bye-bye," he begins to learn that sounds are a part of communication.

Social development takes another big step forward here: the baby now *starts* games himself instead of merely following. Sitting in his high chair, he looks at you with a special gleam and begins to pat his hands together. If you respond and join the game, his face breaks into a huge grin: he has discovered a new way to get people to do things with him—specific things beyond just being fed or picked up. All this helps him to become an outgoing, spontaneous, sociable person.

The Conquest of Space

During his eighth and ninth months, the child gains greater control over the lower part of his body and can cover ground more easily. Some babies hitch along in three-legged fashion, with arms and one leg providing most of the power; others try to crawl on all fours. Although his movements are still poorly organized and there are frequent breakdowns, the child enjoys this increase in liberty.

The playpen may now be too small. A corner of a room fenced off, with nothing in it that can be pulled over, gives scope for exploration and exercise. A couple of months more, and most households are in for the Age of Invasion. If, in addition to scooting around with considerable ease and speed, the child can pull himself up to a standing position, a revolution in household arrangements is imperative. Steam pipes and radiators must be covered or securely blocked off. (Putting a chair in front of them is not enough.) Chairs that tip over easily should be stacked out of the way during his exploration periods. Floors must be rigorously inspected for stray pins, nails, tacks. Electric outlets should be covered against prying fingers. Cords from electric fixtures must be fastened out of the way as much as possible. It may be annoying to disconnect table lamps while baby is on the loose, but often children are cut or bruised at this stage because they pull things down on themselves. Every projecting object is an invitation to tug, every cord or wire will be pulled, the baby waiting with upturned face, eager to see what new prey he has captured.

Having made the home as safe as possible, we are ready to turn our traveler loose—but always with someone around to watch him. For a time he will be carried away with the joy of free movement, darting from chair to chair, pulling himself up and letting himself down incessantly.

It is hard at this time not to interfere, but the youngster should have a chance to find out things for himself, to investigate and experiment, while an unobtrusive presence helps keep him safe.

Bath Play

When the child sits up without support, bath time becomes an important playtime. Floating objects are pursued and captured with zest. These need not be "toys" as we know them. A sponge is probably the most fascinating thing in the tub. Dry, it floats like a ship; wet, it can be squeezed with the most satisfying results. It would be hard to find a more delightful object for sucking, and it is tops for scrubbing the tub side—an activity that the ten-month-old considers his special privilege. Two plastic sponges of different colors, cut to a size that the baby can handle easily, can furnish endless fun.

Once we see how absorbed the baby is in his bath play, it is a temptation to give him too many things. A flood of brightly colored, bobbing objects only distracts and confuses him. We want to aim for calm enjoyment, not hectic activity, at bath time.

The water itself is one of the best of all play materials. The feel of it on the skin, its taste and touch as it is sucked into the mouth, the noise it makes when splashed, the way things float on it—these continue to fascinate children far beyond the first year. It may seem a far cry from the baby's bath to an interest in swimming, boating, and underwater exploration, but these can be direct developments.

Books

During the last two months of the first year, many babies stop mouthing everything they pick up and concentrate with eyes and hands. Among these, the quiet ones may be ready for books. Admittedly, books are not for all children at this age, but those who are ready can learn a great deal from them.

The first books should be of starched cloth or heavy cardboard (limp pages are almost impossible for the child to handle). Pictures should be boldly drawn, the colors bright, and they should be of familiar, everyday objects.

The baby will not be able to turn the pages himself at first, but will look at the pictures as they are pointed out to him. He will listen briefly to "reading"—a few remarks identifying the pictures—then will want to handle the book alone. He will pat and stroke the pages. He may attempt to pick up the designs as if they were real objects, but this soon ceases for he is becoming more sophisticated about third-dimensional cues. Presently he will look at a picture and croon a long series of syllables in a special voice—he is now "reading" to us.

For some time, he may need help in turning the pages and it is important to prevent his being angered or frustrated by their obstinacy. With strong feeling he returns to a lower level of play. He may pick up the book and shake it, or crumple the pages. Heavy Manila folders with bright pictures pasted or drawn on each page will do very well for a first book at this stage.

New Toys for New Needs

The way a home is organized determines the amount of freedom a child can have, of course, but even a crowded household can be managed to allow for *some* exploring of new places and things. The kitchen, where supervision is usually easiest at certain times of day, is a fine crawling place (if hot pipes are covered and the hot stove can be bypassed). Here pots and pans are preferred to toys, partly because they are associated with the all-important mother. Plastic refrigerator dishes offer good sport, especially if they have small toys inside.

In more open spaces, wheeled toys and large balls come into their own. A tough rubber balloon can serve as the object of a gleeful chase.

A trash basket of discarded letters, envelopes, and pamphlets is another object of endless interest. Baby can have the pleasure of pulling out, inspecting, and crumpling to his heart's content. Tiring of this, he may lay one treasure after another at his mother's feet, made happy by her smile and appreciative "Thank you!" for each one.

"Putting in" follows "taking out" in the evolution of play, and as his size discrimination advances, the almost-a-year-old will be able to handle graduated wooden tubes. At first he will hold two such tubes together, knowing vaguely that there is a connection between them but not yet able to fit one into the other. If the two are placed so that the smaller one just touches the opening of the larger he will complete the nesting. In another month, he may be able to do the whole thing by himself.

Old-fashioned clothespins can be fine toys for this age. Lined up on the edge of a loaf pan, they are fun to pull off and put back in the pan. This becomes a social sport if mother or father is willing to line them up again.

Another excellent toy is a plastic medicine vial with plastic stopper, to be found in drug departments of large stores or in dime or variety stores. Some cracker crumbs in such a bottle can serve both as incentive to play and reward—if the bottle mouth is wide enough, the baby may succeed in putting a few crumbs back, and he will enjoy eating the rest.

The First Year Ends

Following the infant through his first year, we have watched him advance enormously. From the first turning of his head toward the light, he has come to the point where he can manipulate objects to a certain extent. He has found that some have insides as well as outsides, that one can swallow up another and be made to disgorge it. He has learned the difference between two- and three-dimensional things. From the first undirected motions, he has gone on to hesitant imitation of simple gestures and from there to wholehearted participation in games of give-and-take and the active use of his whole body in exploratory forays. He has even learned a little about people. Above all, there has been growth in the healthy confidence in his own powers, and an increasing curiosity about the treasures of the world.

Ideally, the first year's learning has been achieved with the help of the creative and rewarding experiences of play. With this solid start we can expect further developments through similar, though, of course, more complex experiences.

CHAPTER II

The Second Year: Enter the Runabout

THE FIRST BIRTHDAY CAKE—what an event it is in the life of a family! It is likely to bring forth a great feeling of expectancy, not to mention tricycles, doll carriages, and footballs. We feel the child has left helpless infancy behind and is now a big boy or girl. Unfortunately, Nature has failed to inform the child of this. He just keeps on doing what he has been doing—more of it, perhaps, and more proficiently, but, for the most part, the same old things.

Still, although nothing startling takes place at this magic moment, the baby's behavior does have a distinctive quality by his first birthday. What used to be done awkwardly, and with effort, now appears easy and smooth. There is zestfulness in his performance, and he is capable of a surprising variety of activities.

The way he handles objects that go together is a good illustration of the halfway state he has reached. He puts his doll's sock next to its foot, for example, but cannot carry the operation farther. He does the same thing with his own shoe, indicating that he knows where it belongs by holding it against his foot. He recognizes that his action is incomplete, gestures to any nearby adult for help, and gives a grunt of satisfaction when the task is performed for him. His intentions clearly run ahead of his abilities at this point, and it is a frustrating state of affairs.

Patience Needed

Watching Johnny at one, we are impressed with his persistence. He tries so hard. He is beginning to handle more than one object at a time, and this is important, as it is the basis for his whole understanding of numerical relationships. But he is apt to stop midway in the process of, say, putting several blocks into one container, and dump them all out. He pulls a peg out of his pegboard and with intense concentration tries to replace it. Over and over he approaches the opening, only to overshoot the mark, or he holds the peg at an angle that makes success impossible. Finally, in exasperation, he may fling the whole thing away, or he may hold out the peg and make pleading sounds for a grownup to help him complete the maneuver.

At this point it is best to guide Johnny's hand so that the edge of the peg touches the edge of the opening, and gently tip it into position. This will encourage him to try again, and eventually lead him to success on his own. If we perform the whole operation for him, he learns only that he can get us to do it, but gains nothing in manual skill.

Lack of skill does not keep the one-year-old from attempting intricate manipulations. Bookshelves are likely to be high on his list of practice places. He scoots from one to the other, pulling out books, intensely preoccupied with arranging and rearranging. Unhelpful as this may be for us, it seems to give the baby a certain feeling of power over his surroundings. Instead of curbing him, we might applaud his enterprise and try to direct it. Many children will respond with pleasure to "Bring it here" or "This is where it goes."

With dangerous and breakable items put out of reach, "No, no" can be reserved for real hazards that cannot be removed, like hot stoves. Even with these, an explanatory word should accompany the "No," like "hot" or "it will hurt baby." General commands like "Don't touch" are not helpful. Young children do not realize that they refer only to certain things; if they are often repeated, the child may come to assume that everything is "untouchable" and that his healthy tendency to explore is a naughty thing in itself. Obviously, when this happens, his development cannot take place easily and freely.

From the healthy baby's point of view, unfamiliar objects are expressly made to be investigated—usually by being pulled apart. Doors that open and shut, drawers that pull out, are much more interesting than his own small toys. If he can reach nothing else, his clothing will do. A period of silence in the playpen often means that the child is busily pulling his garments off. Mothers who do not regard this kind of activity with favor may tolerate it more easily if they think of it as a necessary prelude to dressing himself with splendid self-reliance.

Movement—New Focus of Interest

Shortly after discovering the delights of opening and closing, and taking things apart, the baby notices that *parts* of objects move in other ways. Knobs that turn now take his attention. No radio or television program is safe from him during this period, which may start any time between his first birthday and halfway to his second.

Larger moving objects also fascinate him. He may sit happily in his carriage or at a window, watching cars, bicycles, people. He is less self-absorbed, more and more aware of events taking place at some distance from him.

This interest in movement includes himself, too. He loves to "walk" with support. Confined to one room, he proceeds with determination from one piece of furniture to the next, until he has made a complete round. Scooting swiftly about on his seat, or supported on one knee, is the best game he knows—and it is good for him. Allowed to move freely now, he is being prepared for his later encounters with the world of playground and school, where his degree of initiative and self-confidence will have much to do with determining how the world will look to him and he to it.

Interest in movement and interest in wider spaces go together. The One-Plus is no longer satisfied by the inside of his home. He wants to get out and inspect the larger canvas of the out-of-doors.

Social Life in the Playpen Set

Soon after the first birthday, the baby develops a tremendous enthusiasm for social contact. Chasing and hiding games are his idea of a really good time. He hides behind favorite chairs, and peeks out when he can inveigle someone into an endless game of "Where's baby?" He throws things on the floor, and waits expectantly for them to be returned to him. He also takes delight in giving back objects that are offered to him and can play an elementary sort of ball, rolling the ball back when it is rolled to him. In a month or two, he will be able to *throw* it back, too.

This is the time he wants his fill of tokens of affection. Nuzzling, hugs, caressing the adult's hand—these are favorite ways of establishing contact. The child loves to be hugged tightly and let go, swung up in the air and caught securely. These are loving, sociable games to him.

The child's zestful response to people makes this a good time to further encourage imitative play. Because he likes an audience and enjoys applause, it is usually easy to get him to trot out his little tricks, though not a good idea to insist, if he's not in the mood. Imitation offers a natural and easy path to learning, too, and he will eagerly try such things as scribbling with a pencil, holding a cup, "smoking" a pipe. Telephone-minded mothers find that the gift of a toy telephone is greeted with delight around fifteen months, and used with surprising sophistication.

Coughing, nose-blowing—almost any distinctive noise—can set off a chain reaction of similar behavior in the young observer, and this imitative skill sends his language development forward rapidly. Though recognizable words may still be some time in coming, he often jabbers to himself and has a "vocabulary" of many wordlike sounds that gradually merge into the real thing.

Dogs

The baby's social urge is as likely to include animals as people. He is, truth to tell, not very clear about the difference between them. Everything that seems to move of its own accord appears vaguely human. If he has not been frightened, or made anxious by the attitudes of the people around him, he will respond to small animals with gusto, and even large ones are not likely to frighten him.

This is particularly true of dogs. Kittens are too unpredictable, usually, with their claws—though sometimes an older cat will submit to a certain amount of mauling and tail-pulling, simply stalking away when it has had enough. But there is no more touching sight than a toddler playing with a large, gentle dog. Sometimes the child needs to be protected against the enthusiasm of a young dog, but they often make good companions with a little supervision. The pup is likely to treat the child like another pup, pawing him to restrain him if he tries to creep away. The baby, undaunted, will push the dog out of the way if it gets too obstreperous, and otherwise treat it like something specifically created for his amusement. We have seen year-old children unabashedly yanking at a dog's coat, poking inquisitively at its eyes, and using the animal as a support for pulling up to a standing position, with no more reaction from the dog than a slight movement to get out of range when the going got too rough.

Dogs that have not been frightened or mistreated seem to take special delight in babies, and the two come to terms with only the slightest amount of adult intervention. It is important for someone to be on hand for the first meeting of child and dog, however, to prevent either of them from overwhelming the other. With a little training the dog learns not to be too rough (before the child does!) and he can generally protect himself if his movement is not impeded. The baby who gets acquainted with dogs at this stage, when each seems to have a natural affinity for the other, is less likely to fear dogs and other animals later on.

Another Revolution

At about fifteen months, earlier for some and later for others, the child undergoes his second dramatic transformation. From a four-footed creature, he becomes a biped. Launching himself on his hind legs, he suddenly gets a new view of the world and a new evaluation of himself.

Once he attains the upright position, objects change their relation to him. What was above him is now on his level; what used to be on his level is now below him. The world has a different look, and he *feels* different to himself. Gaining his feet makes him sassy. It is as if he said, "If I can do this, I can do anything—and nobody can stop me!"

At this point, the child may devote as much as an hour after he wakes in the morning to sheer motor play—standing up, sitting down, bending over to look between his legs, circumnavigating his crib. Put down on the floor in a sitting position, he may gingerly stand up and then suddenly launch himself forward, careening erratically until he fetches up against a wall or falls of his own momentum. A pause, a look of astonishment, a peal of laughter or a brief wail, and he is off again.

He seems inexhaustible, but he is not; he simply does not know the limit of his energy. Because of this enthusiasm, the most active babies may have to be restrained gently by being picked up and set at another, quieter activity.

Setting Patterns

At this period parents have the important responsibility of cultivating healthy attitudes toward mishaps, or risking poor ones. If no one runs to pick up the toddler every time he falls, the child will pick himself up. If no one clucks over his little spills and bumps, they will be treated by the child only as momentary interruptions of his more important activities. If someone he loves and trusts helps him to smile at the tumbles, later physical activities will be entered into in a relaxed way and with the confidence that they will prove enjoyable.

For adults, this is often an exacting period. What were formerly outings in the carriage become walks, with the child pushing the carriage. Quiet observation periods in the park are transformed into expeditions of discovery. Treasures of cigarette butts and bits of silver foil lure the toddler farther and farther from home base. For a while he seems dedicated to bright pebbles, desiccated banana skins, and castoff apple cores, which he may sample before offering them in triumph to Mommy.

In his absorption, the youngster may end up against the knees of a stranger instead of his mother. Since most people are gentle and pleasant with little children, this is all to the good. It helps extend the lines of communication, and encourages him to move away on his own without fear.

Onward and Upward

Having mastered the horizontal, the child of a year and a half, or even a bit younger, becomes intoxicated with the possibilities of the vertical. From his point of view, chairs, stools, steps are created for one purpose—to be mounted. Bookshelves, window sills, stepladders make his eyes light up. Whatever offers a foothold is his.

Quiet watchfulness is the attitude for this time. Since the small adventurer needs to savor the magic of his release from former limitations, the wise parent will expose him to challenges that are safe. Low, large, hollow blocks are good for climbing. They can be bought as large as twenty-two by eleven by five inches, or they can be made in even larger sizes. These, coupled with wide planks, smoothed down and shellacked, can be arranged to provide a variety of climbing adventures. Although relatively expensive to buy, these blocks are a good investment, as they can be added to and combined with other equipment later and are useful for six or seven years, after which they can doubtless be sold. A handy father can construct a short set of steps, walled in and ending in a platform, for his young mountaineer. More elaborate climbing apparatus can be purchased at nursery supply stores and is good for both indoor and outdoor play—but it does take room.

Managing Hazards

Active children can get themselves into some pretty hazardous situations during these months if they are not closely supervised. Open windows without window guards, and spiked fences of any kind, even the pretty white-picket variety, can be extremely dangerous. As it is almost impossible to foresee what will or will not present a threat when a youngster is reaching out so actively, yet with so little judgment, supervision is constantly needed when he is on the loose. Interference, though, should be minimum.

When a child does get in a dangerous spot, swift but unflustered action is called for. One mother we observed handled such a situation admirably. While she was in the kitchen, unaware that the baby had left her, her young son had climbed upon the broad sill of a window which was open, without bars or guards, three stories above street level. As the mother entered the living room, the boy was reaching up toward the pull of the window shade, leaning with complete obliviousness to empty outer space.

A cry or a quick dash toward him might have been disastrous. Instead, his mother stopped in the doorway and called him in a low voice. As he glanced at her, she smiled and held out her closed hand and began to move toward him, saying, "See what I have here." Diverted, the baby leaned toward his mother and in a moment she was at his side, lifting him down. He was given a tidbit immediately, so that her "promise" would not seem false.

The important thing at moments like this is to gain the child's attention without startling him, to keep his interest fixed on one's self, and to rescue him without showing fright. Screams, gasps, shouted admonitions may only precipitate a tragedy. And scoldings or emotional warnings which come so naturally to our lips after such an incident had better be held in check, since they will only blast the child's self-confidence without preventing future hazards from arising.

Innovations at Bath Time

Squeezing and pouring, sucking and babbling are still favorite activities at bath time, but something new is added when the child can stand alone. Now he scrambles to his feet and slides down the end of the tub with a splash. As long as someone is at hand to keep it safe, this can be a very good game. It helps develop control in a situation that threatens deliciously to get away from one, but doesn't. In addition, it insures that he will continue to like his familiar friend, water, even when it splashes up his nose and into his eyes.

For such active experimentation, the water should be shallow, of course—no more than a few inches in the bottom of the tub.

Toys for Toddling

Because skills do not change promptly with birthdays, a good many of our suggestions for the almost-year-old still apply during the first months of the second year. But as the crawler becomes the toddler, there will be some additions. He may want to hold something in each hand as he journeys around the house, and soft toys are welcome now. If a supply has been collecting in the closet (people are apt to feel that they are ideal gifts from the moment the baby is born), this is the time to bring them out.

Pull toys also get more appreciation. The kind that makes a sound as it operates is most fun, but the child will use anything he can trail behind him. Toward the latter half of the year, we might appropriately add a hammer toy of some sort. The kind that can be pounded without demanding real precision of aim is best at first. As greater dexterity develops, the child can use a color cone, and often chooses it as his favorite toy.

Some children like dolls at this age; others, not until they are about two years old. If a doll is provided, it should be about eight inches long, made entirely of rubber, without hair or moving eyes. It should be impervious to water, for one of the child's chief joys will be to take it into the tub with him.

Medium-sized trains and other vehicles that can be easily recognized by the child fit in with his interest in action. These need not be realistically detailed, and wood, soft plastic, or hard rubber are the materials of choice. This is a good time for kindergarten blocks to make their appearance—a few oblong units are enough for a start. Many children, though not all, can handle toys using the screw principle by now. There are several commercial versions of this—large screws and nuts, a long spiraled peg and colored squares that screw on and off are common varieties. A screw-topped plastic jar is a good substitute. A covered box with a two-inch square opening, through which large beads and small blocks can be dropped, is another simple device that will hold the child's attention for a good span.

Enter Order

Sometimes the despairing parents of the going-on-two wonder if they must live permanently in an oddly furnished barracks decorated only with large, untippable objects strewn with the results of the child's playtime whims. But just then a new and endearing quality shows itself. For the first time in his life, the young one manifests an interest in order.

This is a beautiful moment, to be grasped before it passes. Although he is still a terror with a wastebasket, and insists that books look best littered along the hall, he also likes to *put things back*. He knows from his earlier free ranging where things are kept, and he loves to put them where they belong.

Now, when the toddler is finished with a play period, he usually welcomes the suggestion, if he is not too tired, to "Put the blocks back on the shelf."

To make the most of his impulse, and to set the stamp of achievement rather than chore on clean-up time, appropriate equipment is necessary. The commonest toy container is a large chest, but this is far from the best idea. Though easiest for the child to dump things into, it makes taking out a specific toy most difficult. Parts of toys get scrambled in its depths; the article wanted is invariably at the bottom.

A set of shelves, with a retaining strip at the front edge, is far better. These should be low enough for the child to reach easily and wide enough to accommodate the largest toy he will be likely to store on them. The retaining strip keeps balls and wheeled objects from rolling off, and the extra width takes care of the child's lack of precision in judging size and distance. Such shelves will be useful for a long time and help prevent many of the family tensions which are apt to arise because of a child's "untidiness" later on.

The World Outdoors

The aptly called "runabout child" becomes more than ever activity-minded in his play. Families with backyards are especially lucky at this time, for a low slide will keep their small dynamo occupied for mercifully long periods.

Sand, or plain dirt, and water now become the child's great friends. The sandbox need not be elaborate—in fact, a sandpile without any enclosure is often preferred. Eighteen-months does not recognize the limits of the box: the dumping which is part of sand play most often takes place outside it, in any case. Just as important as sand, and far less often supplied, is water. When both are offered, the play is likely to be more varied and more prolonged than with either one alone.

If sand is hard to come by or space restricted, a bare spot of ground and a spoon to dig with will be quite acceptable. Even a stick to poke the earth with is often enough, while a pan with a handle, together with a spoon, is a downright luxury. And these are handier tools for this kind of play than the conventional pail and shovel. For loose dirt and gravel, a sturdy plastic salad spoon is very satisfactory.

Part of the fun for the young child comes from being able to mess to his heart's content. This is the age at which demands for cleanliness and control are likely to be frequent, and it helps enormously for him to have at least one place where he can be as messy as he pleases.

The fascination of experiment and discovery also figures largely in this kind of play, for here are substances which do unpredictable, interesting things when one manipulates them. This spontaneous curiosity of the young about the nature of things is worth encouraging. The road from mudpies to real pies, from backyard messes to research in chemistry is more direct than we may appreciate. A little forebearance, a little interest, and above all, a little understanding, bring big rewards.

Indoor Occupations

When we consider the indoor play of the year-and-a-half, we find many of the same values as in outdoor play. Crayons and paper may replace the mud and water (and sometimes snow), and they offer him the same thrill of discovery and achievement.

Because the child's movements still tend to be in broad sweeps and his grasp is an all or nothing affair, the crayons must be large and sturdy, the paper big enough to catch his free-wheeling stroke. His wrist still does not rotate well, and the strokes tend to be made with the whole arm, but the zest, the urge to make an impression is there. One color at a time is best at first. It is enough for the child that wide arcs appear on paper that was blank before. Later he will be interested in different colors; at present, his primary delight lies in making his mark.

The lines the young artist draws are not a "picture" to him; they are a part of himself—an unmistakable witness that he is an individual and wields a measure of power. His enthusiasm may lead to drawing on the wall but this is not malicious mischief. Sheets of wrapping paper, newspaper, or large paper bags serve well for drawing paper at this age. These may be spread on a table, or the floor, but the surface underneath should be able to take without damage whatever goes over the paper's edge. A large rectangle of wall board or plywood makes a good drawing board. The paper may be fastened to it with clothespins or Scotch tape.

Playing with Sound

All sorts of sound-producing equipment are useful now. A toy accordion, sturdy enough to take the vigor of eighteen-month-old activity is a welcome addition, and a small record player is a good gift. Music boxes that produce tunes when a handle is turned are intriguing and may keep the child content when all else fails.

Musical appreciation at this time means participation, and the child "listens" with his whole body, swaying in rhythm to the sounds. A pronounced rhythm is needed to catch and hold attention, and records with distinctive sounds like bells or whistles are asked for again and again.

Books in a Big Way

If books have not been part of the play equipment before this, they certainly should be now. At about one, the baby made a significant change in his approach to pictures—instead of picking at them, he began to point to them, thus showing that he had learned to differentiate them from real objects. Now he can really be read to. Though he still loves to sit and look at a book by himself, he also likes to listen to rhyme, in small doses. Singing rhymes are even more entrancing, especially when the small listener is invited to join in. Pictures, of course, are still essential, and should be of familiar objects or animals, and of human faces. A hint of action keeps interest from wandering.

Although he may be able by now to turn pages by himself, the not-quite-two still needs cloth or cardboard books—otherwise his new liking for order and his impulse to action may betray him into tearing out the pages as he finishes with them. (Old magazines may be given him for this kind of play, although many doubt that it should be encouraged.)

That's That

The tendency to tear a page out of a book as he finishes with it is part of a growing fondness for *endings*. At this point, when he finishes his milk, the child hands his mother the cup, a signal that this particular part of the day's work is over. If she is not there to take his plate at the end of the meal, it is likely to land on the floor. This, of course, is not deliberate devilment, though it may seem so to the adult who has to pick up the pieces. It is, rather, the child's way of emphasizing his new understanding that the things one does can stop as well as start.

Being Part of the Family

As the second year wears on, the child takes on a somewhat staider air. He pays more and more attention to adults, although he may still show some hesitancy in moving out toward strangers. In the home, he often follows grownups around, simply watching. It is hard to separate these observations from his play proper, because they feed directly into it—his dramatic play, for instance. Whole sequences of household activities are played out after he has spent some time studying them.

When Almost-Two wants to participate in household tasks, he should be welcomed. A small dust mop to push along when mother uses hers, a cloth for dusting, a child-size carpet sweeper, will help make him feel he can do it, too. Sharing in household tasks gives him a comfortable feeling of being part of what is going on, instead of being shut out of it.

Playmates versus Playthings

One thing that probably has *not* developed at this time is a feeling of kinship or sympathy for other children his own age. On the contrary, these are likely to be treated as so many objects to be explored and manipulated. As he treated his toys at an earlier stage, so now he pulls, pinches, pushes, strokes, and bites other children. It is unwise to try to persuade them to "play together." The best course, on the contrary, is to interest each member of the under-two set in an activity that will not include the other. When this is achieved, they may play peacefully back-to-back for minutes at a time. Nor is this the time to teach the child to "share." He will come to that later, but right now he is intent on holding onto what is his.

In fact, the child from eighteen months to the two-year mark sometimes acts not only as though he wanted to hold onto his possessions, but as though certain objects were part of himself. He may have a special toy from which he refuses to be separated. He may take a Teddy bear to bed and talk to it much as he used to babble to himself. It is almost as though he did not feel quite sufficient in himself, despite all his bumptiousness about being an individual, and needed his floppy puppy or doll—or some less predictable object—to back him up.

Because they have this additional meaning to the child, toys may be used to help bypass some "unmanageable" moments. Even when commands are resisted, he will follow a toy from room to room and in this way he can be lured from one activity to another without feeling that his independence is being challenged.

Putting Words Together—and Taking Clothes Apart

Perhaps the biggest discovery that Almost-Two makes about himself is his ability to put words together. First he learned how objects fitted into each other; then he discovered that certain bits of behavior went together; now he finds language doing the same thing. "Wha' dat" and "Dat me" (meaning "That *belongs* to me") may make an unending litany for every walk. Questions are asked three times over, without pause, and then again in echoing refrain, right after the answer is given.

Exhausted parents are apt to mistake the sheer pleasure of repetition for obtuseness or spitefulness. They need not fear. Jimmy or Jane is only repeating the familiar pattern of give-and-take, receive-and-throw, stand-up-and-sit-down—but this time it is being done with words.

One development may startle the unsuspecting parent: a certain indifference to the niceties of appearance may now become a sharp hostility against his clothes. Left alone for ten minutes, he is likely to reappear completely bare, nonchalant and absorbed in play. It may be his newly developed respect for completion that is responsible for this, or the pleasure of mastering complex manipulations, but whatever the cause, this is a thing to bear in mind when shockable relatives or friends come to visit.

Altogether, the second year of a child's life is not apt to provide many dull moments. But as it draws to a close, the child has made so many discoveries about himself and his everyday surroundings that he no longer needs to concentrate on these matters so exclusively. From now on, other people become more and more important. The child's growth in self-awareness and awareness of the social world outside himself now go hand in hand.

CHAPTER III

The In-Betweeners: From Two to Three

Between Two Worlds

LIKE THE ADOLESCENT, the two-year-old seems to be caught between two worlds. Though he has left infancy behind, he is still shadowed by some of its helplessness. Liking the taste of independence, he has not yet developed all the skills to support it. He spurns the helping hand and falls flat on his face. An ever-present bruise, like a tattoo, on forehead or nose, is his tribal mark.

Laughter and sobriety chase each other in bewildering succession across the pattern of Two's behavior. One moment he is whooping with exuberance; the next he has disappeared behind the sofa in an excess of shyness. At 9 o'clock he is quivering with his desire for a favorite Teddy bear; at 9:01 it lies abandoned on the floor behind him. You may leave him immersed in a whirl-wind of activity with trains and trucks; a minute later all sounds cease, and you find him sitting languidly on a footstool, a far-away look in his eyes. Two is like quicksilver.

In many ways, however, he is simply more of what he used to be. His looking spells were foreshadowed in fleeting moments of quiet watchfulness during his second year. Now, he is likely to spend a good deal of his time absorbed in gazing. A coal truck rattles up and begins to unload—Two is a fascinated watcher. The men fixing the sewer pop in and out of the manhole—Two cannot be pried away. A steam shovel excavates a building site—Two is the perfect sidewalk superintendent.

Two's looking is far from passive. Only the front seat of the bus will do for him because, even though he says nothing and makes no move, he must help the driver push the bus through traffic. The lights cannot change without direction from him. When the ferry touches the slip, he must supervise the men who secure the ropes.

Two's mother often complains that he dawdles, but trying to hurry him is useless. No promised destination interests him half as much as the things that happen along the way. He is not delaying because he hesitates to turn to something new: he is simply absorbed in whatever he is doing, eager to garner every bit of savor the immediate moment holds. To his newly perceptive eyes, the present holds riches he never sensed before; the future is still dim.

As the months pass, Johnny and Jane seem more and more convinced that change is a dubious thing. They cling tenaciously to favorite toys, favorite books, favorite games. Baths and bedtimes become rituals, lovingly and exactly executed and brooking no interruptions.

The familiar seems suddenly to take on new charms. The sight of Daddy shaving or Mother putting a stew together will hold Two riveted until the process is over. In the midst of a dash across the playground he brakes to a sudden stop to contemplate the children climbing the jungle gym or playing in the sand pile, sights he has seen before innumerable times but now meaningful in a new degree.

Imitating and Pretending

Since all the child has learned before has come through the use of his body in one way or another, now, too, he uses his body to help him understand—by making it take the shape as nearly as he can of whatever he is focusing on. Thus, two-year-olds get down on all fours and mew like cats. They stretch and roll and scratch like cats, too, because this is the only way they have of really understanding the nature of cats.

Partly as a new kind of experimentation, partly because Two has not yet learned fully to distinguish between himself and others, pretending takes the center of the stage some time after the second birthday. The momentary imitative postures of earlier months blossom into sequences of dramatic play.

The girl's doll is no longer just another object to be lugged around. It is tenderly held as mother holds the baby. It may be wrapped in a blanket and tucked into bed or taken for a walk in its carriage. Pretended telephone conversations follow recognizable models: "Hello, Daddy. You coming home? Bring bread. Bye." What the child plays out depends largely on everyday doings in his life. He is apt to drive a car, ride in a train, take care of a baby, clean a house, or serve a meal.

Occasionally the young pretender may startle us with a sudden departure from these prosaic occupations, like the two-year-old who rushed into his mother's kitchen, jerked open the oven door, slammed it shut, and dashed out shouting, "Lion in there!" For the child of this age imagination can be an extremely vivid phenomenon. When Jessie gravely informs her father that she just saw a little green fairy in the backyard, and repeats the conversation they had, she is not lying. Since even reality presents new surprises every day, it is not easy for Two to distinguish between what he thinks, what he dreams, and what is so.

Gagu was a creature who inhabited the house for several months after Anne's younger sister was born. The new baby absorbed a good deal of attention that Anne had formerly enjoyed and Gagu came to solace her. According to Anne, the new playmate was a little man, and she could see him clearly. He had no truck with any of us unless we wanted to sit down. Then he materialized, mysteriously and tantalizingly, in every chair we tried to occupy. "Don't sit on Gagu!" was the signal for a frenzied search for a seat that he had not pre-empted. No matter how fast we moved, he moved faster. After a suitable interval, he graciously offered, through Anne, to permit us to sit down in return for a story or some other prized attention.

Gagu was not the only imaginary companion we have known. The Ginko family came to live with Brenda, a friend of Anne's, when she was twenty-six months old. Mr. Ginko arrived first, shortly after Brenda's ten-year-old foster sister departed for a long visit in Europe. He took up his abode in the telephone plug, and shortly brought Mrs. Ginko and two little Ginkos to live with him.

Mr. Ginko differed from Gagu in many ways. His main function was to counsel Brenda when a difference of opinion about a course of behavior arose in the family. As time went on, the Ginko family mushroomed, until 500 Ginkos inhabited the telephone plug. (Brenda had entered the number-hungry stage a good bit earlier than the customary four years.) After Brenda started to go to nursery school, Mr. Ginko's appearances decreased in frequency, until he was coming out only rarely, to console her in times of great stress.

Favorite stuffed animals often take the place of the Gagus and Ginkos. They are endowed with sensations, given lines to say, and share completely in the child's inner life. They may be inseparable companions for several years, so important to the child that they cannot be discarded even when worn out.

Two's insistence on the reality of his fantasies can be exasperating, but it can also be turned to good account. It is precisely because the work of his imagination is so real to him that Two can accept imagined pleasures in place of those reality denies him. If he cannot go to the beach, he is happy playing "beach" in the backyard. A "party" can be made up of twigs and stones and bits of grass when no cookies are available. If he objects to going to his own room and having his door closed for a play period, he can often be persuaded if mother plays postman and slips a letter under the door. He can sometimes be enticed to bed if he is allowed to pretend that he is a bundle of rags while he is carried to his room, or if he may be a cowboy riding Daddyhorse.

When a new baby arrives, Two's intense absorption in imitative-imaginative projects is sometimes especially helpful. One mother utilized it by preparing a rubber baby doll, a bathinette, and a doll crib for her almost-two daughter when she was expecting her second baby. She saved odds and ends of cloth, and made a nightgown, diapers, and sheets for the doll. The day that brought the new baby home also brought Mary her own "baby" —dressed exactly like the real infant.

Playing Mommy gave Mary a chance to be part of the exciting new developments without getting in the way at crucial moments, and also suggested some of the joys of growing up. There were times, though, when Mary preferred to play that she herself was the new baby. Her mother wisely permitted this without criticism. She entered into the game and prepared a bottle for Mary when the little girl asked for one, and even diapered her and bathed her in the bathinette. A few repetitions of this game were enough to satisfy Mary that nothing very special was being given to the baby that she was not getting, and she was quite content to be mother's "big girl" again.

Dolls

Many youngsters who would scarcely glance at a doll before will welcome one now. Even little boys need dolls at this age—and will for several years to come. A few pieces of cloth to wrap the "baby" in serve as a wardrobe: the two-year-old cannot manage more intricate garments. The first thing he does on getting a dressed doll is to undress it, and he is quite satisfied if it remains that way.

By and large, the child who has a younger brother or sister will play more with dolls than an only child. For the latter, a doll can offer special values. It may help the child to learn some of the lessons of cleanliness that are required—for instance, toilet training may go more smoothly when Janey can rehearse for it by setting her doll on her own small toilet seat and telling it, "Now you go siss in the toilet and not in your panties!"

As household toys accumulate, it is helpful to establish a doll corner in the child's room, if space permits. It is not necessary or desirable to furnish the doll corner all at once. One piece at a time should be the rule, because children need time to assimilate the new. As the year goes on, a small chest of drawers, an ironing board, toy iron, and set of cleaning tools may be added. Size of equipment is very important, for the manual dexterity of the child must be taken into account when buying. Toy stores and toy departments are not always the best sources for play equipment at this age. Small paper-covered lingerie "chests," such as are to be found in the closet department of many stores, make better doll bureaus than most of those offered as toys. Laundry sets manufactured specifically for children are usually too small and not sufficiently sturdy to be really useful. Small metal baby baths or galvanized washtubs are apt to be much more satisfactory, and fullsized clothespins are better than miniatures. Some of the smaller plastic dishes from the tableware counter at the dime store may be easier for the two-year-old to handle than the sets sold for dolls.

A Place for Toys

If toys threaten to inundate the home, two movable single-panel screens, made of composition board and fastened to sturdy wooden bases, can be made to serve as a simple playhouse and to keep playthings within bounds. Windows may be cut through the board, and curtains hung at them to give the cozy look of a real house (the two-year-old does not require this much detail, but we do not see why the adult shouldn't have some fun, too). Portable and flexible, the screen can be set up anywhere in the house, and can be made just right for one child or a group.

If broad shelves like those suggested in the last chapter have been installed, they may take care of current storage problems. Or auxiliary units may be needed. Orange crates, sanded and painted, make good temporary cupboards, and plastic curtains fastened to the front keep out the dust. Toy mops and brushes, awkward to store, can be hung from a row of cup-hooks screwed into the side of the toy shelf. Screw eyes set into the handles, or holes drilled through them near the top, will hold loops for hanging.

Make-believe, of course, does not stop with dolls or household toys, and many of Two's other toys need not and should not be realistic. Blocks that interlock make more satisfactory trains than more realistic trains because they do not come apart as easily, nor overturn. The fact that they do not move unless they are pushed is a definite advantage, because they are easier to control and more specifically within the power of the two-year-old.

However, realistic objects, especially those with moving parts, appeal to him. An eggbeater or a small meat grinder (manually operated, of course, and without the knives) fascinate him. Because his forearm can rotate now, circular movements are easier now than they were earlier. In addition, the child has reached the point at which he can do two things at a time—both manipulate an object and watch the results!

Important Messes

The importance of water play continues, and need not be confined to out-of-doors. In fact, the place for water play is any room where water is handy and where it will do no damage if spilled. Ordinarily, kitchen or bathroom are best. Even in small apartments, a corner can be found that can be arranged for this kind of play. A large sheet of plastic or oilcloth (an old table cover or crib sheet) will protect the floor. A good thick layer of newspapers—about two inches—goes over this to sop up spilled water, and the tub is placed on top.

Equipment for water play can be found in every household. Little children love to dip sponges in and squeeze them. Filling and emptying small pans or pitchers is also fun, and this simple, repetitious play holds their interest for surprisingly long periods, often longer than any other.

Doll clothes or handkerchiefs to "wash," eggbeaters, floating objects of many kinds can be used to vary the play from time to time. A handful of soapflakes makes the play more interesting. A pile of suds follows even a little beating of the water, and adds the joys of achievement to primitive pleasure. Soapsuds are magic to the two-year-old—something he has created by his own efforts. If the child cannot manage a rotary beater, a pastry fork or sieve will create much the same effect. Soda straws and little pipes through which air can be blown into the water are also rewarding. The child who is still using a bottle, or who has just given it up, may find these mouth toys very satisfactory—but they shouldn't be combined with soapy water unless the child understands they are for blowing and not for sucking. The soapsuds game can be given an extra fillip if you add drops of vegetable coloring to the water.

The technique of blowing real bubbles will emerge from simple "bubbling" into the water, but not until much later in the year. When a bubble-pipe can be managed easily, it pays tremendous dividends in feelings of achievement. Lacking a bubble-pipe, the same effect can be gained by using a wooden spool, wetting one end and rubbing soft soap on it. A few drops of glycerin added to the water will make larger, longer lasting bubbles.

If this play produces a mess, let us remember that cleaning up can be fun, too. Unlike his mother, Two likes few things better than wiping up spillage. Keeping large absorbent cloths, old newspapers, sponges, a small supply of soapflakes, pans, washable dolls, floating toys, etc., on a low shelf which the child can reach will make both preparation and pickup easier. A hose which fits the bathroom or kitchen faucets will simplify filling the tub, and may make it unnecessary to move it after it is filled.

A pair of outgrown boots, too small to go over shoes, but large enough to be worn without them, will keep Two's feet dry. Plastic envelopes, for sale at any dime-store kitchen counter, can be wrapped around shoes if boots or rubbers are not available. Clothing can be protected by a waterproof apron, made of a length of old shower curtain or discarded plastic window curtain, with a hole in the middle for the head to slip through. It will be more durable if the cut edges are taped, and tapes can be sewed on to hold it together at the sides. Even without tapes, with a band of narrow elastic or an old belt to hold it together in the middle, it will last for some time.

Plasticene and clay are other excellent creative materials. An oil-based clay that does not dry out, plasticene can be bought in several colors, in any toy or variety store. The color seems to make little difference; the feel and flexibility are the attractions. Before plasticene is offered for the first time, it should be warmed in the hand and kneaded to make it pliable.

Some people feel that clay is preferable because, by the addition of water, its consistency can be adjusted to the needs of the individual child. It is somewhat more expensive and must be wrapped in a damp cloth and put in a covered container when not being used. On the other hand, if it does dry out, it can be reconditioned by breaking it into small pieces, wetting the fragments and, when these have soaked up the moisture, kneading, cutting and rekneading them.

A piece of oilcloth on the floor, newspapers on the table, and a waterproofed board about ten by twelve inches, on which the clay or plasticene is actually handled, complete the preparations. (Any board can be waterproofed with varnish and wax. A large breadboard is a convenient shape.) The best tools at this point are the child's own hands.

Pound and Squeeze

Before we get into two-year-old art forms, we might pause for a moment to clarify our expectations. When children first handle clay, or other plastic materials, they are not sculptors in miniature. They do not set out to make anything. Their interest is in the material itself.

Betty-at-two squeezes and squeezes to enjoy the lovely, live feel of it. She smells it curiously, puts a bit tentatively in her mouth, holds it inquiringly up to her cheek. She wants to know what it is like. Then she wants to find out what she can *do* to the material. She pokes and pounds and pulls off little pieces. If there is water handy, she may pop the clay into that, just to see what happens.

For a long time the sheer fun of such activity may be enough. Young children seem to need something that they can break and mend, over and over again. Perhaps they do so much accidental breaking, bringing so many storms down on themselves, that it is reassuring to have something that they can mend as well as break. In addition, the chance to exert all one's energies without bringing anxious *noes* from parents gives delicious release. Small apartments and city streets mean restraint, an unnatural damming of energy and movement. Children are bewildered and frustrated by the bars to activity that they meet on all sides. As a consequence they sometimes become irritable, and impulsively destructive. Clay gives them a chance to vent their anger and to release the pent up energy. Probably this is why, after a session with clay, irritable children are noticeably calmer and easier to manage.

After Betty and Chuck have had a chance to pull apart and put together, they are ready for the next step, and it is a giant one, even though most of the time it is sheer accident. Betty pokes a finger into her hunk of clay. It leaves a hole. This has happened before, but this time she looks at it with special attention. She has made her mark on a piece of the great outside world, and there it is for everyone to see!

New experiments begin. Clay is rolled, shaped, built into forms. The child can use a little help sometimes. She may find herself in a rut, making the same motions over and over; but the sight of someone else doing something different can be an exciting challenge. It is a mistake for the adult to make finished objects for the child to copy, but new "raw" forms may be demonstrated without harm—balls, long rolls, etc.—so long as they are given no definite names. The privilege of naming, putting together, discovering what the forms look like, is the child's.

After a time, small tools like orange sticks and tongue depressors will encourage further experimentation. With these the child may discover that tools can be an extension of himself— that he can increase and vary the effects his hands alone produced before. From the first primitive pleasure in the sheer feel of the clay to the controlled use of tools is a long step, but it is only one of the many crucial steps the two-year-old takes as he plays between one birthday and the next.

Sometimes a youngster who has been punished for playing with "dirty" things, or who has been asked too early to give up interest in his own body products, needs more of a chance to mess and smear with substitute materials than even clay and water can provide. Cold cream or Vaseline can be offered. Though these may strike the adult as outlandish play materials, they are actually no harder to wash off than other smeary substances, and their use may help to make our social demands for cleanliness in other ways easier for the child to accept.

When our young investigators begin to smear these various materials not only on themselves but on floors and walls, it is time to introduce a surface just for this purpose. Or it may be that the child is ready for finger painting.

Finger Painting

Because finger paint is applied without need for any tool other than the child's own hands, it is considered by many the child's best introduction to creative art. Most children seem ready for finger painting between the ages of two and a half and three. Though they may experiment with painting themselves at first, rather than the paper, those who have had plenty of chance to play with water, mud, and clay soon give this up.

The paint, delightfully sticky to a child, may be purchased uncolored, in the primary colors, and black. The colors can be mixed during painting, of course. The young painter needs only one color at a time at first, although it is a good thing to have two or three on hand, to give him some choice.

The paints are used with specially coated paper which can be purchased in large sheets in most stores which sell the paints. For the very young child, not yet interested in saving his pictures, white oilcloth, which can be wiped clean when he has finished, is adequate. Wrapping paper with a shiny surface can also be used.

Finger paint can easily be made at home. The ingredients are a few cents' worth of gum arabic, half a box of cornstarch, and three quarts of water. The gum arabic is soaked in a small amount of water overnight, then added to the starch, which has been dissolved in cold water. The mixture is boiled until it forms a jelly-like transparent substance, and this is the basic medium. It is colored by mixing into it, while it is hot, powdered poster paints or ordinary food coloring. One tablespoon of poster paint powder to a quart of solution is usually satisfactory, but colors can be made more intense by adding more of the powder.

If gum arabic is not available, a solution made with a half cup of clothes starch to a quart of water can be used as the base. This will not keep as well as the other, but it will serve for immediate use. Since the child is more interested in the doing than in the end product, the plain starch solution may be quite adequate.

The technique of finger painting is extremely simple. If paper is used, a shallow pan somewhat longer than the width of the paper is necessary. The paper, which should be in large sheets, at least sixteen by twenty-two inches, is prepared by being drawn through two or three inches of water in the pan. Then it is laid, shiny side up, on a flat surface, and pulled smooth. Since children need help in preparing the paper, this is another argument for using oilcloth.

The paint is dropped onto the surface, a tablespoonful at a time. The child dips his hands in water and then smears the paint to his heart's content. Since it often goes beyond the edges of the sheet, the paper should be placed on a piece of waterproof material.

Ideally, the paint should be worked with full rhythmic arm movements. When children are not afraid to get messy, the whole body sways with the vigor of their movements. Each stroke of the hands and touch of the fingers brings new patterns, but these are ordinarily only of passing interest to the very young artist—he tends to be absorbed in the feel of the paints, in seeing them spread under his hands, in mixing colors together to see what happens.

When the color flows over to other parts of the room, a gentle reminder that the paper or oilcloth is the place for the paint often is enough to bring the activity back to permitted limits. If inappropriate use of the materials persists, it is advisable to withhold finger paints until the child is older.

Poster Painting

The parent who is eager to open every avenue of self-expression to his child may introduce poster paints sometime after his second birthday. This activity will require an easel, large sheets of newsprint paper, or unglazed wrapping paper, large brushes, and a supply of water-soluble paints.

In a small apartment, a single easel that can be attached to the wall may be preferable to the double easel that stands free. Where space is plentiful, the latter is more desirable because it can be used by two children at the same time, offering a fine opportunity for sociability without interference—just what the two-to-three needs. Single or double, the easel should be adjustable to the child's changing height, permitting the paper to be placed so that its center is at eye level.

A wall easel can be made easily from a piece of thin plywood or beaverboard, about twenty by twenty-six inches, and two blocks of wood about two inches thick. The blocks are screwed to the back of the board at the bottom corners, to give a slight slant to the easel when it is hung. Rectangular cheese boxes may be attached to the lower edge of the board to hold the paint containers. Two holes drilled at the top of the easel, near the corners, can be used for hanging it from screws or nails driven into a wall or door.

Paint containers should have wide bases, to reduce tipping.

Jelly glasses or squat jars are excellent. The child must learn to dip his brush with some care, and to wipe the excess paint off against the edge of the container as he draws the brush out. This requires a good deal of control and the two-year-old needs brushes that are easy to handle. Those with long handles, the bristle end about three-quarters of an inch wide, are best.

The pleasure the child gets out of painting depends partly on the consistency of the paints. They should be easy-flowing without being runny. The paint can be bought in powder form in pound and half-pound boxes in school-supply and art stores. Bright colors are preferable to dull ones. As with finger paints, it is best to present one color at a time to the child under three. Allow him to choose which color he will work with, unless choices obviously confuse him.

A smock will help keep the problems of laundry and self-development apart. An old shirt, the sleeves cut short, and worn back to front, makes an excellent smock.

The "pictures" of the two-year-old are like no others ever seen. They may consist of a few arched or flowing lines on a sheet of otherwise blank paper. A mass of dots is another favorite pattern, and a small area of color scrubbed into the paper is not infrequent.

It is natural to wonder what these pictures mean. By and large, they are self-portraits, two-year style. They reflect the level of the child's physiological development, shown in the way he holds his brush, the skill with which he modulates its pressure on the paper, the sweep of his movements as he applies the paint. They also suggest the way the child feels about the world around him, his courage or timidity in approaching it, and the confidence with which he uses it for his own ends.

After he has had a bit of experience, Jimmy will experiment with different kinds of lines: vertical, horizontal, arcs, circles. He will want to use many sheets of paper, sometimes discarding sheet after sheet with only a line or two on it. But each line or group of dots may be for him a completed experiment. To expect economy at two is to expect the impossible.

Grownups have a way of going to extremes about these early paintings. Some insist on preserving every scrap the child produces; others ridicule or disregard them because they seem to be only daubs. Neither attitude is realistic. The child's work deserves respect as a reflection of the child himself. Painting, he is absorbed in what he is *doing;* he is not consciously thinking about making something. The spread of color on what was a blank surface is enough for him. To ask him to tell what his picture is "supposed to be" is to expect too much. It is not *supposed* to be anything, except marks on paper. After he has finished working, Two is no longer interested in his picture. To him it is simply the dead husk of a living experience; the experience itself is what counts.

Creating Is Important

One cannot be blamed for asking, "What is the use of all this—the clay and paints and finger paints? If the child is not interested in making anything or drawing anything, aren't mud-pies enough for him?"

The answer is not simple. What the child achieves as he messes is a complex process of doing, learning, expressing, and creating all intermingled. We must remember that he has not yet learned enough words to tell us all he feels; he needs whatever help these other forms of expression can give him. Moreover, these materials, which are an important part of our culture and of creative communication, help us all through life to give form to feelings for which we have no words. The child's crude and groping experiences may be the basis for many satisfactions later on—though we are not suggesting that every happy dauber will one day be an accomplished artist.

Further, the materials that a child can manipulate into new forms help him to discover himself. When the two-year-old streaks red paint over white paper, he is not only showing what he can do—he is finding out what his capacities are. Mastery of a new medium, if only in arcs and curlicues or small clay "worms," gives him more confidence in his own resources and in his ability to deal with anything that confronts him.

Out-of-Doors with Two

"Out, out, out!" Johnny at two can't wait to escape from the confines of his dwelling. Once outside, he finds a wealth of chal-

THE IN-BETWEENERS: FROM TWO TO THREE 53

lenge to his growing muscular control. Every time he walks a stone fence successfully, he adds a cubit to his stature. He has solved a new problem. Last year, he conquered the wide horizontal spaces and began his climbing adventures. Now he can cope not only with the vertical but the narrow raised surface.

In equipping the play yard we must keep his new need in mind. One ingenious piece of equipment, called a ladder-box, to be purchased from suppliers of nursery-school equipment or made by a handy father, will satisfy his craving for climbing and balancing and yet keep him fairly safe. As its name indicates, it is a combination of ladder and box, but when combined with a two-year-old it becomes much more.

Approximately four by four by two and a half feet, it has two solid sides and four that are more or less open. Ladder bars cross two, the third is crossed by two widely spaced bars, the fourth has two planks forming ledges for sitting and clambering.

Sturdily built of hardwood or well-seasoned pine, the ladder-box has a variety of possibilities, depending on which side is uppermost. A short wooden ladder, with a cleat nailed to one

end, can be attached to the box simply by hooking the cleat over one edge. A plank, similarly cleated, makes a good slide.

Turning to other equipment, a cleated plank bridging the gap between two large wooden blocks or low carpenter's horses makes a good balancing board. A barrel with both ends knocked out makes a fine tunnel for crawling. Chocks will keep it from rolling, or it can be steadied by setting it in a shallow trench.

Packing cases such as refrigerators come in are treasures for the backyard when sanded and, preferably, weatherproofed. They serve as playhouse, cage, cave, or just something to climb on.

One of the services play performs at two is to strengthen the large muscles of the body. Climbing develops the muscles in the legs, torso, and arms. The use of parallel bars is especially good for arm development. For the very little child they should be no higher than thirty inches, and set about fourteen inches apart, on a firm base. Wagons to pull, large balls to roll and push, outdoor blocks to drag and pile all play a part in the job of developing a strong and skillful body.

Wheelbarrows, wheel toys with pedals, balls to kick as well as throw will offer further exercise for leg muscles. When the child must play alone, a really large ball that can be sat on and rolled over bodily will almost take the place of a playmate. And when large equipment palls, the tot turns again to the well-loved sandbox, now more popular than ever. Pie tin, muffin pan, sugar scoop, strainer: whatever is empty must be filled. Patting, smoothing, piling, dumping, Two is content, by himself or with companions, for incredibly long periods of time.

Social Life

"No! No! No!"

"Don't!"

"Mine! Mine!"

Assorted shrieks and screams of rage are the sound effects of unsupervised group play at two. Not yet a social being, the two-year-old has come only a little way out of the cave. Although he has outgrown the blinders of infancy, he is not yet ready to be involved too intimately with his own kind.

A child of five or six is usually the best first playmate for a two-year-old. The younger child is not as tempted to investigate

THE IN-BETWEENERS: FROM TWO TO THREE

the older by pinching and pushing as he would be with someone his own size, and the older child is far less likely to make off with the little one's treasured possessions. Without the burden of having to defend himself and his belongings, Two can relax while he plays and fully enjoy the pleasure of being in contact with another child. The shift to his own age group can be made gradually by having one other two-year-old join him and his older companion. Eventually the older child need not be included unless he is on hand in the ordinary course of events.

There is much to be said for the mixed-age play group. Older children teach little ones a great deal about social techniques and ways of handling materials, and stimulate them to new ideas in play. The little ones may have to be protected against being bossed too much of the time, but even with this slight drawback, they get more out of mixed groups than out of the exclusive company of their own age-mates.

One playmate or one visiting adult at a time is a good rule to follow soon after the second birthday. The two-year-old is not equipped to deal with the complexities of more than one set of relationships at a time. Fortunately he can protect himself in larger groups by ignoring everyone but the one person who is most meaningful to him. The wise parent will be thankful for this built-in protective device.

When young children are together, the temptation to touch, push, pinch, or bite is often irresistible. That is why they play together more successfully out-of-doors, where they have space to get away from each other. They can stretch their muscles without bumping into things. They can all do the same thing without battling over materials. They can get acquainted while they play the old, familiar games: running in and out of cubbies, chasing each other back and forth, hiding and being found.

As a general principle, materials that can be divided among several children without limiting the play of any are most desirable for promoting harmonious play. Clay, sand, blocks are excellent if enough are provided. A further step in the direction of cooperative play is encouraged by materials that go together, like blocks and a wagon. Two little ones can function together happily with this kind of equipment, since each has something important and interesting to do. One brings the blocks and the other puts them into the wagon. One pulls and the other pushes the load, and both dump it over with equal vigor and glee. The pull-and-push principle applies to tricycles, too.

If the play is to be indoors, it is wise to have the playroom arranged ahead of time. A small table covered with oilcloth, with clay or plasticene set out at two places, will serve as a center of interest. The doll corner, with house-play equipment organized around it, might be another. A book or two might be left lying on a chair or bench. A supply of small cars, beads to string, paper and scissors for snipping, cards with holes for lacing are other possibilities, but should not all be visible at the same time. The young host's particularly prized possessions should be put out of sight when visitors are expected.

Large sheets of paper for crayoning allow the children to give and get ideas, yet to work each on his own project. After the first hesitation has worn off, Two gets special pleasure out of crayoning on his neighbor's sheet, and when there is a double easel available, he may like to crayon or paint on the opposite side from another young artist. Sometimes two of them want to paint together on the same side of the easel, but that is likely to lead rather quickly to a breach of the peace.

Problems of Management

Young Twos do well if they last out an hour in contact with other children. Toward the end of the year, two hours of play are possible if they are divided between indoor and outdoor activities. Sounds of protest, furniture falling over, or disorganized running and jumping are signals for a change of activity. If this happens after the children have been engaged in sedentary play, something more active is in order. Records might be brought out for marching or dancing. A chance to be locomotives or bears or autos lets off enough energy to make another session of quiet play acceptable.

We must realize that the two-year-old does not know when he needs help. It is our job to watch out for signs of fatigue, to step in before disputes develop into battles, and to help terminate play in due season.

Giving warning before a change in play or activity helps keep things functioning smoothly. Phrases like these ease the child peacefully from one activity to the next:

"Pretty soon we'll go out."

"Orange juice is coming now."

"Soon we'll wash hands."

Suggestions should be made in the form of specific statements. A general command like "put the toys away" will rarely work, but "Dolly goes in her bed—cars go on this shelf" stands a much better chance of success. Also, in trying to keep Two's social life smooth, it is best to make definite suggestions rather than questions that may be answered by a flat "No." These phrases were overheard in a skillfully supervised nursery group:

"What else can you use, Mary?"

"Helen needs the wagon; you could use this wheelbarrow."

"Jackie needs this car; let's find another one for you."

"Julius could *tell* Jennie." (Instead of hitting.) "Say, 'No, Jennie.'"

Adding to the Toy Shelf

It may be that you have now accumulated enough toys to occupy the two-year-old happily for some time. However, there *are* some things that a child loves to do now which he could not manage before. If there are gaps in his supplies, here are some suggestions, many of which will serve for months, even years, to come.

Simple puzzles feed the same interest in boundaries that, on a larger scale, drives the two-year-old to walking curbstones. The best ones for this age do not look like puzzles at all. They are simple shapes that fit together to produce patterns. Four or five identical triangles cut out of plywood or fiberboard, three to four inches to a side, can be put together in many combinations. When they are painted different colors, the patterns can be varied in even more ways.

Large circles may be cut into two arc-shaped pieces that are easy to fit together, or into triangular segments, like a pie.

Squares and rectangles cut out of plywood, similarly sized so that they can fit together, painted in bright colors, are also good playthings.

Puzzles that are slightly more advanced may be made by cutting simple shapes out of a rectangle of plywood about twelve by fifteen inches, and mounting the remaining frame on a solid backing. If the cut-outs are painted a color that contrasts with the background piece, they furnish more vivid lessons in shapes and contours.

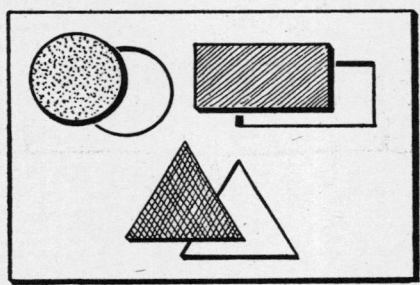

After the child has gained some experience with puzzles, animal shapes may be used for the cut-outs. These should differ markedly from each other in size or outline if several are to go into one framework.

Flannel-play sets are similar to puzzles in appeal, but are less demanding. Although these are available at toy stores under various trade names, they are best made at home for the very young. They consist of a flannel-covered double easel and a large number of pieces of textured material in varying shapes, colors, and sizes. Any material which will cling to the flannel-covered board is suitable: felt, flannel, velvet, etc.

For the two-to-three-year-old the easel should be about twenty-four by thirty inches and constructed so that it can stand up on a table or lie flat. Such an easel can be made by inserting two pieces of cardboard of the right size into a double-envelope flannel slipcover. Ties sewed on the edges of the cover about six inches from the middle on each side will keep the easel from collapsing when it is standing up.

The opening for the boards is at the center of the double envelope, and is concealed when the easel is in use.

The child needs only to place the pieces of material on the board, with a pat to make them stay. With a good variety of colors and sizes to choose from, he can create innumerable designs. There are no clean-up problems to speak of, and children can occupy themselves for long periods. This is especially good for entertaining more than one child at a time, when there is no time for the special preparations involved in the use of clay or paint.

Flexible plastic also offers diversion for the two-year-old. This can be obtained in sheets of different colors, and cut out to please the fancy. A piece of cardboard, fiberboard, or plywood covered with the plastic makes the base. When smaller pieces of the material are laid on, they adhere to it until removed. Sets constructed along these lines are also available in toy stores.

Like other creative materials, these sets continue to be useful for many years—until the child is ten, in some cases. They belong to the general category of materials that change as the child changes, being used for simple expressions at first and more complicated ones later.

Blocks, of course, belong to the same category. Around the second birthday, two-inch-square table blocks are preferred, in bright, solid colors.

Building with blocks rarely comes before thirty months. The first wobbly towers are explorations in the dynamics of balance. These the child must learn before he can go on to more complicated structures. When Libby takes books from their shelves to pile them on top of one another on the floor, the time for building blocks has come.

There are substitutes for the rather expensive kindergarten blocks found in stores. Cigar boxes, for example, make fine large blocks if the tops are fastened down securely. Satisfactory units can be cut from ordinary two by four lumber, in lengths of three, six, twelve, and twenty-four inches. The ready-made blocks, however, have the virtue of being made of hardwood. Besides being practically indestructible, they are smoothly finished.

The recommended set for a two-year-old consists of six of the smallest units (called "half-units"), eight larger ones, and six double units (about twelve inches). In addition, four small triangles, two quarter-circles, two small half-circles, two short rectangular pieces, and two small cylinders, are suggested.

Construction and imaginative play go hand in hand, and a

small supply of little cars, trains, animals, and people enriches block play. The animals and people can be cut out of plywood, or wooden ones may be bought. The vehicles are best made of hard rubber or soft plastic.

Sturdy action toys can be made at home fairly easily. Boxes hooked or tied together make acceptable trains. Spools or button molds wired on for wheels can transform the same boxes into small wagons. A cylinder and a small flat block nailed to a rectangular unit make a fine locomotive. A screw eye will provide a hold for a pulling cord.

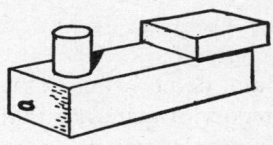

Combinations of cylinder slices and slightly shaped flat blocks produce boats, barges, and ferries.

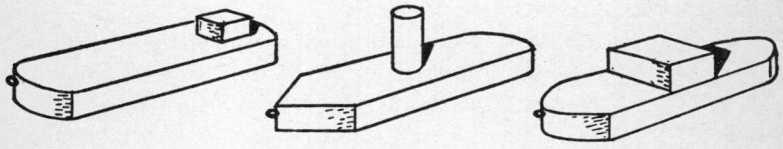

Wooden rectangles about one and a quarter by three by six inches, with ends cut to allow for coupling, make excellent trains and barges. A string of these can be pushed around the room, or pulled with the help of a cord tied to a screw eye in the first one.

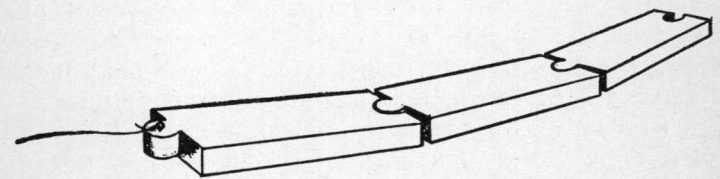

If it is more convenient to purchase more conventional realistic types of trains, special attention should be paid to the wheels. They should be fastened by cotter pins, or bolts. Tracks are not appropriate for this age. The free-wheeling quality of trackless trains fits in with the imaginative flow of the child, and his manual skill.

The child at two, going on three, whose hands have finally consented to obey him, finds small-muscle activities fun. Blunt scissors may be introduced and old magazines donated for snipping. Bead stringing requires enough concentration to make a small triumph of each bead that slides on the string. Wooden beads at least one inch in length are best to start with. Painted spools and button molds can be used with, or instead of, regular beads. The string might be a shoelace, or a special stringing lace with a long, firm tip. If no tipped string is available, edhesive tape or Scotch tape can be used to stiffen the end of any piece of firm cord.

Improved eye-hand co-ordination permits the use of a wooden pegboard, containing many round openings, into which the child inserts quarter-inch pegs of different colors. At first the pleasure comes from achieving an exacting task; later, color-matching and design production take over.

All sorts of little things are welcome additions to the toy shelves—bright pebbles, marbles, tiny bottles, buttons, little books, miniature packs of cards. (These should be offered only if mouthing has stopped, of course.) The age of "beautiful junk" has begun.

Despite his real ability to concentrate on quiet tasks (sometimes fifteen minutes at a time!) Two is still a creature of action. He will dote on trucks and cars from now on. While three- or four-inch vehicles fit in with block play, the twelve- to fifteen-inchers are more suitable for pushing around with engine noises. Rubber wheels are almost a must for indoor play. Bodies of metal will stand up under the usual drubbing meted out to them, but plastic is often too brittle or fragile for this age.

Flimsy toys are always dangerous, and may be the source of destructive habits at any age, but at two special care should be taken to avoid them. Two tends to become attached to his toys; he acts as if they were part of himself. When they break, his anxiety is greater than it was earlier, or than it will be when he is older.

Other items that should be considered at this time are: various kinds of rocking equipment, especially those large enough for two children; tractors and locomotives large enough for the child to ride; wheeled toys with pedals. Before buying a large riding toy that has no pedals, it might be well to consult one's pediatrician. Some question the advisability of the pushing motion necessary to make these move.

Books Again

At two words are wonderful things: sometimes they make sense, and sometimes they don't, but who cares when you can string them together and play with them like bits of bright color or puzzle pieces? This is why nursery rhymes are Two's meat. Maybe he doesn't know what they mean, but they have such delicious sounds that come over and over again—he can even get to know when they're coming.

Mastery is a passion at this age. Being entertained is fine, but learning and repeating is much, much better. The repetitions in stories like the *Three Little Pigs, Chicken Little, The Gingerbread Man* offer double pleasure—the pleasure of familiarity quickly established, and the joys of anticipation. It is recognition, not novelty, that gives the child a thrill. Novelty is old hat—everything was novel only a short time ago.

Imitations of familiar sounds find a welcome in the ears of the two-year-old: the *chug, chug* of the engine, the *zoom* of the plane, the *buzz* of bees. Similarly, stories that repeat his own experiences give him satisfaction. Books about everyday doings—going to the market, a trip on a train, getting a haircut—keep him entranced.

Homemade stories are as welcome as homemade toys. What Johnny did when he went to see Grandmother, what he saw at the zoo, what Katie, his friend, did when she came to his house—these he will ask for again and again. As he nears his third birthday he will demand detailed tales about what he did when he was a baby: how he was bathed, what he ate, how he took his airing. It is reassuring to him to be able to fill out his idea of himself, but perhaps more reassuring is the fact that there is someone who knows all about him and knew how to take such good care of him in the past. It is his hold on the future.

Reading to Two is a cooperative affair. He must look and

touch, and after he has had some experience with a book, he wants to participate by filling in words and phrases he knows. He likes to enumerate parts of the body, or name kinds of animals, and respond to questions like, "Where is the doggie?"

Favorite stories will be called for day after day—and woe betide the careless reader who changes a phrase! To introduce something new the desperate adult may have to resort to guile, using familiar subject matter as a bridge to a new story. For example, if Bobby has been insisting on *The Three Bears* too long, it may be possible to introduce *Ask Mr. Bear* one day, as another book about bears. The "Little" books get ready acceptance because they deal with things the child already knows, *The Little Train, The Little Auto,* etc.

Two enjoys certain kinds of fantasy. Talking animals do not seem strange to him. The nonsense of nursery rhymes is all right because it is heavily laden with repetition and rhythm. For the most part, however, he prefers the factual.

Since fact is at least as strange as fiction to Two, this is not surprising. For our educational ends, factual materials are also best. We are trying to help Two understand the everyday world; why confuse him by telling him about what is not real as if it were real, when he is not yet able to tell the two apart? The world as it exists is still fresh with wonder for him; he would like to know more about it.

Music for Two

The language of the body is still the language our child knows best. His "listening" to music consists of movement. His head nods, his feet tap, his torso sways, his arms swing. Finally he can contain himself no longer: he breaks into a prancing run. If the music moves sedately, his movements match it as he marches in a circle, his Teddy bear in the crook of an arm. Let the music quicken and he is off with it, running, turning in circles, bouncing up and down.

If a record-player is used, it should be down where Sally can watch the record go round. She enjoys it even more if she can put the needle down, or if she can throw the switch while someone else manages the needle. From some points of view, a manually operated machine is more fun than an automatic one, because it can be wound while the music is going.

Markedly rhythmic music is the preference of the youngest set. Ravel's "Bolero," some of Sousa's marches, selections from "The Nutcracker Suite," by Tchaikovsky, Ponchielli's "Dance of the Hours," Rossini's "William Tell Overture," are examples of selections likely to hold their interest.

Like familiar toys and familiar stories, familiar tunes are the best beloved. When rest time comes and Ruthie squirms, a favorite record can help her settle down. For some, records take the place of the bedtime story. At two, when thrusting energies and curiosity make it difficult to let go of the day, this can be a blessing.

Conversely, we can use music to get action. A chant of "Here we go into the house, into the house, into the house," has inveigled many a reluctant little character. "Putting our toys away, putting our blocks away," sung with vigor, can make cleaning-up a pleasant task.

The great thing at two is to be able to do things, with confidence and enjoyment. This is no time for niggling perfectionism. The unself-conscious, spontaneous joy in the song-query that accompanies us as we pass a child—"Where are you going, lady? What are you doing, lady?"—this is what music means to Two, and what we hope it will continue to mean at three and four and five.

Holidays and Parties

With the second birthday, the toddler begins to take part in family celebrations. Earlier he was a beloved onlooker; now he can really participate.

His own birthday party may be the first joyful occasion in which he takes an active part. Planned especially for him, it will be kept simple and within his capacities to manage. Since food is the essence of a party at two, a mealtime is often the best occasion. One friend and the immediate family are enough, as guests.

The cake is the high point. Blowing out the candles, and having "Happy Birthday" sung is sufficient ritual. After the meal is over, it is best to terminate the festivities quickly, to keep the day happy.

Presents must be managed astutely. If there are more than two or three, it is best to distribute them throughout the day, opening one at each meal, perhaps. Family visits should also be strung out, so that the child does not have to cope with more than one visitor at a time.

Aside from his birthday, Christmas, Easter, and Thanksgiving are the other holidays that Two can begin to take part in. He is able to appreciate all of these through ·the concrete things that are associated with them. The bunny means Easter; the turkey, Thanksgiving. Two is not interested in historical or symbolical explanations; they are beyond his comprehension at this point.

The wonder of Christmas will come through the tree that he sees, the pretty cards that he can hold and examine, and his gifts. If there are a considerable number of these, they had better be doled out over several days, to cut down overexcitement.

Places of His Own

Participation in celebrations gives only a faint hint of the way the two-year-old will want to take over the family. As he sees it, his home and his family are all his. He expects and should have at least a little space for his own things in every room in the house. In the living room, part of a bookshelf can accommodate a box of blocks, a few little cars, several baby books. A large square of sturdy cotton material, with loops at the corners, can define his play space. This may be called Two's "rug," and he will soon get used to putting it down when he wants to play. When he has finished, the toys can be gathered up quickly, if there is not time for a systematic put-away, by catching the corner loops together. A round "rug" with a drawstring in the edge serves the same purpose.

The kitchen presents even fewer problems. A low shelf in the cupboard, or an orange crate stood on one end, is sufficient. If the crate is used, a cover of plastic material, with an opening down the front, could make it more sightly and keep out dust. A few spoons, an eggbeater, some old pans, a small apron of his own, would satisfy the child. Macaroni to "cook," a bit of dough now and then, a little water—these are all he needs to occupy him in the kitchen, and to give him the feeling that he has a rightful place there.

Outings and Special Times

Family outings are long remembered with enjoyment. A walk in the park to feed the squirrels, a visit to a neighborhood pet shop, a brief stopover at the playground are highlighted by the fact that the family is all together. The simpler the excursion, the better; one objective at a time, and then home. If the zoo is attempted, remember that the endurance of Two is limited. The monkeys alone may be enough for a single visit.

Every day should hold one time especially assigned to Daddy. Usually this is the hour just before bedtime, after the child has had his dinner. Since this precedes sleep, it is well to keep it in two stages, one in the living room, and one in the child's own room. A little roughhousing is a good thing, if it is followed by quiet play just before bed. Reading or singing together just before the goodnights are said leads gently from the busyness of the day to the relaxation of sleep.

CHAPTER IV

Three: Settling In

THREE IS WISE. Three is sweet. Three is restful. "Please give me that," says Three. "Is this the right way?" asks Three. Compared to the tornado that was Two, Three is a zephyr.

For this there are reasons. Three can hold a crayon with less effort; Three can make a stroke stop almost where he wants it to; Three runs without wavering, in control, at ease. Three has arrived.

Managing Emotions

Three has also made a tremendous discovery: one can get almost as much relief, when anger and resentment boil up, by wreaking vengeance on an imaginary person as on a real one. Punching an object or rubbing soap in the faucet's "eyes," the child finds, is almost as satisfactory and has no such unpleasant consequences as kicking Aunt Laura in the shins or throwing soapy water in Sister's face. This is not reasoned out, of course. But somehow, by his third birthday, the child has found that it is better not to let his emotions explode all over the place, as the infant does, nor direct them without discrimination at whatever sets them off, as the toddler is apt to do.

Children's feelings are not things they *choose* to have. They come without invitation and stay till they are spent. Storms cannot be avoided; frustrations must occur if the child is to learn to take his place in a group. But when the child has reached that stage of maturity at which he can use substitutes for the real objects of his rages, parents can help by providing the substitutes.

The older child can let off steam on the baseball field or in a roughhouse; the adult can put his aggressive feelings into words or read a "whodunit" in which a tough detective expresses his rage for him. But Three needs our help in finding ways to get rid of troublesome feelings without harming others or being made to feel guilty.

"Buffets" to the Rescue

Sometimes a Teddy bear spontaneously assumes the role of whipping boy; sometimes it is a doll. We have found it helpful to provide creatures specifically designed to take beatings without harmful effects. In our house they are called "buffets." Essentially they are rag dolls without bodies. The head may be made of canvas, stuffed, with features embroidered in colored thread. The hair can be painted or made of yarn, strongly attached to resist pulling. A woman's blouse or a man's shirt sewed to the neck completes the creature.

A family of these, representing father, mother, and children, are handy things to have around. If the child's real family contains a baby, the buffet family should have one too. An older brother or sister calls for an older child-buffet. Then, when the storms come, there is an appropriate figure to work them out on.

Anyone who doubts the usefulness of these special dolls need only watch a group of preschoolers at play with them to be convinced. Marie was three when her brother was born, and she immediately named the baby buffet "Tony"—her new brother's name. The day the real Tony came home from the hospital marked the beginning of Marie's favorite game, "spanking Tony." Every whipping was well deserved, of course. Tony was bad; Tony broke dishes; Tony cried at night. Toward the real Tony, Marie was sweet and motherly. The buffet was enough to drain off the jealous feelings.

Tommy had a different problem. His parents quarreled. Tommy's baby buffet lay undisturbed in his box, but Mama and Papa buffets were given plenty of exercise. Whenever a friend came to his house, Tommy offered one of the adult creatures and said, "Let's have a fight." Every such game brought Tommy relief. In his small boy's mind, the fighting of the buffets was like the quarreling of his parents: if the buffets could survive, Tommy apparently assumed his mother and father would, also.

The Uses of Fantasy

Imaginative play takes many other forms between three and four years, when many developmental problems ordinarily confront children. "You're a big boy now," they are told, "Big boys don't cry." Or, "If Jeanne took your pail, you get it back. You have to look out for yourself." In instances like these, fantasy makes possible the relief from tension that the real world does not permit.

While she was coping with a host of new problems, Marjorie found it expedient to become a cat for several months. She meowed for things she wanted, scratched people who got in her way, and ate her meals off the floor. Marjorie's mother was trying to make her into a proper little girl—a clean, courteous, gentle, generous, pleasant little girl. Instead, Marjorie became a cat.

Deep inside, where she could not reach with words, Marjorie was having a struggle. She wanted to be the kind of little girl her mother wanted her to be, but she could not, not just yet and all at once. She had too many bitter, angry feelings when she was smacked for getting dirty. She still loved dearly to explore all the bits and pieces of the world that her mother called "filth," in a frightening, disgusted voice. She could not manage to pass the hours from bedtime to rising without wetting herself, and wettings brought sudden, angry scoldings. It was simply not safe to be Marjorie.

But as she could plainly see, cats lead charmed lives. Nobody expects *them* to stay clean or to remember to use the toilet *all* the time. They may investigate and play with and even eat dirty things from the floor. They can even scratch people who annoy them without being disowned. Becoming a cat was Marjorie's way out of her dilemma.

Larry, too, was not quite ready to grow up. He never had had all the cuddling that he needed. Everything was demanded of him too early, before he could perform with confidence. To try to cope with his own kind at three, as well as with grownups, was a forbidding task.

But the world had been a safe place once—when Larry had been a tiny baby and his mother had been with him constantly, and cared for him tenderly. Larry's answer to *his* problems was to be a baby whenever he could. He curled up in a carriage, contentedly sucking at a bottle while another child pushed him around. He lay down obligingly in the doll bed when his friends played house; and if he could find an adult to play with him, his greatest delight was to nestle in her lap, eyes closed, body relaxed, reliving the pleasures of an earlier, happier time.

Reversing Roles

Sometimes the weak become strong in make-believe. One group of little children who were often threatened with bogymen had this favorite game:

One child would come dashing in, shouting, "There's a bogyman," with hands upraised in horror, as if fighting off the fearful specter. Then all would rush to her defense, strike at the imaginary bogy and run away together, congratulating each other on their escape. This game was a healthy one, because it helped the children keep up their courage. It drained off their fear of the bogy and assured them that they were quite capable of dealing with him.

Grownups can act the part of bogies without realizing it. If they are demanding, stern, and strong, the little child must do as they wish, but in make-believe the child can reverse the roles. Timid Jonathan takes the part of his own overwhelming, bearish father, and threatens his doll children with instant annihilation if they do not go to sleep. Sally, the meekest follower in her play group, is transformed into an aggressive, dominating matriarch, ruling her doll family with a heavy hand. In this way, children prove to themselves that they are not quite as weak and helpless as they fear they are.

Mirror of Reality

Imaginative play also mirrors the child's experiences, showing us how they seem to him. To observe this can be amusing and is always instructive.

Mary, at three, sweeps vigorously in the doll corner of a friend's home. "The party's gonna be at one o'clock," she mutters. "Clean up the house. Hurry up—get the house clean. We having achioni and potatoes and string beans."

She gets her friend sweeping, too. Putting a blanket on the doll in the crib, she says sternly, "Stay there, now. Don't you bother nobody."

Later in the day, the doll is being pushed in the swing when her hat falls off. Mary tries to replace it, sputtering, "You put this hat on your head. I spend my money to buy you a hat—you gonna wear it!"

We might not be pleased with ourselves in our children's versions of us, but they certainly show how we appear to them.

Helping with Social Contacts

Imaginative play helps the child begin the great social adventure. The three-year-old shows his readiness for social contacts in many ways. The word *we* has become part of his vocabulary. He can feel sympathy: "Poor mommy, head hurts." "Kitty hurt—poor, poor kitty," he says. He watches people's faces intently for indications of feelings. His enlarged vocabulary makes contact easier, and he breaks out with tales about himself, his toys, or his family at every opportunity. Most important, if good experiences have quieted his fears about losing his possessions, he can now share his toys.

In addition, a better-developed time sense makes it possible for Three to wait a turn: to understand "When it's time" or "In a few minutes." The urgency of living has worn off a little. Surprisingly, he is a conformist—cooperation comes easily to him. The desires of the group are his desires. He is learning that it is more fun to play with others than alone.

Leave several three-year-olds together in a room, with a few props scattered about, and a game of house flourishes in short order. Each one knows what it means to be a member of a family and each can find a role to fit into. How the child plays his particular role depends on the kind of family experience he has had, but the role itself is familiar to all.

One of the delightful discoveries that children make during their first experiences in playing "pretend" together is that they have the same ideas or feelings, and have been through similar experiences. This makes for a group feeling which encourages greater self-confidence; the group strengthens each individual in it.

Moreover, each child has a chance to change his role—a privilege not often granted in the reality of everyday living. The follower of one day's play can be a leader in the next. Different parts can be experimented with and different techniques for handling people tried out. In this way, make-believe can serve as a bridge to filling a role adequately in real life. The value of this kind of play cannot be overestimated; children who do not have a chance at it may find adjustments to their social groups a bit hard later on.

Since imaginative play is so important, it is worth while to give the youngsters some help when they falter. Tactful suggestions from an adult can help elaborate and enrich the play. If Carolyn has started a tea party, for example, Jane can be brought into the group with "Here's Jane come to call. Wouldn't you like to give her some tea?" Or a fatherless play family can be completed by suggesting, "David might like to be the daddy. Can you give him his breakfast before he goes to work?"

When boxes, blocks, and children are thrown together, train-play seems inevitably to emerge. This is particularly useful for involving a large group, since trains need passengers, conductors, switchmen, baggage men, ticket sellers, as well as engineers.

The variety of play will depend largely on the experiences the children have, so it is a good idea to add to their store. Every excursion is relived in imaginative play. Simple things like visits to the grocer, the butcher, or a restaurant will inspire many rich and fruitful hours. The excursions must be short enough to avoid fatigue, of course, and the situation simple enough so that the child can attend to and remember its important parts. A visit to an airport, a railroad station, a firehouse, the zoo, or a harbor is a special occasion. The subway is fascinating if the young explorer, male or female, is permitted to stand at the very front or to look out the back window of the last car.

Play as Preparation

Visits to the doctor or the dentist can be robbed of much of their terror by make-believe rehearsals. Play kits with fairly realistic implements give the child a chance to become familiar with tools like the stethoscope, the drill, even the hypodermic needle. "Open please" practiced on a friend, on a doll, or on mother, removes the apprehension usually connected with doctor's request.

Playing going to grandmother's or staying at a hotel, or an overnight train ride can make for relaxed and joyful participation when the real event comes up. Here, naturally, the adult must introduce the subject to start the play, and guide it, by telling what might come next. Including friends in these play sessions makes them more fun and gives all the children a point of contact from which they can carry on later, after the actual journey.

Props for Imaginative Play

Three-year-olds can usually convert any handy object to their needs, once a project has started, but having a few props around helps. A costume box, instituted at this time, will be helpful for many years. Old hats (both men's and women's), dresses, shirts, scarves, jackets, gloves, pocketbooks, shoes, lengths of material all make a stimulating collection.

Blocks are the building stones of fantasy at three, and this is the time to increase supplies of both indoor and outdoor units. They make tracks, streets, enclosures for trucks and cars, and tunnels for trains. The child who has watched road builders at work becomes himself a powerful manipulator of machinery as he cranks his toy dump-truck to dump his load of blocks on a fancied roadbed. Another works a bulldozer with great concentration as it plows its way into a pile of block-debris to clear the way for a new building. Steam shovels, wreckers, earth movers combine with blocks to play out the whole drama of man's conquest over inanimate materials. But blocks will not be used for building only. Wrecking is sometimes more fun and just as legitimate for overburdened feelings.

Machines for a Machine Age

A co-ordinated set of toy machinery and vehicles can go a long way towards encouraging group play. A dump-truck alone engages one or two children, but if a road-scraper and a steam shovel are also available, a group of four or five can work out a project of some complexity, involving cooperative activity.

A nursery school can provide such sets of toys easily; for play at home they might have to be the result of neighborly planning. Several parents of three-year-olds who play together could work out a program for birthday and Christmas giving so that the toys coming into the various homes would supplement each other. Then each child could contribute to the play of the group something the others would appreciate, and look forward himself to using a coveted toy not available to him at home.

Help Needed

We need not emphasize how delicately the adult must maneuver whenever he has to step into the child's world. At three he is needed often. Although the child is a better group member than he was at two, he still has a good deal to learn about getting along with his fellows.

Toward the middle of the fourth year, strong friendships flourish. This is a time (the first of many such) of "best friends" and cliques. The timid child, the newcomer to the group, is likely to be frozen out or made a scapegoat. Even the sweetest preschooler will occasionally bellow, "You can't come in here"—especially when supported by a couple of cronies. This is the adult's cue to step in.

Concrete suggestions related to the play that is going on are best. "But Jean is bringing a present for the baby," might get results in one situation. "Harry says he has a load to deliver," might prove the magic formula in another. Other children may be used to help settle squabbles. "What does Dorothy think about it?" may be just the suggestion that is needed.

Painting

Three's awareness of form shows itself in the way he handles all kinds of creative materials: crayons, paints, clay, and blocks. With crayon or pencil he can copy simple forms like a cross or a circle. This means that he has two new achievements to his credit: he can now take in the relationship of parts of a figure, and he can control the movements of his hands sufficiently to make the marks take the direction he intends them to.

In poster painting we begin to see many kinds of designs. Some children fill the paper with solid blocks of color. Others experiment with different sorts of strokes: verticals, horizontals, arcs. Still others use the shape of the paper as their guide, and send color after color flowing along in rough rectangles that may become spirals after a while. This is a step forward, beyond the simple paint-spreading that characterized Two at the easel.

Some youngsters, usually those who have been badgered to tell "What it is," begin to name their productions, but the relation of title to picture is tenuous. However, frequent exclamations of "Look what I made!" show that the child is beginning to pay attention to the *results* of his efforts. Before this, of course, he was mostly interested in the *process*. Now, too, the child dislikes sharing his paper with another. What was good fun at two, when the doing was most important, has become an intrusion.

By the time a child is three, an experienced person can tell a good deal about the state of his feelings by watching him paint, or even just by examining a group of his paintings. "Reading" a painting, however, is a job for experts. What is more important to parents is the value of the painting activity to the child, and that is unquestionable. If at two painting contributed to his intellectual development, and expanded his notions about his own abilities, at three it is an invaluable ally to his emotional growth.

When we place a tense child on a cot and command him to rest we often get only twisting and turning, hair pulling, nail biting, and other small explosions of energy. But give him his easel for a while before his rest, and afterwards he is likely to sprawl into healthful relaxation. There is a magic in it. The things that bother him are channeled off, leaving him free and ready for the next step.

On the technical side, the child approaching four needs and can use more than one color at a time. He has enough muscular control to wipe the brush carefully against the side of the paint container and to put it back in the right place when he has finished. Threes need a separate brush for each color, and they can learn to keep each brush with its own color. At this point, too, the child can wash his brushes, and learn to put them away clean when he is finished.

Finger painting also brings new experiences. Children who luxuriated in the rich feel of the paints at two, show more interest in the effects they can create at three. From its first use for smear- and splatter-play, finger paint emerges as a creative medium. Clay follows the other materials. Cakes, balls, snakes, snowmen, dishes emerge more and more frequently, and are used in snatches of imaginative play.

Roads and tunnels, cakes and pies appear in the sandbox. Sand alone is not enough to keep up with Three's burgeoning imagination. Stones, pegs, shells, small cars, wooden people combine with the sand to carry ambitious projects to completion. A twig makes a candle for a birthday cake; a shell is the window of a house.

Nursery School

As we go on talking about Three's play-day, we notice that we refer to his play less and less as an individual affair and more and more as a group matter. This is unavoidable. The preschooler is group-hungry. He may play alone contentedly in the morning, but if he does, with afternoon he will crave companions. His family is no longer enough for him.

Since this is so, it is natural for parents to begin to think about nursery school or preschool play groups as the third birthday approaches, especially in cities, where both space and appropriate companions are often hard to come by.

Unless there is some special reason to send a child away from home for part of the day when he is younger, it is usually best to wait till this age to start him in nursery school. By three the lure of other children is pronounced enough to soften the effect of separation from home. But where a child still shows pronounced dependence on his mother or other familiar adults, the transition will either have to be carefully arranged or postponed for a bit.

If parents have doubts about the desirability of sending a child to a preschool group, the question can be settled rather easily by considering three simple facts. The three-year-old needs other children to play with; he needs guidance in learning how to manage relations with others of his own age; he needs space and equipment to improve his motor skills. If he can get all these at home, or through the cooperative endeavors of a few families, he has no need of a nursery school. If any of these conditions is lacking in his home environment, nursery school has something valuable to offer him.

Choosing the right school is an important matter. Schools, of course, should conform to health regulations and educational requirements for teachers, but these are only minimal essentials. The emotional atmosphere, which is the real teaching tool at this age, can be judged only by direct observation. Teachers of little children must themselves be mature and stable. Minor crises are to be expected in every group, but teachers should avoid flurry, vexation, or anger.

Here are some questions to keep in mind when choosing a school for a three-year-old:

Is there plenty of space, both indoors and out?

Is there enough play equipment, indoors and out, to accommodate all the children?

Is there adequate space for resting, serving refreshments, isolating a sick child?

Are physical conditions safe and healthful, with due attention paid to drafts, dampness, temperature, light, sunshine?

Is a trained person available for daily health inspections?

Are the teachers alert to signs of illness?

Are the furniture and other fixtures appropriate for children in size and sturdiness?

Do the teachers treat the children with respect and friendliness?

Can they vary their approach to suit individual children?

Do they avoid favoritism?

Are the children encouraged to experiment?

Are toileting, dressing, eating, sex differences treated matter-of-factly?

Do the children seem busy, friendly, happy?

Are they learning to respect the rights of others, yet to stand up for their own rights without becoming bullies?

Really young children often attend nursery school only three days a week, two to three hours a day. This gives them a continuing contact with playmates without enforcing undue separation from their mothers. Five half-days a week are not too many for most youngsters, and some even thrive on eating and napping at school, although this is not generally recommended if it can be avoided.

Frustrated mothers sometimes complain that they "can't get a thing out of" their Johnnies or Beths about what goes on in school. Yet at other times, without prompting, a stream of stories will suddenly spurt forth, about everything from the misdemeanors of the "bad boy" of the group to the peculiar behavior of Myrtle, the turtle.

Three refuses to be prodded, but gradually he begins to bring his paintings proudly home, his vocabulary takes on a fine new luster, and he develops a look of being preoccupied with important affairs. He is off on a life of his own.

New Interests: Words and Books

Three really loves to talk, and goes for certain words like a faddist: *different, surprise, secret* can always arouse his interest. *Help, too,* and *could* (as in "You could do such and such") are effective persuaders. *Big* and *strong* challenge him to try many things.

Leaving the wariness of Two behind, Three rises to the bait of novelty. This interest in what is new makes entertaining Three a delightful adventure. Gone is the need to hear the same old story word for word. Three is pretty sure of himself at home—now he wants to learn more of the wider world. He listens eagerly to information books—either stories, or straightforward factual presentations. If he has been on an excursion, he will be entranced by a book about the same place; the firehouse, the zoo, the city, or the country. He will want to identify the pictures himself, and comments about his own experiences will punctuate his listening. This may, in fact, be the only way his mother ever learns that his nursery group visited the firehouse or that the school bunny died.

Books about animals keep Three entranced, especially if there are pictures on every page. Birthday party books, the doings of picture-book three-year-olds, stories about adventures with familiar things like telephones and trucks help Three assimilate his own experiences. And, no matter what the subject matter, any book that invites some kind of participation is doubly appreciated.

The Music Makers

Threes may justifiably proclaim, "We are the music makers; we are the singers of songs." Always responsive to patterns and rhythms, they have enough control now to *reproduce* sound patterns, and to relate one set of sounds to another, with harmonious results. Three can recognize familiar melodies and sing simple songs, though not always on pitch.

The three-year-old loves to use simple musical instruments. Since shaking or waving, hitting and hammering are natural movements for him, instruments which can be used in these ways are best. Most percussion instruments—bells, gourds, rattles, cymbals, rhythm sticks—are suitable. Large chimes, African drums, and bass drums also give excellent results. The larger instruments, like the bass drum, permit the child to dance as he plays, doubly enhancing the musical impulse.

Small drums can be made by stretching pieces of heavy rubber (sections of old inner tubes) over the open ends of empty paint cans and lacing them tightly in place.

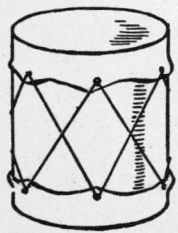

THREE: SETTLING IN

Little Christmas bells sewn to the edges of sturdy paper plates make satisfactory tambourines. Attached to bands of wide elastic, they become wrist bells.

Dried gourds with a few pebbles in them and eight-inch sticks inserted for handles make effective rattles.

Three is too young to make a rhythm band, but can "tell" a rhythm after hearing it by beating it out on a drum. He loves to move to music and to emphasize his movements by the sounds of finger cymbals or wrist bells. With his imagination operating at full blast, playing out songs comes naturally. He becomes a choo-choo train, or a caboose, or a galloping horse at the first note.

Music holds a special blessing for children who move awkwardly, and for shy children. Under its stimulating influence muscles seem to loosen up, and co-ordination increases as self-consciousness tends to fade.

Managing the Music Time

With music, as with everything, it is important not to press. Luring and leading are the maneuvers most likely to be successful. Whether music is to be a group project or an individual one, the child should be master of it. His instruments need a place on his shelves where he can reach them when he wishes.

If the child does not attend nursery school, a regular time at home is desirable, when an adult is free to join in, either by singing, playing, or supervising the use of records. The radio can sometimes be used, though of course one can't be sure of getting something the child will enjoy just at the time it is wanted.

It is not difficult to find appropriate music for home use. The Victor Educational Catalogue can serve as a guide. "Young People's Records," put out by the same company, are excellent, as is the collection called "Rhythms for Children."

A large number of collections for singing with piano are available. A few of these are "Songs for the Nursery School" by Laura Pendleton MacCarteney; "Sing, Swing, Play" by Martha Stockton Russell; "Singing Time" and "Another Singing Time" by Satis Coleman and Alice Thorn. There are many lovely, amusing, and rousing recordings of folk songs, and "activity" records are also especially appealing to the small listener who is a vigorous doer at the same time.

Music time can be made more meaningful if the child is told a little about the instruments or the songs involved. He enjoys looking at pictures of the common instruments, listening to the sounds each makes separately, and handling them. A visit to a music store is a treat that will increase listening interest if the clerks are receptive. The important thing, after all, is to make music a normal part of the child's play life.

Nature—A New World

Three's eagerness to find out about the world that surrounds him leads him to notice all sorts of things—so be prepared for questions! It takes a child to reopen our eyes to the magic of everyday things. The water we take for granted, for instance, is magic to him. The very fact that it comes out of the faucet is a thing to wonder about, but when it turns into a block of ice, or escapes from the kettle in a cloud of steam, or drifts down as snow, it demands special attention.

Anyone can freeze a pan of water; anyone can let it melt. "Let's freeze it again," says Tommy, delighted with his control over nature's sleight of hand. Snowflakes are difficult to make, but a magnifying glass will reveal their resemblance to the tiny particles of ice which a child can make by scraping a block of ice with a dull knife or a board. Setting the ice in a pan over a flame will permit the whole drama of solid to fluid to vapor to unfold, and if the steam is condensed against a cold object, the circle can be closed. Threes do not and cannot understand *why* these things are—it is satisfying and wonderful for them simply to know that they can make them happen.

Making Things Grow

Plants form another source of satisfaction and wonder. The lima bean recumbent on its bed of damp blotting paper illustrates the eternal mystery of life in a way the three-year-old can grasp. He sees roots and leaves and stem develop while the bean grows smaller. With other seeds he can follow the cycle of seed to plant to blossom to seed again in the space of a few weeks. String beans are especially good for this because they develop quickly, are hardy, and have seeds large enough for the child to handle.

The exposed roots of easy-to-grow bulbs like narcissus and hyacinth make it possible for the child to follow the whole growth process without digging up the plant. Other methods of reproduction may be illustrated by rooting begonia slips in water, or starting plants from the leaves of the African violet.

Harvests add solid satisfactions to growing experiments. A window box will do to raise a few radishes or leaves of lettuce if no other space is available. In a large tub in the backyard, Susan may grow a pumpkin.

If the child does the planting, and he should, the size of the seeds is important. Those of the calendula, nasturtium, morning-glory, and zinnia are large enough. These have the additional advantage of hardiness and some reproduce seeds in great profusion. While the seed of the marigold is not as large as the others, the plant's swift germination, hardihood, relatively quick bloom (of the dwarf kinds), and seed production make it a good candidate.

What do children learn from these experiments? The lessons are many, but these are outstanding: the need for food and water that is shared by all living things; the importance of each part for the good of the whole; the way of the unending cycle of life.

Lessons from Animals

Every child loves to watch small animals. If first pets are selected carefully, he can take a real part in their care, and learn the ways of living creatures from them.

We have spoken of the joy that a child can get from playing with a dog. His other pets should be hardy enough to take his handling and amiable enough not to protest against it; they should be easy to care for, active enough to be interesting, and should reproduce fairly freely and easily. Guinea pigs and pigeons are examples.

Other animals commonly thought of as good early pets have

certain disadvantages. For example, handling is generally bad for kittens, young rabbits, chicks, and canaries. Adult cats and rabbits may scratch. White mice and rats will nip. Goldfish offer practically no interest, because they cannot be touched, they eat very little, and they rarely breed in captivity. Guppies eat their young and are apt to be distressing.

The three-year-old who can grow lettuce or carrots for his pet, and use the refuse from the animal's cage to fertilize his garden, is developing a priceless understanding of the interdependence of different life forms. One young member of the preschool set put it this way, "The garden makes food for the bunnies and the bunnies make food for the garden. That's fair!"

At three one wants to know mainly what the animals *do*, what and how they eat, and how they get born and grow. Watching a mother animal taking care of her young relays a reassuring message about one's own mother and one's self. It usually leads to all sorts of questions about the differences among different animals, encouraging curiosity while satisfying it. But best of all, it produces a solid sense of kinship with all living things.

Small-Muscle Play

In our discussion thus far, we have not yet touched on play materials which encourage the three-year-old to exercise his increased dexterity and small-muscle co-ordination. A buttoning book, for example, with pages made of some sturdy cloth, is useful for this. Buttons of different sizes, colors, and shapes are sewn on one page, while facing pages have appropriately sized slits worked into them. The object in using the "book" is to get all the pages buttoned and unbuttoned.

Sorting boxes are also fun for quiet, relaxed times. These may be cylindrical salt boxes, with slits of different sizes cut into the closed ends. The whole top must be removable so that the objects dropped into the boxes may be recovered. A sack full of buttons of varying sizes furnishes the ammunition for this activity. The object is to drop the buttons through the right slits until they are all used up. When small friends come to visit, this activity can keep them amused for twenty minutes at a time, if enough buttons are available. It offers practice in judging size and in the co-ordination of eye and hand.

Hammer and nail sets can be used with profit now. The hammer should have a short handle, and a large, fairly heavy head. The nails should have large, flat heads. Materials for nailing might be scraps of soft pine, balsa, or even composition board, but a heavy board to back these softer materials is a necessity.

Some children enjoy nailing pieces of colored wood to a piece of composition board about eighteen by twelve inches. The pieces can be abstract shapes, or they might be parts of a simple figure—a snowman, the back of a sitting cat, or a stick-figure man.

Bits of gummed colored paper offer opportunities for many experiments in design. These can be obtained already cut in a variety of shapes, or the paper may be bought in sheets and cut as needed. Since the three-year-old can handle blunt scissors, it is good to let him cut his own designs. An occasional suggestion can keep him from cutting the pieces too small. Pasted on sheets of construction paper, these make impressive "pictures" with little effort.

Privacy, Please!

Although Three may have a whole room for himself, he wants to be in the living room when the rest of the family is there, or in the kitchen, when kitchen doings look interesting. But, granted his place in the family group, he still needs to be sheltered against too much social impact.

The easiest way to arrange this double accommodation is to give him a place in the family room that is partly closed off. An armchair in a strategic corner, for example, screens off a cozy place to which Three may retreat when he needs to be away from people, without leaving the family circle completely. Some children find retreats between the sofa and the wall, or under a table. The cloth "dollhouse" or "fire station" designed to fit over a bridge table may be another solution.

Holidays Again

Three can enter into family celebrations much more than Two could, but he still needs specific signs and symbols to mark off holidays. Christmas is signified by Santa Claus and *giving* as well as receiving presents. He can understand the idea of its being a birthday celebration of a kind, and he loves to join in family caroling. With the help of his gummed paper, he can even contribute some decorations for the tree. Stars, circles, and triangles of construction paper in bright colors on which Three has pasted metallic stars will look well and fill him with healthy pride.

Easter remains much the same as it was at two, but Thanksgiving is now enriched by visitors and visiting. Valentine's Day and Halloween begin to take on particular meaning. Sending and receiving cards is concrete enough for Three to know that February 14 is something special, and the jack-o'-lantern is an occasion for high excitement on Halloween.

Food is still the most important part of parties, and a favorite dessert is often enough to mark a celebration. Two or three friends invited to share lunch or dinner make a gala occasion, with the cake a fitting climax for a birthday party.

Three and the Adult

On the whole, Three is a good deal easier on adults than Two was. Tricycle expeditions and climbing forays require less supervision than before. Three's lengthened attention span means that stories and records can be engrossing for longer periods of time. His developing imagination provides aids for managing transitions from one routine to another. A "pretend" nap may take the place of a real one after lunch, but the relaxation will be as complete as his body requires. When clean-up time comes, it is ordinarily enough to suggest playing moving man (with some guidance, of course) to get his toys back into their places.

When Three goes to bed, he often continues to relish stories of what he did when he was a baby, and may even want to act out parts of these tales. If he needs to return to his babyhood very frequently, his parents should take stock of the demands they are making on him. This usually signifies the presence of a burden heavier than the child is ready to bear—an over-fatiguing schedule or too much pressure to conform to adult standards of behavior. A bit more cuddling, a milder approach to training tasks may be all he needs to keep him facing happily forward in his march toward maturity.

CHAPTER V

Four: Age of Expansion

NEW SKILLS, wider perceptions, quick swells of energy make Four a hot-rod model of what he was at three. Everything about him is on the increase during these months—his size, his speech, and his ideas. Hurrying to meet himself at five, he overshoots the mark at times. Boasting, grandiose, chafing at restrictions, his eyes are on the future.

Tolerance Needed

The four-year-old needs more space and more freedom. The old backyard no longer suffices. He must ride his tricycle on the sidewalk; he can no longer match his pace to the pokiness of grownups.

Freedom, however, must be given with discrimination. Although he chafes against them, the four-year-old still needs limits. It is the adult who must decide at which tree or park bench the young speedster is to wait when they are out for a walk together, or how far up the block he may parade without supervision. Given a slight extension of privileges, and a definite, but widened, set of limits from time to time, Four can be persuaded to abide by the rules.

He wants to put his mark on space in all directions. He needs lots of the materials he already knows: paper, crayons, paste, clay, paints—plus a large amount of tolerance. Because his ideas move as swiftly as his body, he never knows precisely where he is heading. The flower he starts to draw may become a baby before he is half finished, and end up as an alligator.

This imaginative freedom shows up in his talk, too. Factual reports are transformed along the way into tall tales. He is apt to be accused of fibbing by bewildered adults who do not appreciate his true quality, but this is a feeble name for the flights of fancy Four presents. More accurately, he is a fabricator, a dramatizer of events that might be. He needs to be led gently to recognize that a difference exists between what is and what he imagines, but we must admit that part of his charm stems from his blithe disregard of that difference.

Guidance Needed

The uninitiated onlooker is apt to be shocked by Four's social crudities. Once a clique has been formed, outsiders may be rudely excluded. If a dispute develops, feelings are expressed in forthright terms. "I'll sock you" is a common threat. Name-calling is at its height. Bragging seems to be the common coin of discourse. Other people's feelings are of no concern to Four.

The clowning, bragging, I'll-go-you-one-better kind of behavior is typical of the four-year-old silliness that often causes promising play to deteriorate into squabbling and tears. Almost any new idea suggested by an adult can avert this and knit the play more firmly together.

Sometimes Fours become overstimulated by the intensity of their own imaginations. An accidental meeting of two tricycles, for example, can start a series of "wrecks" in the wink of an eye. Several children playing together, each earnestly getting up steam to make his wreck more spectacular than the last, can create a dangerous situation. The first crash should alert the supervising adult to the need for diversionary activities.

"Bobby, Tom has had a wreck. Will you be the hospital man and help him?" will give the play a new direction. Or Sally might be detailed to keep traffic going the other way, while Harold serves as a garageman to tow the wreck away.

Compensating Virtues

Despite his crudities and extremes, the four-year-old has some surprisingly mature and endearing traits. He can take capable charge of a newcomer to his group, showing him around and fitting him into current activities. He is almost overgenerous with his belongings when special friends are involved, swapping around until his mother is hard put to keep track of the real owners of all the objects she finds in his room. Even clothing is not immune to exchange, especially among girls.

Although Four would rarely spend a minute alone, if he had his own way, he *can* amuse himself for an hour at a time, provided he has a large enough variety of play materials. He can remain indoors as long as two hours without becoming restive. When we contrast this with Three's need for changes every hour, we can see that Four has come a long way.

Adults Are Important, Too

Four's interest in the grown-up world is even more intense than it was before. This can be sensed from the way he has stepped up his "Whys?" and "Hows?" Some of these he uses for practice in talking and listening, because he is fascinated by the sound of words, but many of them stem from a real desire to know.

Another somewhat disconcerting clue to Four's fascination with adults is his addiction to grimacing. It is not unusual to find a four-year-old off by himself, looking abstracted and twisting his features into strange and awesome patterns. This appears to be an attempt to capture the myriad expressions he perceives on the faces of the adults he scrutinizes so intently. Having begun to master their more obvious actions by imitation the year before, Four seems bent on putting the finishing touches to his impersonation.

He is, however, not content with mere imitating, as Three was. He senses the vast gap in skills and power between himself and the grownups around him, and he seems to be concerned because of these differences. In a thousand ways his play tells us that he is trying to reassure himself that basically he is capable of being as skillful, as powerful and, above all, as strong as grownups.

The Outdoor Arena

The out-of-doors seems the logical place for trials of strength. Since most Fours love to climb and clamber, they need safe and sturdy climbing materials to put together. The well-stocked play yard for the three-year-old will serve Four as well, with the addition of extra packing cases, one or two longer planks and a few objects to haul around. Canvas sacks about eighteen inches long and six in diameter, filled with sand, serve this purpose well. Old tires are particularly good.

Watching a group of four-year-olds from the sidelines, one can conclude only that they are intent on defying fate. Together they struggle to set a packing case on end, so that it stands as tall as possible. Next comes a ladder, set against the side with grunting effort. Four large blocks are painfully hauled up next, to be stacked against each other on top of the packing case. A chair somehow finds its way up to be set against the blocks, and, finally, a plank forms a ramp from the top of the blocks to the roof of the packing case.

After a few trial slides down the ramp, it appears that this intricate device is insufficiently hazardous. More cases and planks appear, until we get something like this:

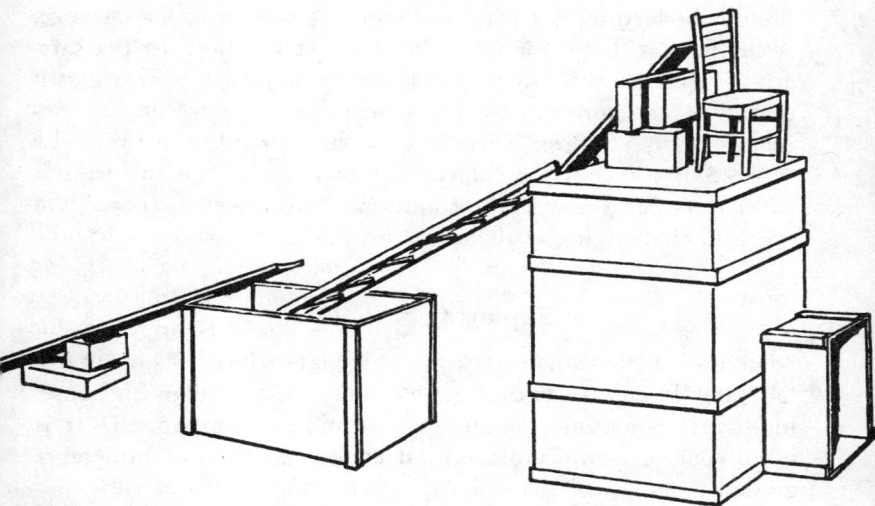

The feats the young space-conquerors attempt will chill the blood of the adult onlooker, but he will do well to interfere as little as possible. To help Four strengthen his conviction of capability the adult must witness his unnerving brushes with danger with equanimity. Every time he emerges safely from a peril he has arranged, something satisfying has been added to his inward vision of himself. However, the four-year-old sometimes bites off more than he can chew. Once Johnny and Victor have built their leaning tower and climbed to the top of it, the ground may look frighteningly far away and they may wail for help. This is the adult's signal to come out of hiding and lend a helping hand. But the hand has to vanish promptly after it has served its purpose, for the *amour propre* of Four is a delicate thing. He does not like to be reminded of his limitations.

Time for New Skills

Despite frequent errors, Fours generally seem to have an uncanny understanding of the limits of their abilities. Only if they are held on too tight a rein are they likely to go out of bounds—and this, of course, because they feel the need of extra effort to overcome the force holding them in check.

Adults can keep the yearning for new conquests within safe bounds by feeding it a little at a time. A new skill, for instance, is challenge enough for Four; he will not kick against the safeguards that go with using it. Feats on a jungle gym are still tentative but more daring and give Four a great sense of conquest. Many children learn to swim and to roller-skate at this time. Skiing is not too difficult on easy slopes. Double-runner ice skates offer a new kind of motion. Two-wheeled scooters are safe and challenging at the same time.

Exploring with Four

Sometimes Four stands stock-still, his glance focused on far distances. He conjectures that there is more to know than his house, his street. Sometimes he runs off to find out for himself. It is usually more comfortable for all concerned to take him on a guided tour.

FOUR: AGE OF EXPANSION

At four, excursions start sooner and last longer than they did at three. Because time has more meaning now than it did before, the four-year-old can anticipate a trip with relish, and help in the preparations for it. Afterwards he talks long about his experiences, reproduces them, and builds on them, until he has assimilated every sensation and each bit of new information. Under the stimulation they provide, his play reaches new heights of inventiveness and grows rich in detail.

If cars and trains and busses are old stuff to him, he will be fascinated by boats and planes and motorcycles. He will look forward eagerly to trips in different kinds of boats, and will want to know what makes them move. (And don't make the mistake of assuming that Joanne and Ruth will not ask questions too!) A ride in a freight van or a pick-up truck will be a tremendous adventure. A hay wagon, a country sled, the back of a pony or burro—the possibilities for investigating means of transportation are endless and endlessly engrossing.

Another way to broaden the horizons of the four-year-old is to give him a complete change of scene. The country child is stimulated by the wonders of the city, if he is exposed to them in small doses. The city child has his eyes opened to innumerable new delights by a trip away from his native sidewalks.

Whether from city, country, or suburb, most children respond with enthusiasm to trips planned around some specific activity, like collecting. What can one easily collect? Beetles, worms, caterpillars, centipedes, millipedes, crickets, newts, frogs, toads, land snails, water snails. Also the cocoons or larvae of several insects: water beetles, stone flies, and May flies, for example. The equipment is simple: a few covered jars and a basket are sufficient.

It is not necessary to bring home all that one sees. The chance to study the hidden things of field and stream, with a knowing adult to point them out, is an exciting experience in itself. Most of the specimens that Four brings home require very little to keep them going. A glass aquarium, even a dish, and a little leaf mold, damp earth, rocks and bark for hiding places, and a jar top of water usually make an adequate home.

A less adventurous collection (from the adult's point of view) might consist of different leaves; a "book" made of newspaper is all one needs for temporary storage.

Tastes and Smells

For an excursion that is a little different, the child might be taken on a tasting and smelling trip, as is done in some nursery schools. Spring and summer are the best times, but even late fall can offer rewards. Along with their search for smells, the children will absorb a good deal of knowledge about insects. If their attention is directed to the fact that some insects go only to one sort of plant, they will become aware that creatures as well as humans differ in their preferences. They may also learn that it is as natural for children to differ as it is for bees and beetles, and this provides a sound basis for the growth of tolerance.

Incidentally, it would be a mistake to confine the search for smells to pleasant subjects only. Skunk cabbage and wild onion are as legitimate material for exploration as honeysuckle and clover. In between these, there lies a wide range of odors—minty, pungent, fruity—to delight and surprise.

By tasting the twigs and bark of sassafras and black birch, the gum exuded by the spruce, the slight bitterness of young dandelions, Four comes to know these in a more intimate fashion than he can by sight or smell alone. Wintergreen, sorrel, and edible berries of many kinds give a full measure of satisfaction to the tasting trip.

Touch and Hearing

Children, of course, have been accustomed from infancy to finding out about things by touching and handling, so they find nature's infinite variety of touch experiences especially congenial. These may range from the smooth, slippery, wrinkled, rough feels of different kinds of bark to the painful but enlightening sting of thistle and nettle. The satiny feel of water-smoothed stones, the velvet of mullein leaves, the delicate silk of wild anemones provide studies in contrast. Live mosses like fur and dried mosses like brushes, the prickly-soft quality of pine needles, the sturdier texture of spruce—all these and more are game for touchers.

For ears the woods have special gratifications. Most of us know about the hidden voices of sea shells, but do we know that a tree also speaks on windy days, if we put one ear against its trunk? And what four-year-old is not delighted with the song of water flowing over stones or under ice? Bird voices are obvious listening-game, but what of the rustle the field mice make in dry autumn grass if one is very still? The cricket's chirp, the peep of frogs, the plop of a toad—these can be excitements to take home from a "hunting" trip.

These trips promote talk about things that are new. An incessant chatterer, Four delights to search out just the right word to describe the scents and sounds and textures he has just experienced. Lacking ready words, he improvises with pleasure, and often with real inventiveness. So vocabularies grow, and words become saturated with the very essence of meaning—the living reality of an actual experience.

Play as Reality

Four shows us how preoccupied he is with the world of grownups when he is playing make-believe. Compared with the activity of Three, his is almost sober. The lions and tigers of his earlier fantasies have largely given way to truck drivers and delivery men. Little girls are mothers and nurses.

From this time on, as the sexes begin to go their separate ways, boys and girls are apt to spend their imaginative lives in different worlds—although a little girl will still invade the boy's province of pirate and space pilot, and the boy may yet cling to the companionship of a cherished doll. Naturally their play reflects what they see going on about them, plus what they have heard about or come to know through radio and television, and these samplings will largely reinforce them in their natural inclination toward traditional roles—with, of course, a few modern wrinkles added. Thus in play they get a kind of preparation for the parts they are going to play as grownups.

It is helpful for us to recognize this added dimension of play in the life of the growing child, so that a difficulty in development can be recognized and steps taken to help straighten it out. Arnold, for instance, was helped because someone was aware of the marked differences between his daily play and that of most four-year-old boys.

At four-and-a-half, Arnold consistently preferred playing house with girls to the more strenuous antics of the boys. This in itself was no cause for concern—as we shall see later, many boys of five and even older still like this form of play and want to have dolls of their own as well. However, Arnold's insistence on always taking the part of either the mother or the nurse, plus his indifference to other boyish interests, suggested that his development might be in danger of taking a wrong turning.

It turned out that the boy lived with a widowed mother who was so fearful for his welfare that she kept him close to her side when he was not at nursery school. He had no contact with any male relatives, and never having experienced that close and pleasant association with men that most little boys have in their homes, there was no reason for him to believe that it would be a good thing to imitate them. This might have meant a situation of increasing difficulty for Arnold, since the boy who does not begin to develop masculine interests during his early years often finds it hard to catch up with his own sex later.

Fortunately, when this was pointed out to her, Arnold's mother understood that her "protection" might be more of a harm than a safeguard. She recognized the need for a man in his life, and a "big brother" was found for him—a high school lad who took him for walks, played ball with him, taught him to enjoy rough play, and showed him how to defend himself. During all this, no criticism of his girlish behavior was spoken, but he gradually began to spend more and more time in the school's block corner with the boys and less and less time with the girls. He needed to be persuaded that being a man was a good thing, that he was capable of it, and that it was a good thing to try. Then he was ready to go.

Working out Personal Problems

In addition to preparing for their future roles, four-year-olds put dramatic play to special, personal uses. They are able to sustain longer and more complicated sequences than they could at three, and they are more articulate. The purpose of their play is, therefore, more transparent at four, although its manner may be more subtle.

For an illustration of this, let us eavesdrop on Harry. He has been having some trouble making a place for himself in his group. He seems too goody-goody, too afraid to fight, to be accepted as a regular fellow. But even Harry has his special pal, and here they are working out their problems in their own play language.

The boys are busy in a packing case with one open side. Harry says, "Let's build a tiger house."

Phil agrees to be the tiger and gets in, but immediately tries to get out. Harry pushes him roughly back in, continuing to build. As the wall grows higher, Harry talks to himself, "I'll build a strong house so that tiger can't get out. *Now* can't get out—you have to stay there, tiger."

Phil finally breaks out, pushes Harry in, and begins to rebuild the wall, repeating, "You can't get out." But Harry does not take this quietly. He paces back and forth, muttering, "I can get out, I can get out, I can get out." And scattering blocks, Harry pushes down the wall.

Harry is using the tiger, of course, for his own purposes: first, to represent the things he is afraid of, and would like to believe that he can master; second, to show that he himself can be strong fearless, threatening. At the moment, these things are not true and his play is only a dream, but he does not give up.

Another day finds him playing car with a different friend. He builds a large car of blocks, and as he gets into it we can see that when he sits at the imagined wheel he is in a cozy, protected place, yet he is also strong and speedy and invulnerable. In a number of different ways, Harry continues to play the boy he wants to be until some of it overflows from play into real life and he begins to see that it can really be so.

One day, playing apartment-house window cleaner, he fights for his ladder successfully, when a rival seizes it. Is this the same Harry who was afraid to stand up for his rights? Harry's growth seems to indicate that play may have solid values. If we let our four-year-olds pretend to be characters they admire, and experiment with a variety of solutions to their symbolized but quite real problems, they have a chance to find their way toward the strength and wisdom and skill they long for.

Toys and "Props"

Four's dolls and Teddy bears need to be sturdy, particularly around the joints, for their clothing gets yanked off and pulled on with force and speed. Wardrobes for dolls were not very important before this, but they are now. The easiest closure for the child is a zipper. Hooks and eyes or snaps come next, buttons last. Hats, gloves, shoes, belts, and pocketbooks are important for the child's dress-up play. If a costume box was begun for Three, additions should be made to it now. Four is inventive, but he is also suggestible. The glimpse of a fire engine inevitably evokes the fireman in him, but there are many other impersonations that might be called forth. We are convinced that boys play father parts so seldom partly because the props to make the role look important are lacking. How many male Fours are given small facsimiles of the tools their fathers use in their daily occupations? How many, indeed, have any realistic notion of what their fathers do when they leave the house for the day? It would certainly enrich their experience and their play if they could see where father works and what he does.

The toy manufacturers have done well for parents. Toys that encourage identification with adults are offered in profusion. Some are of interest to both sexes, and may be strategically introduced at four, when the urge to be big grows powerful. Shoeshine kits and small medicine cabinets, for example, encourage a do-as-I-do routine and help make good habits fun.

Household toys multiply each year. In addition to the usual items, one can now buy packaged cake and dessert mixes in quantities designed to fit toy pans and mixing bowls. These are just right for one-meal consumption. Dish-washing outfits just like Mother's, sets of vegetable brushes, and carpet sweepers that really sweep enchant four-year-old Laura.

Boys, in their new masculine awareness, may shy away from cooking sets, but they, too, love a chance to mess with foods. For them it might be better to use the dessert and cake mixes in household sizes, letting them prepare enough for the whole family. (Girls love to do this, too.)

No four-year-old he-man, however, will refuse a shaving kit with brush, soap, and plastic razor that simulates his father's paraphernalia. Toy electric shavers are available, too, though they are not quite so much fun. Doctor, dentist, and barber sets are perfect for Four. A small lunchbox or briefcase, if the man of the house uses one, will be greeted with glee.

Rubber knives and toy guns are useful as harmless outlets for aggressive feelings. Police outfits, with handcuffs and badge, give Four a chance to be the strong man, and cowboy and Indian regalia are perennially important.

Vehicles

There is little that the four-year-old does not imbue with imagination. Three's love for vehicles is intensified in Four. He derives satisfaction from controlling the large cars and trains he builds of blocks, but he is also happy to be the master of smaller models of these. Although he appreciates more realism now than he did a year ago, minute details are not yet important. Three did not mind pushing block-trains along, but Four wants his trains to have wheels. However, tracks are not yet called for, since Four is usually not dexterous enough to set them up himself, and is apt to be irked by the limits they impose on his train's erratic journeyings. Wooden trains are preferable to the usual light metal ones, and the harder the wood, the more lasting the train.

Planes, trucks, and boats are great favorites, but a word of caution is needed here. Innumerable specialized toy vehicles are offered in shops and one is often tempted to buy something novel, simply out of ennui. Remember, however, that though Four seems eager for some kinds of novelty, he does not like toys that have no link with the world he knows. The child needs to have seen the machine or vehicle in question actually at work, so that he can transfer to the toy the feelings he experienced when he watched the real thing.

Those Invaluable Blocks

Nowhere is this truth better substantiated than in the block play of the four-year-old. He is not shy about telling what he has made. Chattering constantly, he takes delight in pointing out the intricacies of a structure and in demonstrating its uses. His inventive hunger feeds on a large variety of shapes, which he incorporates with ingenuity into his buildings. His final products are usually complex, symmetrical, and extensive.

Harassed parents and teachers often feel that it is not possible to provide either enough blocks or enough space to permit Four to build unhampered. Working in vigorous cooperation with two or three companions, he can cover enormous floor areas with amazing speed. Tunnels stretch across whole rooms. Houses meander indefinitely, developing unpredictable angles and appendages as they grow.

Even more difficult to cope with is Four's great pride in his achievements, for he often wants his structures to be left untouched. Most vexing of all, when a structure is left standing, at his insistence and at great inconvenience to the rest of the family, he may show no further interest in it. It takes diplomatic handling, ahead of time, to get Four to agree to have his blocks put away. It is usually best not to have him present at this operation; to insist that he do it himself verges on cruelty.

Eavesdropping on a nursery school group, we find that Fours are quick-change artists. The block airplane becomes a boat, a fire-tower, or a bus with no trouble at all, and can be all of these in swift succession within a few minutes. Further, in the process of construction, these young engineers can transform *themselves*, too: Billy and Marvin and Tim speak in the unmistakable accents of those who can easily make the "biggest airport in the world," putting to shame the puny efforts of adult builders.

Girls are as likely to find blocks a source of power and magic as their brothers, although they may concentrate on different themes. Bella, for example, builds with nervous eagerness, muttering to herself. At the end, she sits back and gazes at the result in admiration. "Look at my beautiful big building," she says to the teacher. "Look at my great big building." She hugs the teacher in her joy.

Block building helps introduce a shy child to a new group. The child can build alone while he sizes up his peers. When he feels ready to join in, there are so many ways in which he can be helpful that he is rarely rebuffed or made to feel like an outsider. Even confirmed young brigands tend to be more subdued when they are concentrating on blocks; they accept newcomers more easily then than under other circumstances.

One explanation of this civilizing quality of blocks is that they are so well geared to Four's skills that he finds his greatest satisfaction when working with them. We are all apt to be more outgoing and relaxed when we are happy and satisfied. It is therefore not strange that both the shy and the aggressive become better mixers under this spell.

Clay Talk

The clay table is another fine place for Four to break into a new group. Here his conversational powers burst into full flower. As he kneads and pounds, he chatters, usually about what he is doing. Starting with a simple announcement, Four is soon in the throes of wild exaggeration. If one of the group says he is making a snake, his neighbor is bound to make two snakes. These soon become ten and build up in a trice to the largest number any of the children can think of—a thousand or a trillion.

Often the conversation that goes on, involving birthday cakes, worms, puddings, teapots, and bunny rabbits, may seem the height of absurdity to an adult. But this nonsense is the secret fraternal language of the Fours: grownups aren't supposed to understand it. Four starts with an object with which he has had some experience, but he switches without hesitation if some accident of form suggests another possibility. During one short session we witnessed, Benjie, one of our favorite Fours, started off with a coal truck. A piece which fell off the truck conveniently became a man, with a "mouth and nose and eyes and face," but a sudden hard squeeze converted him into orange juice, from which, like a phoenix, an elephant with a long trunk emerged!

During the fun and chatter that goes with clay play, some

interesting things emerge. Children who are wondering about the physical differences between boys and girls, and about their own bodies, may make figures with exaggerated private parts, or with the parts conspicuously broken off or missing. They may talk about "boo-boo" or whatever their private words for feces might be. Whenever the giggling at the clay table is intensified, it is safe to bet that one of these subjects has been brought up. This usually happens when there is no adult around to eavesdrop.

"Silliness" of this kind may be a call for help. Children often wonder if parts of their bodies are detachable, and fear losing some part. It is also hard for them to understand that they can give up substances from inside their bodies without suffering real loss. All this comes from lack of experience and misunderstanding, of course, but it is nonetheless the stuff of which many of the nightmares of children are constructed.

Our present knowledge indicates that it is healthier for a child to express his anxieties about these matters than to keep them hidden. Playing with clay seems to bring many children considerable relief. Others, who are more deeply troubled, may need the help of specialists in child guidance. If the play with clay is exclusively or consistently concerned with "toilet" subjects, it may be time to seek expert advice.

With clay, as with other materials, Four becomes possessive. He is proud of what he makes, and often wants it saved. He usually likes to paint his product after it has dried. Since dried clay is extremely fragile, it might be well to warn Four against carrying the dried piece in his pocket, or bumping it against hard surfaces.

A stiff dough made of equal parts of flour and salt can be moistened, molded, and dried in much the same way as clay. It is brittle when dry, but is a good substitute if clay is hard to get. It is more suitable for use when the children are concentrating on *what* they are making rather than the *feel* of the material they are working with.

Display Space

This is the year of the monster bulletin board—there is no avoiding it. As with clay, so with painting. Four is proud of his creations and wants them saved.

Since the four-year-old paints on large sheets of paper, and is very prolific, it may be well to plan in the beginning for a really spacious display place. Insulating board, large enough to cover a complete wall of the child's room, is both inexpensive and satisfactory. One family devised a charming frieze on a staircase, involving nothing more than a decorative cord and gaily colored plastic clothespins to hold the pictures. Another added interest to a long bare hall by fastening a row of pictures to the walls with Scotch tape and calling it the "Gallery." A name lends the display space character and importance, which Four relishes. It is also likely to be the start of one of those heart-warming bits of intimate family nonsense which we cherish later. In practical terms, it helps to define and limit the space to be devoted to art displays.

"Pictures" at Last

It is usually after his fourth birthday that the child begins to produce "pictures." We begin to recognize what he is trying to draw, although the details are few, perspective is absent, and proportions are unexpected. However, we are getting one version of a child's-eye view of the world.

Most art teachers who have had a great deal of experience with the work of young children agree that the size they give to specific details indicates the importance those details have for the child. That is why people usually occupy more space than things. On the other hand, objects with which the child has had personal and repeated experiences, or which have special emotional meanings for him, are likely to be larger and more detailed than others.

One art teacher points out that the child paints as if he were at the hub of a horizontal wheel. The child represents most objects at eye level; that is, as if they were standing on the same level as he is. Things have to be dramatically higher or lower than he is (the sun, say, or a fish in the sea) for him to put them at the top or bottom of his picture.

It is fascinating to watch a four-year-old at the easel. Quite different from the typical Three, he talks constantly as he paints, naming objects and telling stories as he proceeds. He usually has some plan to begin with, and may start with an outline, which he enjoys filling in. As his ideas shift, his picture changes, and forms flow into one another, taking on a succession of meanings.

Often our young artist is so carried away by the story he is painting that he cannot take time to change to a clean sheet of paper, and paints one picture over another. At the end of the session his product may be quite unrecognizable, but he has had a whale of a time.

Although Four talks more freely about his creations than Three does, it is not wise to question him too persistently. This is a frequent error of well-meaning grownups who simply cannot accept a child's version of his own intentions. "Correcting" the four-year-old too often interferes with his learning instead of hastening it. His ideas can develop only through his own personal experiences, and only as rapidly as his general rate of maturation allows. Too much pushing is likely to bring results like those in the following incident.

Carl is standing near Ollie, who is painting. Carl is showing him how to paint a house. When Ollie finishes his picture, Carl picks up a brush and adds two portholes to it. An adult, who is watching, asks, "What is it, Carl?"

CARL: It's a car.
ADULT: But it looks like a boat.
CARL (*in self-defense*): Sure, but the car is underneath.
ADULT (*pointing to a different detail*): What's that?
CARL: Oh, that's the sun.
ADULT: Isn't it more like the moon?
CARL (*too amiably*): Yeah.
OLLIE (*who has been a bystander*): Mind your own business!
CARL (*in hearty agreement*): Yeah, mind your own business!

Even at four, some youngsters prefer to keep the subjects of their paintings a private matter. Dick was a case in point. He composed a design of dominant strokes in blue, shorter strokes, and tiny dots. Then he swept over the whole paper with red, starting with a scrubbing movement in the center. A mass of yellow appeared near the bottom, and the original blue was overpainted in green. All the overpainting was done with heavy, angry strokes, as if Dick were determined to blot out the blue design completely. When asked what he was painting, he answered decisively, "A stinker," and continued his attack on the picture. The blue strokes undoubtedly meant something to Dick, but he was not ready to tell anyone else about them.

The too-quiet child finds painting an especially happy activity. As he works at the easel his constraint often falls away from him visibly, and he becomes sociable and lively. For these children it is especially important to supply paint in a variety of bright, clear colors, and of free-flowing texture. Red, blue, and yellow are good choices, with a rich black for contrast.

Mixing colors is often as creative an experience as painting. The first time Ruthie helped to get the paints ready, for example, she exclaimed with pleased surprise, stirring yellow into blue, "It's getting green!" Allowed to pour a little blue into the red, she yelled, "It's getting black!" Learning the correct name for the red-blue mixture, she wanted to go ahead, trying one color systematically with each of the others. Ruthie was exploring a world she had not known existed. Wise guidance kept her experience at a high level of satisfaction, encouraging the child to go on to further experimentation, yet forestalling the gray disappointment that would have followed had she been allowed to dump all the colors together.

Music and Dancing

The most noticeable musical advance made by Four is in the use of the voice. With increased control, the child finds it easier to sing on pitch. He can recognize melodies and remember whole songs. He really enjoys group sings and singing alone, because he is more sure of himself.

This is the year when the child begins actively to participate in his musical heritage. Musical games form one introduction to the folklore of his culture. Simple singing games like All Around the Mulberry Bush, or The Farmer in the Dell, are natural choices for this age, because they involve group-play, and the make-believe that Four dotes on. Many familiar songs like "Jingle Bells" can be good subjects for acting out.

Just because Four can follow directions and enjoys conventional group games, we must not forget the enormous creativity of this period. Experiments with different instruments and combinations of notes are still in order. Tone bars are good things to have around the house. Made of separate bars of wood mounted on metal, each produces a single note of the scale. The child can experiment with musical patterns by arranging these bars in different sequences. They invite exploration and incidentally offer effective ear training.

An experienced teacher of music tells the following story (in *Creative Arts for All Our Children,* published by The Arts Cooperative Service) to illustrate Four's sensitivity and inventiveness:

One day, in the music room, there were five children about four years old. Three were sitting on the floor with drums (one with a snare drum, two with tom-toms) and a fourth had cymbals. The fifth was standing by a large bass drum. After they had experimented with their instruments a bit, the boy by the bass drum said, "Listen to me. When I stop, you stop, too." Then he beat out a good marching rhythm, and paused. The rest paused, too. Starting again in rhythm, he led them in the same kind of thing for a short time. Then, without a word being spoken, the children on the floor stood up and began to march around the room, playing all the while. The next time the bass drum paused, they sat down. This developed into a real rhythmic form—march and sit, march and sit—with more meaning than any pattern taught to them could have. This was their own discovery.

The same teacher tells of her experience with a group of children who were listening to a recording made by Uday Shan Kar's Indian drummers. Each listened quietly until one picked up the rhythm he heard and repeated it on his own drum. Soon all joined in, and their listening became active learning. She says, "It was a delight to hear in their quiet playing how many of the patterns of rhythm they had discovered for themselves. Children are like this when given adequate opportunity."

For small listeners, records in the home collection having a bright rhythmic structure and definite tone color will furnish exciting recreation. Debussy's "The Little Shepherd," parts of Haydn's "Surprise Symphony," and "Peter and the Wolf" are enchanting to many. And there is adventure for grownup and child in exploring "ethnological" records similar to the one mentioned above: recordings of African rhythms, music from the South Seas and from the Orient, folk music from our own and other lands.

Movement is still Four's favorite response to music. We may call it dancing if we wish—Four does not care, so long as we permit him to interpret the sounds he hears in his own way, through his body. His movements may be more graceful now than they were before, his patterns more varied, his response to the rhythm more accurate. If they are, we know he has taken many developmental steps forward; if they are not, we cannot hurry him. Tomorrow or next week, the new pattern may suddenly emerge.

The four-year-old will respond to a suggestion to "show how many different things the music says" but he will lose both pleasure and interest if we try to get him to carry out the suggestion in a specific way. If we criticize his interpretation, we get between him and the music and rob it of its meaning for him. It is only what he does freely, prompted from within, that makes the musical experience truly his own.

Many children are introduced to dancing lessons at four, but the only desirable "lessons" at this age are opportunities for rhythmic movement, in which the child plays out a part or a story, to a musical accompaniment. The teacher may suggest what part a child might like to work out, or she may tell the story while all the children dance it out together; but attempts to teach dance technique are premature.

Quiet Time: the Bookshelf

Four's eyes light up when story time comes around. Despite his incessant activity, he dearly loves a session with books—and he is a much better listener than he was at three. He no longer has to have actual physical contact with a book to enjoy it, for example, although he does like to turn pages by himself when he can.

Choosing books for the four-year-old is not difficult, if we keep in mind four of his qualities: his love of exaggeration, his bubbling humor, his interest in new words, and his constant preoccupation with *how* and *why*.

A lover of tall tales, he finds books like Wanda Gàg's *Millions of Cats* exactly right. He feels at home with books that echo his own vivid imagination. *Cats for Sale, And to Think That I Saw It on Mulberry Street,* and *Miss Flora McFlimsey's Birthday* all fall into this category. A book that combines humor, fantasy, and a firm anchorage in reality is irresistible to Four. *McElligot's Pool, The 500 Hats of Bartholomew Cubbins,* and *Mrs. Roo and Her Bunnies* offer this combination of qualities. On a simpler level, *Junket Is Nice* has a similar appeal.

Four is a great inventor, and he appreciates the inventions of others—especially when they deal with words and sounds. He loves rhymes and nonsense words. Books like Lear's *Nonsense A B C* are fine for him, while the delicate fantasy of the Christopher Robin series wins many as permanent devotees. For sheer swing of words, parts of *A Child's Garden of Verses* are perennial favorites.

The realists among the Fours like factual books, plain or dressed up with whimsy. *Mike Mulligan and His Steam Shovel* is one example of a type of book especially interesting to four-year-old boys. Others are George Zaffo's "real" books: *The Big Book of Real Trains, The Big Book of Real Building and Wrecking Machines,* and *The Big Book of Real Fire Engines.*

Fours are becoming individuals, and much depends on a child's special situation. Animal stories continue to be liked, and are especially helpful if the animal heroes have problems that resemble those the hearers are struggling with. Almost all Fours like stories of everyday life told with a light touch and a bit of verse, such as *Stories to Begin On* by Rhoda Bacmeister. Books about children like themselves who do what they would like to do—go downtown with Daddy, have a menagerie of pets, etc.—are good listener-bait.

Since each child is especially interested in the occupation of his own father or mother, the parent may want to prepare a special book. This can be a challenging task, with illustrations cut out of magazines, or photographed especially for the book. The trick is to keep the language simple, and to follow the parent through the day step by step, speaking always of the specific things he or she does, with every step illustrated. A book like this, "made especially for me," will be a long-treasured gift.

Another kind of book that only a parent can make is one commemorating something the child has done—a first journey, a trip on a new kind of conveyance, or even the baking of a cake. This can be something for the child and parent to do together, with the child dictating the text, the parent doing a bit of judicious editing, and both finding just the right pictures for illustrations. A few drawings by the child and stick-figure sketches by the parent will give this "commemoration number" a personal quality that will grow in value with the years.

All books for Four should have clear pictures and brief texts. Listening is a new art and needs to be tied to a more familiar and easier activity like looking.

Books are as useful at four as the Teddy bear was at three. They fill the waiting time between awaking and getting dressed in the morning. They make the afternoon rest tolerable. They are something to be shared in the evening with Daddy, who may be too tired for active play, and they open to the child a set of wider worlds than any he could reach physically.

Quiet Toys

Solitary hours can be very rewarding if a variety of materials are available to challenge Four's imagination and skills. At this age new abilities seem to emerge with every new type of material offered.

These are the hours for the hoarded junk of the household. Scotch tape, package handles, bits of colored string and yarn, paper clips, odd buttons and buckles, feathers from old hats, pipe cleaners, and paste will inspire unpredictably ingenious creations.

For placid, uncreative hours (and these are quite in order), sewing cards are still good. Under supervision, Four can use tapestry needles with string or yarn. Pieces of material, about eight inches square, are good as a base of sewing operations. Four takes great pleasure in sewing two such pieces together, not necessarily to make anything, but simply to *do* something.

Cutting-out is a great favorite with four-year-olds. They can guide scissors along an outline fairly well, but are still apt to snip off small details. Large pictures, heavily outlined, such as we find in magazines, are excellent for practice.

Table blocks challenge Four's inventiveness. One kind comes in five basic shapes which can be snapped together by metal fasteners to make a large variety of things, ranging from a cannon to a mechanical man. Another group has holes and pegs for fastening together. The popular Tinker-Toy operates on the same principle and is well within the range of four-year-old skills. One must not expect realistic objects, of course; abstract design and fantastic inventions are more in Four's line.

Still another construction material is called "Log-Sticks." Made of wood, these sticks come in lengths ranging from one inch to five inches, each one grooved at intervals along its entire length. Crisscrossed at any point, they remain in place. They are fun to handle and adapt themselves to more intricate concepts as the child develops.

Many children like "modern era" blocks, which come in small, flat units, especially adapted to creating modern architectural effects. This may be a detail somewhat beyond Four's appreciation, but he enjoys the unusual and surprisingly impressive structures he can create.

Color cubes offer endless possibilities of design and can be used for building, too. Stone blocks and peg-tables, on which a variety of designs can be created out of pegs with differently shaped and colored tops, fall into the same class of material. Some peg-boards and peg-tables come equipped with small pegged houses, trees, and accessories which make streets and villages when set up.

Puzzles, preferably of wood, are even more intriguing than they were at three. Many Fours can master those of ten pieces or more. Since good puzzles are fairly expensive, a neighborhood puzzle exchange might be a helpful project.

On days when everything else seems to pall, Four might like to make finger puppets out of vegetables or fruits. Potatoes and apples are particularly suitable. A hole large enough for the forefinger can be made with a corer or paring knife. This should be deep enough to accommodate the finger up to a point just below the first knuckle. Features can be made by cutting bits of skin off, by inserting cloves or large-headed pins, or by pasting on bits of paper. With a handkerchief wrapped around the hand, the puppet takes on character, and two children can give an extremely lively performance.

We usually think of quiet play as belonging to the afternoon rest hours, but the time just before sleep at night is also important. Many a Four calms down with crayons and books before having his light put out, and settles down for a cozy spell of Teddy bear talk in the dark after being tucked in. Long, dramatic conversations, with the current cuddly favorite contributing his share, are common. In fact, whole families of sleepy-time playmates often are present in imagination in Four's bed.

Four and His Family

In one way Four has begun to leave his family, finding new allegiance with his contemporaries, but in another way he is taking a firmer place within it. Definitely out of the baby class, he can now hold his own in family conversations. Better still, he has enough mastery of detail and a long enough attention span to play games with tolerant adults. This adds another activity that can be shared by the family group, taking its place with the old favorites of story-telling and listening to records.

Even a simple game like picture lotto, where the object is to match up similar cards, can be a refreshing alternative to activities grown stale. One can easily assemble an assortment of different lotto games—foods, objects, flowers, animals. Each toy season sees new ones issued and homemade boards and cards are not hard to design. The number of subjects need be limited only by the child's experience. A variety of games to choose from lends excitement, and the making of new game-sets can become a good family project in which the four-year-old can participate.

The fact that Four can plan ahead also means more sharing in projected picnics and excursions. Later years reveal how prized the memory of these occasions can be. Father's presence in particular gives week-end doings a special glow. Many fathers enjoy their leisure time with their children more this year than they did earlier because of the children's increased abilities. Games of catch are possible, with Frank or Mary throwing overhand. Some time might be allotted for them to show off their new tricks: standing on one leg for a few seconds, for example. This is a newly acquired skill and legitimate call for admiration.

Celebrations

At four, family festivals can include the child more fully. Birthdays are now anticipated with relish, the child usually selecting his own guests without assistance. An hour of play before the food is served can be included in the planning, providing adult supervision can be supplied.

The most successful birthday for four-year-olds that we ever saw began simply with offering the children different kinds of play materials—blocks, stick-ons, scissors and magazines to cut up—arranged in separate play centers. Utilizing the child's room, a hallway, and her own bedroom for these arrangements, this mother was able to keep the living room clear of guests until it was time to eat. A candy hunt, involving trails of wrapped candies, then led the children to the glory of the decorated birthday table, at which they were immediately seated, and the climax of the celebration was under way without fuss or tears.

At Easter, an egg hunt can be added to the ceremony of the Easter bunny and his gifts. The latter will be anticipated with more awareness than they were the year before. Four is as much interested in what the bunny will bring him as in the bunny himself.

The same interest in gifts extends to Christmas. As with everything else at four, *size* and *number* are important. Christmas means *trillions* of packages under the tree. The four-year-old can help in planning gifts for others, and will enjoy having secrets about them (although he may be unable to keep them). Some religious educators believe that this is the time to introduce the story of Jesus, told very simply, and dramatized by the children. If this is done, a crèche beneath the tree becomes meaningful as an illustration of the story. Others hold that Four is still too young for the story to have any religious value and feel it is likely to be confusing because of Four's very limited understanding of historical time.

Thanksgiving, however, does begin to take on some historical significance. The story of the Pilgrims, preferably backed up with pictures, is treated like any good story. Little girls love costumes suggestive of our first settlers, and boys become friendly Indians with no trouble at all. If the family enacts the story of the first Thanksgiving feast on Thanksgiving Day, the four-year-olds will participate with enthusiasm. Or they might act it out themselves, as impromptu entertainment for the grownups—but there must be Indians.

In some ways, Halloween seems made for the four-year-olds. Dressing up in fantastic costumes is just doing what comes naturally to Four, and the magnificence of the "funniest jack-o'-lantern in the world" is just his dish. The custom of trick or treat has now degenerated in many localities into mere begging for money or handouts of candy. If neighbors are cooperative, however, Four will love accumulating a few small treats. However, in a growing number of localities the custom has taken on new scope and meaning: the children collect money for UNICEF, the United Nations Children's Emergency Fund.

Valentine's Day comes into its own as a day of friendship tokens. The *number* of cards received is very important, and solicitous families do well to have an emergency stock laid by for "anonymous" contributions.

All in all, we must credit Four with trying with all his might to grow up. If he overreaches himself sometimes, an unobtrusive hand stretched out to help can steady him. Given time and tolerance, he will attain an even keel surprisingly fast.

CHAPTER VI

Five: Welcome to Reality

Inspiration from Life

ONE AFTERNOON excited voices spilled out of Mark's room when his friends came to play.

"Give me ten pounds of apples," a little girl's voice exuberantly demanded.

"Got no apples today, only onions," came the masculine reply.

"All right, I take ten pounds onions—here's ten dollars."

"I give you five pounds, that's all I got. Want some lettuces?"

Mark's mother cocked an attentive ear. Sometimes her five-year-old son was angry when she broke into his play, but she was curious enough to take that risk now.

A busy scene greeted her when she slipped quietly into the room where Mark and his friends had congregated. Paper bags filled with blocks, potatoes, and the tops from her morning's purchase of carrots stood on the floor. The scales and quart measure from her kitchen were arranged on a block wall, which was obviously a store counter. Two little girls were industriously rolling plasticene into round and long shapes and handing their "oranges" and "bananas" to the salesman.

At supper Mark told about the trip to the fruit and vegetable store his class had taken the week before. Mark's teacher later told his mother that the whole group had shown an avid interest in activities growing out of this one trip. They wanted to know where different fruits and vegetables had come from, and incidentally learned about the conditions necessary for their growth. Transportation fascinated them, and the ways in which the products they saw were transported to the city formed the basis for another play project. They learned something about different measuring units: pounds, bushels, dozens. Relative prices were discussed and some elementary ideas of economics developed: they began to understand that transportation costs affect the prices of items, and how scarcity might make some things more expensive. Interest in numbers and writing ballooned.

This incident is typical of five-year-old play. The child can now sustain an interest for fairly long periods of time. He is stimulated by playmates, and easily falls into cooperative ways. He has a vivid interest in the here and now, and favorite questions are "How does it work?" "Why is it like that?" "What is it for?" The keynote of five-year-oldness is practicality and conformity. He is no longer so keen on magic or absurdity. The real world holds novelty enough for him, and he has learned quite well to distinguish between what is and what is not.

This is the perfect time for the child to absorb all he can of the facts of everyday life. Actually, almost all his play is devoted to learning. When he pretends to be the garbage man or mailman, he does so with earnestness and exactitude. Although he can accept substitutions in the way of materials, he wants to *do* exactly what the real models of his play do. His projects are elaborate because he notices details and wants to have everything just right. His play has the quality of practice or rehearsal rather than invention; he is a copyist, not a designer.

Trips Are Important

The interests of Five expand as fast as his experiences multiply. That is why it is not enough to read to him or show him pictures: for facts to take on meaning, he must actually be there to feel, to smell, to hear, to be part of the thing he is learning about. So this is an especially good year for trips. The talk of five-year-olds as they play together often provides clues as to the kind of trips that would interest them. The experience of Mark's nursery school group, for example, started with talk among the children about the foods they liked and disliked.

Trips starting with the child's immediate interests do not have to be confined to kindergarten. Indeed, not every kindergarten can supply these experiences, for they require a great deal of planning and organization. It is usually much easier for parents to handle such expeditions for their children and a few invited guests than for a teacher to travel with a whole class.

Favorite visiting places for five- and six-year-olds who live in the city are the post office, police station, car barn, bus depot, a wholesale market, a retail supermarket, a railroad station, the fire station, any bit of building or road construction, a garage, a fish market, a warehouse, a greenhouse, a bottling plant, behind the scenes in any store, a furniture store, a butcher shop. Country children enjoy visiting the wayside store, a farm (if different from the one they live on), particularly one where there are various kinds of livestock, a fox, mink, or chinchilla farm, a milk station, a post office. If trips to a town close by can be arranged, the range of interests will be similar to that of the city child.

Success Depends on Planning

Certain ingredients help make these trips effective and fun for all concerned. Several children—preferably those who ordinarily play together—should go together if this can be managed. Secondly, the children should be prepared ahead of time about what's to come: how they will go, what vehicles they will ride in, about how long it will take to get to their destination, and some of the things they will see. Pictures are especially good in preparation of this sort.

Once there, the adult might encourage them to talk about the details of the scene. At the fire station attention can be called to the pole the men slide down when an alarm comes in, the siren on the hook and ladder, the work it takes to keep the equipment in good condition. At a farm the storage facilities will be a revelation. The barns, silo, ice house, milk house, root cellar should each be explored and discussed. If the excursion takes place while ploughing, planting, or harvesting is taking place, these will also be of great interest to the children. There are many small, specialized kinds of farming to be found around the edges of some cities, such as truck farms, plant nurseries, and establishments devoted to small animals like rabbits, chickens, and goats.

It is important not to tire the child before he reaches the objective of the trip. A car is ordinarily preferable to public transportation, but if one is not available, the quickest route should be chosen. Different forms of transportation are themselves interesting to Fives, but this interest is best served by a separate trip devoted just to the ride itself. Something to eat is essential; carrot strips and apples, cored and cut in quarters, are satisfying and make practically no mess. Crowds must be avoided. Breaking up the actual sight-seeing into half-hour units, with a rest in between, helps postpone fatigue.

Arrangements should also be made beforehand for the children to talk to a knowledgeable person, once the objective has been reached. Any adult can call attention to gates, signals, watertowers, ticket booths, waiting room, bulletin board during a visit to a railroad yard and station, but not everyone knows the names of the different kinds of cars, and what they do, nor the precise duties of all the employees the children will see. Yet it is exactly this kind of information that gives an expedition the concrete and factual quality that makes it a good experience for the five-year-old. The fruit and vegetable store Mark visited with his class differed little from the familiar neighborhood market he had been to with his mother, but on the school visit he could talk to the proprietor and find out how the wares come from central markets, where the different kinds of produce were grown, and what vehicles were used in transporting them from their place of origin to the store.

The Follow-Up

Finally, one has to be prepared for almost anything after the visit is over. Most of its value is realized through follow-up play activities at home. The children will be interested in books and pictures related in some way to the place visited. Unpredictable needs evoked by dramatic play and related construction projects often demand ingenuity.

One group that visited a farm, for example, decided to reproduce it in detail at home. They made wagons of cardboard and wooden boxes with buttons for wheels, but they needed small horses to go with them. The dime store supplied these and some other farm animals. A strip of blue oilcloth became a river, white oilcloth a road, green cloth a field. An oatmeal box was a silo, bits of rubber sponge glued on cardboard stands, wooden sticks, and pipe cleaners, made trees. The wooden people who usually stayed in the block corner came out to run the farm.

The five-year-old definitely needs the adult to help his play along. His ideas are big, but the means to implement them are sometimes a little beyond his reach. Suggestions for how things might be done are not out of place, but the actual doing should be the child's. The grownup can help most as a resource person—for supplies, information, and occasional brief assistance when something "won't work" and discouragement threatens.

Science

One way to prevent a five-year-old from being interested in the world around him is to raise him in a dungeon. Short of that, it is almost impossible to keep him from noticing all kinds of things—and trying to find out how each and every one of them works.

In addition to wanting to know how the creatures that surround him live and what they need, as he did at four, Five also wants to know something about their structure. Most Fives are not squeamish, and a visit to a butcher shop, where they may watch as the butcher draws a fowl, is a treat to many.

A pocket magnifying glass is almost a must for the adult who is coping with Five's scientific interests. It serves, among other things, for examining snowflakes, seeds with wings and "parachutes," and the structure of flowers, stamen, and pistil.

A magnet is a fine filler for Five's Christmas stocking. With a little packet of iron filings, or some nails, it furnishes hours of entertainment and evokes countless questions. Even if his questions cannot be answered completely, the sheer magic of magnetism will keep the child interested. He can help mother gather up dropped pins, he can test common objects to see if they are made of iron, he can control the movement of miniature magnetized animals and figures. He can be introduced to the wonder of the compass, and through that, learn something of the way of the stars, and of woodcraft.

If the five-year-old is allowed to watch and to experiment with common things, everyday life will rarely be dull. The difference in a cake before it is baked and after, the thickening of starch as it is cooked, the way gelatin stiffens when it is chilled—these simple observations are within the reach of every child, and offer powerful stimulation and encouragement for inquiring young minds. It is important that questions bring satisfaction. If they do, the child is likely to continue asking, learning, and thoroughly enjoying himself.

Five Needs to Be Useful

When Five makes something, he wants it to be useful. He uses his blocks to build roads, tracks, bridges, tunnels, garages, airdromes, firehouses. Girls build houses for their dolls and use clay to make dishes, food, animals, ashtrays. Handicrafts are interesting when they lead to finished products that can be given as gifts or used in the household. Mothers are likely to be overwhelmed with mats and potholders. Father must be ready to use large numbers of fragile ashtrays.

Even water play, delightful as ever, must have some form and purpose. If it entails responsibility, so much the better. Mopping the floor or washing a window takes the place of earlier aimless splashing. Dishwashing is enjoyed, in small doses, if there are some unbreakable items to be cleaned. What if the work is crudely done? Its importance lies in the satisfaction the child derives from it. It should be received with thanks and treated with respect—and the child had better not be present when the window is rewashed or the floor remopped.

Wood and Clay—New Uses

We can help the five-year-old in his passionate desire to do something "real" not only by supplying the materials, but by giving him a few hints about their properties. Because quick surface drying puts cracks into clay objects, for example, we can see that his prized creations are covered with a damp cloth until they are almost dry.

For special uses we can provide plastic material which is less fragile than ordinary unfired clay. There is a self-hardening clay which dries to a stonelike final finish. Another material, a kind of soft plastic, can be molded like clay and then baked in the oven until it takes on the consistency of hard rubber. Dextrine added to ordinary clay, one part to twenty, makes it more durable.

At this point, a little technical guidance is not amiss. The five-year-old can be introduced to the use of *slip* for holding the parts of his clay products together. (Slip is clay moistened until it has the consistency of paste.) It can be applied with a soft brush wherever two parts of a creation are to be joined, and the two parts then smoothed together at the surface. Since the five-year-old usually builds his forms out of parts, instead of evolving the whole from one lump of material, this is a very useful technique for him, and one he can handle.

Small clay tools, orange sticks, pallet knives will give Five greater command of his material. Cookie cutters can help him achieve form without frustration, and decorated buttons and small glasses with raised designs are useful in obtaining decorative effects.

Both boys and girls are now enthusiastic about wood working. By furnishing wood that is not too difficult to saw and hammer, and tools that fit their hands, we can make satisfying products possible. The five-year-old can usually learn to handle a small crosscut saw and a brace and bit. Some Fives can use a spiral-blade coping saw. A workbench to which the wood can be clamped, or to which a vise for holding it can be attached, is very desirable. Hammer, nails, tri-square, screws, glue, and sandpaper are the chief tools and accessories. Quarter- and half-inch lumber, pieces of balsa wood, dowels of several thicknesses, manageable sheets of plywood, are the basic materials. Wheels, or good substitutes like button molds, are handy to have.

Five will need help in planning his projects. It is important that he does not undertake more than he can carry out himself without help in the actual handling of the tools, though occasional suggestions from an adult are permissible. Airplanes can easily be made of two pieces of balsa wood, and boats and barges can be made somewhat after the pattern of the ones the grownups shaped for him when he was younger (see page 61). Girls can make doll beds by hammering flat, solid pieces of wood at right angles to a longer section; another parallel section higher up will make this into a toy bookcase.

For gifts, the five-year-old can make simple book ends by piling up graduated squares and nailing them together with edges lined up straight on one side. He can make blocks for a younger brother or sister by sandpapering and waxing pieces of wood he has cut up. Single pieces of thin wood, about six inches square, make good stands, when they have been sandpapered and painted, to slip under potted plants.

The child himself often shows surprising ingenuity when exposed to the tools and wood in different shapes and sizes. But perhaps a word of caution is due here. Because carpentering is considered a manly art, we sometimes feel that all little boys should take to it like ducks to water, just as we tend to expect all little girls to show a proclivity for sewing. Neither may occur in certain cases and nothing is to be gained by insisting that children pursue these occupations when they don't seem to be congenial ones. A boy whose saw cuts are always crooked, and a girl whose "embroidery" is invariably smudged and knotty, may want to come back to these skills later—but not if they are pushed toward them too insistently at this age.

Boys, Girls, and Babies

As we have pointed out, boys and girls by this time are apt to enjoy different kinds of imaginary play. But like all rules about children, this one sometimes seems made only to be broken. Many boys at this time still want a doll for Christmas. If a new baby has recently joined the family, even a six-year-old boy may be avidly interested in playing with baby dolls, washing, dressing, and feeding them. On the other hand, if the boy has been teased about his natural interest in domestic play, he may turn away from it entirely.

Although boys must develop masculine traits and learn to play the role of men in our society, it is a pity to turn them too soon from house play. They are, after all, destined to take a place as a family member when they grow up, and childhood make-believe is one of the ways to prepare them for this role. It is much better to let the boy play house to his heart's content, until he turns from it naturally under the pressure of other interests, than to shame him away from it. Even those who do not show other interests when most boys do, need encouragement, not shame. Humiliating and teasing him when he is little may interfere to a surprising degree with the best kind of functioning as a husband and father when he grows up.

Both boys and girls are intensely interested in babies at five and six. They want to know mainly where the baby comes from and how it is born. This is part of their interest in how things work in general. Sometimes they play out childbirth by putting a doll between their legs and pulling it out. Such play need not indicate any undue sex interest—it is a way of absorbing information similar to the rest of their imaginative play. Occasionally a child who is too shy to ask in words uses this device to show that he wants to know, having perhaps heard something of the mystery from his little friends.

If the parent has not given any explicit information up to this point, he or she might ask, "What are you playing, dear?" This is opening enough for many children; but others may look embarrassed and remain silent. This may be the cue to inquire further, "Are you playing how babies are born? Are you wondering about it?" Usually this helps the child to overcome shyness and the way is open for giving the appropriate information.

Five Rides the Range

The boys who turn away spontaneously from house play at five often break out in cowboys and Indians, and war games. Bombs and six-shooters invade the kindergarten. Bandits and posses whoop around every corner of the block. At five the appeal of this kind of play lies mainly in its opportunity for violent action and noise; at six it may take on a more purposeful character.

So this is the time for those cowboy and cowgirl costumes (if they haven't been furnished at four). Boys and girls alike swagger about with guns slung low on hips, or simply stuck into a belt. Some parents are disturbed by this. They need not be. Five is simply showing awareness of his culture; as long as guns are part of our world, they are going to be part of the world of the five- and six-year-old. Some, in fact, start at two, stimulated by an older brother or sister. The gun furnishes a delightful opportunity for saying "Bang"; it is not recognized as a deadly weapon with any sense of reality. The "dead" are expected to rise again, and quickly; anyone who insisted on playing dead realistically would precipitate considerable anxiety in most five-year-olds.

Homemaking for Girls

Girls, however happy to be hard-bitten bandits at times, are mostly devoted to playing house. They have assimilated most of the household activities by this time, and they repeat them tirelessly with their toy equipment. The shifts and make-do's of a year ago are often scorned. Dolls are dressed and undressed, endlessly fed, bathed, aired, and put to bed; spanked, too, when they deserve it, and doctored. The appetite of the five-year-old girl for dolls is almost insatiable. If she already has the basic equipment for playing house—table and chairs, stove, cabinet, refrigerator, bed, carriage, bassinet, ironing board, bureau—the next most welcome gift will be clothes to fit her dolls.

Doll clothing for this age should be fastened with fairly large buttons and button-holes. As for younger children, homemade clothes may use zippers and hooks, if these are not too small.

Clothing that approximates the child's own will be especially appreciated. Small rubber boots, umbrellas, roller skates, handbags, are greeted with glee. So are pajamas and dressing gowns, outdoor clothing with an approximation of fur, underwear that really fits and can be removed and put on easily.

Necessary Disorder

In the interests of dramatic play, the home may be continually in disorder. A chair and a sheet make a tent. Chairs are frequently set up in rows for trains. A living-room chair may be turned upside down to serve as a cave, and the sofa may become a fort. Wise parents accept this as the fate of homes where

Fives and Sixes live. It is possible to avoid many such upsets by providing for every contingency with ready-made toys, but this robs the child of chances to use his imagination; improvising, as we have said before, adds to his sense of achievement, and hence, of fulfillment.

The Age of Costumes

Although Five plays well and lustily with whatever he has, complete and realistic costumes are especially appreciated now. Four was content with a policeman's badge, an Indian headdress, epaulets to suggest a uniform. Five wants the whole thing.

Boys like police uniforms, complete with handcuffs, billy, and whistle. They also like to don full fireman regalia, the pocketed apron of the carpenter, the breeches and coat of the ringmaster, and the plastic helmet and magic paraphernalia of the space explorer. What will have special appeal depends on what they have seen and what they know. There is little point in giving a clown costume to a child who has never been to the circus or seen it on television. And a doctor's coat will probably give more pleasure to a doctor's son than to a farmer's.

Girls, for their part, delight in dressing up in their mother's clothes. High-heeled shoes, elaborately trimmed hats, and dresses are donned at every opportunity. In fact, the dressing-up part of their play may become so elaborate as to give the whole thing the aspect of a theatrical performance. In addition, girls love the outfits of nurses, ballerinas, and circus queens. On the whole, they go for anything gay and glittering. One toy distributor, recognizing this, offers a finery kit, full of flowers, feathers, and brightly colored shining lengths of cloth. Another boosted his profits substantially with a pair of wooden heels, equipped with elastic bands to hold them on the child's shoes.

Lipstick and nail polish are often passionately desired by girls. Starting at four, this desire does not seem to abate until about eight or nine. Inexpensive make-up and manicure kits, put out especially for children, can save Mother bothersome invasions of her dressing table.

Miniature Worlds

At five the interest in miniature objects of all kinds really blossoms. There are several reasons for this. The five-year-old has usually achieved the small-muscle co-ordination needed to manipulate small things. Also, miniatures give him a chance to represent a wide variety of real-life situations in a small space. And, finally, it is sometimes easier to play out his wishes by pretending that they belong to the tiny people of the doll-house world who cannot object or talk back.

The Day of the Doll House

Doll houses begin to have real appeal for girls at this age. The usual commercial kind is not the best choice now; Five needs more access to the insides of the rooms than these offer, and more space for her hands. Unless a new type of house has come on the market since this was written, the most desirable kind has to be made at home.

Actually, this is very simple. Corrugated cartons, measuring twelve by thirteen by fourteen inches can be obtained from most grocery stores. When these are cut in half, and the top flaps glued down, each carton makes two rooms six inches high. Windows and doors can easily be cut out, and even opened and

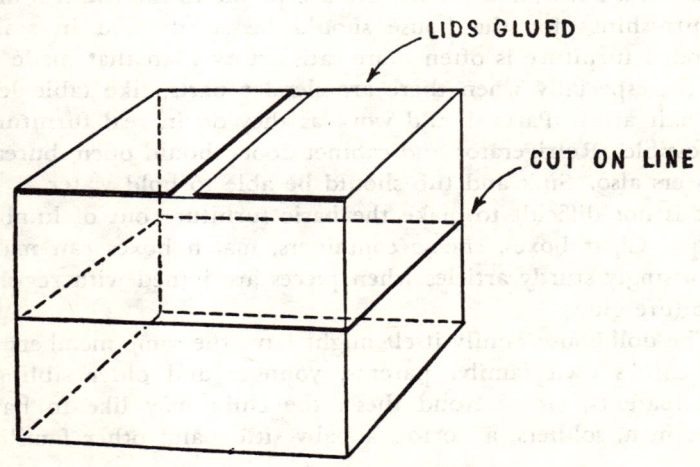

closed if one edge is left attached to the box. A simple poster paint job, wallpaper scraps for the inside, rugs made out of old felt hats, and the job is done. A realistic flat roof with overhang can be made from an extra carton, by cutting around all four sides about one inch from the bottom. The piece that comes off will have a rim; when the corners of this are opened, and the edge flattened, we have a roof in one piece.

Separate rooms can be joined with glue, and openings cut through the walls. Leaving the rooms unjoined has advantages for the apartment dweller; the house can be stacked for storage.

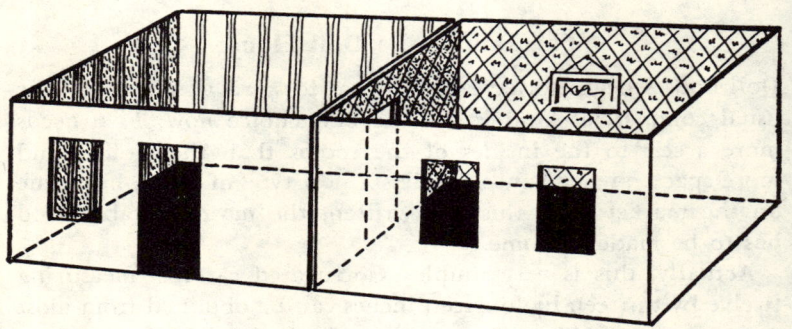

Blocks can easily make a doll house, and are more flexible. A few long units standing on end are enough to suggest the rooms of a house, and usually are acceptable to the five-year-old.

Furnishings for the house should be sturdy and in scale. Wooden furniture is often more satisfactory than that made of plastic, especially when there are slender parts, like table legs or chair arms. Parts should work as they do in real furniture, if possible. Refrigerator and cabinet doors should open, bureau drawers also. Sink and tub should be able to hold water.

It is not difficult to make the basic furniture out of lumber scraps. Cigar boxes, cheese containers, match boxes can make surprisingly sturdy articles when pieces are joined with regular furniture glue.

The doll-house family itself might have the same members as the child's own family: parents, younger and older siblings, grandparents, etc. Beyond these, the child may like to have policemen, soldiers, a doctor, a baby sitter, and other familiar figures. These people come in flexible rubber-like plastic and rigid plastic jointed for bending. The former can be bent into any position, the latter are more limited in the positions they can assume, but both are satisfactory. It is even possible to make families out of pipe cleaners and clay or beads. These are more fragile, and cannot be undressed and dressed as easily as the plastic dolls. For these reasons we do not recommend them unless the others are unavailable.

Vehicles and animals are part of doll-house play. Animals may include pets, farm stock, and even wild specimens. Dogs, kittens, cows, pigs, lions, and tigers usually are not difficult to obtain. These should be in correct scale for the people and furniture. A dog that is larger than its master is an awkward item to fit into one's play.

Small Worlds for Boys

Boys have their own equivalents of doll houses. Toy farms, forts, barracks; soldiers, sailors, farm workers, and animals; miniature models of machinery—these are their means for working out the destinies of small worlds.

Slightly larger than miniatures, but still coming into the class of small toys, are the working models of machinery which are so beloved now in the block corner and in the sandbox. These are much smaller than those we recommended for four-year-olds, and are much more exact reproductions of the vehicles and machines they represent. We have seen sturdy sets of exact scale models from six to twelve inches long of hauling and trucking equipment of all kinds, and of farm equipment, from tractor to seeder and bailer. They are moderately priced and could add a great deal to the play of children in whose lives these activities are important.

Small scale models such as these can pyramid the value of exploratory trips. In preparing for such a trip, it is wise to scout the market for toy replicas which will enrich the resultant play. More and more toy manufacturers are becoming aware of the lure of exact reproductions which really work, and new items come on the market every year. Grain elevators, cement chutes, car-washing establishments, gasoline stations are only a few of the things one might look for.

Out-of-Doors with Five

Almost anything that offers Five a chance to leave the earth appeals to him. He loves knotted ropes and rope ladders, stilts, a trapeze bar, and his performance on the jungle gym is a delight to watch. If he has seen telephone linemen at work he wants to emulate them. (A telephone lineman's outfit is a very appropriate gift at this age.) A circus brings on an epidemic of acrobatic tricks and tumbling. The somersault sometimes appears to be Five's natural mode of locomotion.

If roller skates have not come into his life before, they now present a challenge that Five cannot ignore. He cannot skate for long at one time but with effort he can master the complicated co-ordination of arms, trunk, and feet that skating requires. For social reasons this is also a good time to begin skating. As his sixth birthday approaches, acceptance by children of his own age will become more and more important, and skating is one of the skills on which that acceptance depends. A child's ability in skating and rope-skipping is also a good gauge of his co-ordination. When he has difficulty with these, it will pay to give special attention to the development of his motor skills, since they become more and more important to him as time goes on. Children whose physical skills are poorer than average are often more verbal than motor-minded and may appear more mature and imaginative than their physically agile playmates. Certainly their gifts are not to be underrated. Nevertheless, such a child needs practice at what he does less well, and plenty of interest and encouragement from an adult, to make up for the frustration of poor body control. Swimming often brings great satisfaction to those who can't keep up with land games. For those who *do* co-ordinate well, water seems now to be their natural element, and they usually take to swimming happily.

Equipment and Games

Five's new interest in upper space expresses itself in all kinds of hoisting activities, as well as climbing. It is a good idea to have on hand a strong clothesline, large pulleys, pails, baskets, boards, and boxes that can be assigned to the back yard. A safe climbing place is also important, if our young piano movers and roustabouts are to function without damage to themselves. Some adult help will be needed for rigging up the hoist and pulley system, but once it is established, Five will manage it with amazing adeptness.

Fives are likely to want coaster wagons and full-sized scooters. Swings without backs, seesaws, slides are basic equipment for playground fun. Hoops, large rubber balls, and balloons are good accessories. The sandbox and large, hollow blocks still remain favorites.

Junk continues to be valuable. Old tires and tubes, large rocks, barrels, packing cases, kegs, wooden pails, large paint cans are legitimate back-yard equipment.

One sign of Five's steady advance toward becoming a social creature is his interest in group games. He is not yet ready for competition, because he cannot stand losing, but games in which everyone has a turn—he began learning these at four—are exactly what he needs. Ring Around a Rosey, Here We Go Round the Mulberry Bush, The Farmer in the Dell, Here We Go Looby Loo are fine for him. Drop the Handkerchief is popular with some Fives, but the adult must be sure that slow runners are not penalized and made to feel inferior. Games in which words and movements are repeated with every turn are especially enjoyed.

Handicrafts and Quiet Play

Five is the perfect kindergartener by taste as well as age. He enjoys all the usual kindergarten activities: painting, drawing, coloring, cutting, pasting. Unlike Four, he likes limited periods of activity and models to serve as guides. He likes definite tasks that can be completed in a twenty-minute session, and he wants to have something to show for his efforts.

In a year he has made great strides in what he can do with his hands, but he still has limits. Handedness is fairly well established, but he will still change hands while working, especially with block building, and painting. Five can lace his shoes, fasten buttons, and put a needle through a fairly small hole, but he is not yet able to tie a bow snugly. Although he can sit still much longer than Four can, he does a good deal of scratching, poking, wriggling, and touching parts of his body to show that sitting still is not easy for him.

Now coloring books come into use, but only those with large, simple, outline pictures are suitable. Even with these, he will spill over occasionally. Cut-outs are prime favorites, if the outlines are not too intricate. Small protruding details are still too difficult to manage. Along with cutting out, Five likes to test the steadiness of his hand by simply cutting paper into shreds. His clothes are in some hazard here, for he is not above experimenting on them when he really gets going with scissors.

Five can manage simple weaving and dotes on making paper mats for his mother. Loop looms are a little difficult for some, but others get great satisfaction out of them. A simple heddle loom, set up by the adult, seems easier than the loop loom, on which the loops are forever slipping off their pegs.

Those who can manage the loop loom can also manage knitting spools, with a little help when new yarn has to be attached, or the finished rope removed from the spool. Raffia baskets can be made easily, if a base and pegged frame of wood are furnished. Many useful articles can be made of pieces of cardboard which have been cut in the shape of book covers, picture frames, portfolios and provided with holes for lacing.

Some girls love to sew as passionately as some boys like to hammer. They want to use real needles on real cloth, and to make real things. Large-eyed darning needles, heavy thread or yarn, and loosely woven materials fill the needs of these young creators. With some guidance, they can produce crude bags, mats made of several thicknesses of material sewn together, capes and skirts for their dolls.

Paper plates are a boon to the parent of an enterprising Five. These can be colored to make ornamental wall plaques, or strewn with paper flowers for glamorous party hats; laced together, they make creditable May baskets.

Small beads, buttons, spaghetti broken into suitable lengths and dyed with food coloring, colored macaroni "snowflakes" all make excellent stringing materials. The five-year-old girl is delighted to make necklaces and bracelets for herself, but most of all she is proud to present such ornaments to her mother. Fashion note for mothers: macaroni necklaces are quite *de rigueur* for housework, shopping, and family meals.

Toy manufacturers have produced innumerable varieties of sewing sets to appeal to Five, but with a paper punch it is simple to make one's own cards, using the cardboard that comes in laundered shirts, glamorized with shiny-surfaced construction paper.

Rejoicing in the skill of his hands, Five enjoys working with small construction materials. Sets which combine balls, tubes, and sticks are challenging. Mosaic blocks appeal to Five's taste for order and give him a chance to exercise his skill at copying. Jigsaw puzzles which are difficult enough to challenge him but not too difficult for him to solve still give him a real sense of achievement.

Some Fives can begin to play games like pick up sticks, tiddlywinks, and jackstraws, though for others they are extremely frustrating. Before exposing the child to them, it is wise to estimate his deftness. Often children who are confident on the playground lag way behind at small-muscle tasks. For these, ring toss or ten pins might make better indoor games.

The Appeal of Numbers

One thing that is very apt to distinguish the outlook of the five-year-old is his interest in numbers. Four enjoyed counting his toys; he responded to the challenge of "Can you do that by the time I count ten?" But Five goes much further—he wants to master the shape and sequence of all the numbers that enter his life.

Clocks and calendars are prime favorites at this time. First, the numbers are recognized; then they are proudly marked and read. Five can make his own clock out of numbers he has cut from an old calendar. He can make up simple matching games by pasting cut-out numbers to cards. He tries to write the numbers he has seen, though many are still beyond his skill. If his interest in numbers is kept at the level of play, he will glide effortlessly into arithmetic.

There are many aids the parents can offer in this connection.

Flat table blocks bearing numbers and letters in large clear outlines can be used in many combinations. Ordinary playing cards are good, or one may look for some of the new games that use playing cards with large, clear numbers in combination with plainly marked dice. Domino sets with numerals instead of dots and a simplified version of bingo are also available for the five-year-old. Number stencils which the child can use to color make him more familiar with the detail of different forms.

The alert parent can take advantage of many situations involving numbers and measurements in the child's play and daily doings. How long must he make the sides of his wagon? Out comes the tape measure. Does he need to share his blocks? He can be helped to count how many blocks he needs to finish his building. He can take note of the number of quarts of milk his mother buys when he goes shopping with her, the number of pounds of meat. His own toy telephone may have numbers on its dial. There are street and house numbers to notice on marketing trips—not to mention car licenses. All these experiences are play now; they will help to make play of work later.

Fives who have learned to count up to ten can play table games like Peter Rabbit or Puss in the Corner. In these, the moves are determined by a spinner which indicates how many "steps" each player may move. When the child can distinguish the different values of coins and bills, very simple trading games are in order. Play money and a cash register will also help number interests along.

Alphabet Play

Interest in letters starts, naturally enough, with the child's own name. Many four-year-olds want their names written on the pictures they make; the five-year-old wants to write it himself. He can write a few capital letters, but many will be reversed. It is best not to fuss over reversals at this age; first we must build the child's confidence that he can master this new and intricate material. He may even sense that his letters look "funny," as he knows his pictures look "funny," but for the time being he cannot help it. Copying any intricate form takes tremendous control over hand, arm, eyes, and the writing tool.

Five's protruding tongue tip and tense grip indicate the effort he is making. He deserves the reward of parental appreciation without carping criticism about comparatively minor details. In time the child will come to recognize and correct his errors by himself. The best way we can help Five is to supply him with many different kinds of materials bearing letters, and to give a little time to playing matching games that he can master.

Letter stencil sets, anagram sets, ABC card games especially designed for five- and six-year-olds offer play materials that reinforce Five's interest in words and letters. In addition, table games involving the matching of pictures (some were mentioned in chapter 5) encourage attention to details that later pays off in ease in reading and writing.

One construction toy made up of interlocking plastic blocks which can be put together to form letters or numbers seems made to order for this age. It can be used with or without models, and as the finished products can be picked up and moved around without disturbing them—remember that Five, like Four, likes to keep things he makes—this kind of toy remains useful for a long time because it is so flexible. Additions to the original set will be welcomed eagerly for years, as ideas and projects expand.

If a blackboard has not made its appearance before, this is the time for it. It is now an excellent preparation for school. Experiments with numbers and letters are easier when the unsuccessful ones can be erased without fuss. In addition, there is more outline drawing at five, and chalk is a good medium for this kind of activity. Different colored chalks will be needed.

Critics Not Wanted

Five will glow under praise; criticism, even when well meant, will wilt him. When something at all recognizable emerges from his strenuous efforts, the least we can do is rejoice with him in his triumph. A spot left unpainted, a slightly crooked alignment are small matters. Standards and self-criticism will develop as he grows older, but as with numbers and letters, so with art—this is the time for reassurance and encouragement. He may seem brash and boastful; actually, his confidence is very brittle.

Unlike Four, Five knows what he is after and does not abandon his original idea when his techniques fail him. In painting and drawing he is not distracted by accidental forms he creates. He wants to carry out his first intention, and he does, crude as the result may be. He is sufficiently aware of how things look to know his picture is not like those he sees in books, but he is helpless to do anything about it.

It is too early to try to teach painting techniques. Five has such a drive to complete things that he has to put in everything he knows about his subject matter as well as what can be seen. Thus, Picasso-like, he endows his profiles with two eyes, and insists on showing the back door to a house even when painting only the front. Extra walls may be stuck on at curious angles.

This might be a good time to take inventory of the kind of painting and drawing Five sees about him. Are the illustrations in his books fresh, appealing, and in good taste? Are the pictures on his walls the kinds we would like him to use for models? We are not suggesting that Five be directed to copy anything, but we cannot overlook the fact that he is model-minded. There are many prints of good pictures that appeal to children, and these are not necessarily subjects especially designed for them. With his generous appreciation and few prejudices he is apt to enjoy a Picasso Harlequin quite as much as Albrecht Dürer's study of a hare. Animals, children, and parent-and-child subjects are most likely to be appreciated by this age group. Specific suggestions will be found in the appendix.

Progress and Problems in the Block Corner

The block corner often presents the most impressive evidence of Five's maturity and competence. As with other types of play, increasing ability calls for more supplies. Five often sets out to build a structure like a real building he knows—usually one that has impressed him—and he achieves a surprising resemblance, if he has the variety of block units that he needs. Assuming that he has the basic set of kindergarten blocks we suggested for Three and Four, Five is likely to need the following additional units: two circular curves, two small buttresses, one small bridge, two large cylinders, and four roof boards.

It was possible, though not always easy, to cajole Four into letting his building be dismantled. But Five is adamant—leave it up. About the only way to keep peace in the family is to designate a specific place where structures may be left standing. A table or platform on small wheels that can slide under his bed is one solution for structures of limited size. Given this concession to his needs, Five can be much more cooperative about taking other block structures down at the end of the play period.

Music and Dancing

The five-year-old wants to be assured that the world is a predictable place, and whatever is orderly, definite, and meaningful furthers this belief. Music has both order and meaning, and Five is adept at picking out melodies and tunes. Intent on mastering what he can, he picks them out on the piano. The mother who plays even a little will find she has new charm for her child, and a new companion in her pleasure.

The piano seems the easiest instrument for Five to begin on, during his one-finger, one-hand stage. He has already had a great deal of training with different kinds of sounds and rhythm during his early years. Now this training pays off in helping him detect different sound qualities. The child who has more experience with different kinds of instruments may do better than one with more limited opportunities, but most are responsive to clearly stated melodic patterns.

After Five has acquired a feeling for the orderly progression of notes, he may be able to shift to simple wind instruments: like the song flute, or ocarina. These require more co-ordination than the one-finger exercise on the piano at first; later, when real playing from notes is attempted, the situation is reversed.

Fives can begin to work together in small groups, and follow the beat of the music. Two or three may make up a primitive rhythm band, with someone to lead them at the piano. The band must be kept small, and only the simplest of accompaniments should be expected. The pianist can help by playing in a markedly rhythmic manner.

Instruments for rhythmic work at this age are about the same as those we recommended earlier. They must be easy to hold and operate. The triangle, unless it is suspended so that the child does not need to hold it, may be difficult. Maracas, rhythm sticks, large cymbals and finger cymbals, wood blocks, tom-toms, tambourines, and different kinds of bells are all good. One music teacher reports that a large nail hung on a string and struck with another large nail makes a good substitute for a triangle. Homemade tambourines and tom-toms, described earlier, are still useful.

Five can sing well, too. The usual center of his and her register is G above middle C. The child performs creditably, if the songs keep close to this and do not go on too long. Pieces involving imitative noises—a boat whistle, the chug of a train, animal sounds—have special appeal. Fives join energetically in back-and-forth songs in which an adult sings the verse and they sing back with assorted noises. A great deal of the enjoyment comes from the repetition; between choruses the children wait in a state of delicious anticipation, and pounce with gusto when their moment comes. Song suggestions will be found in the appendix.

Records and radio both attract Five. In the first he likes a combination of words and music which tell a story. In radio, the singing commercials are likely to be the things he picks out to repeat. They are usually catchy, with a pronounced rhythm, and involve the obvious kind of rhyming and repetition he likes.

When Five interprets music with body movements, he definitely dances. The dance is informal and improvised, but likely to have some recognizable form. Because he can skip and gallop, tiptoe and walk crouched and bent as well as upright, his repertory of movement is larger than it was at four. He can also bounce a large ball in time with music and show with his body whether a tune is going up, down, or holding steady.

Five prefers to dance in his bare feet—this helps him to maintain his balance and to move more smoothly. Shoes hamper him and cut down his enjoyment. If bare or stockinged feet are not advisable because of drafts or splinters, soft leather slippers with flexible soles can be bought at most shoe stores. Slippers of chamois or felt can easily be made at home.

Despite his unclad feet, the five-year-old often feels incomplete without something to dress up in while he dances—preferably a straight length of material that can become anything from an Indian's blanket to angel's wings. Although he must still be allowed to use his body spontaneously, Five likes to take a specific role when he dances. He will accept suggestions from the adult readily, but needs to work them out in his own way. He loves to imitate animals, to show how things grow, or to impersonate natural forces like the wind. Once he gets the idea, Five can act out a fairly elaborate story in dance form.

Bedtime is a favorite time for dancing to records. Freedom from clothing may be one reason. Another may be the relaxing effect that comes with rhythmic movement. For Five, who fights rest, music can be a blessed aid in wooing sleep.

Books

Bath time and bedtime are favorite reading hours, and reading has special values at each of these times. If his Mother or Father is busy reading to him at bath time, the job of getting washed is clearly up to Five. Unobtrusive supervision without personal service is just what he needs to help him on to the road to real self-reliance.

For some five-year-olds reading at bedtime is a ritual. Tucked snugly under the covers, they relax imperceptibly into sleep as the familiar voice and the familiar words go on. Sleep time is also the vulnerable time, when the child feels small and fears arise. Accordingly, it is the time for old friends. From this kind of ritual, reading takes on its own power to soothe in later years.

The tastes of Five differ from those of Four. Subject matter may be the same—animals, trains, fire engines—but the period of wild exaggeration seems to be on the wane. Animals and trains and autos may act like human beings, but they are expected to act like credible humans. Repetition continues to be appealing, both in words and actions, and a touch of fun is always enjoyed. Rhyming jingles interspersed throughout a story make it irresistible.

The question of fairy tales often comes up at this time. Parents feel nostalgic about them, and are apt to resent the suggestion that realistic tales are more suitable. Actually, some of the old folk tales are not very different in essence from a number of today's stories. *The Musicians of Bremen*, for example, concerns animals that talk like humans, just as *Peter Rabbit* does, and use their skills to outwit a gang of robbers.

Many fairy tales, of course, are frightening to children, and many are difficult to understand, dealing as they do with times and customs different from our own. Reading fairy tales to Fives is often disappointing because they fail to get the point, or are distracted by unimportant details. At seven, when children are less hazy about what is real and unreal, and about the past and present, many of the traditional stories can be shared with more satisfaction.

If, however, the parent feels an irresistible urge to try out fairy tales, it would be wise to avoid the blood-and-thunder variety. True, some Fives can "take it," but when the choice of enchanting, unfrightening books is wide, there seems little point in forcing the child to screw up courage to deal with such stern subjects as *Hansel and Gretel* and *Little Red Riding Hood*. On the other hand, such tales as *Puss in Boots, The Shoes That Danced, The Six Servants, Cinderella, The Princess and the Pea,* and *The Emperor's New Clothes* offer humor and excitement without making their audience anxious.

Acting Out and Making Up

Being read to is only a beginning for Five. After he knows a story, he wants to dramatize it. He can act it out with friends, or, during quiet hours, he can use puppets or dolls. Sharing the re-enactment of a story with the child is even more intimate a pleasure than sharing the reading, and gives us a partial return for all those times when re-reading is merely a service dutifully performed.

Even more important than dramatizing stories he has heard, Five needs a chance to produce his own. A narrative—perhaps based on a previous excursion—can be dictated to the adult, and she may lead the child to draw illustrations for his story or perhaps to make covers for it and so create a book. When his words are taken down seriously, the child gains a new appreciation of his own capacities and a new impulse to extend them.

Telling his own stories serves other ends, too, for in this way the child gets practice in translating experiences into language and finds he can communicate them to others. Furthermore, the child who is encouraged to give out as well as take in, to do as well as to look and listen, is not as likely to become the listless onlooker in life, satisfied with ready-made entertainment and ready-made thinking.

Here Come the Comics!

The problem of the comic books often begins to trouble the parent of a Five. We cannot deny their appeal for this age group, and there is much to be said for them. The pictures are often simple and satisfactory to the child, the action is swift and obvious, many of the characters are similar to those the child favors in his story books. The problem therefore boils down to a choice. If we offer suitable comics—and Donald Duck comes immediately to mind—we may forestall a hankering for the inappropriate. The trick is not to leave a vacuum.

Comics are valuable as a bridge from listening to independent reading. The text is usually brief enough so that its gist can be recalled after one hearing, and it is so closely tied with the pictures that the latter act as a reminder. A child can "read" his comic books by himself, with pleasure. Gradually, his dependence on his parents for this service lessens. His eagerness to learn "real" reading for himself increases, but it would be idle to say that he will automatically discard comic books for better literature. Real guidance in this realm and the continued sharing of different kinds of stories by children and their parents, will be needed for years to come. But since the comics are very much with us, it is well to recognize their positive values as well as their drawbacks.

Television

Television and radio are commonly part of the child's recreation by the time he is five. It is fortunate that both offer some good programs, for, whether we like it or not, Johnny and Helen are going to look and listen. As with comics, indiscriminate exposure can be avoided by suggesting the few programs that are desirable, and keeping the child busy with other things when these are not available.

The greatest danger this ready-made entertainment holds is its tendency to make a passive spectator of the child rather than a doer. (As we know, it can have the same effect on the adult; parents who spend a considerable part of their time watching television should not be surprised when their children evince the same interest.) Television is especially guilty in this respect. If there are any programs available that invite the child's active participation in appropriate activities while he is watching, these are the ones he should be encouraged to see.

Unfortunately, the commercials are a problem. Until they live long enough to develop some discrimination, most children will fall for every boxtop lure they are offered. Insisting on complete consumption of the contents of the box before the top can be sent in seems to be one way to keep this within reason. Some parents demand that the child pay for the lure of the moment by giving up some customary treat costing about the same amount, when cash is also involved. The perfect solution has not been found, but a succession of disappointments with the tawdry items usually given as "prizes" may be the most effective education of all.

Planning the Day

If the five-year-old does not attend kindergarten, someone needs to give some real thought to his play-day. He needs to know what to expect, and not have things sprung on him, and he wants to be in on the planning.

The five-year-old's day can be planned so that it works in well with his mother's schedule. It might go something like this: a free play period in the morning, preferably outdoors, while the house cleaning is being done; quiet play indoors just before lunch; then a short rest in the afternoon, with reading, if Mother is free, or quiet play in his room, and another outdoor period from three to five.

Shopping trips with Mother might be substituted sometimes for one of the outdoor play periods, with Five on tricycle or pulling his wagon to help bring home the groceries. Above all, Five needs time and space for visits with his friends, and he needs friends. Some Fives prefer children of their own sex, others don't care, but most like children of their own age.

"Best friends" abound at five, and they want very much to visit each other's homes. An invitation for lunch and an hour or two in the afternoon usually works out well. With only two present, play goes smoothly indoors or out. In a group of three, two may gang up on the third, and such a group needs more supervision. However, cooperative play, when it does occur, is likely to be best in groups of three, so the extra trouble entailed may be worth while.

Despite his love of company, Five likes to work on solo projects. At such times he resents interference with his materials, and likes to finish what he starts. If he is asked politely for the use of some of his things, however, he is usually obliging.

The five-year-old is willing at many points to accept adult guidance—in fact, he asks for it. "How do you do it?" is heard often where Fives have access to a helpful grownup. Bragging less than he did at four, Five seems to have some idea of his own limitations. He comes to terms with them by relying on adults to help him.

Five needs much help in taking care of his things. His favorite method of cleaning up is to dump all the offending items in a chest or drawer. As we have pointed out, this is not the ideal method, as another mess is bound to result every time he wants to retrieve a single toy, unless it just happens to be on top of the heap. Nevertheless, it's about the best that Five can achieve without help, and if the start of a good habit and a helpful attitude seem more important now than efficient results, parents may have to settle for this method.

Family Fun

Compared to Four, Five seems to make few demands on his family. But he does appreciate a "little bit of butter to his bread." The "butter" can be fifteen minutes after lunch, when he shares a story with Mother, or the half-hour before dinner, when Dad is free to toss a beanbag with him, or his bath time, when he has an audience for splashing and chattering. If there is time between the end of the family dinner and Five's bedtime, twenty minutes or so might be given to a table game.

At five, there are many choices available for family fun. Games like parcheesi or Chinese checkers are endurable for short periods by even the least game-minded adults. Many materials have real appeal for an age range wide enough to embrace the preschooler and the adult. One father reports that a finger-painting session is as much fun for him as for his little girl, and another likes a session during which he and his child create a whole zoo of fantastic creatures. The adult can also join in playing with materials that are fun just to handle, like the silicone plastic that can be stretched, bounced, and shattered, or the supple metal spring that "walks" down inclines and jumps from hand to hand when agitated slightly. One building set made up of interlocking clown figures often intrigues adults, who build intricate and perilously balanced structures with it, yet it offers satisfaction to the five-year-old, too.

A supply of these versatile items, collected with all the family in mind, is likely to be worth its weight in gold. With them family fun can really be fun and not a routine drearily pursued from a mistaken sense of duty.

Week ends can be treasures of togetherness for Five. He does not care much what is done, but he does want to be let in on plans ahead of time. Some responsibility for carrying out what is planned also heightens his enjoyment. If the treat is to be a picnic, he likes to help make the sandwiches, or help pack the food. If he lives in a city, a picnic in the back yard or a nearby park can be something special. Museums offer him a chance to learn about the home life of some of the birds or local wild animals he has seen. The zoo remains eternally charming. Cooking with and for the family can be the most fun of all. Outdoor campfires or barbecues are understandably exciting, but indoor cooking is also highly satisfying. The five-year-old can scramble eggs and cook frankfurters, if an adult manages the lighting of the stove. Both boys and girls shine in this department. With the aid of modern mixes, they can produce biscuits, puddings, ice cream, cookies, candy, and cake. It is a proud moment indeed when Betty or Ben marches in proudly bearing the family dessert that "I made myself!"

FIVE: WELCOME TO REALITY

With Mother's help, Five can trim cookies, frost cakes, help prepare salads, join in clean-up activities. Fathers who welcome their youngsters as helpers in handyman chores around the house find that the seriousness and satisfaction with which the young apprentice goes about doing his share almost lifts them out of the class of chores. With Five the "what" of his doing does not matter; it is the "with whom" and "how" that count.

CHAPTER VII

Six: A New Beginning

SIX IS LIKELY to appall and baffle grownups. His play is filled with sounds of violence. "Bang, bang, you're dead!" "Kill the rat!" "Let's get 'em!" "Hurry up, you dope!" His favorite taunts are apt to be epithets like "Fatty," "Gimpy," "Two-Eyes," "Butter-fingers," and "Stinker." Girls are not immune to enthusiasm for these expressions.

When Six is not pursuing his fellows with cocked guns, he is rolling on the ground with them in exuberant scuffles. The tattered knee, the shredded elbow, the scuffed toe are his emblems. Not even the cast-iron patch or triple riveted seam can outwit him.

Grownups are apt to feel that chairs are for sitting and the floor for walking. Six knows better. He sprawls and rolls on the floor, uses his bed for a trampolin, makes a fort of the sofa. Outside, any culvert must be explored, all trees and fences must be climbed. It sometimes seems that a chimpanzee and Six have much in common.

New kinds of motion excite him. He begs for a bicycle because his tricycle has grown too sedate. He throws himself recklessly into problems of balance, and he is hungry for speed. Skating, skiing, tobogganing—he is ready to try them all.

More speed means more ground to cover. The back yard has grown too small. Six needs the street, playground, park, and fields for his new ventures in playing and growing.

The Year of the Swarm

Six has outgrown the back yard in another way. He cannot stay there and wait for other children to come to him. He needs to go where they are.

The common formation of the six-year-old seems to be the clump; he rarely appears in public singly. If a few do appear one by one, they soon move together in a close-packed mass.

The members of this swarm are not particularly interested in one another, but they are very much interested in being together. Inside the group, each child seems to be going his own way, without much attention to the others. Little cooperation is visible, yet Six behaves as if he could not live away from the others, almost as if he felt incomplete by himself.

The truth is that safety does lie in numbers for the six-year-old. The wildly surging herds we see are the early beginnings of society. The children have not worked out the niceties of group behavior yet, the give and take of cooperation, the orderly contribution of each to the whole. But, like primitive man, they have the basic notion that there is strength in being together.

Fine gradations of feelings are foreign to Sixes. If you are not in the group, you are out of it. And how can you make sure you are in it unless you are there, physically and in person, every time the group is together? At six it is not very difficult to join a new gang, but, by the same token, it is also easy to lose one's place. A few days' absence, and one has to work one's way in again. It is better to take no risks.

As soon as children begin to look beyond their own families and homes, they sense that man does not live alone in society. And we help them to sense it now, and come to terms with it, by seeing that they have another environment and other companions than those offered by home and family for a good part of each day. But it must be remembered that the six-year-old's tolerance for separation from the familiar varies and that not all can get their bearings in a group at one time. We say "six," but as in our other statements about age levels, this may be only an approximation. Also, it's wise to remind ourselves that getting along easily with the crowd is not everybody's dish at any time in life. The way of the person who likes solitude may be a tougher one because of the standards of society today and because almost everyone craves the feeling of being accepted by others. But solitude has many values which we tend to forget in our natural desire to have our children fit comfortably into the patterns set by their peers.

Making One's Way in the Group

The way is smoother at this point if we recognize what makes a child a group member in good standing, and accept these things, for the time being, as facts of life. At seven things will change, but Six must face them as they are at the moment. To do our job well we need to know what our six-year-old faces: what the customs of his play group are, the skills that are valued, the games he must be prepared to play and that we must live with during the year.

In most groups the rules are simple. You must not be afraid; you must not cry when you are hurt; you must act, look, talk like the others. If you are fatter, slower, clumsier, or afraid to give as well as take physical punishment, the going will be rough, though sometimes boldness and self-confidence or good humor can take the place of physical skills. Fortunately, too, the group is not persistent about driving off the inadequate. The child who can tolerate teasing without giving way, the tenacious hanger-on, can hold his own. This is one reason why it is important for parents and teachers to help children of this age understand that teasing is not fatal.

Some Sixes need to be told that they can meet name-calling with a "So what?" attitude. Others, who are not too sure of themselves anyhow, have to be encouraged to go back to the group and show that they too can play this teasing game. A little family teasing of the kind that is *really* "all in fun" sometimes helps, but not if it sets a tone that a brother or sister can pick up and use in a more strident key.

The little wrestling bouts that go on continually when Sixes get together upset some of the group. Gentle, playful tussling with Father often helps those who are afraid of close bodily contact. Some Sixes need to learn also that the boy who challenges you to a fight may have nothing against you personally, but may simply be looking for someone to fight with.

If a neighborhood bully terrorizes the other children, it is important to show them how they can defeat him by joining forces instead of letting him tackle them one by one. Above all, it is essential not to ask "What's the matter with you? Why can't you fight your own battles?" when Six comes for help. He has a right to be shown how to fight his own battles, if he has never had to do it before.

Active Games

Wind, speed, and co-ordination are important in the play-life of the six-year-old. Older brothers and sisters, as well as parents, can help the six-year-old by challenging him to beat them "to the end of the block" or "down to the bend in the road," and by pacing him so that he has to put out every ounce of effort he has, but letting him win some of the time.

For boys, and some girls, baseball begins to be a major interest. Sixes need practice at batting with a light-weight bat, but pitching is just as essential. Frequent games of catch with a soft ball when Father has time, or with Mother if she is available, will reduce the wild pitches, and make the child welcome on the informal baseball teams that form in every neighborhood.

Marbles also takes the spotlight at this time, and marble shooting can be practiced alone.

For girls, jumping rope and bouncing balls take the place of the tussling and Cops and Robbers of the boys. Hot Peppers and Double Dutch are very serious matters to the girls. Solitary practice is helpful here, but it is not enough. Little girls who hold back from the group, those who are self-conscious or timid, are often deficient in co-ordination and a sense of timing. While time alone often helps considerably, it is not a good idea to depend on it entirely. A helpful adult who will administer practice in graded doses, so that the child starts with something she can do, and goes on gradually from there, can make an invaluable contribution to the child's social development.

The great thing in helping the sensitive Six is to give pointers without making him feel small. The adult who really believes that everyone has his weak spots, and needs more work on those, is not likely to make an error. The one who feels put out because his child is not up to snuff in every skill may do more harm than good in trying to help. Let us remember that a child who needs help does not need scolding, teasing, or a disgusted "Why can't you be like So-and-so?"

It's also our job to look at the child's position in the group with a kind of perspective he can't be expected to have for himself. For instance, we can remember that leadership is not yet fixed. The head man or favorite girl of the crowd today may be a nobody tomorrow. A daring leap from the shed roof makes Tommy the leader one day; the next he is superseded by Phil, whose big brother has made the school baseball team. Charlotte lords it all over the other girls on Monday because she has been to the city and seen a "real play" but by Wednesday her glory has fled and Dodie, champion rope-skipper, has taken her place. When it is our own little boy's or girl's turn to be an "out," it is a good thing not to show too much concern and so add to the feeling of being displaced. We can reassure them that their turn will come again.

Bicycles

The one demand that seems to bother parents more than any other is Six's insistent request for a bicycle. Some immediately buy the most expensive one they can find and are then disgusted because Johnny has difficulty in learning. Others are so fearful of accidents and traffic dangers that they say "no!" without thinking what it may mean to their child to be the only one without a bicycle.

By and large, bicycles are not necessary at six, though they may become so at seven, depending on the nature of the child's group. The child's desire to learn to manage one, however, should not be ignored. We learn best at the moment that we most want to.

It is usually possible to rent or borrow a bicycle to learn on. After the child has mastered the skill the matter of buying may be taken up. The first machine owned might well be secondhand also, since the thrill of having one in any condition, as long as it is usable, is usually enough to cover shortcomings. It is important that the child's feet touch the pedals easily when he is seated, even though a few very skillful children can use machines too big for them.

Before a machine is bought, however, the limits of its use must be firmly established. If there are traffic hazards, the child must understand exactly where he can and cannot take it. No amount of pleading that "the other fellows" ride in the road, or the gutter, need influence one. In this area safety is too crucial a matter to let oneself be swayed by argument. It is necessary, of course, to allow enough freedom so that the child can get some pleasure out of using his bike; if the limits are reasonable, they can be firmly enforced.

Rules and Cheating

Six is still unable to put the rules of a game above his need to win. For the most part, Sixes do not understand that rules are the same for everyone, and that they exist whether he likes it or not. This age is too uncertain of itself to lose gracefully. Every defeat, even in a game, is a real blow to the still delicate ego. Abstract morality is a long way off. For these reasons it is best not to expect Sixes to play games that have rigid rules, and not to be shocked when Six breaks rules that he himself may have made. In two years more, he will become a strict guardian of the law; now he needs latitude.

When the six-year-old tattles on others who have cheated, it may seem comic or deplorable to the adult. However, this is his way of protecting himself against a similar transgression. Because of his own constant temptation, it is important to him that no one else get away with anything. If the other fellow can do what he is trying not to do, he has lost the social support he needs to become a responsible citizen who faces up to his duties.

The Six who tattles should not be ridiculed. When he comes with a story of Mary having cheated in a game, the adult might talk with him about *why* Mary may have cheated. Perhaps she did not intend to cheat; perhaps she did not understand the rules. Or, if she knew the rules, maybe it was so important to her to win that she "forgot" them for the moment. The next time perhaps she might be reminded of the rules by Tommy himself.

This kind of treatment gives the tattler the support he is looking for. At the same time, it shows him that grownups can understand that children sometimes "forget," and teaches him to handle himself while he is ostensibly learning to handle Mary.

Group Games

Six is not ready for competitive games that demand good coordination. For one thing, Six has to learn to work *with* others before he starts working *against* them. To some Sixes, who are uncertain of their status anyhow, competition is completely demoralizing.

Group games which can include everyone, and do not demand special skills, are the ones to choose. Tag and hide-and-seek are probably the favorites, with London Bridge Is Falling Down especially liked by girls. Beyond these, we might turn to Grunt, Pig, Grunt, Bluebird, Bluebird, Which Am I? and Architecture. These, and a number of others, are fully described in *Handbook for Recreation Leaders,* which can be secured for a small sum by writing to the Federal Security Agency, U.S. Children's Bureau, Washington, D.C.

The best competitive games for Sixes are those which have simple rules, and do not require close teamwork, although small groups may play against each other. Relay races and informal volley ball are examples.

Dramatic Play

Something new has appeared in dramatic play since the child's fifth birthday. Now the dramas include more than one or two children, often depend on a leader, and involve give and take between groups rather than single players. In addition, interest in the same subject may go on for several days.

While the rather prosaic experiences of everyday life, like storekeeping and transportation, may take up the greater part of time used for dramatic play, topics that are charged with a great deal of emotion (for adults, mostly) come up rather often. It is not unusual, for example, to see a group of six-year-olds solemnly conducting a funeral service for a "corpse" that was the principal character of a hospital drama a short time before. Facing what he is afraid of in play, and overcoming it time after time, is Six's favorite device for warding off trouble. In a hazy way, the child is afraid he might lose his parents, might have no one to take care of him, might die. Hence the repeated funerals.

A great many children around this age play "doctor" a good deal, and sometimes this indicates that they need more information about the differences between boys and girls or about birth of babies. If the children are obviously playing through some experience one of them recently had, like a tonsillectomy, this explanation does not hold. Operations are frightening events, and they need to be played through repeatedly for the child to get rid of the lingering fears connected with them. If, however, the play has no connection with real experiences, and is monotonously concerned with giving shots and taking temperatures, it may well be an indication that parents should offer information about subjects which are of intense importance to little children.

The play of Six may be full not only of corpses and patients in the worst of health, but of ghosts and witches. Here again he is gaining mastery over his fears by acting them out. If he can summon these scary creatures on demand and make them do what he likes, then he does not have to be afraid of the shadowy demons that come out to haunt him at night and represent many of the things he does not understand.

The interests that Five showed in numbers and in the realities of the market place now combine in an absorption in playing store. All the equipment for the most rewarding kind of store-play can be found right in the home, and most of it—empty jars, milk bottles, fruit baskets—is what we usually discard as trash. Parents who have cellars, garages, or attics for storage spaces are blessed. Apartment dwellers may find it more difficult to keep "store" materials on hand, but a carton full can usually be accommodated under a bed even in crowded places. The greater the variety of can sizes and measuring devices the child has access to, the more he is likely to learn from his play. Toy money, or strips of paper with different denominations marked on them, are usually called for, and are educational, too.

The interest the six-year-old shows in playing store indicates a real expansion of his social outlook. We know that children play the characters that have special interest for them: first, the all-powerful parents, then the masters of machinery and the competent housewives and teachers. Now comes the man of wealth—for anyone can see that the merchant has more possessions than anyone else. And the guy with the mostest is the guy Six wants to be.

Back to Babyhood

Occasionally Six shows by his quiet-time play when he is alone that he is not yet ready to take on the self-control that school demands or the strong-man role he needs for coping with his fellows. Some of the time he needs a chance to relax, to drop his responsibilities, to luxuriate in the tender-loving-care-without-demands that he enviously assigns to infancy. Sixes who have not been intimidated by being told constantly that they are "big" may show this longing by talking baby talk. Others disguise it by pretending to be little animals that get treated more or less as babies. Whatever form it takes, this kind of play is the signal that the child needs to be relieved of his responsibilities. He (or she) might even be told that "It's all right to play baby sometimes." By saying *play* baby we are saving face for Six; it would never do to *be* a baby—the other kids might laugh.

Equipment for Six

Because Sixes are fairly drastic in their handling of toys, it is wise to provide them with rugged playthings. The best of the larger scale models of machinery (about twenty-four to thirty-six inches long) are made of tempered metal, and guaranteed against breakage with reasonable usage. If they do break, in most cases they will be repaired by the factory that makes them, at a nominal charge.

This type of toy (unlike the models suggested for Fives) is a major investment for people of moderate income, equal to a third or half the cost of a bicycle, and warrants care in selection. A highly specialized piece of equipment, like an aerial ladder, may not be as good a choice as a more prosaic piece that can be used in several ways, like a tractor-bulldozer combination. What would be most welcome also depends on what is already available to the group the child plays with. If others already own dump-trucks and graders, a bucket-loader or mobile crane might contribute more to the play of the group and, by the same token, to the child, than a duplication of what others have. Six himself is likely to beg for what others have, but in the case of an important and long-lived toy it is worth at least pointing out to him the virtues of variety. In addition to the pieces already mentioned, it is possible to get earth movers and scrapers, pumpers that use real water, and rock hoppers.

Electric trains still hold the record in number of mentions to Santa Claus, but it is the wise parent who waits two or three years longer before yielding. Although they have a flashy appeal, toys that work by springs or electric power should still be avoided. Six really does not have sufficient control over his movements to treat such toys with the care they need, and nothing is more disappointing than the mechanical gadget that breaks the first day it is used. Besides, mechanical toys become boring in a short time, since the child can do very little with them besides winding them up and watching them. Adults are conditioned to passive play; Sixes are not and should not be.

If the child has been playing with trackless trains, the addition of tracks at this point gives the further touch of reality he seeks. If he has had the small hardwood trains that come with grooved wooden tracks, he will welcome switches and curves that will make more complicated layouts possible. Some Sixes are ready for over-and-under railroading of a mild sort, imitating the clover-leaf arrangements of major traffic crossings. These small trains are especially good for combining with the miniature villages, forts, and farms that Sixes love.

For Girls Only

The little girl's craze for dolls now reaches new heights. The more realistic the dolls and all their belongings, the better. Additional changes of clothing, specialized equipment for feeding and airing, roller skates, rainy-day clothes are prized items. Although dolls with hair are universally demanded, it is a mistake to expect them to be kept looking neat. Six-year-old fingers are not up to giving doll coiffures a professional finish. If one can put up with a slightly bedraggled version, however, there is real value in supplying the bewigged specimens, especially for little girls who wear their hair in braids. Practice in plaiting can hasten the day when the doll's mother can take care of her own hair.

Additions to doll houses are also greeted with joy. Six's fingers are skilled enough to handle two-inch brooms and minuscule platters without effort. Details that escaped Five completely entrance Six. A floor-lamp that lights, a miniature sewing machine with parts that move, a tiny mantel clock bring delight far out of proportion to the size of the object.

Although they are fascinated by exact reproductions of household items, Sixes do not scorn to improvise. A set of tiny interlocking plastic blocks helps to keep doll-house play creative. Ingenious Sixes use these for garden walls, extra tables, beds, stools, even stoves and sinks.

Paper dolls now come along to take their place in the girl's world. Small fingers are finally steady enough to guide blunt scissors along outlines. Tabs may still give some trouble, but there are paper-doll sets available that avoid the problem by supplying costumes with both front and back, or ones that wrap around the doll. In addition, these sets offer sturdy fiberboard dolls, and a paper for dresses that can be washed and ironed. Some may be colored, cleaned, and recolored. This represents real advances in paper-doll design, since it permits fuller activity on the child's part, and encourages some creativity.

Household play goes on merrily, with the emphasis on more and more realistic accessories. Manufacturers have responded by offering replicas, in child-size, of almost every piece of adult equipment, from vacuum cleaners to shopping carts. Ice cream freezers that really work, baby carriers, cooking utensils meant to be used in the oven, dish-washing outfits that include miniature packages of soap and scouring powders are only a few of the items available for the small homemaker.

Dress-up play becomes very elaborate, with attention to small details of grooming and make-up. The make-up and manicure kits we spoke of in connection with Fives are just as desirable for six-year-old girls. Six may want to dress up like a character out of a fairy tale, and she still adores impersonating a ballet dancer and a circus star. She is likely to have a new desire: to be a drum majorette.

The Virtues of Puppets

For six-year-olds, giving puppet plays is sometimes even better than making believe. Many a child who sits wooden-faced and silent in the classroom, or leans listlessly against the porch railing while others play, comes alive when he can speak through a puppet's mouth.

The equipment need be no more than a screen tall enough to conceal the child while he operates the puppets over the top. Hidden from view, the child becomes identified with the puppet character and is free to express any kind of feelings or ideas that come popping out, even where these would be frowned on by the grownups in real life.

Children may need to be "warmed up" by dramatizing stories that have been read to them first, before they are ready to make up their own plays. If they are allowed to choose the stories themselves, the characters their puppets represent will express something of importance to them. After the warming up period, they will want to present their own plays, and in these more personal problems and concerns will appear.

Sixes can make their own simple puppets. Stick puppets—figures drawn on cardboard, cut out, and mounted on wooden handles—are often good enough for their purposes. Or the puppets may be small rubber balls with holes cut in them to admit the child's forefinger, the costume a bit of cloth wrapped around the fist. An old sock (preferably white) stuffed with cotton or rags, the face drawn on the toe, makes another simple puppet. The six-year-old cares little for refinements of expression or movement in his puppets; he is satisfied if he can personify the characters of his story even crudely and carry out the main action.

In addition to helping the constrained child express himself, they permit the child to entertain company without being obnoxious. Many sixes seem unbearable when they do silly things to attract attention when visitors are present, but if we let them take the spotlight legitimately by putting on a show, they can see the justice of our request that they take a back seat part of the time.

The Handy Man

"You don't like me. Nobody likes me." Six looks mournful between periods of boisterousness and waits anxiously for a reply. He is begging us to contradict him, to say oh, we do, we do like him. For Six needs periodic doses of reassurance. He suffers from an occupational disease, a vast sense of incompetence. And what can counteract that so well as tangible accomplishment? Handwork is an excellent way of helping the self-doubting Thomas and his sister of six prove that they can deliver the goods.

As the little girl wants true-to-life equipment for her housekeeping, the boy of six wants real tools and he wants to know how to use each one correctly.

Teaching Six takes a bit of doing, because it is demeaning for him to admit he doesn't know, but tact can accomplish wonders. "This is the way you use this, isn't it?" is one approach that he can accept. "Let's try this out, shall we?" followed immediately by a demonstration accompanied by an educational soliloquy is another. However it is done, it is important that Six gets the feel of handling a tool correctly before he begins to use it by himself. Sometimes his hands have to be guided at first.

Hammer, pliers, brace and bit, crosscut saw and coping saw should be old stuff to the six-year-old. Now he is ready for a screw driver, augur bits, hand drills, hand plane, wood files, and rasps. This supply, fortunately, will serve his needs for several years, and should be acquired gradually, as his projects require the additional tools.

Six is much more critical of his own work than he was a year ago, and likely to be even more so of anyone else's. These attitudes should be understood as developments, for he is showing an increasing awareness of good work. The suffering parent might take comfort from the fact that Six does not apply the same rigid standards to his own performance—if he did, he would never attempt anything.

"But he never finishes anything!" Parents of Sixes will recognize this lament. It is too true. Left to himself, the six-year-old is likely to bog down in the middle of any project. Beginnings are so much more exciting than difficult continuations. With time he may outgrow this tendency to give up—many do. But he would enjoy a sense of real competence if we could help him over some of the hurdles and let him feel the joy of completing what he has started.

Doing this without taking over the work ourselves can be a delicate business. The first step is help in planning. When Six-plus announces that he is going to make a footstool, we might get him to visualize the end product. We can help by sketching various simple models until he is satisfied. Then we begin to measure. How long and wide will the top be? How tall will the legs be? When the measurements are worked out with a carpenter's rule (with Six incidentally using numbers and number combinations constantly) they are noted down. The steps to be followed in the construction are gone over and listed, this information tacked up near the workbench. Perhaps the shape of the top is drawn on the wood. The places for the leg holes are marked. Finally, Six is ready to start with his tools.

This process may sound laborious; actually it takes a short time and is absorbing to the child. The interested companionship of father or mother, the sense of working together, is not the least of its attractions. With a clear notion of the sequence of steps, there is a minimum chance of Six's failing.

Even so, a time may come when the eagerly planned project lies neglected for a day or two. This indicates the danger point. A judicious need on Father's part to make some household repair in the workshop may be all that is needed to get the object finished. For Father's companionship is prized above all (except, of course, the gang's) when one is six. And perhaps, when all is said and done—or rather, *not* done—we should guard against a feeling that it is disastrous if every single undertaking is not brought to completion. We reserve for ourselves the right to abandon an unsatisfactory project every now and then, and there is no good reason why we should demand that a child follow through on every start, though we might encourage him to do so.

As we have pointed out before, girls love to work with wood, too, and should be encouraged to do so when they show interest. Actually, many little girls range rather widely in the so-called boy's area, enjoying many of the games, activities, and skills that used to be thought of as purely masculine. When it comes to carpentry, girls often show a competence equal to boys'. And the adult woman who can use tools will always have a big advantage in this do-it-yourself age.

A good book for the reference shelf is *Let's Build,* by Constance Homer. It contains a large variety of suggested projects that interest Sixes and are within their range of competence, with judicious guidance.

Stories for Six

Six will like most of the books that he did when he was five, but he has a greater tolerance for magic, providing it is *good* magic. Animals that talk are still prime favorites, and Six will relish *Mary Poppins* and *Freddie the Pig* equally.

At this point, however, stories can do more for the child than amuse him or enlarge his vocabulary. They can help him over a tough spot in his development.

Scratch a Six and you find a fear. Children of this age notice much more about the world than they did before and much of what they register they do not understand. In addition, so much is expected of them that they do not feel up to performing. We have to take the fears of Six seriously, for they tell us where he needs help. It is a mistake to expose him to stories that will feed his fears and increase his conviction that they are well founded.

Knowing the common fears that trouble six-year-olds can help us select the literature best suited for them. Individuals differ, of course, and every mother will have her own supplementary list. By and large, these seem to be the most common fears: fear of bodily injury; fear of thunder, rain, wind, fire; fear of wild animals and insects; fear of darkness; fear of attics and cellars.

Stories built around a character with whom the child can identify himself, who suffers from feelings and fears very much like his own, can be extremely effective. Little Hans, for example, is a six-year-old boy who moves into a large house in the country. He has never seen a cellar before. The steps are dark, and the yawning door reminds him of a mouth ready to swallow him up. Nothing will persuade Hans to explore the cellar. One day his pet cat, Martha, disappears. He hunts and hunts, calls and calls, but no Martha. Suddenly he hears a mewing. He listens. It seems to come from under the kitchen. He faces the cellar door fearfully. Finally he girds himself—to recover Martha he will chance everything. Step by step he creeps down, encouraged by louder and louder mewings. Finally he reaches the bottom, and the cellar isn't fearful at all! In fact, it's rather nice, like a cave with shelves, and some light even filters in from small, high windows. He sees Martha, but she does not come to him. Instead she remains curled up on some newspapers in a corner, only looking at him with glowing eyes and mewing. He approaches. Wonder of wonders, there is not only Martha, but five squirming scraps of kittens about her!

An improvised tale like this might be followed by "What do you suppose we'd find in *our* cellar (or attic, or closet, or whatever part of the house is feared)?" and an invitation to explore it then and there. Needless to say, this is not an exercise to try at bedtime.

Other worrisome feelings that can be handled in the same way as fears are jealousy, hostility, and the feeling of not being loved, or having a sibling preferred to one's self. Successful stories of this kind usually detail the events that made the hero feel as he did, devise a climax that shows his parents how he feels, and end with a new understanding all around. A touch of humor is very helpful, and animal protagonists are often better than human.

In this age of whoop and holler, of strenuous overdoing, the reading period serves an important function in giving the youngster a chance to relax from his active play. For the child who fights sleep, books continue to help. Little girls who insist on braids and curls, but dislike the combing out period, will sit contentedly looking at familiar books while undergoing the ordeal.

Sixes continue to enjoy making up their own stories and verses. Some like to keep diaries, dictating day-by-day happenings to their mothers. Girls are apt to like this more, and keep it up longer, than boys. Reading the diary on a significant occasion—a birthday, or the last day of the year—gives it special importance and can become a pleasant family ritual.

Comics, Radio, Television

At six, the spell of the mass entertainments really begins. The child must be able to have the latest information about his favorite characters if he is to take an informed part in his group's talk and play. The animal comics still maintain their pull, but cowboy heroes may reign supreme at this age, closely followed by detectives and space characters. In all these classifications there are fairly wholesome choices to be made.

With television, as with radio, the chief complaint parents make about the programs available for the young is their blood-and-thunder character. Sometimes the fare runs more to spacemen, featuring the same amount of violence but in a slightly more subtle form. Clown and puppet shows are available, as well as old movies of the slapstick comedy type.

Since noise and violence characterize Sixes in their active play, it is not surprising that these elements should attract them in more passive entertainment. It has been pointed out that the fantasies which fascinate the young audience on both radio and television are not very different from those he produces spontaneously: they provide a hero who can be a projection of himself and who is able to triumph over all obstacles. However, the monotony of this type of program is in itself a problem, since it offers children no opportunity to develop individual tastes.

Parents can do more about the situation than complain. We might, for one thing, ask ourselves what alternatives to such programs we give our children. If we simply abandon them to the screen with a sigh of relief, we are not in a very strong position to criticize.

Further, we can use television to widen the horizons of our Sixes if we scan the offerings carefully. Week ends usually offer a wide variety of shows, some intelligently planned and educational in the best sense. They include animated cartoons and programs about animals (usually in zoos), about children from other nations, and about community activities. More programs which encourage participation by the watcher would be welcome. Educational television stations may close this gap eventually, but they need public interest and support.

Comics, radio, and television can be turned to good account by making them family-shared enterprises. We heartily recommend reading the child's comic books, so that their material can be family fare. It is also a good idea to permit the six-year-old to stay up past his usual bedtime once in a while to share with the family a favorite comedy program. These family events will be anticipated with eagerness and recollected with nostalgia. The child who has shared these moments of laughter with his parents is far more likely to accept some of their criteria of good taste than is one who has missed this element of family life.

Six Needs Music

Because the ready-made entertainment of radio and television is an easy road to blessed quiet, we may be tempted to turn away from the experiments in sound that delighted our Fives. However, we must not forget that the stream of creativity does not stop at this age or that, but flows as long as it is not impeded.

Six's need for noise need not be expressed exclusively in the explosion of cap-pistols. He takes as great delight as Five does in cymbals, drums, gong and mallet, bells of various kinds, whistles, castenets, triangles. With more mastery of form than he had before, he can now perform expertly in a rhythm band, putting in his ping or bong when the music tells him to. Alone, he enjoys accompanying brisk march rhythms with his own set of drums, or experimenting with a harmonica or a ukulele. He can master a simple metallophone or xylophone, and with a little help he can relish the joys of musical achievement by picking out songs he already knows. Small instruments, true in tone, can be purchased inexpensively from organizations that deal in school supplies, and in some cases from music stores.

If a rhythm band is out of the question, Six can join in family "jam" sessions. Even unmusical families can have fun with sound, and this may be just the time to try some experiments. Most families have at least one adult member who can pick out a few familiar tunes on the piano. The recorder and the lowly "uke" are not difficult for adults to master, for the fun of variety. Even a kazoo band can be fun and give the young fry a background for percussion contributions.

Six enjoys listening to records, too, if they are brisk and exciting and have a touch of humor. *Tubby the Tuba* is a great favorite; *Peter and the Wolf* is less sure-fire but still good for many. If the record is being used to keep Six resting quietly, it had better tell a story.

Movement can be as relaxing as sitting still, if it is rhythmic, unforced, and unhampered. Like the dancing of Fives, Six's is likely to be most successful when it has some form and substance. Exciting natural phenomena like storms and fire appeal to him. Or he will turn into a witch, a giant, or a kangaroo with ease. The important thing is to give him a role he can sink his teeth into, one that can be executed with force and verve. His sister may like the gentler parts—to be a bird, a fairy, a princess—but she has her witchlike moments, too.

Rhythmic movement to music is considered much more suitable as exercise for the six-year-old than the usual gymnastics because it permits each child to be his own master, to use his body for his own purposes, and to find out what he can do at his own pace.

Table Games and Quiet Play

There comes a time in the life of Six when he must amuse himself quietly at home. Perhaps no playmates are available or he is convalescing from an illness. Some of the activities and toys we have already mentioned will do well for such an occasion. One such is the mallet and nail-a-peg set that comes with a background board of firm but fairly soft substance, and colored pieces of wood in various shapes. The sets of pieces are built around various favorite themes: the West, Circus Days, the Frontier. When several have been acquired (as may happen in the course of several illnesses) a store of pieces is available for original compositions that may leave the manufacturer's conventional ideas far behind.

Dominoes and Chinese checkers are played with avidity if a parent is available for a partner. The lotto games mentioned in chapter 6 are still liked, with real lotto now coming in for some attention. Card games like Cowboys and Indians or Space Race are enjoyed, with only minor wrangling. Simple games like War and Giggle a Bit keep several children occupied hilariously, yet do not demand much play space. (See *50 Card Games for Children,* by Vernon Quinn, for the rules for these and other games suitable for this age level.)

As number combinations are learned, Arithmetic Lotto may be useful. There are other gamelike materials which are designed to help the child learn arithmetic and reading while having fun. These can be found in bookstores near teacher-training institutions and may also be available in children's book departments.

When Six is not busy hammering things together, he likes to take things apart. For this we recommend a supply of old clocks and watches, available free for the asking at many neighborhood jewelers' and watchmakers'.

The Collector

Everything else failing, and sometimes in preference to other things, Six can spend happy hours mooning over his collections. These may be no more than a haphazard assortment of picture postcards, bottle tops, match covers, miniatures of anything, rocks, or just odds and ends garnered from unguarded trash baskets. Since Six goes in for quantity, he is not concerned with intrinsic values. To him, everything he collects has value, though he could not tell you why. The wisest course is to make room for the collections and listen sympathetically if Six wants to talk about them.

Six's interests shift with such rapidity that he may have ten hoards of different objects by the end of a year, all treasured, but scarcely looked at. Should we try to wrest any from him, he will defend them desperately, thinking up reason after reason why they should not be thrown away. The truth is that part of his security is somehow bound up in these objects, and until he feels stronger in spirit he cannot let them go. They may have to be given houseroom for several years, for it is dangerous business throwing them away against his will.

Six Looks at Nature

"My, isn't Mrs. X. getting awfully fat!" comments six-year-old Linda innocently, with a sidelong glance at Mother. If Mrs. X. is within earshot, and she usually is, Linda get shushed, but her curiosity goes on just the same. Most Sixes, even if they have not indicated it by questions or by playing "doctor," are interested in sex differences, mating, marriage, and where babies come from and how they are born. Even if all their questions were answered when they were four or five, they are apt to want more detailed explanations now. This curiosity is normal, part of Six's interest in himself and the world about him, and it can be used to extend his knowledge.

An excellent first step in nature study might be to get the six-year-old a pair of pets that will reproduce (if he has not already had some). Although they are likely to be smelly, white mice are acceptable for this purpose at this age and the offspring can be generously donated to schools and friends. Guinea pigs are more highly regarded because they are not so likely to slip away from eager hands and will not nip, but they do take more room. Besides, they cannot so easily be taken to school.

For city children especially, the birth of a pet is an event of tremendous importance. It is a magical event in a way, and very reassuring to the child who has been speculating about his own debut into the world. The helplessness of the baby creatures, and the sure care of the mother, tell him as nothing else can that there is order and predictability in the world, and that the small and weak are provided for in a beneficent scheme of things.

Of course deaths also occur, but Six can be helped to accept them if they are treated matter-of-factly by the grownups around him. Met in this way the death of an animal can be a preparation for the more disturbing deaths that will inevitably occur later. The dignity of a small ritual of disposal helps to satisfy Six and permits him to return his attention to the fascinating progress of the living.

Birds and flowers become interesting *after* Six has learned about mammals, as a variation of the same theme. Many children, in fact, are not particularly curious about the reproduction of these until they are nine or ten and have thoroughly assimilated the facts of human and animal reproduction. Then they are ready to detach their interest from themselves and apply it to other forms of life.

However, if Six has a garden he will be interested in increasing his crops, even if this means only getting five pods of beans instead of four, and this is a natural point of departure for finding out about pollination and the structure and purpose of blossoms. Bush beans are probably the best subject. The pods are evident so quickly after pollination that six-year-old interest does not flag between the two events.

Window-box gardens in the city can provide dramatic demonstrations of the importance of pollination if they are high enough to escape the attentions of flies. Six can help to pollinate one set of plants, while a neighboring group is left unpollinated. The resultant quick withering of blossoms and setting of pods on the treated group, while the others remain sterile, will be an impressive lesson.

Following such a demonstration, Six may be ready to observe the structure of a blossom under magnification. The large, simple flower of the day lily is good for this. Petals removed, the stamen and pistils are easily seen and their differences recognized. Next, slicing the stamen through the middle reveals the passageway down which the pollen must travel to reach the egg cell and fertilize it.

The activities of bees and other insects take on real meaning after Six has discovered their importance in something which touched his own interest in a direct, personal, and concrete way.

From bees, Six's interest might move on to caterpillars and butterflies. The life cycle of butterfly or moth is easy to learn about through direct observation, and makes a fine introduction to studying that of other common creatures—birds, frogs, fish.

The monarch butterfly and Prometheus moth are especially interesting and may be housed easily in the home. A box with a piece of screening on top, or a cylinder of screening, with a pie-pan top and bottom, makes an adequate home. A cocoon-hunt in the fall can provide material for interest next spring, when excitement mounts high as the children wait to see what kind of creature will emerge.

One good way to give the six-year-old interesting contacts with nature is to make a seasonal plan for excursions and collections. Spring, for example, is the time to collect pond life. The familiar greenish jelly on still waters is treasure for the child when he can take some home and watch the tadpoles emerge in their own good time. Feeding tadpoles opens all sorts of questions about the different things different kinds of animals eat. The gradual loss of the tadpole's tail and taking on of the frog-form make differences between human adults and children seem small by comparison. The final appearance of the young frog rounds out an extremely satisfying experience for the child.

Other specimens that can be collected on a pond trek are small turtles and snakes, snails, larvae, small fish, and water striders. The last four can live amicably in one container, while the first two can share another. Preparing the aquarium with some of the pond water gives Six something active to do and provides the best kind of learning for this age level.

Birds are a natural focus for nature interests in the summer. The Six who lives in the suburbs or in the country can build up quite a proprietary interest in the birds which nest near his home by leaving appropriate nesting materials where they can get it. Small feathers from hat trimmings, bits of colored yarn and string, strips of cloth will be picked up by the eager nesters. A nest hunt with a small telescope or field glasses is next in order. Once the nests are located (and often they can be identified by glimpses of the distinctive material the child has supplied) the progress of eggs and baby birds can be followed day by day. When the latter arrive, the child's attention is sharpened if he tries to find out how many times the baby birds are fed in an hour, or where the parent birds get the food. He might even try to find out if both parents do the same amount of work, or if the mother bird is the only working member of the family.

Insects offer special summer interest. Grasshoppers, crickets, and katydids will reward care by giving evening concerts during August if they feel comfortable in the home provided for them. One can readily be constructed from a baking dish, four rectangles of glass about eight inches high, and a piece of window screen. The glass can be cut to order by a glazier, and forms the walls of the cage when fitted together in the dish and held in place by a deep layer of damp earth. A layer of pebbles or gravel under the earth is an aid in keeping the soil moisture constant. The corners of the glass walls should be tight—they might be taped together—and the tops level. The screen top for the terrarium is made to fit tightly by bending the sides down about an inch all around. Small plants make the home attractive, and odd bits of sticks and pebbles can add interest. A small medicine bottle, buried in the earth with only its neck protruding, makes a good fresh plant holder, and a glass coaster can be used for a feeding station.

If the captured cricket does not "sing," it is likely to be a female. Some compensation for her lack of song may be found in watching her lay eggs, which she does over a long period of time. She can be seen busily cleaning the spot where she intends to lay, forcing her ovipositor tube down into the earth, withdrawing it part way, changing the angle, shoving it down again, each time sending an egg through it into the earth.

When the cricket babies hatch, they put on a show of their own. Although the size of a pinhead when born, they grow rapidly, frequently splitting off their skins and eating them. When the old skin is shed, the cricket is nearly white, gradually darkening as the new skin hardens. It emerges from its last molt with wings, and may be singing an hour afterward.

Fall is filled with natural events that pique interest and provoke questions. It is the time to collect old nests, trying to identify the summer occupants. Again, a bit of fluff or yarn built into the structure may identify a certain nest as having belonged to birds that Six supplied with homemaking materials.

Fallen leaves offer fun and things to do—raking them, piling them up and jumping into them. The child who helps mulch flower beds with them learns how eternal the life cycle is. While they are still brilliant with end-of-summer color they can be dipped in paraffin and preserved. Six also likes to draw outlines around their edges and try to color the pictures to match the models.

Winter brings its own special birds to be cared for. A Christmas tree for them, with decorations of suet, popcorn, small ears of corn, and bunches of seed-bearing grasses is a project Six can undertake and execute with pride. He can count the number of different birds that remain after the others have migrated, and learn to identify them easily, since they are so few. He can make friends with them by leaving food in the same place every day, preferably a place where he can watch them without disturbing them, such as a feeding-station attached outside a window.

Snow and ice come to mind inevitably as subjects for winter nature study. The freezing and melting experiments suggested for younger children are appropriate for Sixes if they have not had them earlier. Freezing a bottleful of water, with a loose cork in the top, is always a dramatic experiment. Two bottles, each full to the top, one with a tight cover and one loosely corked, offer even more intriguing possibilities.

There are numerous other simple experiments, not necessarily connected with the seasons, which will help to answer the questions which are Six's stock in trade—and start him off on others. Water poured over a heap of earth and stones may suggest something of the might of rainfall and rivers to the six-year-old who has seen riverbeds and gulleys. A saucer held over a candle will gather a layer of soot. Where did it come from? What made it? The wonders of chemistry are opened up.

Certain bits of equipment are extremely valuable. An air pump and a bellows lend excitement to experiments with air, and give Six something he can manipulate. Measuring aids are almost necessities: compass, ruler, measuring cups and spoons, scales, plumb line, and level. Mirrors and prisms are needed for finding out about light, while a small sundial and hourglass give time the concreteness that Six loves.

Painting and Modeling

Although Six may not look at them for days at a time, his easel, paints, and brushes are waiting in his room. Painting is one of the most valuable allies the parent has in the struggle to give the child a few relaxed moments in a hectic day. It is a refuge from the stress of the crowd-world, which demands constant adjustments, strident self-assertion. Painting, Six may once again "be himself," tranquilly trying out his skills, quietly digesting some of the phenomena of the big outside world which are increasingly rushing in on him.

The art of Six is actually less interesting to look at than that of Four, because the six-year-old is so much concerned with presenting realistically the things that interest him. Painting airplanes, trains, boats—objects they know and want to master—boys are sensing new details. Devoting themselves mostly to people and houses, girls are actually learning more about them.

Six can learn to mix colors, if he has not already done this, and if he has not spontaneously developed a feeling for color values, he can profit from some instruction now. He can learn to test his colors by applying them to a separate piece of paper before using them on his picture, and he can keep his colors clear by washing his brush thoroughly before dipping it into another color. Beyond these small advances, his technique remains his own.

Harum-scarum in many ways, Six can also remain interested in a project for several days. Clay-modeling may become fairly ambitious. A damp-box to keep the unfinished work in is needed at this point. This may be a large tin can, with smooth edges, or a large glass or plastic bowl. A bowl-cover made of plastic will prevent the piece from drying out. If it is too large to fit into a container, it will remain workable if it is covered with a damp cloth and a piece of oilcloth, well tucked in all around.

Games with Rules

Although creative and spontaneous play is important, there is now a place in a child's life for some games with rules and organization. Rainy days are apt to call at some point for things like horseshoe pitching (available in rubber sets), quoits, table tenpins, or magnetic darts. Magnetic darts are a happy development, because they do away with the problem of supervision. The marked metal target can be hung on a wall or set up on a table. The darts are small bits of magnetized metal with feathered backs to steady their flight. Unlike suction-tipped darts, which rarely work well, these really cling to the target.

In buying games for the six-year-old it is important to remember that the more rules there are, the greater the wrangling we must expect. Movements must be simple, better ruled by chance than skill, and no great concentration demanded. Games with many small parts should still be avoided. Six likes to keep score, but the process must be simple enough to fall within his writing skill, and demand no greater number combinations than he has learned. Additionally, playing directions must be simple enough for Six to remember from one time to another, and the game's dependence on reading should be minimal.

Managing Six's Play

Despite his truculence, the six-year-old needs a manager. He boasts and brags and belittles, but he does not know how to manage himself or his new life alone. He is beginning to feel the tug of war between the standards of his own age group and those of his parents that will be a problem for years to come.

As parents, we can ease the problem by bringing the alternatives together. If we can accept some of the behavior the group demands, Six can accede more easily to some of our decrees.

One way to show the six-year-old that we are ready to be reasonable is to throw the home open to his friends. They all need a chance to work and talk and plan together, away from the hampering effect of adult eyes. They need a chance to explode, a place to spread, an opportunity to be noisy, energetic, inquisitive.

A cellar or attic, or the child's own room, can be converted into a meeting place. The garage might do if none of the others are available. Equipment need not be elaborate. A pair of hand rings and a trapeze bar might be installed, with an old mattress to pad the floor. A workbench, with hammer, nails, and bits of wood is good for implementing inspirations—more dangerous or delicate tools had better be kept where their use can be supervised. A few indoor floor and table games complete the roster. The important thing is to have a place where the children can make their fill of noise.

Although this assumes a need that some six-year-olds do not have, we might suggest a few dates with *individuals* from the child's class or playground gang. We might even have to make the arrangements if the Six in question is a bit shy; the gains the child will make in adjustment and acceptance in his group will repay us manyfold. It is a good idea to have cookies and a favorite drink where Six can get them himself. The less adult intrusion, the better. The home remains a center, but now it is the *child's* center, where he can bring his friends and where he is the host.

We must also accept the responsibility of alternating Six's active play with quiet hours. He is so full of a number of things that he exhausts himself unless he is firmly led to a recuperative activity. When he comes home from school, he may be itching to rejoin his friends, but he needs a rest before he gets started again. Quiet conversation about what happened at school, a few minutes of reading together, or listening to a favorite record might be all he needs. The institution of milk and cookies is a great help in providing a break.

In a similar vein, Six has to be prevented from undertaking too much at once. He wants to master all skills at the same time —pitching, batting, cycling, swimming. He would start a dozen projects a day if he were permitted to. It is up to us to decide how much he can do at once without too much frustration, and to see that nothing new is started until there has been a little achievement in what was begun first. No prescription can be given for this kind of regulation, but it is a safe bet that keeping interest up in the first project will work better than forbidding others.

Also, we must be ready to help when the intensity of Six's interests and feelings gets in his way. For example, many Sixes get so engrossed in what they are doing that they wet or soil their pants. They feel intensely humiliated by this, and it is up to us to restore their self-respect. If we accept what has happened casually with something like, "I know it must be uncomfortable; next time try to come in a little sooner," we will be helping Six re-establish control.

Play is our ally and the child's, if we exploit it fully. For instance, some Sixes go to pieces at the slightest scratch or abrasion. Presenting Six with his own supply of Band-Aids, and showing him how to apply the antiseptic himself, heightens his feeling of being in control. Permitting him to take on the doctor role for other members of the family when they undergo minor damage further assures him that scratches and cuts are not the devastating events they seem to him. If the six-year-old has not had a doctor or a nurse kit before, playing with one of these may also help.

In somewhat the same way, we might try to make a friend of the dark through games like Sardine, which demand absolute darkness, and yet are neither frightening nor startling. Played in familiar territory and close to a trusted person, they may connect darkness with hilarity rather than terror. This can help attics and cellars to become friendly play spaces instead of haunted corners to be avoided. Frequent exploration with an adult at first, then with children of the same age, should desensitize the child in whom the fear is not deeply rooted. Finally, fixing up the attic or cellar as a workshop or meeting place should remove the last shred of threat.

Company Manners

Marie's mother waited until all the guests had departed after her daughter's sixth birthday party. Then she rushed to her bedroom to fling herself on the bed and weep with anger, disappointment, and embarrassment. Many parents can feel with her, after a party involving a six-year-old.

Marie's particular crime had been a temper tantrum, accompanied by "I hate you!" to her mother and grandmother when they tried to placate her. What precipitated it? A simple thing —she could not arrange the seating of all her guests as she had been planning to for weeks before the event.

When she was calm enough to talk, her explanation was reasonable enough. It was her party, wasn't it? Then why couldn't she tell people where to sit? Why should her four-year-old cousin be allowed to choose his own seat? Why was her aunt permitted to interfere with her plans? What was the good of having a party if she couldn't boss it, just this one day that was supposed to belong to her?

This example pretty well sums up what parents are up against when they try to include six-year-olds in social events. Six wants to be boss. He cannot tolerate a great deal of social stimulation without losing control. In the face of frustration or disappointment he goes to pieces.

The lesson is plain. Parties for Sixes should be kept small—preferably four or five close friends. Six should not be promised what is not possible—and it is not possible to predict how other children will behave. Finally, and essentially, parties should be short. An exchange of presents, refreshments, and Six is ready to go home. If entertainment is planned, it should be well organized—a game or two, or home movies, is enough. There should be enough prizes for all the guests, if any are given at all. Favors are a must, for Six feels cheated if he has no loot to take home in exchange for the gift he brought.

Entertaining adults with a six-year-old present involves slightly different, but just as pressing, problems. A good deal depends on the guests, of course. People who look through children and speak over or around them bring out the worst in Six. A natural seeker of the limelight, Six is likely to try to monopolize the conversation, insist on telling his own variety of jokes, or invent show-off stunts on the spur of the moment. "Hey, look what I can do!" is a typical beginning. Ignoring Six is a dangerous procedure. His bids for attention will simply grow more and more desperate.

A simple way to handle this situation is to prepare for it, bow to the inevitable gracefully, and let the child give a performance of some sort, like the puppet show we suggested earlier. It is important to reach a firm agreement beforehand on exactly what the performance will consist of, including the encore. Otherwise Six may suddenly turn coy and clownish, or insist on coming back for more and more applause.

Another wise precaution when guests are expected is to brief Six in advance. Because of his new status, he really does not quite know how to treat adults outside of the family. In his embarrassment he is likely to resort to the obnoxious "So what?" attitude. If he is told exactly how to greet the company, and given some definite responsibility in welcoming them, he will feel more comfortable, and behave more acceptably. Six does not mind rehearsing the whole visit on a make-believe basis; this fits right in with what he has been doing all his play-life.

Parents Needed

To abandon the six-year-old completely to the company of his age-mates, would be as great an error as keeping him from them. Six needs his parents very much, although he may spend comparatively little time with them.

Both boys and girls prize leisure time spent with their father more than ever before. They love to help him in his chores around the house, garden with him, take walks with him. Boys are beginning to feel a little closer to their fathers because they are definitely marking themselves off from the female part of the population. Girls, on the other hand, value their father's attention almost as if he were their cavalier. They glory in having him take them to the movies (if they are ready for such adult entertainment) or in an hour with him in the park.

When parents can unbend enough to play games or do with their Sixes something of special interest to that age, they are showing in the most effective way their love for each child as he is, with all his needs and problems.

CHAPTER VIII

Seven: The Socialite

Gerry holds an apple aloft for all to see. "Who likes apples, raise their hands," he commands.

Marcia stretches her hand above her head. Ed holds his near his chest. Pete sits on his.

Sue has a cookie. "Who likes chocolate cookies?" she calls.

Three hands shoot up. Then Pete stands up, to raise his hand higher. Gerry climbs on his chair. Marcia puts two hands up.

Pete sits down. "Who likes spinach?" he asks.

The other children huddle under the table.

This kind of thing can go on by the hour. It is a major time-passer when Sevens must remain in one place for any length of time. They vote for things they like, things they do not like, people they like, people they do not like. It is play, of course, but it holds a deeper fascination, being a way of advertising that one is part of a group. You come together to vote, whether you agree or not.

Every organized group in our society has a body of customs, knowledge, traditions, beliefs, and rituals which are shared by the members of that group alone. Taking part in them marks the members as "belonging"; those who do not know about them are outsiders. Seven passionately wants in.

For the first time, the child seems to realize consciously that he *is* a child, and to measure himself as a child against the adults around him. The early fantasies of omnipotence are gone. On the other hand, the grownups who were the source of all help in the past, suddenly seem to have little to offer. They cannot pass a miracle and make Seven suddenly big. Short of that, they only emphasize his own littleness and comparative dependence. Among others of his own age, however, he counts for something. This explains why the opinion of other children is so much more important to Seven than the opinion of adults.

Cliques and Outsiders

At six, outsiders stood a good chance of getting into any group simply by attaching themselves. At seven, the task is more difficult. The group is not giving its bag of tricks away for the asking.

It is not unusual to see a lone youngster sobbing his way along one side of the street while a cluster of four or five follow him on the other side shrieking "Cry baby, cry baby, run home and get a bottle!" It is not a happy experience for the victim. Yet the persecutors are not really moved by dislike or meanness. It is simply that by turning against this one child they are doing something *together*. Furthermore, if they make it very clear that he is "out," they can assure themselves that they are "in."

Seven is a for-or-against age, an age of gratuitous insult. In their casual play at this age children turn against each other frequently. Their need to be against something or someone may take a regrettable turn. If the children come from families where race hatred or religious prejudice is manifested, they will readily turn their hostility toward children of other races and faiths (although without the parental example they might not). Then little neighborhood gangs may form and wars may start. These organizations and their activities are very hard to stamp out, and what started as a natural development becomes a warping experience for hater and hated alike. Parents who have conscientiously not passed on prejudices to their children may have the unpleasant experience of finding that the attitudes have been acquired in a school or neighborhood where intolerance exists.

However, these are often not difficult to eradicate. A firm refusal to condone them, a matter-of-fact explanation that they are based on ignorance or misconception, and some pleasant experiences with members of the maligned groups are usually effective in combatting them. The child may still give them lip service when with his gang, but they will be discarded when the gang changes. If they seem really well entrenched, it is time for parents to examine their own attitudes honestly, or to find out why Johnny needs a scapegoat.

The grownup must also be prepared for the fact that seven-year-olds may despise him as a matter of course. This is not necessarily true hostility but may only be a way of making the child feel closer to his group.

Parents and teachers naturally want to do what they can to help a child who is a long-suffering "out." However, overprotection will only separate him further from the group and make it harder for him to get back in. Nor does it help to think of the aggressors as little beasts and roughnecks, for this time it *is* "only a phase." The grownup needs stoicism; the child, sympathy and careful coaching.

Even at the most amiable gatherings of seven-year-olds the adult must be on his toes to prevent "ganging-up." Constructive group play can become gang warfare in a flash. Luckily, however, the young gangsters are quite susceptible to the reliable old tactic, having their attention diverted. Fortunately, too, the adult has on his side a new, positive quality that Seven possesses: his basic sympathy with his contemporaries. Since he thinks about himself more than he used to, he is beginning to recognize certain feelings and to give them names. With help, he can recognize the same feelings in others.

The seven-year-old likes his contemporaries just because they *are* his contemporaries—unless, of course, they are against him at the moment. If he is ready to criticize (and he is), he is also ready to help. At this age, even where there seems to be undying enmity between two youngsters, it is not uncommon to find them suddenly becoming "best friends." Two little girls can be seen in the corner of the playground earnestly learning rope-jumping tricks from each other. "No, not like that, like this," says one. Or, "Hold the cord straight and then jerk it fast," one small boy explains to a friend, demonstrating the proper technique with tops. A casual word from the adult, suggesting one of these "show us how" sessions, can sometimes turn the beginning of a brawl into a pleasant practice period.

Rules and Standards

Ask Seven whom he likes best in his class or play group, and he answers without hesitation. He is equally positive about the child he likes least. Then ask his reasons for liking and disliking certain individuals, and the code by which Sevens are shaping their lives becomes clear.

Daniel comes out poorly in a poll because he is a poor sport: he is afraid to fight; he gets sore too easily. Johnny is disliked because he acts silly: he disturbs everyone when the group has a serious project on; he gets into trouble. In contrast, Alan is well liked because he is a good fighter; he is fair, generous, and a good pal, and he is always ready to help. These are the actual reasons given by a group of seven-year-olds who were asked to choose the "best" and "worst" children in their class.

Girls seem to have other sins. Marcia is criticized because she tells lies; Amy is repudiated as a tattle-tale, Thelma is "too proud because her father is a doctor." Alma, chosen most frequently as "best," is described as being helpful, and not silly, a good fighter and one who is fun to play with because she has lots of ideas.

Sevens know what they like, and many of the characteristics they choose sit well with adults. However, the qualities that appeal to them are not subtle. They are what have made life better for this age, but they are hardly the best for every age.

Seven knows that rules exist and wants to observe them, but is extremely vague about how they operate. Up to this point, "rules" were chiefly what some grownup told him he could or could not do. So the idea of a rule by itself, without an adult around the corner, is still unfamiliar to him. Also, because he is still largely self-centered, it is hard for him to think of rules except in personal terms. He sees nothing odd about insisting that certain rules in a game apply to everyone except himself.

Furthermore, the actual content of the rules of the games Seven wants to play are not clear to him. He still sees things outside himself in broad outlines. Baseball consists of pitching and batting, catching the ball, and running around bases. Finer points escape him. What does it matter if a team has an extra outfielder or two, or lacks its full complement of players? As long as he can get some action, Seven is satisfied. If a situation comes up that is not covered by the rules as he knows them, he is quick to invent his own. Waiting until the official rule is forthcoming would impede the action. Seven largely plays by ear.

There is one point, however, that he is very sensitive about. He insists on fairness. As this "fairness" consists of interpreting rules as he understands them, and as his understanding is often extremely personal and sometimes unique, hassles are not infrequent. Adults can help enormously by being on hand to give information when rules are in question, by making sure that all participants in a game understand the rules that will govern them, and by acting as a referee when disputes arise. Scrupulous fairness is a necessity, if the child is to learn to be fair himself, and later, by extension, to grasp the meaning of law and democratic government.

Perhaps because of his uncertainty about them, the seven-year-old is peculiarly fascinated by rules. One of his (or her) favorite games is making up rules for the whole group to follow, rules which he knows are extremely difficult to obey. The familiar "Silence in the courtroom, the monkey wants to speak" is an example of this kind of game. A cluster of tittering and sputtering Sevens, waiting to hail the first of their number to become a "monkey," may not look like a group of apprentices in the art of citizenship, earnestly practicing an important skill, but that is what they are.

In many situations it is wise to encourage Sevens to make their own rules, because these seem easier for them to follow than those imposed by other people. However, they need some examples of the way authentic rules operate. Class elections and parliamentary procedure of a simple sort are important in school groups. At home, the seven-year-old might be given a choice of chores for which he (or she) will be responsible. As a group member he participates in making the plans and in carrying them out.

Boys and Battles

As we have noticed, physical combat goes along with the age of seven, especially among boys. Sometimes the fighting is in earnest, resulting from a disagreement the children have not learned to resolve in other ways. More often, it is a sport, starting with a challenge. Whether you like it or not, you are supposed to accept any such challenge. Otherwise you are a " 'fraidy cat."

The boy who is afraid of being hurt and the one who expects to be beaten are at a disadvantage. A certain amount of alibiing is excepted, because all Sevens tend to excuse themselves when things go against them. Thus, a youngster can often get away with claiming he lost a fight because the sun was in his eyes, or because his shoulder hurt from a previous tussle—but refusing to fight is not tolerated.

What, then, can we do to help the child who is timid and withdraws from rough physical contacts? Certainly we do not say, when he appears disheveled and sobbing, "Don't come running to me; get out there and fight your own battles." But we can explain to him that fighting is like baseball or swimming—it is something you can learn to do, and something you need to learn if you want to be part of the gang. We can go further and see that he gets some training in the techniques of fighting he needs to keep up his end.

Seven's battles are a mixture of wrestling and boxing, with more shoving than punching. They are rarely deadly serious. The participants spend more time scaring each other than pummeling. Some *talk* a good fight, stopping every few minutes to discuss another "rule." The bystanders contribute most of the ferocity. "Beat him up. Knock him down!" They dance up and down excitedly, getting more release vicariously than they do when they are actually doing battle themselves. The fight over, one antagonist may help another up, proclaiming, "We both won."

Baseball

Baseball ranks with fighting as a prime occupation for seven-year-olds. Most Sevens know when the baseball season starts, are familiar with the names of a few outstanding players, and root for their favorite teams. As with fighting, Seven talks a better game than he plays. In pitching, his windup is more impressive than his control. Batters may swing ten times before they connect with the ball. Catchers and fielders are active and zealous, but flies are rarely caught. The complex co-ordination between trunk and legs, hand and eye, called for by the game is still beyond Seven.

Still, baseball skills are extremely important for most little boys and for some little girls. For one thing, the team is a well-defined social structure in which each individual must fill a special role for the good of the whole: the child may even have to sacrifice individual glory for the greater glory of the team. To remain with the team he accepts criticism, even guying, and comes back to try again. He goes off by himself to practice pitching or hitting in a far more mature manner than he practices the piano. Also, baseball almost forces self-criticism. It is hard to look at one's skill through rose-colored glasses when one strikes out time after time. There are always eyes quick to detect a pretender, and the candid opinions of one's team-mates leave little room for self-deception.

Fortunately, everyone is learning and blundering. Despite the exceptional performers, there are enough mediocre players to support the ego of the clear-eyed Seven who realizes the limits of his own abilities. No one *need* feel too far out of the running at this point.

A little help with skills can go a long way at this point. Seven may want to concentrate on his batting, because that is the road to glory, but most children also need practice in catching. If parents have only limited time to devote to helping Junior become a star, it will probably be put to the best use in catching and fielding. Batting and pitching can be improved by solitary sessions, with the help of special equipment.

A tether-ball arrangement can be used to improve the eye-hand-body co-ordination needed in batting: a baseball is suspended by a length of strong elastic from the branch of a tree or a one-armed support set in open ground. The child intent on improving his pitching control will find a target painted on a wall or set up firmly in a field a big help. Rubbing the ball in some substance which will leave a mark where it strikes will help him estimate his progress accurately.

Seven's absorption in improving physical skills deserves as much respect and consideration as the scholar's silent concentration on his books. The fact that he can recognize the need for improvement, and devote himself to the task without external urging or praise, indicates that he has taken a long step toward real maturity. Seeking an effective place in his group, he has become aware of, and accepted, one of the most important facts in social living.

Playtime Variety

More self-conscious about his skills than he was at six, Seven wants to acquire new ones. Archery attracts him, and it is worth while to buy him real target equipment rather than toys if this interest is to be encouraged.

Indeed, when the seven-year-old enters a new activity that may last, expert instruction is something to think about. While most children can master enough of a sports skill by trial and error to have fun, good guidance in the beginning leads to faster progress and more satisfaction. This is especially true in swimming, skiing, and riding, all sports suited to Seven's level of physical development.

Of course, professional instruction in *too* many sports is not only a strain on the pocketbook, but can make the child's life a series of regimented lessons. Directed work needs to be balanced with sheer fun.

Aside from sports and physical triumphs, Sevens (like Sixes) have two loves—tops and marbles. No city street is complete in springtime without its clusters of small boys playing marbles or, in the fall, spinning tops. Marbles especially are treasures and, since the game is played for "keeps," stores of these objects are apt to accumulate in bags, boxes, and drawers all over the house.

Sugar and Spice

While little boys are rolling and tussling over the ground to prove their manhood, most little girls go on with their imaginative and household play. In the park, under trees, in whatever shelters they can find, they spend most of their time playing cooking, washing dishes, feeding the family and entertaining guests. Sometimes they are princesses riding in fairy-tale coaches, sleeping beauties waiting for the prince to come, or royalty going through the ceremony of coronation. Occasionally they are horses, drivers, riders, or grooms.

By and large, girls seem to prefer playing in smaller groups than their brothers. They walk contentedly about the playground in twos, arms about each others' waists, exchanging views and news and secrets. Some bounce balls by themselves, trying to better their own scores in the rhyme-games like "One, two, three, O'Leary." Others jump rope by themselves, intent on jumping longer or faster than they ever have before.

A few larger groups gather to play jump-rope games like In and Out or Double Dutch, or leaping over the barrier. Penalties attached to failure are not radical—the child has to give up her turn to the next in line. There is little social censure attached to poor performance, though the admiration of the group goes to the skillful jumper. Most girls at seven are not very skilled at rope skipping, and the slow one still has a chance to catch up.

Girls' activities involve less competition and less elaborate group structures than boys' do.

Common Ground

There is, however, a growing group of activities shared by girls and boys. Some girls can be found with bat and ball, and if a girl lives in a neighborhood where baseball is taken up by the girls, she also may need help with the skills of the game.

More common, perhaps, are the running games that include both sexes—tag and hide-and-seek are at their peak at this age. Bicycles also occupy both sexes. The importance of bicycling at this age depends largely on where the child lives. If everyone else in the neighborhood can ride a two-wheeler, the child who cannot is obviously at a disadvantage. If there are only a few bikes in the crowd, and lending is customary—as it is in many places—the pressure is likely to be less.

Roller skating is one activity in which younger and older children frequently unite. Most Sevens have learned to keep their balance on the straightaway, and are beginning to work earnestly for speed. A few are starting on figures. Since roller skating retains its popularity until adolescence and later, it is worth some real effort and attention.

Water sports and winter sports engage the attention of girls as well as boys from now on. More girls than boys now show promise as horseback riders (and are apt to be more faithful in caring for their mounts) but some boys love horses, too. Riding and skiing, like swimming, may hold happy surprises for the child who shrinks from team sports. Here he can use a different kind of co-ordination and progress at his own pace.

Imaginative Play

Limp figures strew the ground. One moves and groans faintly. From a rude shelter two large-headed shapes dash to the groaner and lift up his shoulders. Hands under armpits, they tug and drag his dead weight with effort until they reach the shelter. Head lolling, eyes closed, he seems to be past help. Hurriedly a doctor sits astride him, apparently administering artificial respiration. The space-men have scored their first shot of the day.

The names change, a few details of the play change, but the pattern seems never to change: one group of boys and girls flings itself recklessly in pursuit of another, which flees, darting and feinting, finally turning and chasing the pursuers. Hunt and chase games go on, perennially.

Seven shows his greater sophistication by varying the roles he plays. Bandits, space-men, commandos join the simple cowboys and Indians of a more innocent time. Guns, noise, vigorous movement still characterize the play, but more realistic details have found their way in. Now the wounded are removed from the battlefield and cared for. Each side is organized and several kinds of roles must be filled. Doctors and nurses, for example, are felt to be as necessary to war as fighters.

Emblems of belonging are prominent. An army must have a uniform—even if it is only a paper bag worn over the head. There are rules: the dead cannot be killed again; help must be given to a man who asks for it. Each group has a definite organization, or at least a leader.

Seven needs his romping, shouting play for much the same reason that Six did—as an outlet for feelings which do not fit into orderly social life, and as a means of letting off steam. It is especially valuable during this time because so many of the child's other activities are governed by rules that diminish spontaneity and freedom. Holding a place in a group requires that he accommodate himself to the requirements and notions of other people. All this is good and necessary if the child is to become a smoothly functioning part of a complex social system, but it leaves him less leeway as an individual.

This is the price we all pay for the security we get from group living. But we cannot really destroy parts of ourselves. When society gets through with us, we all have feelings, needs, longings, desires, thoughts, fears left over that do not fit into the general patterns of behavior that the group demands. These make up our most intimate selves, the part of our personality that has most meaning for us as unique individuals. If we are to function well in our social guises, we must find some means of expressing these other aspects of ourselves. Some of us take to daydreams. Others paint, or write, or make music. We use the bits that do not fit the outward pattern. And Sevens, in search for both outlet and self-expression, play.

Frightened Children

There are more frightened Sevens than adults know of, and they are all busy saving face. The Seven who yells "Beat him up!" most loudly from the sidelines may be one of the timid and overobedient children who are torn between wanting to be one of the boys and wanting to please the adults.

Retreat is Seven's favorite method of dealing with difficulties. If things go badly at home he threatens to run away. When a decision goes against him at play, he is more likely to quit than to stay and try to win. Among his favorite words are *gyp, mean,* and *unfair*—directed against others, of course. If he cannot run away from defeat, he makes excuses. His inner image of himself is so precious and so perfect that he cannot bear to acknowledge that he might have a fault or two.

Candidly, we do not know whether this is a necessary trait, arising from the vast difference in skills and power that Seven suddenly perceives between himself and adults, or whether it develops because we expect more from Sevens than they are able to give.

Children who have been made to feel weak or foolish and without value will find the increasing competition of group living hard to face. If a failure has been made a bugaboo to them, they feel that people will like them only when they are successful. Rather than chance being defeated, they avoid the contest.

What these children need more than anything is the heartfelt assurance that there is more to life than besting the other fellow; that the kind of person you *are* is more important than what you *do*. They need to experience the simple homely comfort of being accepted on any level, without any strings attached. Then they will be better able to face the prospect of some failures with equanimity.

"Wanna Swap?"

While seven-year-old pugilists grunt and strain, and future baseball kings hold sway, quiet twosomes dot the edges of the playground—usually girl with girl and boy with boy.

"I'll give you this one for that one."

"I'll give you two of these." And pasteboards change hands; the shuffling resumes.

These are the swappers, another guise in which Sevens appear. From seven to ten, trading cards and their equivalents are inescapable. Swapping enables Seven to be in touch with his (and her) playmates in a relaxed, nontaxing fashion. It is a comfortable way of being sociable, and extremely rewarding to the unathletic type, who may prefer to exercise his business ability.

One warning to parents of a swapper: funds for buying trading cards should be limited to the general level of the group with which the child associates. Unlimited funds permit him (or her) to evade competing on an even-Steven basis. Under such circumstances, participation can become bribery or sheer showing off, neither of them healthy forms of social behavior.

Group Games for Outdoors

Parents of seven-year-olds need to know a few group games that can be pulled out of the hat when the moment beckons. Outdoor

SEVEN: THE SOCIALITE

birthday parties, backyard picnics, father-son and mother-daughter affairs are only a few of the situations which might call for an organizing hand.

As we have suggested before, Sevens love the idea of teams, but are not ready for complicated team responsibilities. For some, the usual hunt-and-find or run-and-chase, in which *one* person is "it" until he captures a replacement, is agony. An ideal group game should have lots of action, give everyone a chance to contribute to his team, and make no individual stand out because of lack of skill. Among many others, Pom, Pom, Pull Away fills these conditions. To play it, a space large enough for marking two lines thirty feet apart is necessary. The players all stand behind one of these goal lines, except the one who is "it"; he stands in the middle, between the two lines, and chants:

"Pom, Pom, pull away! If you don't come, I'll pull you away!"

At this, all the players must run across the open space to the line on the opposite side, with "it" tagging as many as possible before they reach safety. Anyone tagged must help in tagging others as they run across the open space. After the untagged players have reached the goal, "it" gives the signal again, and the uncaught players make another dash. This is repeated until all have been caught. Then the game starts over, with the first player tagged in the preceding game becoming "it" in the new game.

A game that ministers to Seven's love for rough and tumble, but omits the rivalry, is Ride Him, Cowboy, a version of Crack the Whip. Groups are divided into cowboys and bronchos, with two or three cowboys for six or more bronchos. The bronchos form in short lines (four or five children), each player clasping the waist of the one in front of him. The cowboys "ride" the bronchos by clasping the waist of the last broncho of each line. By turning and twisting, the bronchos try to throw their cowboy. If he can stay on, he becomes a broncho, and the first child in the original line becomes a cowboy.

Crows and Cranes, Stealing Sticks, Spoke Tag are other action games suitable for this age. (Rules for these, and many others, may be found in the U. S. Children's Bureau's *Handbook for Recreation Leaders*, already mentioned.)

Keeping groups within bounds and having a good time is not difficult, if one follows a few simple rules. Specialists in group recreation make the following suggestions:

1. Understand thoroughly what you want done and make your directions brief and clear. Demonstrate the action when possible.

2. Stand where you can face everyone. Speak so that you can be heard, but do not shout.

3. Go into the first game without hesitating. Choose something that is familiar, or that is easy to explain in a few words, and get the group actively interested at the very start.

4. Play a game until it is almost at its best, then change to another.

It is better to stop while everyone wishes to go on than to let even a few players feel bored by too much of one thing.

Problems that arise in the course of organized group play can be handled simply. If boys and girls are unwilling to take each others' hands, for example, we might begin with games in which the players stand one behind the other in lines, as in relay games. Then one can shift to double-circle games, and then to the single-circle games which require taking hands. By the time two or three team games have been played, self-consciousness will be gone.

Bossy children are often useful as bases for relays, as judges, or as assistants to pass out materials. Plenty of work keeps them from spoiling the fun of the others. Shy children do well if they are permitted to lose themselves in a group at the beginning; they need a chance to observe the game and get thoroughly familiar with it before taking a conspicuous part. If they can be put into situations where they are sure to win, they will thaw out quickly.

Faced with managing a group of Sevens, the best guarantee of success is to have plenty of material planned ahead of time. Active games should alternate with quiet games, but game formations should be used in succession—a circle game following a circle game, a line game after a line game. Musical games and motion songs are particularly good for endings. The following one is just silly enough for Seven to love:

The Crocodile

Oh, she sailed away on a sunny summer's day (*flutter hands*)
On the back of a crocodile (*make crocodile mouth by flapping hands*).
"You see," said she, "he's as tame as he can be (*pat back of hand*);
I'll speed him down the Nile" (*flutter fingers*).
The croc winked his eye as she bade them all good-bye (*wink, point to eye, wave hand*),
Wearing a happy smile (*outline smile with finger*).
At the end of the ride (*whirl hands*)
The lady was inside (*hands on stomach*),
And the smile was on the crocodile (*outline smile and make crocodile mouth*).

To Camp or Not to Camp

Early in summer, railroad stations bloom with banners: Camp Wookytookit, Texas-on-the-Hudson, Merryall, Tot's Delight. The annual hegira is about to begin, official signal of the start of another camp season.

For many Sevens this is the year of the Great Separation. From some points of view it seems the natural time to start the camping adventure. The seven-year-old needs companions of his own age; he may need to get away from parents for a while; he needs to learn how to live as a member of a group. Good camps satisfy these requirements and in addition offer space, a chance to get acquainted with nature, practice in the skills that are increasingly important during the middle years of childhood, and a desirable balance between outdoor exercise, rest, and creative activities. On the surface, the picture is completely rosy.

Why, then, the furtive tears and the anxious looks? The answer: many children are not ready to leave home at seven . . . or at eight, or nine or ten. And no child should be forced to leave home until he himself wants to go. Many fathers are tempted to send their sons to camp to toughen them up. Often the result is quite the opposite—the timid become more timid, the physically backward find active sports more distasteful than ever.

Typically, the child who is afraid of competition and who is not easily accepted by his age-mates is reluctant to go. This kind of child may need a summer or two of gradual "hardening off" before he is sent away. Day camps and boarding camps that accommodate parents as well as children may accomplish this.

If you decide to send your child to camp, for the child's first summer away it is important to choose a camp where he will not feel lost. It is usually best to start him off in a small one, where each counselor is responsible for no more than four or five children. Noncompetitive camps are preferable for younger children; many prefer them for children of all ages.

Good health and safety standards are essential, of course. (The American Camping Association issues a brochure on these.) Most camps have a trained nurse on the staff, and some large camps also have their own doctor. For others there is a doctor on call.

Most approved camps have satisfactory equipment, but personnel must be judged carefully, and by personal contact. The director of the camp will set the tone for the whole program. He will choose the counselors according to his ideas of what is important for children. Therefore he is the key to the whole setup.

One can find out a good deal about a camp director by letting him talk and noticing what he emphasizes. Does he try to impress parents by talking about his plant, the cabins, showers, grounds, etc., or is he more concerned about the children? Does he speak of the maturity and sensitivity of his counselors, or does he stress their skills in specific activities like swimming, and riding? Above all, does he seem interested in finding out something about your child or is he mostly intent on impressing you?

Good counselors will see that each camper gets enough personal attention, a balanced program and a chance to pursue his own interests. They will keep him from feeling left out. Such people will be alert to see a child's need for help and know how to give it to him. Without them, camping is a risky proposition, especially for the young child. With them, almost any camp can offer a great deal.

Parents needing further guidance might wish to consult *How to Choose a Camp for Your Child,* by Ernest Osborne, of

Music

"And the rest will be green, green, *green*," sings Laura as she paints.

"Isn't this dumb? Isn't this dumb?" Jonathan chants. Around the room the lilt of familiar tunes arises as others bend over clay boards, or sprawl over drawing paper.

Seven loves to sing. He'll hum under his breath as he works, or gladly stop what he is doing to join in a community chorus. He probably knows a wide variety of songs—folk tunes, holiday and seasonal compositions, nonsense songs, marching melodies, rounds—and is always eager to learn more. He especially enjoys repetitive and additive pieces.

The second grader recognizes tunes and rhythms easily. He likes to play "What am I humming?" or "What am I clapping?" in which one person hums a melody or pats out a rhythm, and the other tries to guess the name. Drums delight him, and he can accompany a record with a fair degree of accuracy.

If our seven-year-old has had a chance to experiment with simple musical instruments, and has served his apprenticeship in a rhythm band, it is now time to introduce him to some of the elements of the orchestra. He will enjoy being able to identify the sounds made by different instruments, especially the more outstanding ones like the double bass or the piccolo. Unusual sounds will pique his interest—the howl of bagpipes, for example, or the peculiar resonance of Javanese gamelan music.

Margaret Thorne, a music educator of long experience, suggests we use the sounds of nature to sharpen young ears. How many different tones can we hear in a thunder storm, for example? Who will be the first to identify the notes in the cricket's chirp, or the boom of the bull-frog, or the little tree frog's peep? Bird calls offer a reservoir of music fun. The seven-year-old can make a "collection" by learning to identify, imitate and keep a record of the calls of birds at his home grounds, country cottage, or in the city parks.

Music Lessons

Some seven-year-olds can pick out tunes on a piano or xylophone. (The piano is a source of fun if it is sometimes left open so that hammers can be seen striking the strings.) Some want to take music lessons. At this point parents often begin to harbor unrealistic expectations.

There are good reasons for deferring formal study. This is a sampling age, an age for plunging impulsively into new activities, for wanting everything in sight. But Seven's experience is too limited to enable him to judge his own capacities or the work involved in a project. As a consequence, he often takes on more than he can carry out, and the year is littered with abandoned undertakings. Hand, finger, and arm co-ordination may not be developed sufficiently to make music practice easy. Note reading may pose another problem, because even word reading is not well established.

Group lessons offer one way to satisfy the first flush of enthusiasm without disappointment. The groups are usually small, five or six children of about the same age. The study thus becomes a social affair, but with a regular schedule and definite tasks that are not too demanding.

If group lessons are not available, better delay lessons for a year or so, unless the child evinces a consuming interest.

Dancing

Watching Sevens trying to dance in time with music reminds us how unfinished they really are. They can skip, gallop, and step-clap with great aplomb, but rhythmic leaping or a combination of steps and leaps is still too difficult. When they are asked to run with the music, someone is always either a little ahead or a little behind.

As we might expect, slow music seems harder for Seven to follow than fast. At any rate, he *enjoys* speed, and he likes an organized exercise better than abstract movement. Boys will be airplanes with enthusiasm, but ask them simply to step to the beat and clowning breaks out. A good game of skip-tag or a sham battle played out to a musical background can still keep their interest. Girls are more amenable, and seem to enjoy the sheer control involved in doing exercises to music.

The question of dancing lessons comes up in the homes of many girls at this age. Most modern teachers believe that dance disciplines involving rigidly defined patterns of movement are not yet suitable. Thus, they would endorse a free-flowing type of dancing, but advise delay in ballet training. Tap dancing may be fine for some well-coordinated Sevens, but baffles those less advanced.

Books and Stories

About halfway through the eighth year, something new is usually added to the child's life—he discovers that he can read! Familiar words spring out at him from newspapers, signs, breakfast-food boxes. Old books go through a transformation because they now make sense in a new way. The world of the grownup, represented by those mysterious magazines and papers in which parents bury themselves, is closed no longer; slowly it yields up its secrets, and the child becomes a member of the privileged group made up of people who can read.

In our enthusiasm we must remember that his comprehension goes far beyond his reading ability. He will read by himself the simple books that he can, but he will need help with the more advanced material that he can understand but not yet read.

Seven is a good listener, and he likes twice-told tales. The reading period is a time of relaxation for him, a special luxury because he is working so hard on reading himself. He will ask "Is it real?" over and over again. He now knows enough to distinguish between make-believe and reality, and he is busy exploring each one. His approach to the world of fantasy is different from what it was before because now it is quite deliberate; he knows that different rules apply to reality, and he is busy marking out the boundaries that separate the two worlds.

What shall we read to Seven? To know, we must ask *"Which Seven?"* because tastes are becoming more and more individual. Choosing a book is a more personal matter than it used to be, and the child himself is our best guide.

We can offer prospective donors a few general hints. Most seven-year-olds have a taste for the sensational and dramatic.

Accidents, disasters, narrow escapes hold them enthralled, providing the escape is made safely, and the disaster ends well, of course. Fairies, supermen, magicians offer delightful release from a humdrum world. Myths and fairy tales are fine for the child who feels secure in his general approach to life. But fantasy needs to be balanced by books about the here and now. Seven has a great deal to learn about the real world, and he is an eager pupil. He likes to read and hear about cowboys, army and navy life, airplanes, what is below the surface of the earth, how animals live. Girls also like stories about animals. If they are at the beginning of the "horsy" stage, they will be avid collectors of pony stories. They love stories about cheerful family expeditions and situations, provided there is a bit of drama involved. No one knows why, but girls seem to have a much wider range of interest than boys and will often enjoy a book intended for boys, whereas boys firmly refuse to read stories in which the feminine interest predominates. Both boys and girls like reading about heroes and heroines their own age.

Stories about people who live far away or long ago do not seem to appeal to most Sevens as much as down-to-earth tales in settings they can recognize, or out-and-out fantasy. There are always exceptions, of course; *Heidi* is well liked by many girls at seven, and most youngsters of this age enjoy simple Bible tales.

Humor has a universal appeal. Any book that combines animals, humorous rhymes, funny predicaments, narrow escapes, and adults shown in a slightly ridiculous light is almost sure to be a success with Sevens.

There are many ways in which we can encourage the child to use books independently. Getting him a card at the local library is one important step. Borrowing books can add to his sense of importance and competence, as well as to his enjoyment. We can keep books around to pique his curiosity, well-illustrated volumes about subjects with which we know he is concerned. We can show him how to use a dictionary—there are some good ones prepared especially for his age level. We can include him in the family reading circle by taking a newspaper with comic strips that appeal to him, and by getting him a subscription to a magazine planned for his age. When he needs information for some special project, we can help him find it in reference books. Even if he still needs it read to him, inviting him to go along on the search reveals new uses for books.

It is even more important than it was in his younger days that he have his own library, keeping it in his own room or in a special section of the family bookcase. If he can carpenter his own bookcase, so much the better.

More than a Listener

"Know what *I*'d do?" says Seven when his story-book hero is thrown into prison. "I'd take that stinky old guard and knock him out, that's what I'd do," and he flourishes clenched fists. No passive listener, he projects himself wholeheartedly into the story, identifying himself with the most sympathetic figure. He likes few things better than acting out the part of a character from a familiar tale, and can stay in the role from beginning to end of the dramatization. Books are beginning to feed into his dramatic play, and by playing out the parts, he makes the books come alive.

Seven likes to compose his own stories. Mostly they are about things that have happened to him, with emphasis on the factual, but they tell us in a way that nothing else does what seems important to him, what he notices, how he feels.

"This afternoon I went to see some little new mice," dictated one seven-year-old, about a very important event in her life, "and you could see one of the mice's hearts beating!"

"The mother was rough with them, but she took care of them," another dictated; "she didn't lose a one!"

It is important for Sevens to have a chance to tell stories, as well as listen to them, to help them keep their feeling for the spontaneous, imaginative use of language. The books they are able to read themselves are necessarily simple in style and limited in vocabulary. Without continuing encouragement to express things in their own way, children may make this flatness their own.

Comics Can Be a Blessing

The comics seem to gain in fascination with each year. Our discussion in chapter 7 applies as well to Sevens as to Sixes.

Tastes do not change much from the previous year. Now and then we hear of a child who tries to "fly" in imitation of some airborne hero, but by and large there does not seem to be much harm in this type of story for the healthy child: the forces of good still triumph over the forces of evil, and action rather than gruesomeness is their major attraction. For general appeal, it is hard to beat the comics in which children get the better of grownups, or the underdog upsets stuffy authority.

Radio, TV, and Movies

Adventure and shooting programs on the air are still the greatest favorites, but others also have some appeal. Comedy and quiz programs gain more fans, and girls often listen to "soap operas," as one way of sharing in the adult world.

The programs that are "good" for Six are also to be sought for Seven. The added year of maturity makes possible more "participation" for those who live in cities with television studios. These seven-year-olds can be taken to selected shows that have live audiences. With persistence, it is possible to arrange for a visit backstage, so that he can see how the cameras work. He and his friends can play "television studio" after such a trip, and he can make up his own programs at home and present them to the family on special occasions.

Many programs have children as guest performers; Seven can write letters to the studios, trying for a chance to participate, or to get tickets for the audience shows. The child who has no access to a live show (as well as those who have) can be helped to follow up on science programs with home experiments. He can use the gags and stunts he sees on programs with his playmates. Fully exploited, television offers many opportunities for exciting activity.

Since the advent of television, one hears less about the movie problem than before but it still needs consideration.

Many seven-year-olds are capable of sitting through a full-length feature picture, but more than that is definitely too much for them. If the youngster is to sit through ninety minutes of looking, he must at least be permitted to wriggle. Matinees especially designed for children, during which they are permitted to cheer on the hero and hiss the villain, imitate gun noises, jump up and down in their places, may be horrible from an adult's point of view, but they provide the kind of freedom Sevens need.

Anything that is undesirable as TV fare is also undesirable in movies, while humor, adventure, and action are as attractive on the larger as on the smaller screen. The old-fashioned serial which left the hero hanging by his fingertips from the edge of a cliff at the end of each episode is definitely not to be recommended.

Additional Forms of Entertainment

Because entertainment by TV, radio, and movies is so easy to come by, parents sometimes overlook other offerings in their communities. It is worth while to keep an eye out for those groups of entertainers specializing in children's programs which nowadays put on productions in many towns and cities. Among these, magic and puppet shows are apt to be the most reliable and popular. Dramatizations of fairy tales are fine if they are well done, but acting for children is an art that cannot be conquered by good intentions and tinsel crowns. Where the requirements of the child audience for clarity and diction and plenty of action (but no confusion) are understood, these plays can be delightful and memorable occasions.

Special dance groups, giving story-ballets designed for the young, offer a rare treat where available. Some communities have orchestras which present regular concerts for children. The best of these give the young audience a chance to get acquainted with the different instruments of the orchestra, and use an appealing commentary to focus attention on the music.

Tastes and interests differ widely among Sevens. Some are ready for selected adult entertainment. Little girls enjoy some of the classical ballets that dramatize stories. Before they are taken to see the ballets, they should, of course, become familiar with the stories involved. Both boys and girls enjoy band concerts, community sings, folk-song offerings. Hillbilly music, Western ballads, folk music of the less plaintive sort have a very wide age appeal. Simple square dances can be mastered, especially if a misstep or two can be overlooked. Seven is ready to go out into the community; it is time to find out what the community has to offer him.

Painting and Drawing

A display of seven-year "art" is like an echo of Grandma Moses. We find the same attention to vivid detail, a similar flat look that comes from distorted perspective, and a noticeable concentration on realistic subject matter. Sevens are not accurate about the comparative sizes of details, and three-dimensional and two-dimensional representation in the same picture, but they show the beginnings of sophistication.

The child is not yet able to draw what he sees. Instead, he draws the conventionalized forms he has learned. Thus, a tree is likely to be a straight line with a handful of smaller lines fanning out at the top, or with individual leaves marching along its branches. Houses are usually drawn in crude perspective, with front and side showing. Flat surfaces, like gardens, are still pictured as if the artist were looking down on them from above.

In subject matter, Sevens seem to be on a seesaw. Some swing from down-to-earth scenes they experience every day to wild fantasies of bombing and shooting. Others use realistic techniques to picture fantastic themes—a cow with her tail going down a chimney, for example. On the whole, though, even fantasy seems to follow conventional lines. The shootings, ship-sinkings, and airplane battles seem to characterize the work of boys; girls tend to express themselves through scenes taken from myths and fairy tales.

Unlike younger children, Sevens often prefer pencils and crayons for their drawings. They work quickly and vigorously, and crayons seem best for this. Waiting for one water color to dry before applying another along its edge is hard for Seven—once started, he wants to sweep on to the finish. Pencils are probably favored because mistakes can be erased—a toeful of erasers is a most welcome Christmas stocking gift for this age.

Given plenty of space, however, Seven enjoys slashing both crayons and paints across large sheets of paper. Teachers find that murals are excellent projects at this age, affording the children an opportunity to work in a group, which they relish.

Large sheets of wrapping paper taped or pasted edge to edge and tacked to a wall, offer enough elbow room for several to work at the same time.

Children who seem young for their age might find pastel chalks appealing. Firm enough for drawing outlines, pastels also offer a chance for "messing around" in the spreading of the colors. Mistakes are easy to rectify since the figures can be rubbed out if the artist is not satisfied—an important point in this hypercritical age. Another drawing material, called Payons, might be tried. The sticks are used like crayons, but the effect of water colors can be created by a judicious wetting of the finished product.

Attitudes and Meanings

When Seven speaks of his own work, he is likely to say something like "I didn't make mine any good." He is in a hurry for results, and quick to reject what does not come up to his demanding standards. Working in a group, he is eager, sociable, expressive, free with advice and criticism. He may keep moving around, as if he must have a finger in every pie. At the same time, he shows by his earnestness and the care with which he chooses his colors that he takes a deep pleasure in his work. He makes comments that indicate his drawing represents an experience that is vivid and real to him. "This guy's running to get to third base," he may say, "and the ball is coming faster than he is. He's gonna be out—" Or, "Colors are nice, aren't they? This pink looks pretty next to the blue."

Absorbed in his work, a little tense about getting just the effect he wants, Seven may be touchy about sharing his materials. However, he is not averse to swapping, even if he will not lend.

Particularly at this age, when the individual is competing so hard in the group, solitary sessions with paint or clay may have special value. In the company of their fellows, Sevens seem almost to repress their individuality. Each seems to be trying to speak a common idiom—to draw and paint themes that the others will recognize, in a manner they will approve. In private, however, the artist may give more of his own individuality— assuming that the parent does not goad him toward perfection.

Clay, Collages, and Constructs

Seven, the self-critical, welcomes and needs a chance to relax from his own exacting standards; in working with clay he finds it. In modeling, more than in painting or drawing, we find the first hints of the wide individual differences that children show increasingly as they grow older. Subjects now range from animals to houses to decorative tiles. In one small group we found a swan, a cliff dwelling, a face, an ashtray, an alligator, and an Empire State Building. Generally, there seems to be less interest in making objects for use than at six, and much more in producing a piece of work for its own sake.

One teacher suggests that some seven-year-olds are ready to learn the coil method of making pottery. They can also learn to make small figures from one piece of clay instead of forming them out of separate pieces stuck together. In the one-piece method, the head is pinched out at one end of a clay cylinder, arms are cut and spread from the sides, and legs and feet are produced by splitting and shaping the lower end of the cylinder. If tools and the use of *slip* (see page 120) have been introduced earlier, the child will have enough technique to produce many different objects and figures.

But clay is only one of the three-dimensional art materials available to this age. Papier-mâché can be tried—admittedly messy, but lots of fun. And we must not neglect collages and constructs.

Victor D'Amico, director of the children's educational section of the Museum of Modern Art, in New York City, speaks of "feeling pictures" "seeing pictures" and "space designs." The first two are made by pasting various materials and objects on a background sheet of paper, wood, or metal. The last is built up of a variety of things that bend, have interesting shapes, or are just fun to look at or through when suspended in the air. Since all of these may be abstract in design, they offer another haven from unattainable standards of realism.

For "feeling pictures" any kind of material with a distinctive texture may be used. Mr. D'Amico suggests rough cloth (burlap or wool), smooth or slippery materials (glazed paper, satin), corrugated cardboard, feathers, cotton, sandpaper, steel wool.

The child will enjoy adding others from household supplies—bits of sponge, fur, pipe cleaners, Turkish toweling, yarn, metallic coils from dishwashing aids, bristles from old toothbrushes, etc. These are mounted on a backing so that they present an interesting succession of "feels" as one runs one's fingers over the surface. Since no standards exist for "feeling pictures," Seven can be quite comfortable about anything he produces.

Collages are somewhat similar but are made for eye appeal rather than touch. They are usually abstract designs constructed from such materials as bits of shiny or dull cloth, tinfoil, pieces of mirror, patterned gift wrappings or wallpapers, colored string, colored cellophane, lace, mosquito netting, all kinds of sheer materials, bits of bark, pebbles, shells, seeds, feathers, etc. Whole families can have fun constructing collages, and as there is no "right" way to make them, so also there is no "wrong" way.

Space designs may appeal to Seven most of all, because he is becoming aware of spatial relationships of many kinds. These are built on a base of clay, cardboard, wallboard, wood, or a flat box. All of the materials we have already mentioned may be used for them, and in addition, some of the following: wire of different thicknesses, rubber bands, tinsel, old movie film, cellophane drinking straws, tongue depressors, toothpicks (plain and colored), dowel sticks, drink stirrers, bright plastic spoons, corks of different sizes, bottle caps, Christmas tree ornaments, bright buttons, bits of costume jewelry. The idea is to produce three-dimensional designs that stand free, with or without parts that can move.

The following tools will be found helpful for all these constructions: scissors, paper punch, stapler, paper clips, wire cutters, pins, Scotch tape, and glue or paste.

Handwork Is a Hobby

If finding a place for himself with his age-mates is the seven-year old's main business, handwork is his hobby. He turns to it with eagerness, because it is familiar and rewarding in a very tangible way. He now has some control over his tools, and finds the rhythm of their use enjoyable. Both boys and girls find the simple repetitive movements of sawing and hammering pleasant, especially if they result in something appealing to the imagination.

Seven has no time for elaborate plans. He loves to *invent*. Meccano sets, ends of wire, gears from old clocks, and nuts that won't fit anything are his raw materials. With these he creates weird and wonderful contraptions that won't do anything, but are impressive to behold. (There was a seven-year-old who made such a "thing" for his father's Christmas. The daddy expressed wonder and gratitude. Finally the little boy said, "But, daddy, what *is* it?")

Because Seven is in a hurry for results, he may not produce the best workmanship of which he is capable. Children who are overconfident can profit from a gently worded suggestion for improvement, but others, especially those who are quick to run down their own work, do better with encouragement and an accent on the positive.

The range in the quality of handwork at seven is enormous. Some children are good with words but clumsy with their hands. For these, even a crude product represents a great deal of effort and should be treated as a real achievement.

A junk box is a good source of ideas. This is the place for flashlights that no longer work, bits of rubber tubing, worn-out washers, empty spools, hubcaps, pulleys, old clotheslines, clothespins of various kinds, discarded doorknobs, drawer pulls, etc.

Tools

For youngsters a hang-up place is bettter than a toolbox. Hooks in a wall are good; a pegboard hang-up is positively fascinating. It is as easy for the child to hang up a tool when he is finished with it as it is to throw it into a toolbox, and edges are better preserved. Besides, exposed storage makes for a proud array rather than a concealed mess.

At seven a child can saw soft wood and nail pieces of it one upon another. He probably cannot saw along a line. He may plane sporadically, but for smoothing, not for fitting. He can sandpaper, but not for long, for it is not exciting. In addition to the tools and materials suggested for five- and six-year-olds, Seven would relish shingle nails and brads. (The brads, driven in a quarter-inch, have a dozen uses that every seven-year-old knows.) The family hammer is too heavy for him. The family saw is too big, and will become dull for you, besides losing its set. If there is a family block plane, let him use it with permission, but *not* chisels or drawknives. Permitting him to use some of the family tools once in a while puts a premium on special jobs and shows him that he belongs to the group, too.

Myth, Magic and Messes

One of the startling and delightfully perverse characteristics of Seven is his interest in magic. Just as we begin to think of him as a prosaic, down-to-earth citizen who wants only what he can see and test, he brings us up short. Magic tricks fascinate him; stories of spacemen enthrall him. The myth of Santa Claus is now scorned, but creatures of other planets are accepted with sober wonder.

Seven enjoys trickery as a debunker. He wants to master tricks to fool others, and he likes to be "in the know." His attitude is that of the experimental realist. Electricity and chemistry suggest tremendous possibilities, half magic, half real. He becomes an alchemist in the kitchen and concocts mixtures of flour and water, oil, sugar, glue, bits of food, and calls these messes "poison" or earnestly assures one that they have mystic properties. These culinary exercises give him a feeling of control in a world whose complexity is becoming daily more apparent to him.

Children of seven (and sometimes six and eight) often like to work their fingers through material softer than clay. Sand, dirt, and mud are of course the answer for those who have back yards. Sawdust or soapflakes are good possibilities in an apartment, if they can be used on a table with an edge around it, or otherwise kept within bounds. This sort of material can be taken up with a vacuum cleaner without much trouble.

The Feminine Angle

In addition to many of those enjoyed by their brothers, girls have special interests. If boys "invent," girls "design." They create costumes for their paper dolls. Weaving is easier than it was at six; bedcovers for dolls, carpets for the doll house, belts for themselves come increasingly from their looms.

Looms which they make themselves are especially dear to them. A frame loom for mats and bags requires only four strips of wood, a few nails, and cotter pins. Simple directions for making several other types can be obtained from the sources listed at the back of this book.

Box-head puppets are good "do together" projects for mothers and daughters. The child can make the head with very little help, requiring the adult's services only for the fine points of fitting and fastening the dress to the head.

To make such a puppet, cover a small empty box, about the size of a cough-drop box, with flesh-colored paper, and glue on yarn or crepe paper cut in strips for hair. Features can be drawn or painted on, or made of bits of felt or contrasting paper, glued on. A piece of cloth about nine by eighteen inches makes the dress. One seam, a hem bottom and top, and a gathering string run through the top hem, gives the basic form. One end of the box is left open for the child's middle fingers; that end is then slipped inside the top of the dress, the string is drawn tightly, and the dress is sewed to the bottom of the box. A bit of trimming covers the raw edge, and a crepe paper hat may be added to the hair. Slits cut near the top of the dress allow the puppeteer's thumb and little finger to act as the puppet's hands.

The seven-year-old girl is no more a natural sewer than she was at five. When she does want to sew, she is not interested in making fine seams. She may want to make a dress for her doll, or, better yet, something that her mother can use. She can make a skirt for a large doll, or a peaked hat, if the material is cut out for her and she is told which edges to sew together. Whatever she makes should be large enough to be handled easily, and should not involve fine matching of edges or small stitches. Most commercial sewing sets are unsuitable for this age because they usually require too small stitches and offer too little material for a firm hold.

Nature Supplies the Handicrafter

We are all familiar with the daisy chains and burr-baskets of childhood. Most of us, however, overlook the abundance of other raw materials for handicrafts that nature provides.

Two pine cones of unequal size, a pair of pipe cleaners, and a small feather can create a charming small bird. Thin sheets of birch bark (*found,* not stripped from a living tree, of course) can be made into all sorts of small containers by over-edge sewing with string or raffia. A small section of a birch log, with a hole drilled part way through, makes an attractive candleholder.

Stringing materials of many kinds can be found in woods and fields. A tiny steel drill for boring holes will convert pumpkin, squash, and watermelon seeds into beads. Acorns, small seedpods, and small cones are also good candidates for this treatment.

Shells of all shapes and sizes can be glued or bonded together to become candleholders, tidbit dishes, tiny boats, flowers, and even—with the aid of ambroid cement and some pipe cleaners—small figures for the doll house or doll collection.

Crushed oak galls can be used to make magic ink. Placed with an equal amount of crystallized ferrous sulphate in a cup of water, one or two will produce a kind of ink in an hour or two. This is almost invisible at first, but turns black as air and light work on it.

Trips to look for handwork materials are incidentally excellent introductions to nature study. Seven is interested because he is looking for something that will be useful to him. At the same time, his attention is subtly directed to the infinite variety of shape and pattern the natural world presents; his curiosity can be titillated by bits of information about the why and how of eye-catching phenomena like fungi, and his own urge to investigate will do the rest.

Collections and Such

Hobby handicrafts and trips for nature materials can feed right into Seven's mania for collecting. What began formlessly at six continues and expands at seven. Quantity is still important, but there is now less miscellaneous collecting. Little girls especially love tiny glass and china animals, tea sets, boxes, and figurines, while boys go in for soldiers, small frontier figures, different types of airplanes, cars, or ships.

Though collections can be very messy, they are exceedingly dear to their owners. We can help the child, and ourselves, by suggesting orderly ways of storing and exhibiting beloved objects. Coin folders are available for coins ranging from pennies to silver dollars. Candy boxes and shoe boxes make useful storage units for trading cards. Ordinary magazines will keep paper dolls and their equipment from getting battered—simply place the dolls between the pages of the magazine. Transparent refrigerator dishes permit miniatures to be seen without getting dusty. An old set of bookshelves can be converted into a display cabinet by the addition of a wooden frame, to which a sheet of clear pliofilm is tacked. The frame can be attached to one side of the bookcase with hinges, and fastened to the other with a hook and eye to form a door. Large scrapbooks help keep pictures of dogs or horses, also popular items, under control.

Puzzles and Games

Although jigsaw puzzles are not so appealing as they once were, Seven still finds them fun. He approaches them more systematically than he would have at five or six, looking for clues in continuing patterns and matching colors. He does best with subject matter that is familiar to him. Puzzles that are too tricky soon make him fidgety, but on the other hand he quickly loses interest if the pieces are too big and "babyish." When he's through, it's worthwhile helping him collect all the pieces in a box with a tight-fitting cover—there's nothing more exasperating than to find next time that pieces are missing.

As soon as the child can easily recognize numbers through thirteen, he is ready for a dozen different card games. The simpler types of rummy are played with zest. *Menagerie, I Doubt It, War, Hearts, My Ship Sails, Round the Clock, Down the Stairs* are others that the seven-year-old can learn. Directions for all of these are given in *50 Card Games for Children*, mentioned in chapter 7. Games at seven are more peaceful than they were at six, because the child can understand the meaning of rules somewhat better, and is a more graceful loser.

The repertory of table games can also be expanded. Some Sevens learn to play checkers. If they are not overmatched they can manage trading games like *Monopoly;* each year brings out several simpler versions designed for children rather than adults. Bingo and dominoes continue to be useful games to have on hand.

Magnetic games are fun, and they come in many forms, from magnetic pick-up sticks through the dart game described in an earlier chapter, to small pairs of magnetized figures that affect each other in various ways, depending on how they are manipulated.

Even a piece of colored string can keep Seven occupied for a surprisingly long time. Dropped from a height onto a solidly colored background, it falls into shapes which he enjoys naming and completing. With the help of a few bits of colored felt or paper, he can make cartoon faces and weird animals out of this twisting line. Used to play cat's cradle, it gives him a chance to demonstrate his dexterity. *Fun with String,* by Joseph Leeming, describes a few of the simpler string figures and tricks that the child can do by himself. He will need help at the beginning in following directions, but once he has caught on, he will be able to perfect his performance himself, and will go on to invent his own.

Crayons and coloring books are still liked and the pictures can be quite complex. For variety, letter and number push-out-and-paste sets, or reading and spelling puzzles can supplement the coloring materials.

Parties and Holidays

Is any day more important than one's birthday? Certainly not at seven. Every other festive occasion must be shared—only the birthday is exclusive property. It gives the seven-year-old status in his own eyes, and can be used to promote his importance among his age-mates.

The time when a birthday was a family celebration is past. Now it is the child's day, and he looks forward to it, counting the months, sighing, "It's awfully long till your next birthday." Invitations to a party at seven can be a medium of exchange—or a bribe. The five-year-old invited "best friends"; Six wanted the whole class or the whole neighborhood included; Seven is canny. A party invitation can help him gain the favor of a popular child in his class; withholding it can be used to get even with someone who excluded him.

However chosen, the guest list should be short: ten second-graders can get out of hand very rapidly. One must be prepared for clowning, nonsense and noise—Sevens are often having the best kind of times when they are at their silliest. But silliness deteriorates into wild, almost eccentric behavior unless the party is given form and organization.

To keep the occasion happy, the tone should be set as soon as the first guest arrives. A make-it-yourself bar for party hats provides a focus for attention and something to keep each one busy until all have arrived. Supplies might include crepe paper or shiny coated paper in bright colors, gummed stars, strips, and the like for decorations, odd flowers and feathers from old hats, Scotch tape, a stapler, and yarn or thin elastic to hold the finished hats on. Girls would enjoy the additional luxuries of tinsel, sequins, veiling, and crepe paper for matching aprons, sashes, or big, artificial flowers. Prizes might be given for prettiest, funniest, most original, and so forth.

Active stunts and quiet games should alternate for the body of the entertainment. Team stunts are excellent for keeping Seven within bounds while he is letting off steam. Balloon kick and stick wrestle are fun for boys or girls. (Directions for these and many other games are in the *Handbook for Recreational Leaders*, already mentioned.) Quiet games might include contests to see who can draw the funniest face, paper and pencil games like Dots and Lines or Humbug, or stunts which are arranged ahead of time, like "mind reading" or "thumb choice." Dumb Crambo and This Is My Nose are usually hilariously successful, and involve the whole group while confining it to a relatively small space.

Favors may be placed at each table setting or taken from a grab bag. All prizes and favors should be equally attractive and appear to be of equal value. Small packages of trading cards, mechanical pencils, false mustaches or noses, magic tricks, compasses, small pads of paper in different colors are all welcome. Girls also like toy jewelry, accessories for doll houses, toy compacts and make-up kits, small bottles of toilet water, bubble bath, beads and charms to make ornaments for their dolls.

Parties run most smoothly if all contests and stunts come before the refreshments, and if the young guests depart immediately after. Cake and ice cream, with something festive to drink, are the simplest and most satisfying fillers. Providing paper bags for carrying off the favors and prizes helps wind up the party with dispatch.

There seems to be no limit to the ways in which Seven can contribute to traditional holiday celebrations during the year. Girls and boys both love to help bake and decorate cakes and cookies.

Valentine's Day may call for really big doings. A supply of red construction paper, paper doilies, white paper for the message, and one is all set. A simple and satisfactory form of Valentine consists of a rectangular piece of red paper, folded in the middle like a book, with a somewhat smaller piece of white paper of the same shape folded inside it and stapled down the middle. The message is written on the white paper, with crayoned hearts as decoration. A bit of the lace border from a paper doily ornaments the red cover for an air of elegance. Seven can perform all the operations involved in this without help. Another simple and effective Valentine consists of a red heart attached to a lace paper doily. Any Valentine which is to have a message written on it should be large enough to accommodate Seven's large and erratic printing.

Mother's Day and Father's Day are extremely important to many a seven-year-old, as are the parents' birthdays. These are times for "secrets" (which always appeal to Seven), for a delightful feeling of being in on something special, for creating new bonds between the partners in plotting. In addition, these occasions give Johnny and Mary a chance to make some return for all the love they have received. Children need such opportunities: their dawning sense of fair play is reinforced if they can tender a visible symbol of their love to the people who are always giving them things.

Fathers and Sons

Seven is the year when Pop takes over. We noted portents of this development at six; now it comes to full flowering.

Johnny wants to go on long walks with his father, without any "women" around. They talk about masculine affairs—how bridges are built and tunnels dug, how coal is gotten out of the ground, and which baseball team will win the pennant. The family car forms a bond between them; the mysteries of defective spark plugs, the need for oiling and other attentions form the basis of many conversations.

Seven has enough stamina to go along on a not very strenuous camping trip; to join in an afternoon of fishing. Some communities offer special father-son activities—church dinners, school athletic events, open school day for fathers. In large cities, families may have to create their own men-of-the-family doings. Baseball games, boat and auto shows, shopping for sports and hobby equipment are some of the opportunities for Father to show Seven that he is a welcome member of masculine society.

Older brothers come in for more attention. Pests to Seven before, they become assets now. If they are successful in their own group adjustments, they are looked up to as guides and mentors. Seven may want to trail along when Ten goes out to play with his team; if he is allowed to serve the older boys as batboy, for example, he is happy.

Mothers and sisters may be treated with condescension by the male Seven. There is nothing personal in this; it is only his way of emphasizing that he is not a sissy. Up to this point, his mother has been his main source of comfort and support; it is not easy for him to give her up. Because it is difficult, and because he is afraid to show how much she means to him, his reaction may be overdone. An easy, good-humored acceptance of the boy's bid for his place as a male soon restores his equilibrium and helps him see that he does not have to hate women to be a man.

Daughters and Fathers

Johnny may temporarily turn his back on Mom; Dad gets no such treatment from Jane. Often tomboyish, she appreciates his interest in skating or swimming, and is not above coaxing him to a bit of batting practice.

Fathers are very important also in helping a little girl appreciate her own femininity. An occasional invitation to take a walk, serving as a willing audience for her shows, participating regularly as a bedtime reader, a compliment when she is dressed for Sunday School or a party—these things let her know that growing up does not mean losing out. The interested companionship of her father at seven—as at five and at eight—lays the foundation for wholesome and satisfying experiences with other men at seventeen and twenty-seven and all the sevens thereafter.

All Together

Near the end of dinner at the Tilsett home, Dad takes a firm grip on his coffee cup, anticipating the whirlwind, composed of Danny, nine, and Helen, seven, which will sweep the table clear with the last gulp of dessert. Most days, Dad obligingly lifts his cup and saucer so that the cloth can be removed from under it, and the cards or games brought out while he finishes his leisurely sipping. It's family game time at the Tilsetts'.

Dominoes, bingo, parcheesi, and lotto are the staples. A simplified version of casino (with no "building"), rummy, Old Maid, I Doubt It, and an occasional hilarious game of Menagerie make up their card fare. Mother, Dad, Danny, and Helen take turns choosing the game of the evening, and seven-thirty is quitting time. Having a set time to end the play takes care of Helen's tendency to insist on playing until she wins.

Since the game hour was instituted, the Tilsetts have no trouble in getting the children to the dinner table promptly. They watch the clock jealously, to be sure that they will not be cheated of a precious minute of playing time. Helen, who used to sulk every time she lost a game is gradually learning that the rules work in her favor as well as for others; the fun of playing is becoming more important to her than winning. Then, too, it is easier to learn a new game at home than with her friends. Parents have more patience with mistakes than playmates, and do not mind stopping to explain a point she missed. It is much easier to introduce a game to her group after she has become sure of it in the comfortable atmosphere of the family.

Family good times pay big dividends all along the line, but they have a special contribution to make now. Sevens are essentially serious children. So much of their playtime is actually devoted to work—the perfecting of skills, the anxious mending of social fences—that at this point the light touch relaxes the child and reminds him that pure pleasure is as much a part of life as rivalry and achievement. Then too, at this time of intensive life with the gang, when Seven sometimes acts as if all adults were his enemy, it is good to know that those rebellions which are a necessary part of growing up are not held against him—that though this is a year of breaking away, Seven is still very much part of his home and all that goes on in it.

CHAPTER IX

Eight and Nine

EIGHTS AND NINES are like Sevens, only more so. They want to rebel, but they want to belong. They want to make rules, but they want to break them. They are even more full of paradoxes. On occasion they can be even fresher. Eights and Nines become so absorbed in new exciting activities that the ordinary routines of life are often forgotten. They may wear watches but be oblivious of time. They seem to use every conceivable means of asserting themselves and denying their heritage: slang (or worse), back-talk, ridicule of family patterns, sloppy clothes and manners.

But look a little closer, and you will see that these youngsters, for all their bravado, are not nearly ready to navigate on their own. They want to break loose from the home, but they fall right into the hands of another family: the small-boy gang. The clothes they wear are the gang's clothes, the language is the gang's, the daring they display is the gang's and not their own. Don's clubhouse in a tree is actually a home away from home, for in it he finds the safety of a group that accepts him for what he is. He belongs. But it is also something beyond the home, and a real taste of the world at large. For to remain a member in good standing he must constantly prove his worth by competing with others and conforming to the code of the group. Many of the values he meets have never been stressed at home: physical strength, agility, daring, ingenuity, comradeship. But they are worthy values, too, and the kind that help the boy become a man.

Often parents look askance at these small-boy gangs and small-girl cliques. They say, "But why do they have to be so mysterious?" "Why do they spend so much time just sitting around talking?" "Why do they take up with tough kids?" "Can't they find other kinds of play?"

The secrecy of the gang is a major part of the fun, and a reflection of these children's needs. They are trying their hand at forming a society of their own and secrecy is their gesture toward privacy and individuality. It is also a protective device, for they are self-conscious in taking this new step, and perhaps a bit ashamed to admit that there really isn't much to tell. Secrecy is dramatic, too, and a challenge to parents to trust them and have faith that they can handle themselves on their own.

As for "sitting around talking," here, too, there is something positive. In bickering or just idle chatting, these young boys and girls are testing their ideas on others. They are getting grievances out of their systems. They—the more mature Eights and Nines—are sharing their doubts and worries. They are learning how other families live and meet their problems. But they are also learning the technique of carrying on a conversation and preparing themselves for the highly social world in which they are going to live. Here is proof that play does not have to be active to be productive.

And what about those tough kids? One or two in a gang will not spell doom for our children. In fact, it is important for them to learn to hold their own with all kinds of people. In some instances, too, they may be a healthy antidote to over-cautiousness instilled by anxious parents. Moreover, the toughness may only be a rough exterior, and when you get to know the boy or possibly girl in question, you probably will understand why your youngster insists that he or she is a "good kid."

Ways and Means

All parents of these growing children have a right, and a responsibility, to become acquainted with their friends. One sure-fire way is to let the gang come in for snacks every now and then, particularly on cold or rainy days. But there are other ways to help them get more out of group play. We can provide them with an indoor meeting place in the cellar or attic, and give them a hand in planning it and cleaning up. (In return, we will probably get some shelves or a closet made of old lumber.)

Let's be on the lookout for the kind of play materials they are likely to want. Boys can always use old shingles, tarpaper, or bricks for their hideaway. They are likely to want stray pieces of wire for a telegraph system, or sheet metal for an armored tank they are making. Girls (whose "gang" may be only one or two close friends), and often boys as well, will be delighted with old furniture to paint or recover, ancient draperies to use as stage curtains, cloth for costumes, bric-a-brac to sell to secondhand shops as a means of swelling their club treasury. Often we are saving these things for some future need; but what better use could there be than creative play?

If we do not have the usual supply of attic treasures, or if we live in an apartment where there is no space to keep things, we might take the gang on a trip to lumber companies, junk dealers, or automobile graveyards on the other side of town. The girls, too, will enjoy an excursion in search of materials—perhaps to outlet stores for remnants or to factories for rejects.

Boys and girls of eight and nine, however, need more than the mere materials for play. In spite of their urge for independence, they are frequently unable to turn these materials into successful products. The tree house—if it is ever finished—falls apart; the complicated doll house won't stick together; the ship won't float. They are constantly overreaching themselves, since they still lack basic knowledge and skills. On the whole this experience is a healthy one, since in revealing their limitations it also indicates what they must learn. But it indicates, too, that these youngsters need the guidance and help of adults. Therefore, one of the best ways for parents to maintain contact with them, in spite of their urge to be with the gang, is to show them how to do things and how to get things. This is the time for parent and child to develop a special project—one too ambitious for the child to carry out alone, and at the same time rewarding for the mother or father. To suggest a few: experiments with raising plants in water (hydroponics), turning a wagon into a "sports car," repairing toys to be sent to hospitals, fixing up the home workshop.

The Collections Continue

The great majority of Eights and Nines have a collection of one sort or another: stamps, coins, postcards, stones, butterflies, bottle caps, shells, dolls, or models of old cars. Often two or three of these objects are collected at once, but unlike earlier ages this is usually done because it reflects special interests, and not for the sake of mere accumulation. In one group of third and fourth graders whom we studied, wooden animals, good books, and pictures of dancers were listed as subjects. Such individuality should be encouraged.

Few children at this age have developed their collections into a full-scale or even orderly hobby. The act of collecting is primary; classifying and studying are distinctly secondary and frequently do not enter the picture at all. The suggestions made in chapter 8 for storing and displaying still apply, although Eights and Nines show more ability and patience than Sevens in making showcases and devising exhibits for school or Scout fairs. In most cases, the sheer size of the collection generally means more than its uniqueness or worth. This is especially true of trading cards and comic books, where the fun is almost entirely in haggling or acquiring a complete set.

Organized Play

The organizations that have done most to satisfy the double need of these children—the need for the gang and for guidance—are the Scouts. The Brownies, for girls, start at seven; the Cubs, for boys, begin at eight. The benefits are many. The experience with organized group life helps them learn to act as a team and to adjust themselves to definite regulations and requirements. It focuses many of the energies which were so hard to direct a year ago. The individual and group rewards—feathers, pins, titles—are a powerful incentive to productive play. Parents are drawn into the activities as both spectators and participants, and the Scout leaders provide an opportunity for contact with adults who are neither parents nor teachers. Membership in a large, national organization gives our children perhaps their first taste of a relationship with the wider reaches of society. But most of all, the Scouts give them the kind of group play they want and need most.

A glance at some of the projects of the Cubs and Brownies will not only show what types of activities they pursue, but suggest ideas for groups in Y's, churches, or community centers. Here are a few examples:

A circus, put on by an entire Pack (comprising six Dens of about five boys each), with the aid of the Den Mother. Each Den is responsible for one act: clowns, acrobatics, chariot race with soapbox cars, wild animals, etc.

A television variety show, in which one group constructs a mock camera and set, while others present various acts "written, directed, and produced" by the boys or girls.

A pet show, given by a Brownie group, in which every pet (toad, snake, mongrel, lizard) is on an equal footing with every other one. Features are a turtle race, trained animal acts, an exhibit of the proper food for each kind of pet.

Crafts exhibits, with booths constructed by the youngsters out of rough lumber and covered with kraft paper or burlap. Exhibits might include not only finished work but demonstrations of whittling, weaving, plasterwork, mask-making, with the children explaining how the work is done.

A trip to the moon, with appropriate space gear, and as a climax the discovery that Cubs or Brownies are there, too!

A transportation exhibit, showing the transportation methods of many periods.

A classroom scene, with children as teachers.

A mock Scout meeting, in which the parents are Cubs or Brownies and the children are parents. The parent Scouts, of course, behave very badly.

Stunts, Tricks, Experiments

Though organized activities have high value, it is a mistake to make all the child's experiences into major enterprises. The sporadic, transient interests are also important. For instance, Eights and Nines love stunts of all sorts. The cruder kinds of magic intrigue them—tricks that bring as much laughter as mystification. Many that they could not do at seven, they can now perform handily. They like to jump spoons into a glass, balance a cork on a pin by sticking two forks into it, do mirror-drawing, make shadow figures on the wall. Match tricks, wire puzzles, and blocks puzzles are equally fascinating, and with a little encouragement children will sometimes devise their own.

At seven the interest in facts—especially scientific facts—began. Now it has become a hunger. Some children are more interested in science during the middle years than they ever will be again. It is worth making something of, for they learn much about the world and how it is put together. It is an ideal age for table-top physics and kitchen chemistry. Of course the science they like best is the kind that "does something." They are ecstatic when the sodium bicarbonate solution turns blue as the vinegar is added. They want little theory and plenty of results.

Good suggestions and clear instructions can be found in a number of books, such as the Scout manuals, *Fun with Chemistry* by Mae and Ira Freeman and *Experiments in Science* by Nelson F. Beeler and Franklyn M. Branley. Usually, help will be needed both in obtaining materials and in following the directions. We must remember that even the most routine operations, such as twisting a wire around a screw, are new to the child and require patient explanation and repeated practice.

Beginning at eight, practically any youngster will become absorbed in such demonstrations as the following:

Making rain by allowing the steam from a kettle to condense inside a glass held over the spout.

Proving that air is a thing by stuffing a handkerchief into the bottom of a glass, and plunging it upside down into water. The handkerchief will remain dry because of the layer of air between it and the water.

Showing how a compass works by rubbing a needle on a magnet, then putting a little oil on it and floating it in water. The needle will point north.

Although the child is not ready for complex explanations, practical facts and analogies are within his grasp—for instance, the fact that mist drips down a cold window like rain, or that the earth, its poles affecting a compass needle, acts like a huge magnet. Wherever possible, let him draw the conclusion, and give him plenty of approval when he thinks things out for himself. This is the way to lay the basis for a lifetime interest in science.

In the eight to nine period boys and girls are usually not ready for complicated handicrafts or fully developed hobbies. Rather, it is a time of self-discovery, a time to explore new materials and new processes. As one example, the world of electricity is opening up, and boys (and girls, too) are ready to learn the rudiments of wiring and following a diagram. They soon learn to make a crude electromagnet, and to attach signal devices and other accessories to an electric train. And nothing is more thrilling, in these days of ready-made appliances, than for a youngster to build a crystal set and make it work. Fathers who made these sets in the early days of broadcasting will find a special satisfaction in reliving their own first experiences with radio.

Something Out of Nothing

The number and variety of things to make is virtually endless. Some are utilitarian, others purely decorative. A toothbrush, a piece of screen, some water colors, a stencil of the right design, and drawing paper are all that Eights need for spatter printing. (Place the stencil on the paper, hold the screen over it, dip the brush lightly into the paint, and draw it gently across the screen.) Those serpentine coils you throw at carnivals can be rewound in various colors, varnished or lacquered, and made into waterproof coasters. When combined with pipe cleaners and bits of colored paper, wooden spools of all sizes become a whole menagerie of amusing animals. The lowly potato can nourish the soul as well as the body, for artistic caricatures of people or animals can be made of potatoes dressed up with bits of cloth, using toothpicks for arms and legs—and when potatoes are cut in half, a simple relief carved on the flat surface, and ink or paint applied, they can provide our youngsters with their first experience in block printing. Ordinary milk cartons, when carefully cut and glued, become bridges, railroad cars, barges, and buildings. Even dried corn husks have their use; they can be split into lengths and woven into mats and sandals, or fashioned into imaginative dolls. And of course tin cans have innumerable possibilities. When punched with holes, in interesting designs, they become ornamental lanterns; when flattened out, they can be cut and shaped into animal figurines, costume jewelry, small trays.

The creative play of Eights and Nines will be greatly enhanced if we take the time to show them the basic techniques and operations they will need in making things—how to open a knife and use it safely, how a cotter pin works, what types of knots are best for different purposes, how to saw wood rather than fingers, how to handle tin without getting cut. The manufacturing ability of these children has grown in the last year or two. Instead of merely nailing one piece of wood on another, they can now, with little direction, make objects that require some fashioning: bread boards, key racks, book ends, bird feeders. These will be produced with much love and some care. Eight still can't do much fitting, and his planing is sporadic, but he *will* use sandpaper. If someone will help him paint or stain the finished job, he will be in seventh heaven. If he is making an ambitious boat, let him try a spokeshave and even a gouge. If he uses his hands well, there are many things he can cut out of plywood (still using a coping saw: an electric jigsaw will be dangerous for a good while to come). Show him how to draw his own animals and other figures on the wood (or how to trace them from a magazine), then saw them out and paint them.

Sports and Nature

Outdoor sports of Eights and Nines are primarily of the large-muscle, rough-and-tumble variety. As a rule, they are not ready for games that require extreme control and precision, such as tennis and golf, and they still cannot be expected to grasp the finer points of baseball and basketball (although much depends on the school coach or the father's interest in these games). They revel in hopscotch, bicycling, roller skating, kite-flying, rock-climbing. In Scout groups, they enjoy marching and simple formations, such as Indian rituals. Wrestling in all its forms appeals to most boys: hand wrestling, pole wrestling (wresting a stick from the opponent), mat wrestling. The body-to-body contact of wrestling gives them an opportunity to feel their growing strength and measure themselves against others. It also helps them drain off energy that might otherwise seek an outlet in pure restlessness or destructive pursuits.

During this period our children may, with encouragement, achieve a fuller appreciation of the great outdoors. They have the endurance required for hiking and climbing, but they also like to wander aimlessly in the woods or sit idly on the bank of a stream. Every child, from the city as well as the country, should have an ample opportunity for both the energetic and the more passive approaches to nature. So, too, they should have a chance to learn the lore of nature while they are coming into direct contact with it—why lichens grow on only one side of a tree, how squirrels help to replenish our forests, which bears hibernate and which do not. They will be eager to learn how to make and control a fire, what the various trail signs mean, how to use a compass and read directions from the stars. Parents, Scout leaders, and teachers must be ready to answer their myriad questions, or help them find the answers for themselves.

At this age, a picnic is still the acme of fun, whether it is in the back yard or deep in the woods. But now the children will want to build the fireplace and fire by themselves and play active games after the meal is over. This means that parents won't get much chance to sleep in the shade—at least until after they have hunted for buried treasure, stalked wild game, or followed an Indian trail with piled stones as markers.

There are many ways to make a child's discoveries in nature meaningful. As always let's watch for the signs of budding interests, and be ready with the help that is needed. Does the child ask how the weatherman knows it is going to rain? Let's have on hand, or get, a picture-book on clouds and wind and atmosphere. Do they ask about the sun and the stars? Let's get a chart of the sky at the different seasons, and a book of ancient legends that will tell about Cassandra and Orion and Sirius. Let's take them to a dairy farm, a plant nursery, a fish hatchery, a planetarium if there is one within a hundred miles. Let's see that they have good books on mountains, wild flowers, trees, animals. When they come to us for subjects for stories or poems at school, let's suggest that they draw on this wealth of nature lore.

But most of all, we need to encourage a fuller contact with nature itself. Collections of leaves, rocks, and insects will help.

Homemade scrapbooks and exhibit cases or shelves will be needed. (It's still too early to worry too much about our child's messy room.) And if the child has that urge, which comes to so many, to sleep outdoors, we can usually satisfy it by letting him share an army pup tent with a friend, right in our own back yard. If an inexpensive tent cannot be found, the youngsters will enjoy making one out of sheet plastic. But why stop here? A far better solution would be a real camping trip with Dad or the whole family. This is the kind of experience a child will talk about for months and even years to come.

The World of Books

Eights and Nines have mastered the basic mechanics of reading, and are ready to roam widely in the world of easy books and magazines. The ability to read by themselves is still a fresh experience. The power of the printed word to evoke images and fantasies still has a magical quality. Their wide-eyed curiosity makes reading an exciting experience—but an experience that must be *kept* alive and exciting in the face of competing interests.

This is an age of stories. Both boys and girls delight in legends and folk tales of many kinds: stories of American Indians, people from other lands, and such classics as *Aesop's Fables, Rip Van Winkle* and *Pinocchio*. Frequently they want to read for themselves the fairy tales they have only heard—but just as frequently they will look upon them scornfully as "kid stuff." However, animal tales are still fascinating, particularly the kind that throw some indirect light on humans: the adventures of a trained seal or a clever rabbit. They love the nonsense and slapstick in these stories, and will perhaps imitate the antics of the animals for hours on end.

But in this period of discovery, our youngsters are reaching out for life as well as laughter. They are becoming more aware of themselves, more concerned about what is right and what is wrong. The search for models and standards for their own lives is beginning, and its natural consequence is an intense interest in biography. They love to roam Kentucky with Daniel Boone, harness lightning with Ben Franklin, entertain guests in the

White House with Dolly Madison. And their imaginations are fed by heroines and heroes of more recent times: Florence Nightingale, Edith Cavell, Charles Lindbergh.

Finally, our Eights and Nines come right down to earth in their reading interests. They want stories about everyday people in everyday situations—farm stories, and stories about offices and factories, military service and circus life; how the nurse's aid, the bus-driver, and the tunnel-digger do their jobs; how ordinary folk live and dress and work in other countries. We must not make the mistake of demanding that all their reading be "literature," and all literature an escape into imaginary worlds. These vital boys and girls appreciate facts. To keep them reading, we must provide them with books that satisfy their healthy curiosity about real people and real events.

During the eighth and ninth years, reading rarely reaches its peak. Rather, it is the first great period of discovery, when the door to the world of the printed page is just swinging open. Don't be worried, incidentally, if that door swings back and forth a bit. If we want our children to step across the threshold, we must make sure that this world is presented in its most appealing light. This is the time to confirm the pattern of going to books for information, for inspiration, and especially for enjoyment. The interests of Eights and Nines have not settled into a groove, and their lives, though busy, are not so full as they will be later, when team sports, clubs, homework, and other activities occupy so many of their out-of-school hours. Here, then, are a few pointers that may keep us from missing the bus at this crucial period:

1. Help them find books that are easy to read in language, content, and print, and liberally sprinkled with attractive illustrations. Antiquated or specialized language and unrelieved pages of type discourage many young readers.

2. Help them establish a personal relation with their books. They will now certainly want a bookcase of their own if they haven't had one before, and their own name-plates in their books (the name-plates preferably of their own design—making these can be an absorbing project in itself). When books have to be weeded out for lack of space, let the children choose the ones to keep, even though the choices may seem unreasonable to you.

3. If they are particularly delighted with a book, help them find others along the same line, or by the same author. At the same time, make it easy for them to sample the many kinds of books that generally appeal to Eights and Nines.

4. Give books as presents on birthdays and holidays, but don't limit book-buying to these times. Bring home twenty-five-cent editions from the drugstore or supermarket, and suggest that your children look over the racks when they go with you. Maintain a balance between the cheaper and better editions.

5. Encourage your children to visit the library regularly, not just when someone happens to think of it. Get to know the children's room and the librarian in charge. Go with your children once in a while to help with selection.

6. Suggest exchanging books with friends and if possible start a book exchange at school. A P.T.A. meeting on children's books, and a book fair, will add to your own interest and information, and through you, to your children's.

7. Bring books and reading into the conversation at home. Talk about your own reading as well as your children's. Listen with both ears when they tell you the stories they've been reading, and give them your help and approval if they want to dress up like the characters or act out the story.

8. Remember that the reading habit is encouraged not only by books of high literary value, but by looking things up in understandable encyclopedias, atlases, and books on birds and flowers, as well as by the better children's magazines.

The Easy Media

During the period from eight to nine, the average youngster devotes many hours per week to radio, television, motion pictures, and comic books. The reasons are clear enough: they offer the kind of material these children can enjoy, in ways they can understand. Intricate plots, subtle characterization, delicate shading are still beyond them. They are looking for clarity, dramatic impact, colorful action—and they can have these merely by twisting a dial or spending a few cents of their allowance.

The tastes of boys and girls, which once were quite similar, are beginning to diverge. More boys than girls revel in heroic exploits, racket-busting, and slapstick humor. Tarzan, Dick Tracy, Captain Video, Abbott and Costello are especially appealing types. The girls, on the other hand, turn more often to husband-and-wife comedy, films of the *Red Shoes* or *Black Beauty* variety, and musical comedies or variety shows. The romantic songs and scenes in these productions appeal to girls while the comedians appeal to their brothers. Yet there is still a large common ground of interest as well. Many family stories and shows attract both sexes, many westerns, tuneful fantasies like *Hans Christian Andersen,* situation comedies such as Jackie Gleason's, and always the comic books and films of the "Little Lulu" and "Donald Duck" variety.

The outstanding characteristic of this period is the fluidity of the child's interests. The world of the mass media, like the world of books, is opening up. The high-pressure MC's have not taken over completely; crime and mystery have not caught hold as yet —at least not a strangle hold. When asked to name their favorites, a gratifyingly high proportion of third and fourth graders include in their lists the more educational radio and television programs and informative adult magazines such as *Life* and *Look*. Frequently, too, children are as interested in enlightening short films as in the main feature at the local movie house. We hope that soon the tawdry second features will be entirely replaced by imaginative and informative shorts.

This is a time for action on the part of parents. We can "explore the air waves" with our children, and explore the newsstands, too, to find the most suitable fare for our children, while still respecting their love of lively action. We can begin to cultivate the idea that comic books are not really books but transient fillers between activities. We can now explain to our children why we won't let them see or hear certain programs or read certain magazines—and be ready with absorbing substitutes. We can be on the constant lookout for budding interests to be fed by books, play projects, creative games—and help the feeding along by our own interest, approval, and encouragement.

The Arts at Eight and Nine

The increase in manipulative skill and co-ordination that generally occurs during the eighth year is reflected not only in the urge to make things that move and work, but also in the desire to translate feelings into form and perceptions into design. Both boys and girls love to draw "just for the fun of it," and the easel which was set up three or four years before can now be used not only for water colors but for casein paint, which gives them the feeling of painting in oils because of its thickness. Finger paint is still a favorite medium. There is rapid growth in the plastic arts: the child can now learn to use plaster of Paris for making both useful and decorative objects, and can try his hand at a copper enameling kit. Even paper takes on new possibilities—for example, for "paper sculpture." To make a human head out of a cylinder of heavy white paper, eyes and mouth are cut out, their outlines are painted, then nose and ears are inserted into slits and brightly colored wool or paper hair is pasted in place.

At this age girls are becoming increasingly interested in costumes (either doll-size or full-size), and that interest is stimulated by their school plays and Girl Scout skits—which are, in turn, frequently inspired by the folk tales they read and the television programs and movies they see. Boys as well as girls like to collect props, build and decorate scenery. Both find dramatic play as absorbing as ever, but now it frequently reflects real situations outside the home or school (accidents, air raids), and such real-life figures as skin-divers and air-stewardesses.

To enliven a party for Eights and Nines, you have only to suggest a song that requires clapping, stamping or shouting—or one that involves gestures and pantomime of almost any sort. As at earlier ages, they like their music active—but now they are ready for a more disciplined approach. Entire folk dances of the simpler variety can be performed. "Bow, Bow, Belinda," enjoyed at seven, grows into the Virginia Reel; and children themselves can act as callers for "Turkey in the Straw" or "Four in a Boat."

But you don't have to wait for a party. Now that the children can read lyrics, and perhaps read music as well, musical fun can become a more exciting part of family life than ever. This is the time to get a good book of folk songs, and have it ready for everyone to "gather round" on a week-day evening or a rainy week end. Songs like "Hi, Betty Martin," "Row, Row, Row Your Boat," and "The Bridge of Avignon" will lure almost any father away from his newspaper.

The urge to play an instrument seems to reach a peak at eight or nine. If our children have had experience with the rhythm instruments we recommended for earlier ages (bells, triangles, drums, etc.), they will probably now want to try the autoharp, ukulele, children's Sousaphone, or toy clarinet. At the same time, we should keep adding to their collection of records. They are now ready for story records of the great composers; more folk music, such as the Burl Ives records; "Hansel and Gretel"; and those excellent introductions to the different instruments, "The Concertina that Crossed the Country" and "Rusty in Orchestraville."

Eight (sometimes nine) is the age when most children are finally ready for piano lessons, and possibly such instruments as the recorder, flute, or even violin. Our job is not merely to keep them playing, but to keep them enjoying it. Success depends on many things. First, our child's readiness for music. If he has had the creative fun with music we have described on preceding pages of this book, he is likely to be interested. However, not all eight-year-olds are mentally ready to understand more advanced music or physically ready to perform it. The first lessons should therefore be considered a trial period, with no blame attached if things don't work out.

The second requirement is the right kind of teacher—someone who not only has the skill, but the ability to instill the joy of music in our particular child, and make learning a pleasure instead of a chore. Modern teachers have discovered many ways to keep the lessons alive and stimulating. They start out with simple tunes and give them an interesting name; they have the child use the left hand as well as the right at the very beginning, so that he can boast of playing "with both hands"; they teach melodies from the great composers so that he can say "I am playing Mozart already"; they tell stories about the pieces and about the composers; they cut down on scales and exercises by carefully choosing pieces that give them the practice they need.

As parents, we have as much responsibility as the teacher for making music lessons fun, and study a form of play. Here are a few cues: Avoid the word *practice* and use *play* or *rehearse* instead. Play duets with your child, if you can. Listen wholeheartedly and approvingly to each new accomplishment. Occasionally have him play his simple melodies while the whole family gathers round and sings. Take him to children's concerts. Don't make him play for your friends and don't force him to play in recitals. Don't insist on having him play when he is tired or distracted by an important ball game or school play. Help him schedule his week so that lessons and practice do not conflict too much with other activities. Encourage him to pick out melodies he hears, and improvise tunes of his own. Above all, if you want your child to play music because he loves it, make yours a musical home—a singing home, a dancing home, a listening home.

Dancing

At eight and nine, boys will have little interest in dancing of any kind except perhaps the gyrations of acrobatic dancers, the swift and noisy movements of tap dancers, or the antics of comedians. These they may try to imitate, ending usually by collapsing on the floor in a hilarious heap. Dancing school at this period would be no better than a stiff and formal affair for them and would be likely to generate lasting distaste, faulty habits, and the jeers of their contemporaries.

With girls, however, it's quite another story. Given the opportunity, many of them will begin to acquire a genuine appreciation of classical ballet, and probably the same girls will appreciate the modern techniques of the Martha Graham type of school. Television will be a source of inspiration to many, and so will the occasional musical comedy that comes to town. However, teachers frequently find that their students try to imitate what they see on the stage and screen and thereby lose their spontaneity.

Eight and nine are ages for girls not merely to appreciate but to learn to execute some of the ballet techniques, although it is too early for them to go on toe. It should be recognized, however, that ballet training is not simple preparation for ballet. Today more and more teachers and artists believe that it is an excellent foundation for modern techniques; it is an interesting fact that Mary Wigman, the originator of the modern approach, now has a classical ballet instructor in her school. Moreover, ballet is also an effective preparation for acrobatic dancing, tap dancing (particularly the Paul Draper variety), and social dancing as well. And its benefits in terms of posture, grace, strength, and health can hardly be estimated.

At these ages—and before, as well—girls will benefit immensely from another approach that borders on the dance. In a growing number of communities, dance teachers and physical education specialists are offering classes in "rhythmic exercises." These exercises are done preferably to piano music (though a tom-tom can also be used) and frequently incorporate some of the techniques of ballet. They are designed to develop control over muscles and to induce the habit of rhythmic movement and good posture. Not the least of the benefits is derived from the fact that the work is done in groups, and the child learns to move and respond with others. The better schools adapt the exercises to the individual needs of children—better posture, development of specific muscles, improvement of balance and co-ordination, and the like. More than that, they do not limit themselves to set exercises, but offer frequent opportunities for free expression and interpretation of musical themes or dramatic situations. For example, the pupils may be asked to act out their own version of an automobile moving cautiously through a fog at night, or the group may imitate an elevator rising from floor to floor, its door opening and closing at each level.

CHAPTER X

Play in the Preteens

PREADOLESCENCE, or the years ten to twelve, has been called the most neglected period in our youngsters' lives. Both parents and psychologists tend to focus their attention on the more dramatic and crucial stages in development, particularly early childhood and adolescence. But the Tens to Twelves should not be skipped over lightly—they're going through too exciting and challenging a period for that!

Let's look at some characteristics of these preadolescents, then see what they mean for their play life. Physically, this is a top age for health, activity, endurance, and vitality. Growth is slow and regular; manual dexterity is high. Skill in sports means a great deal to both boys and girls. Socially, they are joiners; they join teams, clubs, gangs, and cliques of their own sex in an effort to establish themselves outside the home and gain the emotional support of a group. Emotionally, this is likely to be a rather stable, secure age when fears and worries are at a minimum and the desire for independence is gathering force. Intellectually, they are reaching out for information and new experiences with avid curiosity. Life is an adventure and they are eager to explore all kinds of activities and interests.

To satisfy these energetic preadolescents, and to further their growth, it's up to us to offer them a varied diet of play. We must give them a chance to try their hand at many sports and games, many arts and crafts. We, their parents, must be willing to help them plan their playtime as we help them organize their school work.

But let us be sure that our concept of play is broad enough to fit these expanding personalities. For them, anything is play that is absorbing and exciting—and that covers a wide territory. They want to "go places and see things"; therefore let's take them not merely to amusement parks and ball games, but to an automobile factory, a newspaper plant, a farm co-op. They are old enough to try overnight camping, an overnight bicycle trip, or a short fishing or canoe trip (all these with an adult, of course), or a visit to one of the rebuilt early American towns. With their hunger for group activity, they are generally ready for informal clubs of their own—a sewing club for the girls, a model-airplane or nature club for the boys.

Now, too, they will want to earn money—usually working alone, but in some cases teaming up with one or two others, to cover a paper route, sell magazine subscriptions, raise pigs or rabbits, mow lawns, wash cars, collect metal or paper, deliver groceries. It is too much to expect them to "save up for a college education"; a camera or a new bicycle is about their speed. If their saving project is worthy and costly you may wish to bring it closer by doubling what they earn. But no matter what use they make of their earnings, they will always gain what every preadolescent wants more than anything: a feeling of independence.

Getting More Out of Sports

The boundless energy of the preteener finds its most typical outlet on the playing field. Boys and girls alike are eager to develop their skill and prove their prowess. Often they seem to feel that success in sports is the key to both self-respect and social acceptance. Large-muscle activities such as baseball, volleyball, and hockey are most appealing, since they satisfy their restless urge to rush about, and the desire to feel their energy translated into action. Team sports are chosen more often than individual sports, not only because the gang urge is still strong but because they feel less conspicuous when playing in groups.

Typically, too, these preadolescents are even more conscious of the rules of the game than they were at seven, eight, and nine. They often bicker endlessly over decisions and argue heatedly about what's "fair." The competitive element is likely to be strong; they put their heart and soul in the game and fight for the team and for personal glory at the same time. Since skill and experience are only beginning to develop, they frequently expect too much of themselves and are as often discouraged by failure as thrilled by success.

This is the period when as much attention should be paid to our youngsters' attitudes toward sports as to the development of skill. Are we to let the competitive element overshadow every other drive? Should we encourage team sports at the expense of individual sports? Must every child be good at one of the standard sports, such as baseball? And how can we help our children get the greatest benefit from sports—not for their physical well-being alone, but for their character and personality as well? The following paragraphs offer some concise suggestions, based on studies of child development as well as observations made on the playing field.

Instruction is essential. A new sport should always be started under the guidance of an expert. The habit patterns formed at the beginning are basic and cannot easily be changed. A good coach instills confidence in his pupil and lets him develop at his own pace. Moreover, the first lessons indicate whether he is ready for the sport and has the physical and emotional aptitudes for it.

Don't force them to participate. Ambitious parents frequently push their children into sports too soon. When they fail to learn, the parents are disappointed in them and the children lose confidence in themselves. Sports require a combination of coordination, strength, concentration, and understanding, and it takes time for this combination to develop. Don't forget that games should be fun, not a chore.

Adults should be present at some team games. Naturally our youngsters will play many informal, pick-up games. But since the preteens are a learning period for most sports, some of their games should be supervised by recreation leaders, teachers, camp counselors, or interested parents. This will give every child a chance; teams will be equalized and weak or inexperienced players will get special practice and instruction. The presence of an adult will also put the game on a high level of sportsmanship and prevent it from degenerating into a quarrel or free-for-all. If parents supervise, they should try to forget that their own children are participating.

Encourage practice. In tennis, golf, baseball, and other sports, so much emphasis is put on playing the game that practice is often neglected. Yet regular practice and correction of faults will add immeasurably to the fun later on. It not only develops greater skill, but fosters habits of perseverance and self-improvement. For example, Bill Tilden once found that his backhand was not up to par; he refused to enter a tournament for six months, to give himself a chance to work on it.

Correct form is important. There is, of course, some difference of opinion as to what comprises good form in tennis, swimming, and other sports, but in general it is better to begin with tried and tested methods and let individual style come later. Poor techniques are a handicap. It's like typing: you might get along fairly well with the hunt and peck system, but your potential is at least doubled if you take the trouble to learn to type correctly.

The head is as important as the hands. Games and sports should not be approached as mere physical exercise and muscular activity. Many mental processes are involved in effective play: planning ahead, testing an opponent's strengths and weaknesses, using a "system," devising clever signals, etc. The child who lacks brawn can often hold his own if he uses his brain. A study of the fine points of the game adds to both enjoyment and skill, and gives parents and children an opportunity for interesting discussions and closer contact.

Discourage playing only to win. Although boys and girls should be encouraged to do their best, nevertheless they should play for the sake of the game more than for victory. Playing only to win makes them tense and anxious, decreases enjoyment, and often leads to defeat and discouragement. Moreover, it produces bad techniques, such as constantly cutting instead of stroking the ball in tennis, or using an awkward swimming stroke because for the moment it "gets you there." Betting should be discouraged for all the reasons mentioned.

Encourage noncompetitive activities. Today the competitive side of sports is overdone; everything is a race, a contest, a fight. It is essential to teach children that beating others is not the supreme objective of life. Moreover, many of them cannot "take" severe competition and feel inadequate if they do not do well. These youngsters should be encouraged to explore noncompetitive activities and be assured that they are just as good as the competitive type. In fact, they frequently have values that cannot be duplicated: hiking and skiing bring them close to nature, group bicycling provides companionship, folk games and square dancing are unsophisticated fun as well as good exercise.

Individual sports are as good as team sports. Emphasis on team sports in schools and on playgrounds may make some children feel that individual sports are second best. The reason team sports are stressed is often only practical: it is easier to keep children busy in groups. Although every child benefits from group games, some are far happier with individual sports such as archery, target shooting, riding, tennis, fishing, pitching horseshoes, or skating. Some of these involve tremendous skill and carry over to later life far more than sports like football or water polo. Let's not neglect these activities.

Don't limit them to the most popular sports. Why should we try to make every boy a ball-player? The less popular sports provide just as much fun, just as much chance for exercise, the development of healthy attitudes, and great skill. Badminton, gymnastics, and fencing are examples. Other team games, such as volleyball, that don't single out the individual have much in their favor. They should be as acceptable to parents and school administrators as the more usual sports. In fact, they may help to make a child more distinctive and interesting.

Let them concentrate on one or two sports. Your youngsters should have a chance to try many kinds of games, but they will get far more satisfaction if they develop their skill in one or two instead of trying to become all-around athletes. This doesn't mean that if they play tennis they should never touch a basketball; naturally it is an advantage to be able to join any games that are suggested. A boy or girl would do well to concentrate on a single sport in each season of the year. But if they regard one or two as their games, and become fairly proficient at them, they will feel more secure and confident than if they try to master everything. They will also be preparing for high school and college, when skill counts most, as well as for adult life when they will need athletic interests for reasons of health and well-being.

Finally, let us recognize how much of our children's personality is formed by their participation in games and sports. They learn to follow rules and respect law and order. They practice teamwork and cooperation in a setting that makes these qualities most attractive. They learn to assume responsibility for others as well as themselves. Loyalty, fairness, and honesty are cultivated through action rather than mere precept or preachment. Energetic activity helps them relieve tension and releases bottled-up feelings. Competition prepares them to hold their own in a competitive world. Through victory they experience the thrill of achievement; through defeat they learn to be good sports and sympathize with the underdog. The exercise keeps them healthy in body; the confidence they gain through developing their abilities keeps them healthy in mind.

There is little doubt about it: the playing field stands next to the home and the school in its influence on our children's lives.

What Games Can Do for Your Children

During the two or three years before adolescence, your children's interest in games will probably be at its height. Practically every type will appeal to them—serious games and silly games, indoor games and outdoor games, word games, puzzles, board games, card games. They will have an intense, absorbing passion for one game after another, and you will very likely wish they would show the same degree of concentration with school work.

What is this magic that games exert, and why does it operate at this particular period in our youngsters' lives? The reasons run something like this. During preadolescence, children feel their growing strength, their skill, their mental abilities (and their oats, too) more acutely than ever before—and they like to use and develop these qualities to the fullest degree. Games are a special challenge to their expanding personalities. They sharpen their wits, increase their fund of knowledge, perfect their dexterity, make them socially adept. Moreover, the competitive nature of most games gives children an opportunity to test their abilities and measure themselves against others, enabling them to see if they are keeping pace with their fellows. Other activities can accomplish these purposes to a large extent—exercises in the gym, classroom studies—but the beauty of games is that the spirit of play prevails, and so often more can be gained in an atmosphere of fun and enjoyment than in one of dead seriousness.

The very fact that our preadolescent youngsters have such an avid and often undiscriminating interest in games gives us, their parents, a special opportunity. Since they will try anything that looks like fun, we can steer them to games that will have some particular value. Dominoes and card tricks will help the child who is having trouble with numbers. Action games such as "balloon blow" will arouse the apathetic or slow-moving, and give the tense child a chance to let off steam. Scrabble is wonderful for spelling and vocabulary. Charades is a "natural" to bring the timid out of their shell, though you'll have to lure them into the game subtly. Some games induce better habits of concentration, others improve observation, while almost any game increases alertness, encourages obedience to rules or principles, and provides practice in fair play and good sportsmanship.

Let's not overlook the fact that *making* a game can be as much fun as playing a game. With a little ingenuity and help from father and mother, practically any of the common games can be constructed at home. Anagrams can be made out of squares of cardboard or wood. All that is needed for ring toss is a half-dozen circles of rope or a set of jar rings and a wooden stake. Bean bags can be sewed by any boy or girl, with the target cut out of plywood or heavy corrugated board. Wooden matchsticks make good darts, with old phonograph needles or pins for points and "feathers" made of crossed paper inserted in slits at the other end. The family can divide into two teams, each making up a quiz with which to challenge the other. In creating these quizzes, the youngsters will get some excellent practice in using encyclopedias, maps, and almanacs.

Many of these games can be bought for a few cents, but the joy of making them cannot be measured in money. Moreover, the child who makes his own games will probably keep them longer and play them with special care. You might also suggest that they make first-rate presents for other children's birthdays.

You can often spot a child's needs through games. In playing checkers, one youngster may be so disorganized that he can't "think straight"; you may find that too much pressure is being put on him at home or at school. Another may reveal that he needs extra help with spelling or geography. Still another will confine himself to a type of game—solitaire, for example—that will help him dodge the risks of competition. It will be up to us to find ways to bolster this child's confidence and help him hold his own with others.

Let your child try as many types of games as possible—and suggest some new kinds if he runs out of ideas. Each game has values of its own. To prove that there is a game that will foster practically any quality you can name, we will now offer a brief inventory of indoor games, classified according to the characteristics they most prominently promote. You will also find some useful game books listed at the end of the book.

Vocabulary games: anagrams, ghost, crosswords, Scrabble, derivations (make twenty-five words out of "stripe" in five minutes).

Observation games: What Do You See? (cover ten small objects with a cloth; take it off for two minutes and put it back; ask participants to write down all they can remember). Find It! (before a party, place ten small objects in various prominent places in the room; give the guests five minutes to locate and list all they can find, without moving them or telling each other).

Number facility: Dominoes, Fizz-Buzz (sit in circle; the first player calls "one," the next "two," etc., except that Fizz is used for five or any multiple of it and Buzz for seven or its multiples).

Memory: When I Go to California (each successive person says "I will take with me" some object; he adds a new object, but must repeat all that have been mentioned before, in order).

Information: Famous Persons (what person is associated with a kite, a slingshot, a footprint, etc.?).
Geography (many types; e.g., naming cities, each player giving a name beginning with the last letter of the city last named).

Quiz games of all sorts—but concentrate on useful information.

Dexterity: Pick-up Sticks, Marbles, Darts, Ring Toss, Jackstraws, Tiddlywinks.

Activity (and release of tension): Musical chairs (Going to Jerusalem); Balloon Blow (blowing a balloon over a horizontal string); Paper Bag Relay (running to goal, blowing up and bursting a bag, running back); Shoe Scramble (everyone puts his shoes in a pile; at a signal, each is required to find and put on his own).

Quickness: Grab (a card game).

Reasoning: Checkers, Twenty Questions, Who Am I?, puzzles, Black Magic (a leader and accomplice decide secretly on signals; the accomplice is sent out of the room, while the group selects an object; by questioning the leader, he tries to discover this object when he returns).

Acting: Charades, Gestures (leader tells a story in gestures; the group write down their versions individually); Hollywood (acting out common scenes: woman trying on a hat, listening to gossip on the telephone, different characters watching a movie).

"Let's Make Something"

During the lull between sports and games, or when there's no one around to play with, boys and girls are as busy as ever, one with hammer and nails or knife, the other with needle and scissors. In a word, when our children aren't playing something, they're making something. This is the period when they are developing an interest in manual skills and constructive projects It is the ideal time to introduce them to handicrafts of many kinds, so that they will gain firsthand experience with different tools and materials, and then concentrate on the ones that are most congenial to them. These handicrafts, as well as many of the other activities discussed in this chapter, may develop into worthwhile hobbies in the teens (see chapter 12).

If our children fail to experience the enjoyment of making things between the ages of ten and twelve, and if parents neglect to bring handicrafts into their lives, the chances are that they will not discover their value for years to come—and perhaps never. Adolescence with all its turmoil will soon be upon them, and they will hesitate to embark on this new field of interest. But if they have already tasted the satisfaction of creating things, they will have a happy refuge from the storms to come.

What *are* the satisfactions in making things? Through handicrafts, the growing child learns mastery over materials and over himself as well. He develops control over his fingers, learns to co-ordinate hand and eye. He explores the physical properties of a variety of materials: the grain of wood, the malleability of metals, the pliability of leather. He learns many productive processes—sawing, gluing, stitching, splitting—and finds many short-cuts and ingenious techniques of his own. He is stimulated to make original designs or carry out the designs of others with care and precision. He develops skills which others recognize and admire, and raises his level of aspiration as his work improves. He forms habits and attitudes that will serve him well for the rest of his life: a workmanlike approach, methodical thinking, persistence, resourcefulness, pride in doing a good job. There is no better spur to growth than handicrafts, and no better example of creative play.

How, then, can we help our growing boys and girls to channel their urge to make something, so that it will give them the most lasting satisfactions and contribute most fully to their development? It is all very well for them to fix a household gadget here or make a model there, but these sporadic activities add up to very little. We cannot, of course, expect these preteeners to be perfectionists about their handiwork—in fact, they are usually quite uncritical—but we *can* give them the opportunity to see how manual work can be further developed and become one of their greatest sources of pleasure. Here is how to do it:

See that they have a good place to work. The kitchen table is no place to carry on a handicraft hobby, nor is the desk in the child's room. These are associated with other activities and must always be cleared off after use. A workbench in the garage or basement, or better yet, in a corner of your youngster's room will act as a stimulus to constructive work. There must be an adequate place for tools and for storage of materials. Planning and building this work corner can be an absorbing project in itself, one that will probably require Dad's help and certainly his interest.

Help them obtain good tools and materials. There's truth in the saying that you can judge a workman by his tools. There is nothing more frustrating than a poor tool and nothing more gratifying than a good one. Good tools encourage good work and are no more expensive in the end than poor ones that have to be replaced. Many of the materials can be homemade—salt dough for modeling, for example. Others, like scraps of wood, can be picked up here and there. Metal, plastics, leather, etc. will generally have to be bought. Remember that materials of good quality inspire good work.

Keep that junk box handy. Your child will probably want to try his hand at making all kinds of things, and then settle down to one main hobby. By now he may need an even larger junk box. He will get ideas of his own from all sorts of materials and gadgets: wire, cloth scraps, Christmas cards, discarded costume jewelry, string, candles, old kitchen utensils, light switches—many of which he may have started to collect two or three years before. Rummaging through the box will stimulate his imagination, lead him to devise his own projects. Although special materials are needed for many activities, we should also continue to encourage our youngsters to "make something out of nothing" and enjoy the thrill of finding new uses for old things.

Avoid too many "packaged" handicrafts. Many companies are putting out complete kits for model-making, leatherwork, weaving and so on. Some of these require a good deal of effort, and they do teach the child to follow directions, but generally speaking they provide too little scope for ingenuity and creative expression. Realism has its value but imagination must not be ignored. Moreover, these cut-and-dried kits make children think that handicrafts are just a simple, undemanding pastime. The kit habit will lead them to believe that they are really making something, when all they are doing is putting it together. Producing a belt out of prefabricated links and a prefabricated buckle is an extremely limited activity. The first belts children make for themselves may not look as neat as a prefabricated one, but the experience will be many times more meaningful.

Help them get detailed information from experts. Visits to experienced hobbyists or people employed in a particular handicraft will help to develop a child's interest and knowledge. Watching a professional jewelry artisan or cabinetmaker will be a stimulus to better work, and the child may form a valuable friendship to boot. Teachers can often supply information, and every good library has books on the major hobbies and crafts. Such books make excellent birthday presents. If there is an arts and crafts show anywhere in the vicinity, be sure to take your children to see it. And consider the possibility of following one of these pursuits *with* your children. Perhaps you can attend a Saturday morning class with them. Learning together would be a stimulating family experience.

Gear your expectations to your children's abilities. Don't judge your youngsters' work by adult standards. If your expectations are too high, you may discourage your children. Handicrafts will become more work than play, and the emphasis will be put on the product instead of the joy of producing it. If you find that it is too early for your boy or girl to handle a saw or a crochet needle, or if no facility is shown, be prepared to suggest something that will be within reach. Don't go overboard with praise and call everything they make "just wonderful," but give them your enthusiastic encouragement when they show improvement, your help and support when things don't turn out right.

Lead them into handicrafts through other activities. A party can be an incentive for making original place cards, favors, and games. Gifts can be made for birthdays and holidays without any strain on the allowance: ash trays, jewelry boxes, leather purses. Make it a point to say, "It's so much nicer to receive something that's handmade," or words to that effect. Occasionally suggest things your children can make for the home: a wastebasket, a figurine, a telephone book cover. Preteeners like to make practical articles and see them in use.

Trips to museums or historical places can also stimulate interest in folk crafts.

Develop a handicraft interest of your own. The pattern you set will make the difference between a creative and an uncreative atmosphere. In a home where parents make and repair things themselves, the children are almost certain to be constructive. Their interests will not necessarily be your own, but that will make for variety in your home life. Each will appreciate the perseverance it takes to complete a project, and there will be no lack of interesting conversation at the dinner table.

The Manual Arts

Preadolescence is still an age of experiment rather than skill. Our ten-to-twelve-year-olds are exploring at the same time the wealth of the world and the richness of their own interests and capacities. Though they range more widely than they did at seven or eight, their excursions into the manual arts are in the nature of an adventure, and therefore they shift their attention from one pursuit to another fairly rapidly. This is to be expected during an age of discovery.

Your child, however, will need some guideposts for his explorations. There are wide variations among preadolescents in their handicraft interests and abilities, yet it ought to be useful to consider some average expectations. Note that we do not offer separate lists for boys and girls. The more we study children, the more we realize that the old distinctions do not run very deep. In particular, we don't want to perpetuate the notion that girls are necessarily sedentary in their pursuits and boys more energetic and interested primarily in muscular activity. Nor do we agree with the idea that artistic activities are feminine, or even that males must not learn how to cook and sew. And we can point to many homes where the mother is far handier than her husband with hammer and saw, and every bit as efficient in diagnosing an ailing lamp or washing machine!

Clay modeling. By nine or ten most children have had considerable experience with clay. Now they will be ready to make useful and decorative articles of their own design, such as tiles, candy boxes, and lamp bases. By twelve they are ready for modeling tools and possibly a potter's wheel, and can use non-firing or marble glaze to give figurines and jewelry a more interesting and durable finish.

Papier-mâché. This activity *can* be started before ten years of age, but then it is largely an occasional school project. After ten it will be a means of producing useful articles for the household, for Halloween, Christmas, and Easter, and for special events like pageants and plays. Most common articles are: masks, bowls, trays, puppets, ornaments.

Model making. This activity cuts across many crafts, since models may be made of wood, cardboard, metal, and all other common materials. Generally, kits that supply uncut and unshaped material are better than those in which the model is all but finished. But it is still better for the children to study the car, sailing vessel or stage coach they want to reproduce, and then make their own design and pattern. The more they learn about the history and specifications of these objects, the greater the incentive for accurate, careful work, and the more enriching the experience.

Weaving. Younger adolescents who have not had any experience with weaving should start with finger weaving or a simple loom. In finger weaving, warp threads are merely looped over a piece of broomstick; yarn, raffia, jute, or roving may be used. Older preadolescents are usually ready for a harness loom, on which they can make rugs, belts, bags, and scarves.

Woodworking. By ten most boys and girls can handle planes, chisels, and hand-drills, but they need a good deal of guidance from an experienced person. Let them practice on scrap wood, and they will soon be making practical articles, such as shelves, shoe boxes, and toys out of soft pine and plywood. By twelve they can make simple articles (trays, for example) out of maple and other hard woods, fitting and finishing them with some degree of skill. Preteeners are not ready for power tools.

Metalwork. Have them begin with very thin sheet copper or tin; it can be cut with scissors and tooled simply, to produce book ends, tea tiles, bracelets. Later on they can make jewelry, trays, and bowls of heavier metals, using hand saw, drills, files. Articles made of tin cans can become more elaborate as eleven- and twelve-year-olds learn to use a soldering iron.

Plastic work. Ten-year-olds can make aprons, bibs, rain kerchiefs, and place mats out of thin plastic sheeting. It comes in colors or clear, but special dyes are available and easily applied. Designs can be traced on plastic curtains and stuffed toys, then colored with a dauber. Twelve-year-olds can use stiff sheet plastic, fashioning it into boxes, trays, table decorations, buttons, and jewelry with the aid of hand saws, drills and etching tools.

Cardboard work. An endless variety of useful objects can be made out of ordinary cardboard and corrugated cartons. The only tools and materials needed are heavy scissors, glue, glued tape, a strong knife or razor blade (with holder), paper and poster paint. Some articles to make: waste baskets, doll houses, buildings for the train set, stage scenery, knickknack boxes.

Puppetry. By ten, puppets can be made more elaborate and imaginative, though still from common materials such as tennis balls, crepe paper and bits of cloth. Nose, mouth, ears, and eyes can now be made out of odds and ends like corks and buttons. By twelve, more permanent puppets can be made out of papier-mâché or carved wood. A carton or wooden box may be used as a stage, with painted decorations and scraps of cloth as a curtain. At this age, too, many children can make and manipulate marionettes, controlling the strings with a simple cross of wood.

Bookbinding. Ten-year-olds should start with slit binding, to make scrapbooks and booklets. About fifty typing sheets are stacked evenly and clamped temporarily near the edge between two rulers. Slits are cut half an inch deep and half an inch apart, then woven with thread, glued, and covered with paper or fabric. With practice, a youngster can be ready for commercial-type binding by twelve or thirteen years of age.

Leather work. Inexpensive calfskin or steer hide can be fashioned into many useful articles: wallets, stamp boxes, belts, purses, bookmarks, clothing ornaments. Patterns should be made by the child wherever possible, and original designs encouraged. Twelve-year-olds can learn tooling and dyeing.

Carving. Let them start with chip or surface carving in soft wood, making decorative box tops and plaques of their own design. Panel or relief carving is more advanced; it is deeper, and includes carving pieces of wood glued to the surface to make the design stand out. Tools needed: quarter-inch chisel, gouges, veining tools for fine lines. Preadolescents are generally not ready for figure carving.

Basketry. Preteeners can be taught to make baskets that have plain, simple shapes, to be used for fruit, waste paper, bread, etc. Split wood, reed, raffia, and grasses are most commonly used.

Cloth work. Both boys and girls can now handle a needle and thread with some dexterity. They are able not only to do simple mending, but make useful articles such as puppets, costumes, pencil cases, shoe bags, aprons, beanies, and boleros. They should be encouraged to design the article on paper, make a pattern, and try different materials and colors in order to achieve interesting and original effects. With some general explanation by the parent, a child can learn to read and use commercial patterns for sewing.

Other Crafts

Preteeners get excited about many types of crafts that capture their interest for short but intensive periods. Some of the most satisfying are: candle-dipping, kite-making, crocheting, lantern-making, doll-making. Sometimes the interest remains strong and can be developed into a full-fledged hobby. For example, after a visit to a museum, or as a result of interest aroused at Christmas time, the youngster might experiment with different types of candles, or explore their fascinating history and the kinds now in use in different countries.

We'll have more to say about hobbies later on.

Fun with Music and Art

In music, as in other things, our "tween-agers" are exploratory and experimental. Their tastes may seem fickle and transient, but at least they will "try anything once"—particularly if we present the new experience in a spirit of fun. Steven, who has been playing the piano for two years or so, will want to see what it feels like to blow a horn or clarinet. Judith, who has never taken lessons of any kind, may easily be enticed into trying her hand at the guitar, ukulele, autoharp, or harmolin. Instruments of the latter kind have a special attraction at this period for several reasons: they can be played passably even without instruction; they are portable and can be taken on trips or hikes; they are associated with recreation more than education; they are highly social—a few strummed notes will put the whole gang in a singing and dancing mood. The youngster who masters one of these instruments in preadolescence will find the teen years more enjoyable and more comfortable.

The preteener's love of group activity carries over into music.

Nothing gives them more pleasure than singing together around the campfire, in the family playroom, in the classroom. Group singing has a special attraction because it helps them lose self-consciousness and gain a sense of power and unity with others. Folk songs are particularly appealing and wherever possible should be sung in their original language: "Alouette," "La Cucaracha," "Swing Low, Sweet Chariot," "Erie Canal." To get the most out of these songs, let's encourage our youngsters to talk about the lives of the people they depict, and act out the stories spontaneously. In some instances, too, they will want to improvise costumed skits around the songs.

Folk Dancing

Like younger children only more so, energetic preteeners are not content merely to listen to music—they react to it with their whole bodies. Not only do they enjoy clapping and shouting, like the Eights and Nines, but they are ready for the more organized movements of square dancing and other folk dancing. These dances appeal because, as in sports, the children like to "follow the rules" and feel that they are members of a team. Moreover, they come into contact with members of the opposite sex while keeping some distance from them. Though at the present time there are rarely enough opportunities for these activities, we would recommend group singing and folk dancing as one of the best bridges between the sexes just before adolescence. If they engage in these active kinds of fun, they will undoubtedly be better prepared to take the later boy-girl relationships in their stride.

The Dance

This is the time for an interest in the dance to blossom into an enthusiasm sometimes bordering on an obsession. Girls who have been studying some of the basic techniques of ballet or other dance forms are likely to develop rapidly now, and latent talent will come to the fore. (And if it doesn't by twelve years of age, with proper teaching, it probably never will.) By now they have lost the silliness of the Eights and Nines but have not yet acquired the self-consciousness and tensions of the teen-agers. It is easy, for instance, to get ten- and eleven-year-olds to take turns leading the group or giving their own interpretations of a dance theme—in fact, they are likely to be so eager that the teacher will be flooded with volunteers. During this period, girl dance students are capable of concentrated attention to technique and can follow more complicated instructions than before. And where technique is lacking, enthusiasm will often carry them through. Teachers report, too, that girls of this age are fun to work with because they put everything into the lessons and enjoy themselves at the same time. Body control and balance have improved to a point where the dancing is beginning to "look like something." Just as important, in the authors' opinion, is the fact that girls who receive this training have a far better than average chance to go through adolescence without becoming leftish and ungainly. The awkward age is by no means an inevitable affliction.

During this period, when interest runs so high, many girls begin to aspire to a career on the stage. That aspiration is, of course, legitimate and we have no desire to cut down on the number who choose this profession. Nevertheless a warning is in order. The dance profession—particularly modern and classical ballet—requires an almost unlimited amount of training, hard work, and downright sacrifice. It is not a decision to be taken lightly, and certainly not from parental pride and pressure, nor from a desire to see one's name in lights. A girl, and her family, must do a good deal of soul-searching to see if she has the requisite stamina and self-dedication before taking this step. On the other hand, a girl who takes the training and then decides to give up the career in favor of marriage and children can still reap most of its benefits in terms of health, grace, and self-expression. Moreover, if she keeps her eyes open, she can find many opportunities to practice her art informally and can keep herself in good trim for the rest of her life.

Records

It would be unwise to associate music only with action. Preteeners need quieter forms of play, and an expanding library of records is one of the best answers. Let's take them on frequent trips to the record shop so they can make their own selection. At the same time, we can see that they are exposed to a wide variety of recordings, since in their enthusiasm they might limit themselves to one kind, such as hillbilly songs. These passing tastes are fine, provided they also get a chance to hear such types as the following: dramatic, pictorial compositions such as "Danse Macabre," "The Sorcerer's Apprentice," "Peer Gynt Suite," portions of the "Grand Canyon Suite"; story records such as "The Emperor's New Clothes" (for Tens more than Twelves) and "The Underground Train" (both from the Young People's Record Club); American folk songs such as the spirituals sung by Marian Anderson, and the songs of Stephen Foster; folk songs from other countries, such as "Songs of the South African Veldt," "Pancho Goes to a Fiesta" (Tripp), "Mexican Rhapsody" (McBride), "Latin-American Folk Songs" (Coelho); selections from the better musical comedies, such as "Show Boat" and "South Pacific."

Those children who are seriously studying music will want to have records of compositions or composers they admire.

Concerts

Preteeners will get most of their music from records, radio, and television; but they are not too young to be introduced to the delights of going to a concert. In certain fortunate communities, there are special symphony concerts for young people or recitals by folk artists like Burl Ives and Dyer-Bennett. In smaller communities, band concerts are sometimes held on the village mall, and children make up a large part of the audience. The informality of these concerts, and the fact that whole families can listen to music together, are special advantages. But in the more formal concerts, buying tickets ahead of time, planning the evening, and talking about the program in advance add luster to the musical experience. So does a bite to eat at a restaurant afterward, a discussion of the merits of the performance, and the eager perusal of newspaper reviews the next day. Moreover, attending a concert is often a greater stimulus to constructive follow-up activities than simple listening to music via electronics. Their own music lessons are more likely to benefit from the inspiration, and their reading may be expanded to include simplified biographies of composers and stories about the countries or parts of America from which the music comes.

Art for the Joy of It

Tens to Twelves tend to be a down-to-earth lot who like to make things for use. But to help them achieve a balanced play life, we need to show them how to make functional things attractive, and introduce them to art forms that are simply amusing or different or decorative without any further use. Of the many ways to achieve the first aim, we will mention only a few: point out the difference between a utensil or appliance that combines good design with efficient functioning, and one that does not; show them that a few simple lines—even a semiabstract form—on a Christmas card can be more artistic, and suggest more, than a realistic picture; plant the idea that a piece of work is really unfinished if its surface or form is not pleasing to the eye.

Given half a chance, preadolescents will continue to experiment with the "free" art forms that may have been introduced at six or seven (see chapter 8). They will be more particular about the variety of textures used in their collages ("feeling designs"), and will create more complex patterns. These may be either nonrepresentational designs, amusing caricatures, or fairly realistic pictures such as boats steaming along. Their mobiles, or "space designs," will also be made of a greater variety of materials —cardboard, tin, scraps of aluminum, or pieces of thin wood— cut in geometric shapes, such as different size triangles or circles or free forms, and suspended from wire arms so they move about in the air. Color will be used in more sophisticated ways—for example, surfaces may be red on one side and blue on the other, so that as the structure flutters in the breeze, it changes kaleidoscopically. They may also explore the possibilities of freezing their mobiles into a "stabile" by using wire in place of thread, and placing them on a table, instead of having them float in the air. Children who show little skill with the more earth-bound materials, such as clay, can frequently produce truly exciting mobile designs for room decoration.

A new art form may be introduced in this period: the diorama. Both boys and girls enjoy making these three-dimensional scenes built into half a hatbox or carton that is open in front. Human or animal figures are made of pipe cleaners, trees of colored sponge pasted on trunks made of dowels or lollypop sticks, with painted backdrops and perhaps a piece of blue cellophane stretched over an opening in the top to give the impression of sky. The scenes themselves will be inspired by their reading, schoolwork, or interesting experiences. With some encouragement, they will enlarge the art experience by making up a story or playlet to go with the diorama.

Museums

Adults are often apt to overlook the fact that just *looking* at things can be a creative experience for children. Spectatorship has values of its own, and no better illustration can be found than wandering through a museum. Boys and girls in the preteens, living at the height of both energy and curiosity, will not be deterred by long corridors and endless displays. (Again, adults sometimes discourage their children by thinking of museums in terms of aching feet instead of inquiring eyes.)

Children absorb an immense amount of knowledge and feeling from objects of natural history such as stuffed birds and snakes, the flora of different regions, and the re-creations of the life of primitive peoples. They will want to return again and again to see their favorite exhibits at museums that show collections of armor, pottery, mummies—because the very old has a special fascination for the very young. Though collecting objects like Indian relics has its advantages, just *seeing* them in a large display is bound to give our youngsters a new feeling for the culture from which they stem. Similarly, although we welcome a chance to study a single Rembrandt, we get a different impression of that painter if we see a large collection of his paintings at once.

Even the smallest museum can leave an indelible mark on our children's memories and on their taste as well. Perhaps an exhibit of Aztec pottery, or pictures of painted buildings of Nuremberg, will determine the color scheme of a future living room. A fossil exhibit may lead to research in paleontology in high school or college or later life. A visit to a museum or antique shop where old furniture is shown may stimulate a lasting interest in a particular period of history. But even without these direct results, there are immeasurable benefits from just looking and absorbing a bit here and a bit there, for these are experiences that enrich the mind and add meaning to life.

Reading and the Spectator Arts

The interest in radio, television, and motion pictures continues unabated. By now, however, the youngsters have abandoned the puppet and story programs designed for small children, and are beginning to classify most comic magazines as "kid stuff." Perhaps the key to the entire issue of these spectator arts is to recognize that many passing enthusiasms develop at this period, and to be ready with new suggestions at the slightest sign of boredom or waning interest. We all know that most youngsters of this age still like the rapid-fire action of westerns, space serials, police stories; the homely humor of family comedies; the obvious antics of the comedians; and we realize that the girls are beginning to "eat up" musicals, costume pictures, and sentimental singers. These interests need no encouragement from us—in fact, they frequently need curtailment. We might better appeal to their exploratory impulses, and help them find films, programs and the few comic books that deal with travel in other countries, hobbies and how-to-do-it, the elements of drawing, scientific demonstrations, great events of history, real adventure and discovery. Documentaries and other informative films can be found on television or rented for use on a home movie projector. There is ample room in the lives of preteeners for relaxed viewing and easy reading, particularly when these contribute to sheer amusement, broader acquaintance with the world, and creative activities of their own.

In spite of competition from radio and television, the years from ten to twelve are likely to be the heyday for reading. Our observation has been that the period of complete absorption, when children "read all day long," which used to occur at about eleven, is now moved ahead a half-year or a year. Sometimes the reading is all the more intense because it comes as a welcome change from the repetitiousness of the easy media.

Probably at no time in the child's life is there a more varied diet of reading. In fact, one of our jobs as parents is to keep up to date on publications, through the Child Study Association,

Parents' Magazine, The Saturday Review and the book review sections of the Sunday papers. Since new books are constantly appearing, we shall limit ourselves to the general types that interest preteeners most—books that satisfy their love of action and excitement, their need to find heroes in the past as well as the present, their strong desire to overcome their own limitations and come into touch with a wider world.

Adventure. Life on the sea (pirate and sailing stories); exploration (Columbus, *Kon-tiki*); frontier life (including but going beyond westerns to include pioneering).

Fantasy. The Arabian Nights; the Oz books; *Alice's Adventures in Wonderland;* stories of Greek and Roman heroes and gods. (Fairy tales have lost whatever appeal they have had.)

Biography and historical fiction. The Barbary pirates, Robin Hood, Kit Carson, Clara Barton, William Penn, Marco Polo, Leif Ericson, stories of the age of chivalry. (Interest in biography reaches its peak; full-length portraits now instead of mere action stories.)

Mysteries. Stories of the secret-panel, hidden-treasure types, with boy or girl detectives; emphasis on action and excitement rather than logical detection; suspense without horror or murder.

Westerns. Stories of ranch life, in which right always triumphs.

Sports. Stories of school and college athletics, with emphasis on teamwork and fair play. These are for boys more than girls.

Animal stories, dealing with raccoons, deer, hawks, dogs, and above all, horses. (Talking-animal stories now have little appeal; more interest in the way animals grow and live, and in stories involving both children and animals.)

Scientific discovery. Stories of Edison, Bell, Watts and the great men of medicine, with as much emphasis on their lives as on their discoveries.

Information and how-to. Books on everyday machines, the stars, the weather, Diesel trains, the earth's beginning, atoms; recreational interests such as camping, sewing, ballet, cooking for young people; simpler books and pamphlets on handicrafts. (Whole books on elementary science will be read, not just directions for occasional experiments or projects.)

Planning for Play

In this chapter dozens of activities have been suggested for our preadolescent youngsters. The years from ten to twelve are the time for the most intense interest in sports and games and for exploration of a host of handicrafts. Reading and interest in the mass media also reach a peak during this period. Gang life is going strong, and Scouts or Campfire or "Y" groups claim much of the preteener's attention. Music lessons are in full swing, and perhaps there are hobby classes once or twice a week. Everything comes at once!

How can our children absorb so much at one time? How can we help them arrange their lives so that each interest gets the time and attention it needs? How can they keep on the move without driving themselves, and us, to distraction?

Part of the answer lies in the immense energy of the average preteener. He is at the height of vitality and doesn't seem to know fatigue. Never before and never afterward will he be capable of so much sheer activity and movement. But this is just the trap that we are likely to fall into. Because preadolescents possess so much restless energy, we may encourage them to be on the go continuously; and before we know it, our children will be not merely active, but *tensely* active, driven by an inner compulsion to dash from one pursuit to another. If that happens, they will have neither the leisure nor the time to absorb the benefits of their many activities. Instead of relieving tensions, play of this kind—if it can be called play—will increase them.

What is more, our youngsters will be forming attitudes and habits that will affect both their work life and their play life in later years. They will be unable to relax. They will develop a fear of idleness and a feeling that they are wasting time when not outwardly occupied. Their leisure time will never be spent in a leisurely way.

The immense variety of play, which we have set out to describe in this book, is not meant to be an invitation to feverish activity every hour of the day. In fact, our very point is that it is not enough simply to be busy, but that *when* our children devote themselves to play, they should be encouraged to play more creatively—in ways that will enrich their personalities and promote their growth. But how can anyone be creative if he is constantly on the move? There must be time to ponder, time to let experiences sink in. This is the only way to be sure that our children benefit from play in their own individual ways. It is far better for them to engage in fewer activities and have time to develop them and feel their effects, than to put them on a conveyor belt that carries them swiftly and thoughtlessly from one pursuit to another.

The metropolitan centers provide the best examples of assembly-line play. In a compulsive, usually competitive effort to give their children "all the advantages," many parents shunt them continuously from one organized activity to another. We believe, as we have said all along, that many sports, games, arts, and crafts should be pursued under the guidance of adults for at least part of the time, particularly during the learning period. But there must also be ample opportunity for free activity when our children can take it easy and let their motors idle. It is during these hours that they frequently create their own forms of play—which they would rarely do if their activities were constantly blueprinted and controlled by others. When they are on their own, they devise new wrinkles in their hobbies, new twists for old games. And they get what every child needs to help him grow: the opportunity for independent action, and for organizing and managing his own time.

Parents who push their children to the limit usually have the unfortunate tendency of starting them too soon and expecting too much. Their youngsters go to camp before they are ready for it; they take piano lessons before they are capable of developing an appreciation of music or the skill to perform it satisfactorily; they are given courses in tennis, riding, and crafts at a time when they are either bound to fail and become discouraged, or succeed only in becoming robots that perform mechanically. As a consequence, they acquire a distaste for these activities before they have a chance to develop a real interest in them. The spirit of play is lost, and with it goes all spontaneity and genuine enjoyment.

Even though each family must find its own ways of pacing the play life of its children, a few general suggestions might help.

Try the "quiet hour" idea, particularly on Sundays and during the summer vacation. A full hour of quiet play—reading, writing a diary, sewing—will refresh the fast-moving preadolescent. It works at camp, and it can work at home.

Don't overschedule. Although over-all weekly planning is helpful, scheduling every minute of every hour will do more harm than good. The object of planning should not be to see how many things can be gotten in, but to see that there is ample time for both absorption and leisure.

Let them drop activities that lose their appeal. Many activities that pall now can be taken up later; many others are merely experimental but leave a residue of useful experience. Don't make a fetish of "seeing things through."

Don't feel that all play should be "good for the child" in some practical or psychological way. Although this book urges you to look for the benefits and values in a wide variety of activities, be careful of making a "problem" out of play. None of the values can be achieved in their full degree if we take the playfulness out of play and make it a duty rather than a delight.

Discourage the idea of doing things just for a mark or credit. The child who rushes through the instructions in the manual, and hastily completes a project of no practical value, may be earning an arrowpoint—and missing the point of the project completely.

CHAPTER XI

What Play Can Do for Teen-Agers

THERE ARE MANY WAYS of helping our teen-agers over the hurdle of adolescence. We can give them more love and understanding. We can listen sympathetically to their doubts and worries. We can treat them in more adult ways, giving them both increased independence and increased responsibility. We can try to ignore their rudeness. But there is one instrument that can be particularly versatile and effective, though it has never been given enough recognition or sufficient chance to work its wonders. That instrument is play—creative play.

At first mention, play may appear a frivolous answer to the plight of the teen-ager. Yet it would be hard to find a single area of his life where some form of recreation cannot come to his aid. Like every other person, the teen-ager is called upon to adjust himself to life in a variety of ways. He is asked to be physically fit, intellectually alert, socially congenial, emotionally mature. Although play is no panacea, it can be of immeasureable value in meeting every one of these needs.

Let's begin with the physical. Teen-agers are acutely aware of their bodies, and any departure from the norm—or what they consider to be the norm—is baffling and embarrassing to them. A full program of sports and games will keep them in good condition, and many are mature enough to recognize that the health of their minds is partly dependent on the health of their bodies. Even those who are temporarily gangling or scrawny can find perfectly acceptable games, such as table tennis, that will give them the exercise they need, and with it the fun and companionship they require just as much. A good many slight defects, such as poor posture and bad co-ordination, which teen-agers worry about, can be improved by a sensible program of athletics. In these cases, however, it is wise for them to obtain guidance from a doctor, physical therapist, or experienced instructor. Many a frail young man has been lured into an unsupervised course of weight-lifting by dramatic advertisements, with the result that he has overstrained himself; and many a stout girl has tried to combine a rigorous, self-imposed diet with strenuous exercise, only to find herself utterly exhausted—and hungrier than ever.

Physical conditioning will serve our children in the future as well as the present. The skills they develop in sports are the kind that are readily recognized and applauded by others. This will add to their poise and confidence. A body that is alive and alert will help them withstand the strains of life. The "exercise habit" will enable them to relieve pent-up feelings and keep them on a more even keel.

Teen-agers are, if anything, even more concerned about their social life than their physical well-being. Typically, they wonder if they will make the grade with others, and they worry about the right thing to say and do. Those endless telephone conversations of fourteen-year-olds are largely an attempt to check their own social behavior against that of others. The mirror on their wall sees many a rehearsal for life.

The notion that personality is formed and fixed during the first few years of life is a gross exaggeration. During adolescence, which is sometimes described as a second birth, our boys and girls have a new opportunity to develop better relations with other people. A full recreational life will give them the chance they need for testing themselves out and discovering the social roles that are most congenial to themselves and most acceptable to others. These teen-agers need, above all, to join clubs and organizations, to dance and sing and play games in mixed groups, and if possible to have a recreational center, a "teen canteen," of their own. A lively, varied social life will bring them into contact with many types of young people and help them feel at home in many kinds of situations.

Our boys and girls should be encouraged to be active in their social relationships—to join a committee, to devise new games or unusual refreshments, to hold their own in conversation, and to do these things with tact and consideration for others. The ideal is not to be the life of the party, but to contribute one's share to the fun. Knowledge and skill are always useful. The boy or girl who can show the others a new step will be admired by the group, but so will the one who can type out invitations to a meeting or explain a rule in wrestling. Hobbies, too, offer social rewards of many kinds. An interesting collection has started many a friendship; experience with ceramics or woodcarving puts the hobbyist in the position of specialist, where others ask his opinion and respect his judgment. Active interests of this kind give substance to social life.

A Place of Their Own

If you are looking for a healthy answer to your teen-ager's love of fun, the place to find it is in a Teen Canteen, Gals and Pals Club—or whatever it may be called in your locality. Let's hope there *is* one within range of your boy or girl, since these centers are built to order for the "high school crowd." Above all things, these young people want to mingle with members of the opposite sex, they want to laugh and dance and make noise, they want to talk and eat in groups—and they want all this in a place they can call their own.

These canteens are an outgrowth of the war, when so many teen-agers were roaming the streets with nothing to do. Today they have become a regular part of community life in about three thousand neighborhoods throughout the land, and their number is rapidly increasing. In a west-coast city not long ago, several hundred teen-agers were asked what their city could do for them. Their answer was overwhelmingly, "We want a teen canteen!" When some public-spirited citizens got together to bring a canteen into existence, however, they soon discovered that the young folks did not want it handed to them on a silver platter. The young people insisted on a major voice in organizing and running it right from the start. This was the only way they could feel that it was their own.

Let's say there is no teen canteen in your neighborhood. How could one be created? No two are exactly alike, and no two neighborhoods either. Nevertheless, the most successful of these centers have many things in common. You might use these features as guides for your own community.

1. *Getting started.* The committee that gets together to plan a canteen is made up of adults and young people in about equal numbers. If the idea is initiated by an adult group, they generally bring in representative teen-agers from the local high school or from churches, "Y's," Scout groups, etc. If a group of teen-agers starts the ball rolling, they will need the approval and cooperation of adults, and probably financial and legal assistance. In either case, the project ends up with a composite committee.

2. *Supervision.* There is always adult supervision of the activities. Usually this means that a congenial parent, teacher, or recreational worker is present the entire evening. At the same time, officers of the canteen take responsibility for behavior of the members as well as the program that is offered. The supervision, however, is the most unobtrusive possible; teen-agers rightfully resent any implication that they cannot be trusted.

3. *Organization.* When the members have had a chance to get acquainted, they hold a meeting to elect their own officers and create their own committees. The various jobs are spread as widely as possible instead of being concentrated in the hands of a few. Adults constitute an advisory board or become members of the executive committee. Together the teen-agers and adults determine all matters of policy, rules and regulations about hours, petting, stag lines, etc.—but most of the suggestions should come from the young people.

4. *Physical setup.* The physical setup is as simple as possible. The search for adequate quarters is a constructive experience in itself. Rooms at a "Y" or community center, the basement of a church, the gym at a school, even an empty loft or warehouse, have been transformed into teen canteens. The more the members put into it themselves, the more satisfying and successful the whole project will be. The young people can make draperies

and curtains, finish the woodwork, paint murals, wax the floor, rebuild discarded furniture, construct their own soft drink bar, plan the arrangement of tables and chairs. Here is a first-rate opportunity for young people to use their skills and imagination in a practical way. It is creative play at its best.

5. *Business details.* The business details are usually more complicated than they appear to be at first; but they provide an opportunity for useful experience. Teen-agers are generally eager to prove that they can manage the finances themselves and make ends meet on a small budget. There are endless discussions about admission charges, how to pay for the juke box or band, whether to have a concessionaire provide food and drinks. Adults must realize that these problems have great value in stimulating thought and sharpening wits. Some canteens help to pay the bills by using the quarters only three nights a week and renting to outside groups at other times. They may also take a percentage from a food and drink concessionaire (large canteens only), or stage a vaudeville show or play with an admission charge. In any case, every effort should be made to make the canteen self-supporting. The teen-agers like it best that way, since above all things they cherish their independence.

6. *Activities.* In most canteens, the young people do much the same things they would do at their corner meeting places. They dance, sip drinks, eat hot dogs and potato chips, chatter about teachers and parents or their own futures. But they do these things in the secure atmosphere of a place they can call their own, where they feel a special pride and sense of responsibility. Moreover, some of these centers promote activities that help the members express themselves and develop their abilities and community consciousness. This, to our minds, is a measure of a good canteen. Talent programs, art exhibits, and hobby shows should be an integral part of their activities. So should community service. Many a teen canteen has become a center where hospital aides can be recruited, where clean-up and paint-up drives can enlist energetic workers. This is another illustration of the way play and recreation can be integrated with the rest of life instead of being left in a compartment of their own.

If there is no canteen and no practical way at the moment of starting one, a substitute might be found in church groups, discussion groups, or interest groups (such as square dancing or hiking groups).

Too Old for Games?

Our older teen-agers, from fifteen or sixteen up, usually consider themselves too sophisticated for indoor games of any sort. These they shrug off scornfully as "kid stuff," and go back to their dancing. However, television is reviving the interest in parlor games and it is getting easier to convince young people to give them a try. Once they get into a well-planned game party at home or at the canteen, they soon discover that they have been missing a wonderful source of fun and laughter, and an opportunity to show their skill and be themselves. Games, too, give the boy or girl who is not a good dancer a chance at social acceptance. With a list of absorbing games to choose from, our teen-agers' night life will be more varied—and they will be less likely to turn off the lights for lack of something else to do.

Number one on our list of games for teen-agers is charades, and its variation known as "the game." It should go well with these young folks since they are living through a dramatic period and may throw themselves wholeheartedly into acting; at the very least they will profit by the opportunity to let themselves go a bit more than usual. The best way to set up this game is to divide the group into two teams. Each team goes into a separate room to compile a list of five or six proverbs, slogans, or titles that are particularly hard to act out in pantomime. (How would you do "Sweet land of liberty" or "Absence makes the heart grow fonder"?). Making up the list is fun in itself. When it is completed the items are written on slips of paper and the teams come together for the game. Each member performs in front of his own team, acting out an item chosen at random from the list made up by the opposing team. He does the best job he can, so that his team will guess correctly as quickly as possible. The teams take turn, and the one that takes the least total time wins.

Here is a fascinating variation on charades. The game is the same in every way, except that instead of acting, the performer tries to convey the idea through drawing. All that's needed is an easel (however crude), paper, and crayon, although in one form of the game two easels are used at once and the two teams vie with each other to see which one guesses first. Skill in drawing is not necessary—in fact the crudest drawings are often the most expressive, since they put meaning before art.

Two other guessing games are particularly appealing to teenagers, once you capture their attention: Who Am I? and Twenty Questions (also known as Animal, Vegetable, Mineral). In the first, you remember, a name is pinned to the back of a contestant and he is required to find out who he is by asking a series of questions. In the second, two teams are used and each one tries to guess an item of any kind whatsoever that has been chosen by the opposing team.

No game is more effective in bringing a group of teen-agers together than "Le général a dit," to use its French title. The whole group forms a circle. A leader, standing outside where he can see everyone, shouts one command after another. These must be obeyed *only* if they are preceded by the phrase, "The general says." If he calls, "The general says to raise your right arm," everyone must obey, but if he says, "Sit on the floor," no one must move, and anyone who does is out of the game. The group is commanded to march, turn about face, walk backward, stand on one foot, etc., with or without "the general says." The result is sheer hilarity.

Now for a couple of dancing games, both importations from Europe. In the first, which is called Statues or Hold that Pose, the couples are instructed to keep dancing until the music stops. They must then stop at once and remain in the exact position until told to relax. If either person moves, the couple must retire to the sidelines. The second game requires a top hat, or any other kind of amusing headgear. While the dance is in progress, the leader puts the hat on the head of one of the boys. His partner must immediately take it off and put it on the head of another boy, whose partner must in turn try to get rid of it as quickly as possible. The music stops without warning, and the couple who have the hat in their possession are out of the game. This goes on until only one couple is left, the winners of the hat dance.

For further sources of teen-age fun, we strongly recommend

singing games and folk dances. Practically every young person of this age knows the words of "I've Been Working on the Railroad," "Oh, Susanna," and "Good Night, Ladies." If not, they can be learned in a few minutes. To get the most fun out of these songs, however, the host or hostess should devise action to go with the choruses, or follow the pattern suggested in the following sample.

Tune: "Oh, Susanna."

Words: 1. Oh, I come from Alabama with my banjo on my knee.
2. I'm going to Louisiana, boys, my true love for to see.
3. It rained all day the night I left, the weather it was dry.
4. The sun so hot I froze to death, Susanna don't you cry.

Chorus: Oh, Susanna, don't you cry for me, for I've come from Alabama with my banjo on my knee. (Repeat chorus)

Formation: All stand in single circle, girls on partners' right.

Action: 1. While boys clap, all girls take four steps to the center and four back. 2. While girls clap, all boys do the same. 3. Girls to the center and back. 4. Boys to the center and back.

Chorus: All face partners and take right hands. Girls move clockwise, and boys counterclockwise in a grand right and left, alternating hands and shoulders as they pass each other by. On the second chorus each boy takes the nearest girl for a partner, joins hands in a skating position, and promenades her counterclockwise around the circle. The game begins again with the new partner.

Singing games are an excellent introduction to more complicated folk dances that require a caller (live or on a record). The Ace of Diamonds, the Chimes of Dunkirk, the Swedish Clap Dance and the Virginia Reel are as enjoyable now as they ever were. Alternating these older dances with the newer steps makes for a lively and varied evening, and gives those who are poor at social dancing a chance to participate.

And there is just plain group singing. Anyone who has been in a bus or train with a group of teen-agers traveling to or from a camp has experienced—sometimes painfully—this activity.

Parties

For a party, as opposed to an informal get-together, written invitations are preferable to oral ones. To save embarrassment about bringing presents, mention should be made if it is a birthday party. The party in a sense begins with the invitation, since it sets the tone and atmosphere. Therefore your teen-ager should try to think of something original and amusing to say or draw. Invitations to parties for younger teen-agers should state the hour at which the party is to end as well as begin. This makes it easier for parents to call a halt to the fun.

The major items on the agenda of teen-age parties are usually dancing and eating. However, there are bound to be a number of boys and girls who do not dance well. Sometimes they can be drawn into the dancing games we have suggested, but there should be time and opportunity for other activities as well. With older teen-agers, conversation corners are a "must," as well as things to look at and talk about, such as albums, art books, and collections. These teen-agers will probably consider themselves too sophisticated for party games, but not so the younger ones. Some of the games require considerable organization; and, if the party is large, it may be advisable for an older person to handle them. A college student who is studying to be a recreation leader might be available at a small cost, or the father of the family might come in just for a game or two.

As for food, younger teen-agers are generally more interested in quantity than uniqueness. Hamburgers or the makings for sandwiches are their speed, plus plenty of ice cream and cake. Since some boys at this age are likely to cut up, it is usually best for the mother to help out with the food. Also, good manners are suggested by asking them to put on their jackets before coming to the table, and a judiciously planned seating arrangement might also help. With older teen-agers, refreshments can be quite a different affair. The table should be decorated much the same as for adult parties, with flowers, place cards, amusing paper napkins, and perhaps candlelight and soft background music. A buffet supper, with the guests seated at separate card tables, might help to complete the adult atmosphere. Food must still be plentiful, but now the main dish can be something of an unusual nature, particularly if the party is given by a girl. One suggestion: Fondue Bourguignonne, the latest rage in Switzerland. A metal bowl containing a mixture of oils is set on a flame or hot plate on the table. The guests then spear chunks of raw meat with a fork and put them in the oil until done. The cooked meat is then dipped in various relishes and eaten with potato salad, tomatoes, cucumbers, or potato chips.

Dancing

Dancing in the teens need not be limited to the social variety, especially for girls. Those who have had some introduction to the techniques of the modern dance will now find new satisfactions in this medium. Body conditioning through exercise will counteract feelings of lassitude that so often descend upon teen-agers. Greater physical control may well bring greater emotional control; and, as they feel more in command of themselves, they are likely to become more confident and optimistic in outlook. Those who have no interest in athletics or who simply "aren't the type," may still experience the benefits of exercise and feel that their bodies are working with them instead of against them. Those who have trouble learning the advanced social dances will surely find them easier after practice in the rhythmic, patterned movements of the modern dance.

In addition to these benefits, there is one other that comes to the fore in adolescence. We have spoken in earlier chapters of the emotional satisfactions derived from moving to music. Among teen-agers, these satisfactions are particularly profound in view of the new realms of feeling now opening to them, as well as the tensions and internal pressures that beset them. Typically, they find it hard to communicate these highly personal reactions in words, and in many cases they hesitate to try. But through the dance they learn to use their bodies as instruments of expression, and in movement they may successfully exteriorize even the feelings they are unable to understand. Moreover, the teen-ager's urge to dramatize himself, often expressed in posing and posturing before a mirror, can find a legitimate, acceptable outlet in the relatively free movements of the modern dance. To this end, it is important to give them an ample opportunity to create their own sequences and express themselves in their own individual ways.

Generally speaking, it is too late to start ballet or modern dance during the teens. However, we again remind our readers that exercise to music may be the answer for many of these young people. Under the leadership of a skillful teacher, this medium offers the physical advantages of calisthenics without its dullness and repetitiousness. Likewise, it provides practice in the rhythm and control of the dance without requiring a great deal of preliminary training—in fact, those who find it difficult to dance, or who resist it, may do very well in rhythmic exercises. The appeal to vanity can be used as a particularly effective lure at this period, for every teen-age girl wants to be slim, supple, and poised. Expression, too, may be free at times, giving the girls an opportunity to draw on their own imagination and express unspoken feelings. Moreover, since many teachers look to both ballet and modern dance for inspiration and ideas, the pupils will have a taste of both, and some may still find it worth while to "graduate" to one or the other of these dance forms.

Talk Fests

Teen-agers love to talk, and they should have an opportunity to make the most of it. Undoubtedly just "gabbing," no matter what is said, has something of the release value of a psychoanalytic session and acts as a safety valve for inner tensions. Some of it, however, is merely a substitute for activity, and adults have a perfect right to limit the use of the telephone when it is constantly pre-empted.

Real issues are often skirted in teen talk because of self-consciousness, but close companions (usually of the same sex, and more often girls than boys) will sometimes unburden their worries and doubts and face their problems together. When this is done in a group, as in a hen party or sometimes in an all-male bull session, the discovery that everybody else is beset by much the same difficulties itself provides reassurance and a greater sense of security. Real information is often exchanged in these discussions: ways of coming to terms with trying parents; how to act in social situations; interesting activities when things are dull; suggestions about grooming, style, and etiquette; comments about teachers and, always, about members of the opposite sex. Each one has a chance to compare the patterns of his own family with others, usually to find that some things are better and some are worse. Practically anything that appears queer, unusual, off-beat, comes in for discussion—partly to see if it really is so, partly to gain security by revealing special knowledge: "Did you know that . . ." and "You should have seen . . ." are favorite expressions. Among older teen-agers, half-formulated opinions about experimental movies, progressive jazz, foreign vs. domestic cars, renting vs. buying a home, and political issues may be advanced to see how others respond. Among both the older and the younger, feelings are gradually crystallized and tested out against the reactions of others—and, through this process, attitudes and standards are formed, and a permanent personality begins to emerge.

Teen-Age Reading

During the teens the door to the great world of books opens wide. All the reading interests of the preteen period remain alive—at least in the early teens—but every one of them can be fed by books that offer meatier fare. For teen-agers are reaching out to understand human relationships, the ways of the world, and the realities of life as never before. Hero-worship is still in evidence, but it gradually changes from blind admiration of distant, legendary, or superhuman personalities to those more closely akin to the actual world and realistic aspirations. Adventure tales reach farther out into space, higher up real mountains (such as Annapurna and Everest), deeper into science. The folk stories read by preteeners are gradually replaced by full-length portraits of life in other countries and at other periods. The teen-ager's desire to be creative leads him into books about dancers, artists, musicians and writers. Fully developed hobby pursuits bring him to whole books about separate interests instead of simplified sets of directions of the how-to sort.

But teen-age reading is not simply a variation on old themes. Radically new interests develop. In the middle and late teens, romantic novels capture the interest of girls, and less often of boys. The adolescent urge to improve the world and relieve suffering on a wholesale scale gradually comes down to earth, and books like *The Grapes of Wrath* begin to attract. The doggerel and simple rhymes that intrigued the earlier ages make way for the appreciation of great poetry. The approach of the time when they must choose an occupation leads the young people to career guides and vocational stories. Books labeled "juvenile" are frequently scorned, and teen-agers from fifteen up will dip more and more into the volumes they find on their parents' shelves. Some read both—voraciously. We may find it wise temporarily to remove a few of our own that seem unsuited to their age, and leave such titles as *Kon-Tiki, Lost Horizon, The Good Earth, Room for One More, The Sea Around Us,* and *Arrowsmith*. By discussing these books with our growing sons and daughters, we bridge the gap between juvenile and adult reading, as well as the gap between their thinking and ours.

Again we shall not attempt to suggest a full list of books, but rather give samples of the most suitable and enjoyable types. Library bulletins, magazines, and some bookstores and book services are excellent sources for current titles. The book by Josette Frank, *Your Child's Reading Today,* is a mine of information and understanding on this whole question. She reminds us of the wide variations in teen-age taste: "The reading adviser cannot answer the question, 'Please tell me a good book for a thirteen-year-old boy.' For this age there is no longer a general prescription. The book has to be chosen for the particular girl or boy, to meet the individual interests and tastes of that young person, as for an adult." Moreover, there is always the possibility of awakening a totally new interest through a fascinating book. For this reason we shall try to illustrate the widest possible *range* of teen-age reading in the categories that follow, and hope that our suggestions will help to enrich leisure-time reading in the years from thirteen to eighteen.

Biography, keyed to the aspirations and idealism of young people: books about such social leaders as Joan of Arc, Gandhi, Franklin D. Roosevelt, Eleanor Roosevelt, Albert Schweitzer, Lincoln; about scientists and doctors, such as George Washington Carver, Einstein, Galileo, Elizabeth Blackwell; about artists and writers, such as Leonardo da Vinci, Pavlova, Walt Whitman, Cézanne; about other great people, such as Helen Keller, Louis Braille, Houdini, Robert E. Lee.

Historical fact and fiction, focusing on dramatic events as well as people: *Marco Polo*, by Manuel Komroff; *The Prince and the Pauper*, by Mark Twain; *Wagons Westward*, by Armstrong Sperry; *The Lost Queen of Egypt*, by Lucille Morrison; Hendrik Van Loon's *The Story of Mankind*.

Discovery and exploration: under the sea, in *The Silent World*, by Jacques Yves Cousteau; up the highest mountains in *Annapurna*, by Maurice Herzog, and *The Story of Everest*, by W. H. Murray; into the polar world, in *North*, by Kaare Rodahl; through outer space, in *The Conquest of the Moon*, edited by Cornelius Ryan.

Adventure stories: Treasure Island, Robinson Crusoe, The Three Musketeers; and more recent books, such as *Stories of the Sea*, selected by Phyllis Fenner; *The Lure of Danger*, compiled by Margaret C. Scoggin; *Five Boys in a Cave*, by Richard Church; *Copperhead Hollow*, by Gerald Raftery; *Space, Space, Space,* by William Sloane.

Science: The Sea Around Us, by Rachel L. Carson; *The Story of People*, by May Edel; *The Wonderful World*, by James Fisher; *Explorations in Science*, by Waldemar Kaempffert; *Great Discoveries of Young Chemists*, by James Kendall; *Engineers' Dreams*, by Willy Ley; *Man, Time and Fossils*, by Ruth Moore; *The Fabulous Insects*, edited by Charles Neider; *All about Language*, by Mario Pei; *Treasury of Science*, by Harlow Shapley; *Explaining the Atom*, by Selig Hecht.

Poetry: Sonnets from the Portuguese, by Elizabeth Barrett Browning; *Come Hither*, edited by Walter de la Mare; *Poems*, by Emily Dickinson; *The Prophet*, by Kahlil Gibran; *Poems Selected for Young People*, by Edna St. Vincent Millay; *100 Story Poems*, edited by Elinor Parker; *Complete Poems*, by Carl Sandburg.

Science fiction: The Caves of Steel, by Isaac Azimov; *Science Fiction Omnibus*, edited by E. F. Bleiler and T. E. Dikty; *The Martian Chronicles*, by Ray Bradbury; *Seven Science Fiction Novels*, by H. G. Wells; *Omnibus*, by Jules Verne; *Undersea Quest*, by Frederick Pohl and Jack Williamson; *Adventures in Time and Space*, by R. J. Healy and J. F. McComas.

The world of work: career stories and informative accounts of all major vocations, as in *Sue Barton, Student Nurse,* by Helen Dore Boylston; *Deadline,* by William Corbin; *Your Career in Motion Pictures, Radio and Television,* by Charles R. Jones; *Curtain Going Up: the Story of Katharine Cornell,* by Gladys Malvern.

Stories of life and love, written with an understanding of the teen-ager's interest in personal relationships: *To Tell Your Love,* by Mary Stolz; *Karen,* by Borghild Dahl; *Laughing Boy,* by Oliver La Farge; *The Bridge of San Luis Rey,* by Thornton Wilder.

Life with nature: animal stories, outdoor life, pets. Such books as *My Friend Flicka,* by Mary O'Hara; *The Call of the Wild,* by Jack London; *Let's Go Camping,* by Harry Zarchy; *Strange Animals I Have Known,* by Raymond L. Ditmars; *Man-Eaters of Kumaon,* by James Corbett; *You Train Your Dog,* by Frederick Reiter.

Hobby books: Photography for Boys and Girls, by Stanley W. Bowler; *The Young Collector's Handbook,* by A. Hyatt Verrill; *The Betty Betz Teen-Age Cookbook;* books by Joseph Leeming and Harry Zarchy; and books about crafts and use of tools.

Sports stories that offer excitement, information, and stimulus to good relationships. Among these are *All-American,* by John R. Tunis; *Jackie Robinson,* told to Wendell Smith; *Captain of the Ice,* by Charles Verral; *Judy, Tennis Ace,* by Helen Jacobs.

Kitchen Fun

The frequency of teen-age raids on the kitchen, and the rapidity with which all kinds of food disappears, points unmistakably in one direction: Show them that cooking can be fun, and help them learn to make their own snacks and refreshments! We hope they have already experienced many of the delights as well as the chores of the kitchen in the years before the teens—but if they haven't, it is not too late to begin.

Preparing food can be one of the most satisfying and creative forms of home entertainment for young people of both sexes. Fun in the kitchen is a palatable way of preparing for family life in the future. If strict rules about waste and cleaning up are made and enforced, this kind of play can help lighten the burden on harried mothers. Girls will find their delicacies effective "date bait," to use the title of a recent book on teen-age cookery. Boys will be intrigued by the chemistry and gadgetry of cooking, and will sometimes develop specialties of their own. And girls and boys will get to know each other in a working environment, not merely in the parlor, the recreation room, or the movies.

No room in the house is more closely associated with work than the kitchen, yet none has greater possibilities for play. We shall briefly list some of these possibilities, with the reminder that teen-agers usually need a mother's patient cooperation in learning to read recipes, select and measure ingredients, and plan the whole procedure. While nothing is so encouraging as a batch of cookies that comes out right, nothing is more confusing and disheartening than a lot of pots and pans and ingredients that refuse to come together.

1. Encourage your daughter to make at least one interesting dish when she has a party or invites a few friends to the house. Some of these she can perhaps devise herself; others could be bacon rolls, shish kebab, baked Alaska, a multicolored jello salad, unusual drink combinations such as ginger ale with grape juice or dessert combinations such as frozen orange juice with ice cream.

2. Suggest making fudge, cup cakes, or cookies *during* a boy-girl date—for consumption the same evening. If this sounds like asking for trouble, because of the mess in the kitchen, you can remind them about your rules for cleaning up and the fact that you are supplying the ingredients. Kitchen fun of this sort will help keep them home for a change, and give them something concrete to do.

3. Acquire some books on special kinds of cooking: casserole cookery, salad-making, stick-cooking for out of doors. Let your teen-agers experiment, or help you experiment, with new dishes —especially when they complain about the sameness of the home fare!

4. To give them a good start, let younger teen-agers use the ready mixes. This practically insures success, and makes cook-

ing less forbidding. Encourage the young cooks to add their own variations and original touches.

5. Teen-agers might take over one or two meals a week completely; for instance, Sunday breakfast or supper. It will give them a chance to exhibit their skill, and to relieve their mother in a most welcome way.

6. If your teen-agers have friends from different nationality backgrounds, you might suggest inviting them in to show how to make their native dishes. A party in which several different types of dishes are served will be particularly exciting for young people.

Camp Experiences

The present tendency to start children at summer camps at seven or even sooner (already discussed) often has the effect of associating this experience primarily with the younger ages. Boys and girls who begin so early frequently feel that they have had "enough camp" by the time they reach ten to twelve. This feeling is often quite justified, particularly if they continue to go to the same camp or the same type of camp for several years in a row. Unless a great deal of attention is paid to the youngsters' growth needs, the experience becomes repetitious and the luster is lost.

These facts tend to obscure the many values of camp for older children, and may cause us to overlook special types of camp that appeal particularly to teen-agers. In fact, so much can be offered to this age group that there is something to be said for starting the experience at a later age, say between ten and twelve.

Camp offers the teen-ager a much-needed and much-desired opportunity to get away from home and fend for himself. It gives him the experience of group living at a time when his social needs are at a peak. It provides healthy outlets for tensions that are bound to beset him. It enables him to associate with responsible leaders who are not too many years older or too far removed from his own worries and confusions. The outdoor life keeps his body in good working order at a time when growth and change are rapid; close contact with nature helps him maintain his perspective.

Camps should be chosen with full regard to the needs and interests of the particular child. Some may profit from a coeducational environment more than others. Some may want to specialize in certain activities such as sailing, horseback-riding, or crafts. Some may benefit from competition more than others, although we believe it wise to avoid camps where competition is extreme, as, for example, camps that climax the season with a bitter and prolonged "war" in which all the campers and counselors are divided into two rival groups.

There are certain general considerations to be borne in mind in helping any teen-ager choose a camp. The camp should be either limited to older children, or have special activities and special living arrangements for the older group. They need their independence and should not have to mingle constantly with younger campers. (Sometimes it is desirable to choose a camp specifically for teen-agers in order to separate the older child from a younger brother or sister, who might go to another camp.) The program for teen-agers should be even more flexible and individualized than the program for younger children. They should have a full voice in planning activities, and there should be plenty of nonscheduled hours when they can read, relax, and talk things out with their bunk mates and counselors. Older teen-agers should be required to take on definite responsibilities around the camp; they will benefit particularly from experience in leadership and from practical work activities.

A good many teen-agers are happiest and profit most at the specialized camps. We would like to call particular attention to the work camps that are now springing up in many parts of the country. Most of them are farm camps—some coeducational, some for boys only. In addition to the experience of farming, the campers generally have a chance to live a more rugged and independent life than at most children's camps. They repair or construct buildings, fell trees, build paths, clear fields—and still have time for sports, dancing, dramatics, and other creative pursuits. Contact with counselors and supervisors is on a more adult level, and the entire atmosphere is one of democratic participation. Often, there is some study of the camp area's social and economic background, sometimes leading to construction of community resources such as playgrounds. (The Quaker work camps are especially effective in this field.) Some of these camps are interracial and interreligious and therefore offer varied social experience. All in all, they are particularly suited to young people from cities and larger towns who have had little opportunity to do manual work, or who have little appreciation of it. They also provide a welcome change for those who have had years of standard camping.

Among the other specialized camps are sailing camps; canoe camps; mountain-climbing camps; aquatic camps; camps for dramatics, riding, painting, music, or dancing. An interesting and successful project is the yearly "Encampment for Citizenship" conducted by the Ethical Culture Society in New York City. Young men and women from many countries and backgrounds meet and discuss social questions, visit the United Nations and other points of interest, engage in a varied program of cultural and social activities.

There are also a number of touring camps, generally conducted by an educator who takes a group of young people across the country by bus on a camping and sight-seeing trip. In addition, we would suggest that older teen-agers and their parents look into the growing network of Youth Hostels in this country, and obtain information from the national organization. These hostels are supervised, inexpensive, and usually located within a day's hiking distance from each other.

(Names and addresses of specialized as well as conventional camps can be obtained from the American Camping Association, 343 South Dearborn Street, Chicago 4, from its recent survey of 12,600 camps in the United States. Some of the leading magazines, including *Parents' Magazine*, conduct camp advisory services.)

Are teen-agers too old or sophisticated to go on a car-camping trip with the rest of the family? Certainly not, as a general rule. Many of them are included in the family groups (said to number in the millions) who spend their vacations in tents and trailers. Living together in the out-of-doors is one of the best ways for members of the family to rediscover each other, and one of the better ways to bring teen-agers back into the fold after years of going away to summer camp.

Family Doings

Are teen-agers too independent or too sophisticated for family activities? A study of school children's opinions on family happiness, made by the author (R.M.G.) indicates that the reverse is nearer the truth. They want *more* family activities, not fewer—and they even express a need for guidance from their elders along with it, provided it isn't given in a "preaching" manner. There's still room in the lives of busy teen-agers for games with the family (both table games and active games), for "fixing up" a room together, for trips to points of interest, for watching and discussing special television programs together. Let's not forget that the family gives our uncertain teen-agers a much-needed home base.

However, teen-agers are likely to prefer activities alone with their parents rather than with younger children included, for the more they are treated like adults, the better they like it. Moreover, the older children frequently don't get enough exclusive attention from parents and appreciate, quite understandably, activities in which younger ones are left out. Going to a play or concert together, or simply out to dinner at the home of friends or at a restaurant can be a high point in their lives. Exchanging books, and comments on them is a particularly satisfying and enriching experience for them. We suggest that it shouldn't be hampered by overconcern that the books will be too "advanced" or "give them ideas"—especially when we know what they are reading and are willing to discuss it with them in adult fashion.

Going It Alone

Are we giving our teen-agers enough experience with independence? Are we trusting them to hold their own and "know the ropes" when they're away from us? Some families deliberately give their teen-age sons and daughters a chance to visit other cities or go on camping trips during the summer. We have recommended youth hosteling at another point, but it deserves a second mention here. Naturally we don't suggest sending them on their own too abruptly, any more than we'd suggest throwing a child in the water to get him to swim. There must be a good deal of preliminary planning and a reasonable number of cautions and warnings, though not enough to make them anxious and spoil the fun.

In one case we know, a fifteen-year-old girl and two friends of about the same age traveled two hundred miles to Washington and spent several days there during their Easter vacation. Their parents had arranged accommodations at a hotel that was well known to them, and helped them with traveler's checks and other necessities. In addition, they were armed with telephone numbers of friends in the vicinity in case of emergency, and they didn't balk at the idea of calling their parents once or twice to give them a three-minute report. Guide books and even history books were consulted beforehand, and a tour plan was made, but with time left for things that would crop up in the course of their visit. Budgeting, too, was done ahead of time, and a careful record of expenses was kept. Not the least of their triumphs was the discovery of a restaurant with a lobster dinner for $1.50 —which their parents had never found on their own visits to Washington. Results: "Fabulous!" "We know each other better, too!" "Let's start planning another trip for next year!"

Ask a Busy Teen-Ager

A section of New Jersey was desperately in need of a hospital. An entire valley, comprising several towns, had only one sickbed for each 800 inhabitants, as compared with the minimum standard of one to 200. The citizens were slow in organizing to meet the need, and the communities were tired of campaigns. But a group of teen-agers from one of the high schools stepped in and took over almost the entire responsibility. Organizing themselves into six districts, they used practically every known means of raising money—cake sales, variety shows and plays, collection boxes, spaghetti dinners, card parties—plus some unique projects like delivering business directories, and charging admission to see a builder's model house. Today, as a result of their efforts, the hospital is a reality, with an especially well-equipped children's wing which the teen-agers have adopted as their own. What is more, when news of this triumph got around the country, teen-agers in several widely separated towns organized for the same constructive purpose.

Can this undertaking of the Jersey teen-agers be classified as play or as work? Does the story of their endeavor belong in a book on recreation? We believe it can be called play in the sense that it was a freely chosen activity which occupied their spare time and afforded them genuine enjoyment. And it belongs in this book for the very reason that a new, enlarged conception of play is needed, one that includes the constructive use of leisure time. When a girl chooses to bake a cake during her spare time, or when a man builds a chair on his day off, we call it play rather than work. The fact that it benefits the whole family makes it no less play. Similarly, why should we not include activities that benefit the whole *community* in our concept of play?

The ideal time to instill this idea is when our children are in their early teens. Typically, these youngsters have a special urge to prove their worth, and one conspicuous way to do this is to make a recognized contribution to the community. Their idealism stands ready to be challenged and turned to good purposes. They resent being treated as children and are aching to show that they aren't immature. Most of them have reservoirs of energy that are waiting to be channeled and organized, and even those who appear inert and apathetic rarely lack the energy—it is only blocked by conflicts, self-consciousness, or feelings of inadequacy. It can be released, and their difficulties relieved at the same time, if they discover new opportunities to work constructively with others. Moreover, many teen-agers are bored with endless hours spent in "just sitting around gabbing," to use their phrase for it. They are ready to "do something"—and it's up to us to show them the possibilities that exist practically at their doorstep.

There is an old expression that has a good deal of truth in it: "Ask a busy man." Yes, if you want to find somebody to do a job, look for a person who is already active. Communities have long been familiar with this idea, and the work has piled heavily on the shoulders of a few willing and able people. But today this notion is being revised. Social organizations are looking everywhere for new faces, not merely because there is plenty of work to be done, but because participation in community activities helps people grow. Now, the largest group of new faces is to be found among young people who are still in school. It's high time we changed the old saying to, "Ask a busy teen-ager."

To prove this point, and to suggest some stimulating forms of leisure activity, let's glance at a few teen-age achievements. In Westchester County, New York, teen-agers, working through the Community Chests and Councils, combed the entire area for swimming pools, approached the owners with the request that they allow them to be used by polio victims a few hours each week. Many of the teen-agers now go to the pools with the children to help them have a good time and build up wasted muscles. In Dayton, Ohio, a gang of fourteen-year-olds descended upon the Volunteer Bureau in a body. They wanted something to do, but they had to "do it together." Their assignment was clearing away land to be used by a "Y" camp. Several Saturdays in a row they picked up rocks, cut grass, tore out bushes and weeds, and enjoyed this rough and ready work "even more than baseball." If you have ever been in the Harlem section of New York City, you might scoff at the idea of planting trees amid the stony tenements. Yet, under the leadership of a lively settlement worker, a barren, littered street has been transformed into a tree-lined avenue in a few short months, and the "men" who did the job were all under eighteen.

Does your town library need someone to alphabetize books? Ask a teen-ager! Are the people in the old-age home aching to hear a concert? Your high school can supply talented musicians from among its students. Is there a convalescent home or hospital for crippled children in your vicinity? Teen-agers are the ideal persons to teach the patients games and crafts. (See chapter 17 for details and chapter 12 for other service hobbies.) Just name it—any community need whatever—and you will find a place for teen-agers. Give them the opportunity to feel useful and use their leisure time creatively! The idea that they are "just children" who should be protected from life and its responsibilities is fast fading out. Never underestimate the power of a teen-ager.

Leisure for Leisure's Sake

A book such as this one that suggests the benefits and values of the many forms of play may give the impression that one's leisure time should be as crowded with activity as one's work hours. Indeed, merely bringing together such a large number of possibilities for recreation may itself have an overwhelming effect on the reader. He may feel tempted to try them all, like the child in the candy store, and he may be as concerned about what he is missing as about what he chooses. Too, he may feel hard pressed by the fact that there is "so much to do and so little time to do it in." Indeed, the busy teen-ager can be too busy. All of which makes leisure impossible and defeats the very spirit of recreation.

Actually, of course, our play life is a matter of exploration and selection, like everything else in a life that offers so much. However, there is one use of leisure time that is as much a question of necessity as it is of choice. It is the use of leisure time for *leisure*. Let us not forget that our spare hours should not be wholly filled with "activities" and "pursuits"—words we have frequently used—since we are also in need of relaxed hours when our only purpose is to pursue nothing at all. We require these hours for both body and mind—for our nerves, our blood pressure, our muscles, and above all for the refreshment of our spirit.

In a day when we feel driven from one activity to another, the ability to be leisurely does not always come by itself. It has to be cultivated. We have to practice letting go without feeling let down. We have to school ourselves to drift without asking "Whither?", and make a habit of "unwinding" for a while each day.

Any number of recommendations can be made for the leisurely use of leisure. Here again it is a question of personal choice and knowledge of ourselves. There is browsing in books, quietly reading instead of actively studying their contents. There are slow walks and meanderings rather than hikes to "get places." There are the wanderings of the *mind* "over the wilderness of Being," to use the phrase of Santayana. And communion with a painting or piece of sculpture, quite apart from its name or date or the "influences" that produced it. The silent companionship of a dog may be the answer for some of us, as it was with Emerson. Or fishing that is not done for the sake of catching, sunbathing without competing for a tan, canoeing in which we drift as much as we paddle. And sitting quietly in a house of worship, reading poetry, conversing without "carrying on a conversation," or listening to music in the dark.

In a word, every one of us needs to escape from "reality" at times. It renews our energies, corrects our perspective, "it restoreth the soul." The play of feelings and images and ideas that takes place is one of the most fruitful of all forms of play. We all need to cultivate what has been called "the fine art of beneficial floating."

CHAPTER XII

We All Need a Hobby

Finding a Hobby

As a small child, Frances always liked "little things." Her parents would save every small object they came across—hairpins, thimbles, spools, pillboxes—and she would play with them for hours on end. Today, at twelve, her hobby is figurines—tiny animals which she started to collect on a trip out West. Interestingly enough, her handwriting is small and she prefers dresses that are decorated with small designs. Her hobby seems to be admirably suited to her personality.

Steven arrived at his hobby in quite a different way. During the war, when his father was a pilot in the Army Air Force, he used to save airplane pictures from cereal boxes and magazines. Soon he was able to describe and spot every type that was used in the war. This interest led to several years of model making. Now, at sixteen, he is already something of an authority on aerodynamics, and is by far the best student in his physics class at high school.

In Allan's case a hobby grew out of a gift. His uncle had bought him a small camera on his tenth birthday, and the boy soon developed the knack of taking first-rate pictures. At Christmas time he sent out clever photographic greeting cards to his friends and relatives—including, of course, his uncle. They were so striking that people began asking him to make up cards on order. So far he has put the money he makes right back into his hobby, and he now has the most fully equipped darkroom in town.

These brief stories indicate that hobbies originate in a variety of ways. A few, like the collection of figurines, seem to stem directly from the personality, although the particular form they take is usually determined by chance experience. Some arise from following in the footsteps of a parent, teacher, or friend of the family; others are initiated by a gift or stem from activities at school, camp, or scout meetings.

A hobby is not a mere pastime. Nor is it a form of dabbling. It is a leisure-time activity which we follow with intense interest and develop through persistent effort. It can be called equally "work done in a spirit of play" and "play carried on in a spirit of work." As it develops, new facets are constantly coming to light and the experience becomes deeper and richer.

In general, hobbies are not only absorbing in themselves but keep us and our children in touch with the world in which we live. Many different interests are fed by hobbies. Some of us may be fascinated by the growth of animals or plants, others by mechanical processes, still others by the challenge of games like chess or by the cultivation of manual skills as in weaving.

Although children are likely to develop their own hobbies despite adults, let us suppose that your youngster has not developed any interest to a point where it can be considered a hobby—yet he admires the hobbies of others and feels he would like to have one of his own. What could you do?

1. *Sit down with him and look over his life,* in an effort to find the things that have excited his interest most. First, consider what activities hold his attention longest? What has he quizzed you about most persistently? When he talks about the hobbies of his friends, which does he dwell on longest? If his school offers arts and crafts, shopwork and experiments in science, see which activities attract him most, and which call forth his most creative efforts. These interests may be anything from driftwood sculpture to electrical gadgets to semiprecious stones, but they will at least suggest clues to possible hobbies.

2. *Watch the workings of his mind and hands.* Does your boy or girl love to keep things in order, with a place for everything and everything in its place? Perhaps he would be interested in a collection of some sort, neatly stored and carefully displayed. Is he adept with his hands—high in "manual dexterity"? A

hobby like metal work, needlework, or weaving might be the answer. Does he show a flair for the graphic arts such as painting or drawing? One of these fields might become an enduring interest—or perhaps some more specialized form of art such as caricatures or animal sketches. Does your child have a particular affinity for nature—does he like to walk in the woods, climb mountains, pick berries or flowers? Nature study in one of its many forms may be the hobby for that youngster. On the other hand, your child may be of a scientific turn of mind, always looking for whys and wherefores. Perhaps he is fascinated with machines, or is constantly constructing gadgets of one kind or another. Models of cars or trains may become that youngster's consuming interest, or perhaps he will concentrate on repairing household appliances or building radio and television sets. In any case, start from where the child now is, and see what hobbies might be congenial to him.

These are only a few of the inclinations that feed into lasting hobbies. The problem is no simple one, however, for most hobbies result from a combination of interests and abilities, and do not stem from a single factor. Gardening may express both an interest in nature and a desire to study soil chemistry; it may also reflect an urge to do heavy muscular work or even a desire to find refuge from competitive sports and games.

In any case, try to help children find hobbies that are keyed to their personalities and abilities or try to help them avoid making a haphazard, unthinking choice. It is better to uncover their real interests than to impose activities because we ourselves like them, or because we think they are good for them. An avocation, like a vocation, must fit the person.

3. If no single interest is outstanding, make it possible for your child to explore a number of fields. You may find that he barks up a good many wrong trees; but in so doing he will learn something about himself, and you will know him better, too. What if your son takes a leathercraft course and drops it in the middle? Does it really matter if your daughter experiments with costume jewelry and later turns to flower arrangements? Hobbies frequently become lifetime pursuits, and a few weeks or months of trial and error will do more good than harm. Moreover, each time a boy or girl tries a hobby, he is experimenting with possible occupation, or an area from which a vocation may ultimately be chosen. The process of finding the right hobby is therefore a constructive experience in itself.

If your child is having difficulty in selecting a hobby and wants some guidance, the check list in the next section may help to narrow down the field of exploration. He might also make a scrapbook of magazine articles that deal with different leisure-time activities. Suggestions for preteeners (pages 242-245) apply even more at later ages. Books on hobbies are available at any good library. Specialists in different fields can be found among teachers, Scout, or "Y" leaders, and the parents of friends. It will be a fascinating experience for the boy or girl to visit them, to see various hobbies in operation and learn about their values first hand. Let them make a hobby of finding a hobby!

4. *Observe your child's needs as well as his interests and abilities.* In many cases a word or two of encouragement, or a carefully chosen gift, may lead to a hobby that will help a child overcome personal difficulties and even change the course of his development for the better. There are hobbies that encourage sociability, others that promote self-assurance or stimulate the use of the imagination.

5. *The choice of a general hobby is not the whole story.* To get the most out of an interest like photography or cooking or coins, it is far better to specialize than to try to cover the whole field. The girl who concentrates on salads or pies will develop her skill to a far greater degree, and have something far more interesting to offer others, than the one who occupies herself with cooking in general. Photography is a huge, overwhelming field these days; trying to be an expert in all phases is apt to be discouraging. But even a youngster of twelve or thirteen can make headway if he specializes in one phase, such as making enlargements. The coin collector will have a more challenging and unusual hobby if he limits himself to one type of collecting, such as shapes other than round. As always, quality means more than quantity, and it is better to concentrate than spread one's self thin.

It is wise, then, to start in with a general hobby in order to explore the field as a whole; but a *specialty* is more likely to be creative and to stimulate habits of perseverance, thoroughness, and systematic effort. Moreover, it will better express the hobbyist's individuality and take on the color of his personality. But most important, a specialty will bring more downright enjoyment.

A Hobby Check List

Some activities, like the youngster's card-trading or match-cover collecting, are too limited to be called hobbies. Others, such as polo, are too expensive to be within reach of more than a few. Still others, like palmistry and numerology (often included in older hobby books), are based on superstition and induce undesirable habits of thinking. There is no point in encouraging these interests when many more constructive and satisfying hobbies are available.

No single classification of hobbies can be fully satisfactory, since the categories are bound to overlap. The following list, however, contains most of the popular activities, as well as some more unusual pursuits. It is offered with this reservation: the most rewarding hobby is likely to be the one that a person devises to suit himself.

Scientific hobbies

    astronomy (star-observing, making and operating a telescope, etc.)
    microscopy (specializing in any objects that arouse interest)
    electronics (radio, television, intercommunication systems, phonographs, calculators, etc.)
    meteorology (weather study, weather maps, forecasting)
    chemistry (experimentation, making plastics, etc.)

Amusement hobbies

    puppetry (making puppets, writing shows, staging and acting)
    magic, sleight of hand
    checkers
    chess
    bridge
    dramatics
    charades
    other card games and board games
    crosswords, anagrams, Double Crostics

Manual hobbies

model-making (ships, automobiles, trains, sailing vessels, wagons and coaches, airplanes, houses, etc.)
woodworking (carpentry, cabinetmaking, whittling, carving)
metal working (ironwork, brasswork, pewter, jewelry making)
printing
bookbinding
weaving
upholstery
leather work
sewing, dressmaking, dress designing
knitting, crocheting
cooking
repairing appliances
glass blowing
plastic work
rebuilding antique cars

Art hobbies

a. Graphic arts
- sketching, drawing
- water colors
- oil painting
- engraving
- woodcuts
- etching
- pastels
- cartoons

b. Plastic arts
- clay modeling
- ceramics
- plastics
- sculpture

c. Photographic arts
- black and white
- color
- stereoscopic
- microphotography
- motion pictures
- scientific photography

d. Musical arts
- piano
- violin
- accordion
- banjo, guitar, ukulele
- trios, quartets
- percussion instruments
- singing (individual, choral)
- composing
- band, orchestra

e. Dancing
- ballroom
- tap
- acrobatic
- folk dancing
- adagio
- ballet
- choreography

Animal hobbies

- dogs
- cats
- tropical fish
- birds (canary, parakeet, pigeon)
- hamsters
- lizards, snakes, turtles, ants, bird-watching
- white mice
- rabbits
- guinea pigs
- bees
- farm animals

Gardening hobbies

- indoor; outdoor; greenhouse
- flowers, vegetables, rock garden, water garden, fruit trees, berry bushes, roof garden, window garden, dish garden
- scientific plant breeding
- chemical gardening (hydroponics)
- special varieties: roses, gladioli, cacti, etc.

Collections

- stamps
- coins
- rocks
- semiprecious stones
- insects
- leaves
- jokes, anecdotes
- souvenirs
- maps
- theater programs
- canes
- ivory
- cigar bands
- stuffed animals
- butterflies
- coral
- wild flowers
- metal ware (flatirons, etc.)
- guns
- paintings
- recipes
- plants
- autographs
- dolls
- figurines
- menus
- posters
- recordings
- china
- calendars
- Indian objects
- spoons
- bottles
- beads
- knives
- clocks
- prints
- lace
- keys
- fans
- hourglasses
- pewter
- pottery
- samplers
- shells
- tiles
- snuffboxes
- Bibles
- bookplates
- dime novels
- wallpaper
- first editions
- lead soldiers
- post cards
- glassware
- buttons
- bells
- antiques (chairs, etc.)
- old weapons
- cameos

Sports hobbies

Team Sports: baseball, basketball, crew, hockey, soccer, softball

Individual Sports: archery, badminton, bowling, boxing, fencing, golf, gymnastics, handball, horseback-riding, horseshoes, quoits, roller skating, shuffleboard, squash rackets, table tennis, tennis, track, volley ball, wrestling

Water Sports: aquaplaning, canoeing, diving, rowing, sailing, skin diving, swimming, water polo, water skiing

Winter Sports: curling, ice-skating, skiing, snow-shoeing, tobogganing

Outdoor Life: bicycling, camping, fishing, hiking, hunting, mountaineering, coaching, managing teams

Service hobbies

(Children can engage in the first six on the list; the remainder are for older teen-agers and adults)

- toy reconditioning
- collecting for campaigns
- town clean-up program
- organizing teams
- used clothing collections
- companionship for handicapped

- driving patients for Red Cross, etc.
- teaching arts and crafts to the handicapped
- assisting in physical therapy
- hospital auxiliary
- Red Cross work

- youth council work
- health council work
- Scout den mother, father, or adviser
- teaching in adult education program
- community music program
- church service work
- Volunteer Service Bureau
- day-care center work
- PTA committees
- lodge service work
- work for improved sanitation, safety, summer play camp, library, etc.

Putting Hobbies to Use

We have already pointed out that even small children might occasionally sell things they make. They derive a special kind of excitement and inspiration from creating articles that are acceptable enough for others to buy. Nevertheless, there is some danger of developing a commercial attitude toward play and, in extreme cases, of having the child lose interest if he is not paid for what he produces.

There are two or three ways of handling this problem of recognizing material value without overemphasizing it. The monetary value of the gifts a child makes for members of the family may sometimes be mentioned in passing, to show him that they *have* such value, and that he is actually helping the family save money. (At the same time we might point out that the real value cannot be measured in dollars and cents, but in terms of the pleasure they give.) Second, we might allow the child to sell some of his handiwork for the express purpose of buying material and equipment which he wants for developing his play interest further. This will increase his independence and at the same time teach him the price of things and the need for careful selection when resources are limited. A third solution is to encourage the sale of his work only for the benefit of others who are less fortunate. Instead of simply giving money from his allowance, or collecting it from others, the boy or girl would sell greeting cards, pot-holders, or other useful articles of his own making, and donate the proceeds to the cause. This is sometimes done by school classes, Scouts or clubs, but it might also become a family custom.

Constructive hobbies go far beyond the sale of handiwork. All over the country, school children are beginning to turn their skills and interests to community benefit, as our list of service hobbies and our discussion of teen activities (chapter 11) have indicated. A teen-age service to the handicapped is discussed on page 360. Clearing empty lots and replacing unsightly refuse with attractive flowers and useful vegetables can be a regular pursuit instead of a one-time affair. In a number of communities, young people from ten up are forming "Junior Improvement Associations," and by concerted effort are transforming the appearance of whole neighborhoods. In at least one instance, in Worcester, Massachusetts, "junior citizens" have formed their own incorporated community (Garden City), and elect their own mayor, city council, police force, and other officials. This "city within a city" has been responsible for countless community improvements.

Many schools and youth groups hold "hobby fairs," not only to exhibit their products and collections, but to exchange ideas and arouse the interest of others. The National Science Fair has stimulated thousands of children to create and submit projects. School children have also scoured many localities in search of Indian artifacts and other historical relics; many exhibits and several local museums have resulted.

In addition to specific community work, such as the hospital campaign mentioned in the previous chapter, in a number of communities, groups of teen-agers have "adopted" old age homes, convalescent centers, and institutions for the handicapped. They put on shows, organize picnics, and play games with the patients. They are also helping to organize baseball and basketball teams among the smaller children. Parents, too, are being drawn into these activities, and not only parent-child teams, but parent-child orchestras, choirs, and hobby classes have come into being.

All of which proves that hobbies do not have to be private and self-centered. Nor do they have to be concerned with useless pursuits (though we do not disparage this type). In other words, the hobbies we ride need not be rocking horses that keep us going but never get us anywhere.

Not only do hobbies lead to new usefulness—they sometimes lead to a vocation as well. Usually this happens in one of two ways. In the search for a congenial hobby, we may try many different activities, and in this exploration we may unearth a vocational and not merely an avocational interest. A glance at the hobby check list a few pages back will show that any one of them can lead directly or indirectly to our life's work. Science, art, craftsmanship, athletics—all represent fundamental areas of interest and productivity, not simply activities to fill, or kill, time. What is play for one person is work for another, and what is work for one is play for another. It would be surprising indeed if the chosen hobby did not sometimes become the chosen vocation.

This is bound to happen most frequently in an ever freer society such as ours, where people have increasing opportunities to follow their own interests instead of their father's footsteps or the custom of their "class." More and more young people are using hobbies as a testing-ground for future vocations. More and more older people are switching the focus of their attention—and their livelihood as well—from jobs that have grown dull and routine to fresher interests that have been discovered and developed as hobbies. The teen-ager who loves camp and camping becomes a junior counselor, a senior counselor, then goes on to organize after-school play groups as a permanent vocation. The adult man (or woman) whose most vital interest is a gardening hobby may open a garden shop or nursery on a part-time basis, without giving up a regular job. Later on he may find it possible to swing over and combine business with pleasure completely. Naturally, long and careful consideration is necessary before deciding to change in midstream—and one important consideration is that the same interest may not be nearly so appealing when pursued for a livelihood as it is when pursued as a hobby.

Footnotes on Hobbies

The following remarks are not meant to be an exhaustive study of different hobbies, rather they are designed to suggest some considerations that will help us guide our children.

Crafts Hobbies

Crafts that were taken up in a transient and often desultory way in earlier childhood gradually assume the aspect of hobbies during the teens. Early craft work was discussed in chapter 10. When a craft becomes a hobby, new skills develop and new satisfactions emerge. The potentialities and limitations of such materials as clay and leather come more fully and strikingly to the fore; the child learns what he can do with them and what he cannot. This, however, does not depend entirely on the material itself, but on the nature and ability of the boy or girl who uses it. In the hands of one young person, wood or metal may "come alive." The child establishes a truly personal relationship with the material—and the two come alive together. This is particularly evident as the hobby develops: what was difficult or seemingly impossible a few months ago is second nature now. Moreover, the older child, like the younger, gains in confidence and security as he achieves greater control over the tools and materials.

Still another satisfaction is experienced as these young hobbyists become more mature. Their chosen craft gives them a chance to express themselves in an individual way. They develop their own style, and should they arrive at a point where others can *recognize* their work by the imprint they have put upon it, they receive a thrill that is hard to match. They have come into their own.

Some Specialized Crafts

In line with our view that concentration on one phase of a general hobby is more rewarding than trying to cover a whole field, we will look briefly at a few of the more specialized crafts. Since teen-agers are generally able to use the more advanced books to advantage, we shall mention a few representative volumes, and leave others to the Appendix.

Lamps and Lamp Shades are seemingly limitless in materials and design—as you will see if you consult the book of that title by S. Palestrant. Shells are collected by practically everyone who visits the seashore; but *Shellcraft* is a source of a surprisingly large number of useful and beautiful objects, as Ruth L. Walworth's little book will show. The relatively new art of mobiles is fully illustrated in *How to Make Mobiles* by John Lynch. If you want to explore the myriad articles to be made from boxes, you can even find whole books on the subject—such as *Boxcraft*, by Joseph L. Leeming. The casual whittler may decide to make a hobby of whittling if he reads Harry Zarchy's book by that name. The ancient art of etching and engraving on glass would seem, on the face of it, to be beyond the average hobbyist, yet in his book *Handicraft Hobbies for Profit*, Robert Scharff shows that it is well within his abilities. Pewter work, soap carving, raffia work, bookbinding, string craft, poster-making, bird carving, gem cutting, restoration of old furniture, and tin can craft —each of these has been developed to a point where there is at least one excellent manual available. Would you like to decorate your own fabrics? Then look into *Printing on Textiles* by La Verne Moritz. Does flower-making attract you? Then try Clara Kebbell's instructive book. Or perchance you have an interest in rope and knots—then you will want to read *Square Knot Handicraft Guide* by Raoul Graumont and Elmer Wenstrom, and learn how you can put the ancient art of macramé to use in making handbags, camera cases, slippers, and other articles.

Plastic Craft

An entirely new field has been opened up by the development of plastics. For hobbyists, the thermoplastics, which can be bent and shaped under heat, are generally best. Simple candleholders, pen stands, boxes, and book ends can be made out of sheets, tubes, and rods with no more complex tools than drills, coping saw, file, and stylus. For more advanced or quantity work, starting in the later teens, a power saw, lathe, drill, and grinder are advisable. The various processes of heating, drilling, shaping, cementing, and polishing can be readily learned by the fairly experienced craftsman. So can the molding of liquefied plastics. Special decorative effects can be attained by dip-dyeing and painting; but the most startling effects are achieved by interior carving of flowers and other forms, accomplished by boring into the plastic sheet with burrs that resemble dental drills. Harry Walton's book *Plastics for the Home Craftsman* is one good book among many on this subject.

Scientific Hobbies

Any science, from archeology to zoology, can become a hobby. The number of specialized scientific hobbies is limitless. One person may concentrate on motors and make miniature gasoline, electric, steam, or even solar engines; while another may go into the history of perpetual motion machines. Fossils and relics of ancient cultures attract many—in fact, a large percentage of archeological finds have been made by amateurs. Scientific fiction can itself become a hobby, and a study of past predictions and early attempts (for example, Leonardo da Vinci's aircraft) can be an exciting interest. Again, we suggest that concentration on a narrower (but not trivial) phase of a chosen subject is generally more satisfying than attempting to keep up with an entire field.

Let's take a single example of a scientific hobby—astronomy—which turns out to be not a single interest but an aggregate of many. The philosophically inclined can make a study of the earliest cosmologies, as well as the various scientific hypotheses of the origin of our solar system. Those with artistic interests can derive pleasure from simply gazing at the ever-changing beauty of the night sky and from the identification of the heavenly bodies and constellations. The mathematically inclined can find in astronomy an application of every branch of their subject from algebra to calculus and beyond. Those who love literature and history may prefer to concentrate on the mythology of the sun, moon, and stars; and those who incline toward anthropology will compare the legends of different cultures. Still others will focus their attention on the mechanics of the telescope, on chronology and calendars, on astronomical photography.

Hundreds of amateur observers record comets, meteors, fireballs, and the movements of variable stars; and professional astronomers depend a great deal on amateurs' observations. So extensive is this hobby that there are dozens of clubs and organizations for amateurs throughout the country, and there are several of national dimension, including the Amateur Astronomers Association, the Junior Astronomy Club, and the American Association of Variable Star Observers.

Amusement Hobbies

Games like chess, bridge, and charades become hobbies when we develop them fully and systematically instead of simply playing them sporadically. In chess we can not only make a thorough study of the moves and systems of play, and improve our technique—we can read books and articles on the subject, join or form a club, learn about the great players of the past and present, follow local, national, and international matches, and collect chessmen. There are many checkers clubs, as well as groups (usually unorganized) who meet fairly regularly for charades and other games. A devotee of crosswords or Double Crostics has an enduring interest in these games and makes them a major source of diversion, conversation, and study. Any one of these game hobbies brings rewards in terms of sociability, mental exercise, increasing skill, and relief from tension.

Photographic Hobbies

It would be hard to find an activity that more successfully combines art with science and social with personal satisfactions than photography. Here is a hobby that sharpens observation, trains the eye for esthetic perception and the hand for skill and precision, brings first-hand acquaintance with basic physical, chemical, and mechanical processes. No one who compares the work of an experienced photographer with the crude attempts of a beginner can fail to recognize its genuine creativity. (With some, of course, photography has become a cult more than a hobby, an investment in gadgetry more than an art or craft; and a few seem to restrict their lives and observations to "picture taking possibilities.")

The facets of photography are so many that we can do little more than list a few of them here. Through this hobby we can record our travels and the development of our family; we can use our photos for decoration in home and office, make up "picture stories" for special occasions, after the manner of illustrated magazines. We can specialize in portraits, nature studies, abstracts, "effects." We can go in for color photography, stereoscopy, motion pictures. We can participate in exhibits and contests, sell occasional pictures to magazines and agencies, and apply the proceeds to the purchase of new equipment. We can develop our own film, build our own darkroom, make our own enlargements, mountings, and frames.

Some of the more specialized photographic interests will be found in the previous check list, but two hobbies with a community angle are worth particular mention. Both apply particularly to adults, but may well attract older teen-agers or college youth as well. One is active membership in a local Motion Picture Council which works for better pictures at public theaters. The other is the study and selection of educational films for use in schools and organizations. Either hobby offers broad scope for service and enlightenment.

Collecting as a Hobby

When is a collection a collection? A true collection is far more than a mere accumulation. It requires knowledge, skill, artistic sensitivity—and it may bring a multitude of satisfactions. It may give our trips and vacations a new point. It may encourage an interest in classification and orderly arrangement. It may stimulate research into scientific and technical matters, and into the history of culture as well. It offers an opportunity to join with others in local, national, or even international clubs and organizations. It may involve special crafts: construction of exhibits and displays, writing and printing of placards and signs. It may provide the personal satisfactions of acquisition and ownership, bring recognition and admiration of others, supply grist for conversation—and in general may make us more interesting, more valuable, and more secure personalities.

Home Repair

Many people, young and old, make their homes their hobby. The do-it-yourself trend extends to every type of repair and redecoration. To the child who is interested in tools, perhaps from watching his father use them, or the child in a fatherless home, who has a sense of being needed, this activity will be particularly intriguing. There are special tools and simplified techniques for practically any job: replacing window glass, repairing a leaky faucet, freeing a sticky door, fixing a cold radiator, refinishing furniture, replacing shingles or roofing, patching plaster. Tools and materials should be kept on hand for many of these needs since they are almost certain to arise. It is also advisable to follow the new developments in "home" magazines and to have on hand a general book on home repair, as well as books and pamphlets that give directions for special jobs such as painting and electrical work. The home hobbyist is constantly adding to his skills and taking on jobs he used to hand over to mechanics quite automatically. Few hobbies are more productive or more gratifying—and the man or woman, boy or girl who keeps his home in good shape can more truly call it his own than one who merely lives in it.

Hiking

Anyone who thinks that hiking is merely taking a long walk should consider the following ramifications, which represent only a few of the interests of the genuine enthusiast. The experienced hiker makes a study of the equipment and clothing he needs, often buys them in special stores. He may make his own rucksack, pack basket, ditty bag, even cooking equipment. He knows how to use a compass; he reads topographical maps with ease, perhaps makes a study of rocks, plants, animals, trees, and geological formations. He acquaints himself with the park areas of the country—county, state, and national—and he probably has an ambition to repeat a historical march or hike along a major portion of a famous trail, such as the Appalachian or the Pacific Crest. He carries first aid equipment, knows the hazards of the out-of-doors and how to deal with each. He has learned how to break and mark a trail, how to cook under the most adverse conditions, where to find water and shelter. And he is probably adding immeasurably to these satisfactions by belonging to American Youth Hostels, by passing forestry and guide tests and by joining one of the hiking clubs that are found in practically every locality. There's more to hiking than meets the eye!

Sailing

"Sailing along with the breeze" is an experience that knows no equal—especially if you know your boat as well as yourself. Actually, enthusiasts spend as much or more time keeping their boat in trim and studying navigation as they do in sailing— which only means that this is a hobby and not merely a sport. They speak a language of their own, talking about gaff rigs and Marconi rigs, catboats, yawls, ketches, hoisting and trimming the jib, tacking and coming about. They not only know the classes of boats, but the special uses and values of each. Some make a study of the history of sailing, collect old sailing prints, or decorate their homes with souvenirs of the sea. Others belong to yacht clubs, make a hobby of racing, plan week-end trips, and pore over coastline maps for hours. Still others make it a year-round activity by rebuilding their boat or putting together a new one from a do-it-yourself kit—thus bringing the joys of sailing within reach of strictly limited incomes.

Fishing

As a hobby, fishing offers many satisfactions beyond the thrill of the catch. It combines healthy recreation and direct contact with the out-of-doors with an appreciation of new techniques and equipment, the skill of the craftsman and the homely wisdom of the nature lover. Fresh water fishing offers many choices, many variations. What is the best place and best equipment for catching perch, trout, bass, pickerel? Which reel, which line, which lure? Will it be bait casting or fly casting, still fishing or trolling, skittering or spinning? Do you know the fisherman's knots, which fish are good eating and when, different ways to cook your catch? Will you spend winter evenings repairing equipment and tying flies? Salt water fishing offers even more variety, running all the way from simple bottom fishing for weakfish, porgies, fluke, or flounder, through surfcasting for striped bass and others, to deep-sea trolling for the "big ones"—tuna, sailfish, marlin, swordfish—and the thrill of a lifetime. Few can afford anything but occasional deep-sea fishing with rented boat and equipment. Still fewer will be in a position to pursue such specialties as spear fishing (sometimes combined with skin diving) and winter fishing through the ice—but these hobbies are not lacking in devotees.

Study Hobbies

One of the most enriching of all hobbies arises out of the selection of a particular subject for intensive research. It may be as narrow as the life and ways of a particular insect or as voluminous as the varieties of religious cults in America. It may have some ulterior objective such as writing a book or giving a series of lectures—or it may have none at all beyond immediate enjoyment. The only criterion for selection should be personal interest, since this is one area in which we can and should express ourselves as freely as possible. Some of the fields that have aroused the enthusiasm of adults are the following: the history of exploration, mythology and folklore, the story of philosophy, the study of words (philology, etymology), criminal investigation, ballistics, folk music, the history of science. In their full development, these interests apply more to adults than young people, but any of them can be started in the teens and continue for a lifetime.

CHAPTER XIII

Ready-Made Play: Television, Radio, Comic Books, Movies, Records

WHEN WE THINK of Johnny or Joan at play, our minds automatically picture children romping about on the lawn, making a sailboat or sewing a doll's dress. These youngsters, we say, are active, not passive, because their muscles as well as their minds are *doing* something. In contrast, when they are sitting in front of the loudspeaker or the motion picture or television screen, they appear to be inactive—absorbing, not doing; spectators, not participants. The difference between active play and passive pursuits seems obvious.

Yet that distinction begins to break down as soon as we look more closely at these children. When Johnny watches a high-jumper perform, he *may* be "taking it all in" idly, but more likely he is leaping over the bar with the athlete or even making up his mind to beat the record himself when he grows older. Joan, too, is active, mentally at least, as she watches the home economist make a salad. She is probably going over the steps inwardly, perhaps planning to show her friends at the next Scout meeting. Spectatorship, then, need not be purely passive; our children don't *have* to behave like sponges, absorbing what they see and hear without reacting.

We believe that the easy media can be a stimulus to creative activity and make a genuine contribution to growth. But the problem is, How can this be done, and what role should we, as parents, play in the process? How can we encourage our children to be more selective about what they see and hear? Is there a danger that the mass media will warp their values? Can we do anything to improve these media? How can we keep them from dominating our children's leisure time? And can we keep them reading in spite of the lure of looking and listening? In seeking answers to these questions, our plan is first to focus separately on radio and television, comic books, motion pictures, and records, then to offer some suggestions that apply to all these fields together.

Television and Radio

Four youngsters were grouped, wide-eyed and silent, around the television set. Suddenly one of them shouted, "It's time for the fight! Here they go! Yippee!" The other three screamed and clapped in delight as the villain and the marshal began to slug it out with murderous intent. The two powerful men rolled over and over, threw chairs at each other, landed resounding blows—and by the time the fight was over, the four youngsters were literally jumping up and down with excitement.

Were these children, and thousands like them, little demons, taking delight in homicidal assault? Or was television debasing the taste and arousing—or instilling—violent impulses in decent American children?

Many have been asking such questions as these, and many have been the answers. We therefore felt that it would be of service to our readers to compare our own views with those of colleagues from related fields, to see if a common denominator of opinion could be found. A questionnaire was drawn up and sent to eighteen authorities, including a child psychiatrist at a leading hospital, the director of an extensive project on juvenile delinquency, the head of the Child Study Association of America, a pediatrician (author of the most widely read book on child care), the medical director of a national mental health organization, as well as school superintendents, sociologists, psychologists, and family-life experts.

The quotations in the first four paragraphs that follow have been drawn from their answers and combined with comments of our own. We hope they will clear the television air and help to achieve a level-headed and constructive approach to this medium and to radio as well.

Is television responsible for juvenile delinquency? "No, the argument is the same as for comics, movies, radio—no evidence that delinquent acts have been due to any of these alone. Delinquency is due to deep-seated conflicts, discrepancies and deficiencies in the personality. Children are too complex to react directly and only to some one immediate stimulus such as a TV program." We agree with this point of view, but also with the warning that "An occasional program may be provocative to an already disturbed, antisocially motivated youngster." (Simply turning off the set, however, does not correct the disturbance.) There is also danger that a steady diet of violence will degrade the *taste* of average children even if it does not make criminals of them. For this reason, the major networks have been eliminating many of these programs and editing others; unfortunately the same cannot be said for some independent stations that show one crime film after another.

Are westerns objectionable? Although not always enthusiastic about westerns, our colleagues generally found them acceptable: "They serve more as a harmless, vicarious outlet than as a harmful influence." In other words, the four youngsters mentioned above were probably getting quite normal feelings of belligerence out of their systems in a healthy way. The reason these programs are not classed with the usual crime stories is that they are far removed from the child's life in time and place, and become so stereotyped in action, with the good always coming out ahead, that children do not take them seriously. They should be counterbalanced however, with more realistic stories in which people are not all good or all bad, and in which situations are met by cooperative action instead of by a single unconquerable hero who takes all responsibility, and sometimes the law itself, into his own hands.

Should parents control the amount of time the children spend on television? There was a unanimous Yes to this question—including our own opinion. Typical comments were: "Same rationale as limiting the number of desserts and requiring reasonable number of hours of sleep," and "In those homes where the children seem to profit most from television, the family has worked out both the amount of time which the children normally watch television, the types of programs—and in some instances the specific programs." Notice that the family works this problem out together. We add that by limiting the amount of time spent on television and radio, children are often prompted to be more selective and to lead a more balanced life. Again we cannot help pointing out that parents who spend hours every evening in front of the home screen, or keep the radio turned on all day, can hardly expect their children to do otherwise.

How can we help our children develop good viewing taste? Practically all put the responsibility on the shoulders of the parents. One respondent pointed out wryly, "So often parents blame the child for poor viewing taste, but actually most parents look to the TV set as an excellent baby sitter," while another said, "It's a teaching process, as anything about rearing children is. Parents can accomplish a lot by pointing out sequences of bad taste, by reacting themselves to elements of bad taste, by appreciating aloud or indirectly programs which are in good taste. We do this with clothing, manners, and in other connections all the time. Why not in connection with television programs?" Again, this does not mean selecting all programs for our children: "They should be permitted to sample a wide variety of programs and should be helped to choose discriminatingly."

How can we keep them reading? The ominous predictions made near the beginnings of both radio and television, that children "would never touch another book," have not materialized. True, there has been an over-all drop in quantity of reading (surveys show 10 to 15 per cent) but this is partially offset by an increase in quality. Librarians throughout the country have been reporting that television, more than radio, has opened new horizons and has turned both child and adult reading in fresh directions.

However, the fact that the situation is not so alarming as anticipated is no reason for complacency. As each new medium captivates our children, we have to make greater efforts to keep them reading—for instance, by finding attractively illustrated editions, by giving books as presents, by starting a "book exchange" among our friends or at the school, and by maintaining our own interest in good reading.

One of the most promising ways to attract our children to books is to use television and radio as points of departure. Here are a few suggestions on this score. Keep track of stories dramatized on the air, and suggest books by the same authors (*Huckleberry Finn, Heidi, Moby Dick,* and *Twenty Thousand Leagues under the Sea* have all been presented). Put up a Television Bookshelf (a good do-it-yourself project), and stock it with books that will be particularly appropriate to programs the children watch; for example, an atlas, books of science demonstrations, a book on weather, an almanac, a dictionary, and ideally an encyclopedia for ready reference at all times. Keep an eye out for special programs that will open up new areas for reading. (The number of "high level" programs has almost doubled within the past three years.) Through these programs our children will get a vivid *introduction* to other countries, folk music and folkways, unusual occupations, literary classics, phenomena of nature, as well as the inside of factories, laboratories, and museums. Television and radio are bound to arouse many passing interests; it's up to us to feed the ones that merit cultivation.

Just how can television and radio lead to creative activity? Earlier in this book we suggested ways for children to become participants instead of mere spectators—for example, by visiting a studio, and by repeating experiments performed on science programs. Here are a few more suggestions. Keep drawing, coloring, and crafts materials in a drawer near the TV set, so that younger children will follow directions given on their programs. Stimulate activity through approval and recognition: when Anne learns to make a pot-holder, be sure to use it in the kitchen and show it off to friends in her presence; if Stan gets deeply interested in dog-training via television, take him to a "school" for dogs or try to get an expert to organize a class. Play the games presented on television and radio, but encourage the children to create their own variations; for instance, they can make up their own quizzes, impersonate people they know instead of "personalities," devise new stunts, celebrate a birthday party by writing their own lyrics to music they have heard.

Sporadic interests are fine, but we should also be on the lookout for full-scale projects. To illustrate, take the case of Marilyn. This thirteen-year-old girl often watched a program that took place in different locales, using travel posters as a backdrop. Curious to see what these posters looked like in color, she visited a travel concern and got to talking with the friendly agent. He happened to have two copies of a lovely French poster, and gave one to Marilyn. However, he warned her that it is not easy to obtain posters, and discouraged her from trying to make a collection of them. Marilyn's mother, on the other hand, saw the possibility of an absorbing and productive project. She and Marilyn made a list of well-known agencies for ships and airlines; they also got in touch with two friends who were planning to take a trip abroad. Within a few months the collection was well on its way, with posters from Italy, France, Switzerland, and Sweden. Mother and daughter now have an exciting common interest, which has gone on from posters alone, to include the customs and costumes of the countries depicted on them. One of these days they will exhibit their collection at Marilyn's school, carefully mounted on hardboard prepared by her father . . . and it all started with a "spectator medium"!

How to Judge the Comics

Why are forty million comic books still sold every month, despite the beckoning fingers of television, radio, and other competing media? The answer can only be that they are geared closely to our children's inner lives. Within their covers, youngsters find welcome relief from a world that is often confusing and confining. The pictures and words and ideas are readily understood. The stories "come out right," and bring with them the assurance that life will be on their side. The tempo is swift and the action dramatic—keyed to their own restless energy.

These are only the most general appeals of the comic books. Others, more specific, are just as powerful. The action stories offer our young people the thrill of high adventure and the chance to worship heroes who fulfill their aspirations. Science fiction gives their imaginations full rein, and makes them feel at home in an expanding world of mechanical marvels. Through the slapstick activities of animal characters and caricatured humans, they get into mischief without consequences, and escape into a happy-go-lucky realm where nonsense prevails.

All these needs are basically sound, and the comic book is one way of meeting them at the child's own level. But there is an immense number of titles available on every newsstand, with great variations in worth. The problem, as we brought out in chapter 6 is one of good management and thoughtful guidance. The only way to solve it is to study our children and bear in mind the principles that make for good selection. Let's begin with the latter, and then see how they apply to the various types of comic books now being published.

To judge comic books, take into consideration both form and content. There is nothing subtle about the drawing and color in these books, and the paper stock is generally pulp. Nevertheless, colors can be bright without being garish, and cartoons can be either crudely or cleverly done. The language should be within the reading ability of the child, and while we can't expect all the words and expressions to be of the utmost refinement, we can at least expect the hero to speak correctly since children tend to identify themselves with him. Comics have been found to help many children with reading, but language that is consistently poor and print that is crude and crowded will do more harm than good.

If a child has shown no interest in comic magazines and is reading books, we see no reason to attract him to this medium. But if he does read them, we suggest that you have a first-hand acquaintance with the following general types of comic books. This will enable you to call your child's attention to the more acceptable varieties instead of simply denouncing the medium as a whole.

Science fiction. These modern tales are closer to reality than the legends and fairy tales of old; they may arouse an interest in science, though the emphasis is on gadgets and action rather than theory and research. The youngster's frequent question, "Could it really happen?" is an excellent opening for giving him realistic information. In most of these stories the emphasis is on positive forces for good. A few, however, go out of their way to depict scenes of terror and horror. Such comic books should be kept from the child—and off the newsstands. Too steady a diet of fantastic stories of any kind is unhealthy for children who are very sensitive or disturbed.

Crime and detective. While these stories generally show that crime does not pay, many of them spend so much space blueprinting the offense that the final outcome is all but neglected. A few even make the life of the criminal appear attractive and inviting. While most specialists agree that antisocial behavior stems from deeper sources than reading stories, nevertheless it is better to have the child read material that accents the constructive side of the crime picture. For this reason, mystery stories are usually preferable to outright crime stories; heroes who use intelligence and modern methods of detection are preferable to those who resort only to action and gunplay; and stories that give the reader insight into the workings of law enforcement agencies are superior to those of the "lone wolf" type.

True stories. In recent years a number of comic book series have been based on stories of real figures and great events. Exploration, discovery, heroic exploits, and feats of sportsmanship are the themes of these books. The heroes are active in many fields of endeavor, current and historical: politics, science, social service, military life, sports. In these stories there is a happy combination of inspiration with information, without sacrifice of excitement and drama. Through them the child learns that reality can be just as absorbing as fantasy.

Condensed classics. Specialists are divided on the merits of these pictorial digests of literary works. Our own attitude is largely negative since they cannot begin to do justice to the originals and too often make the child feel he knows the story too well to read the book. However, since they concentrate on the more intriguing aspects of the stories, they may occasionally serve to lure a child into reading them in full. But this fond hope must be given substance by parents who show an interest in the classics themselves, and make them available in attractive editions.

Romance. Although the interest in romance is high among teen-agers, it is hard to find any comic books that present this theme in acceptable form. Instead, a host of suggestive stories of the "confessions" variety have appeared in the past few years. Neither the themes nor the pictures are suitable for adolescents.

When a girl or boy is attracted to them, it is up to us to sit down and patiently explain their limitations—then see that more acceptable means of satisfying romantic interests are provided through novels, motion pictures, parties, a teen canteen.

Animal stories. The all-too-human antics of the Disney species of animal have a hypnotic attraction for most young children and frequently for their parents as well. The reasons? They are a gay and lively combination of humor with fantasy, yet behind the ludicrous action lie the secret urges that hide within us all. The animal dares to say and do what the child and the adult must constantly suppress. These cartoons are the kind of light-hearted fun we all need.

Westerns and adventure stories. Westerns generally center around the exploits of modern equivalents of knights-in-armor as they defend the innocent against villains defying the law. Action is swift and suspenseful, and as in the TV programs already discussed, the youthful reader undoubtedly finds in them an outlet for his own pent-up angers, fears, and heroic urges. Though there is plenty of shooting, there is little or no killing, and the average child realizes that "it's only a story."

Most of the other adventure stories are acceptable (within comic book limitations): jungle stories where man fights beast, airplane stories involving heroic pilots, stories of men endowed with superhuman powers. But there is no excuse for the lurid comic books that revel in scenes of cruelty and torture, particularly when these are linked with sexual suggestion.

Informational comic books. Comic magazines of an educational nature are rarely found on the newsstands, but an increasing number of organizations have found this format to be vivid, eye-catching, and compelling. Some of the subjects most effectively presented are: atomic energy, facts about race prejudice and discrimination, Bible stories, the teen-age narcotics problem. Here is another place where a "play" medium can be turned to unexpected, constructive uses.

Going to the Movies

Going to the movies has long been something special in the child's life. Even today, when films have lost their novelty and are meeting strong competition, our youngsters greet the suggestion of a movie with delight. Like their elders, they like to "go out," and the trip by car or bus heightens their feelings of anticipation. The outing gives them a chance for companionship with their parents, or the excitement of independence if they go with friends. But above all, they like the movies because the screen transports them to distant worlds, where they can live for an hour among conquering heroes, uproarious clowns, fearsome savages, and daring pirates of old.

We have already traced the motion picture interests of children from the early ages on up. Here we propose to focus on three special aspects of films: the encouragement of creative activities, the cultivation of good taste and judgment, and the value of home movies.

The glamor of "seeing it in the movies" can be exploited as a stimulus to activities of all kinds. Many a youngster has been moved to read classics, adopt a new hobby, look up information, or inquire into a specific vocation depicted in a film. As always, a boy or girl will be more likely to follow up a newborn interest if the parents are alert to it and offer enthusiastic support. The following is a case in point. Johnny, age seven, was fascinated by a time-lapse "short" that dealt with the growth of plants from seeds. His father, who watched it with him, suggested a simple experiment. He had the boy place ordinary beans in a saucer of water, and within a few days healthy sprouts began to appear. Delighted, Johnny gathered all the seeds he could find—grapefruit, orange, birdseed, etc.—and tried them all. The interest grew like the plants themselves, until today, at nine, the boy has a small window greenhouse in which he raises seedlings, later to be planted in a garden outside. He and his father built the greenhouse together, and they already have plans for a larger one. Johnny's favorite present on his ninth birthday was a subscription to *Audubon Magazine* and membership in its Nature Program.

The problem of cultivating taste for good films is much the same as in radio and television—in fact, it coincides with the latter since so many programs present films. (Unfortunately many of the smaller stations persist in using second- and third-rate pictures, sometimes of questionable taste and shown when children are likely to be watching.) It is well to remember that even a single picture on a dramatic subject such as race riots or war can have a lasting effect on a child's attitudes, as psychological studies have shown. That effect may be constructive or destructive, depending on the plot and characterizations. But the fact that films can be so effective means that we, as parents, should not use the theater merely as a means of getting the children off our hands for a few hours. It also points to the advisability of seeing particularly provocative films together, so that we may discuss the story and portrayals with them. If they should see a picture without us, it is a good idea to ask them to tell us about it. This will encourage them to express themselves and develop critical judgment. It will also give us an opportunity to explain things that trouble or upset them, and to counteract influences that we consider undesirable.

As children grow older, film tastes become more highly individualized and permanent preferences begin to appear. Although historical, biographical, and the usual entertainment films are likely to be most appealing, children might also be exposed to films that deal with questions of social significance, such as lynchings, prejudice, alcoholism, and the uses of atomic energy. The age at which this might be done will vary with the child. In the middle or later teens, young people begin to appreciate the motion picture as a form of art. This is the time to draw them into discussions of photographic techniques, lighting, accuracy of detail, good and bad acting, interesting characterizations, and turns in the plot. The habit of looking at films with a critical eye is a sign of maturity and a healthy antidote to "spectatoritis."

Home movies provide a particularly rich source of enjoyment and enlightenment. Although relatively few can afford to own the full equipment, it can be rented for special occasions. Some families have been getting together on the expenses, and have regular showings at small individual cost. The number and variety of 16-mm. films are virtually inexhaustible—in fact, about a thousand new releases each year are listed in the H. W. Wilson Educational Film Guide. To convey some idea of the wealth of subject matter, we shall mention a few recent winners of the

Golden Reel Awards, selected at the annual American Film Assembly:

History and Biography: *Saugus Ironworks Restoration* (American Iron and Steel Institute)
  The Face of Lincoln (University of Southern California)
Human Relations: *And Now Miguel* (U.S. Information Agency)
  The Way of the Navaho (Columbia Broadcasting System)
Industrial Processes: *Glass and You* (Association Films)
  The World that Nature Forgot (MPO Productions)
International Understanding: *Asian Earth* (Atlantis Productions)
  The Family of Man (Columbia Broadcasting System)
Natural Resources: *The American Flamingo* (Carlin Films)
  Man with a Thousand Hands (International Harvester Company)
Recreation: *Split the Ring* (Indiana University)
  And So They Grow (Campus Film Productions)
Safety: *Paddle a Safe Canoe* (Aetna Casualty and Surety Co.)
  Play It Safe (MPO Productions)
Science: *ABC of Jet Propulsion* (General Motors Corporation)
  The Colour of Life (National Film Board of Canada)
Visual Arts: *From Renoir to Picasso* (Brandon Films)
  Color Lithography, an Art Medium (University of Mississippi)
Instructional: *How to Make Papier-Mâché Animals* (Bailey)
  You Are There: The Emancipation Proclamation (Young America Films)
  The Steadfast Tin Soldier (Brandon Films)
  The Story of Light (General Electric Company)
  Industrial Arts: Chisels and Gouges (Young America)

The World of Records

It is one thing to have a phonograph and a few records and play them for occasional enjoyment; it is another, and a far richer experience, to explore the vast territory of recorded sound. It would be hard to find a more varied and imaginative medium than the recordings of today. In fact, just keeping pace with what is happening in the field can be an absorbing pursuit in itself.

Now that unbreakable records are made for every age and taste, and inexpensive players are widely available, every member of the family can enjoy this medium. If you are hesitant about going "all out" for records because radio and television offer so much music, consider the advantages of the phonograph. You and your children can play the music of your own choosing when you want it. Your children can gain in dexterity and independence by learning to make their own choices and by operating the machine by themselves. No one has to "pay" for the privilege by listening to commercials. Selections can be repeated as often as you like (children increase their understanding by playing records over and over). Your children can sing or dance or act to the music when they get to know it well. Each member of the family may have a collection of records, expressing his own individual taste. In one word, recordings are in many ways the most flexible and personal of all the mass media. Though they come to us ready-made, they can be *used* creatively

Through a careful selection of records, we can introduce our children to this inexhaustible reservoir of enjoyment and develop an appreciation of the beauty of sound at an early age. As we have already seen, young children need only the barest encouragement to make music a rich and full experience. Just watch the radiant glow on the face of a five-year-old when he recognizes the Peter theme in "Peter and the Wolf," and his "pretend" scowl when the wolf arrives on the scene. He will spontaneously act out the dramatic sequences of "Genii, the Magic Record," or "The Little Fireman." He will learn the words of folk songs without being taught. Later he may go to the piano to pick out melodies, and name the instruments he hears on the radio or sees on television. If he is restless on a rainy day, playing records will keep him absorbed. If he is tense and overactive, a "music hour" will quiet him down. Such is the versatility of the phonograph.

But that is not all. Consider the way records can help to produce changes in the still-plastic personalities of three- to six-year-olds. Anne is overly quiet and passive. Her nursery school teacher selects a recording of "High-stepping Horses," remarking casually, "I'll bet you'd make a good horsey, Anne." During the first few bars, Anne moves hesitantly, but as the music becomes livelier, she drops her caution and by the end of the record is stepping up and down with complete abandon. Jimmy, who ordinarily keeps completely to himself, always comes out of his shell when the game of musical chairs is played at a party. Allen is generally so scattered and disorganized that he cannot co-operate with others in any way. Yet when "Parade of the Wooden Soldiers" is played, he immediately falls in line with the other kindergartners—and what is even better, he is more orderly and co-operative for the rest of the day.

Older children, too, can be guided to a fuller enjoyment of records. Listening in silence has its own rewards, and need not be embellished. Yet it can often be made more creative by encouraging the listener to make comments of a critical or appreciative nature, and by having on hand books about the outstanding composers, the history of music, and stories of the great operas. Some teen-agers make a game of identifying themes and composers.

Collecting records is one of the most rewarding hobbies a young person can have. It will last through the years, and become a social asset, since others will want to hear them. As with most collections, it is better to specialize in a particular phase of the subject instead of spreading the interest too thinly. The boy or girl who makes a hobby of collecting piano concertos, folk songs of a particular country, or early jazz will add the gratification of being an expert to all the other joys of owning records.

Still other satisfactions can be found in the study of the faithful reproduction of sound. Though some have made a cult of the *science* of "hi-fi," most young people find in it a means of enhancing their enjoyment and appreciation of both the art and the science of sound.

Last but not least, the development of the tape recorder is opening new avenues of leisure-time activity. Young people and adults are using it to preserve and reproduce amateur theatricals or radio and television performances that would otherwise be lost. Others are adding a new dimension to their musical and dramatic efforts by listening to playbacks of their work. Still others are performing ingenious experiments with sound; for example, they make two separate recordings of a song performed by the same person in different keys, then reproduce them together for interesting effects. Undoubtedly we are only beginning to discover the possibilities of the tape recorder; there is a wide-open field for creative applications of this instrument.

Managing the Mass Media

To conclude this chapter, we have gathered some suggestions designed to help children make the most of the mass media, and to help us with the problems of management.

1. *Keep track of what is available.* Maintaining a list of programs, records, etc., that sound appealing makes an excellent family project. It is also a reminder to explore new material. A scrapbook containing reviews and recommendations made by organizations is also useful. Some families post a weekly schedule of programs in order not to miss special presentations.

2. *Help your children budget their time* to insure a balanced diet of play, and enough time for school work and home responsibilities. When children have trouble getting everything in, take a single representative week and list all activities and the time spent on each. This will usually lead to cutting out repetitious programs on radio or TV.

3. *Talk over the material they see and hear*—but remember that their taste need not always coincide with yours. Induce the habit of criticism by asking such questions as, "Did the plot really hang together?" "Was the comedian clever, or just loud?" "Is it a good idea to give such big prizes for such small performances?" Listening and viewing together, like reading together, can be one of the most enjoyable and profitable family activities.

4. *Watch their reactions to exciting stories.* This may bring to light unsuspected fears and anxieties, since radio, television, and comic books can be used as a rough barometer of children's emotions. A boy who remains glued to the set may not have the confidence to step out and fend for himself. A girl who steeps herself in comic books may not have developed the skills that would make her acceptable to her age mates.

5. *Gradually attract the children to richer, more adult fare.* Although children enjoy what is supposed to be typical children's material—thrills, action, sheer nonsense—they have an equally strong desire to learn and to grow up. With a little

urging, they will give the more informative, enlightening broadcasts, records, and reading material a good try. Make the new interests "stick" by following them up with books, visits, round-table discussions, and by showing them how much their school work and their play life will benefit.

6. *Work with organizations for the improvement of the mass media.* Criticisms and constructive suggestions from P.T.A.'s and other groups receive careful attention from networks and publishers. Joint action has kept many lurid comic books off the newsstands. Motion Picture Councils review films in many communities. The Children's Film Library of the Motion Picture Association of America has been organized to bring good pictures to children. Local groups can arrange to show many of these films, and also obtain transcriptions and kinescopes of many network broadcasts.

CHAPTER XIV

They All Want Pets

IF YOU ASK any group of children what they like most to do, their answers will almost invariably include "play with a pet." Hardly a child will say he does not want a pet; far more often the youngster will say he wants one "more than anything." Ask these same youngsters *why* they like pets, as we have done in hundreds of instances, and the very young will reply simply, "Because I like them," or "It's fun to play with them." Older children, more sophisticated, find in pets "a friend to tell my troubles to," or "company when you're lonely." When favorite animals are mentioned by name, by far the most frequently chosen is a dog. But high on the list will be cats, turtles, goldfish—or several of these at once, as with the boy who answered, "My dog, my lizard, my three pigeons, my snake, and my nice family!"

What Pets Can Do for Your Child

No one can deny that there is a special affinity between the animal world and the world of childhood. Probably one reason, beyond those voiced by the children, is that they can escape from the demands of the adult world while playing with their pet. There is no need to be on good behavior or even to carry on a conversation. For the most part, play is of the simplest and most primitive sort—just romping or tending to the animal's basic wants. Temporarily, at least, eight-year-old Andy does not have to be "constructive." With his pet he feels that he is loved for his own sake, and not for what he accomplishes or how he behaves. In turn, he can lavish unlimited affection without fear of arousing jealousy in others. On occasion, too, he can boss the animal around and make him a target and outlet for angry moods. Whatever he does, he is completely accepted and his pet will always come back for more.

Each child finds the answer to his own particular needs. Little Johnny is a sickly child and spends a good deal of time in bed. A look of profound contentment comes into his eyes when his small dog is permitted to lie on a chair beside him, hoping but not demanding to be stroked now and then. When the other girls on the block leave Judy out of their play, she can always count on her kitten for silent solace. The fact that the animal cannot speak is of no importance, since the feeling of kinship and understanding goes deeper than words.

Pets, then, have much to contribute to the child's need for the simple satisfactions of affection, acceptance and playfulness. But there are many other benefits as well. The five- or six-year-old is used to being taught and trained by larger, older people who have an air of authority. With his pet, however, he can at last reverse the roles and become the leader, the master, the all-knowing "big person." This gives him a sense of power and assurance, and the identification with adult behavior gives him an extra push to grow up. He is rehearsing for the future and trying himself out on his dog or cat.

At the same time that the child is learning to take the lead, he is also finding out what it is like to have another living being dependent on his care. Perhaps for the first time he experiences the feeling of being needed. Moreover, he is beginning to feel genuine sympathy for other forms of life, and learning to protect those weaker than himself. It is not generally recognized that children do have to learn to be sympathetic; they are not simply born with the ability to project themselves into the mind and feelings of others. Caring for a pet hastens this process.

Pets have a way of bringing out the best in children. Not long ago a sixth-grader rushed into his classroom fifteen minutes before the morning bell, and told the teacher, "I just saw something terrible. A dog got run over on the highway. I think it was Ronnie's, but," he added thoughtfully, "maybe we oughtn't to tell him till we're sure." The teacher, knowing Ronnie's love for his dog, rushed over to the highway in her car, identified the dog by the name on his collar. Back at school, she called Ronnie's mother, then brought the boy and his smaller brother, Danny, into the office to break the sad news to them. Ronnie was able to master his grief, but when he noticed Danny's lips trembling, he asked if he could take his brother for a walk. Hand in hand they left the school together—the first time in months that Ronnie had outwardly shown his feeling for his brother. A few days later, when their father offered to buy them another dog, their answer was, "Not now, Dad. It wouldn't be fair to Chappie. Let's wait till after the summer and see how we feel about it."

Adults, including some psychologists, are apt to place primary emphasis on the training in responsibility which owning a pet entails. No doubt feeding an animal regularly, and keeping it clean and well-behaved, are tremendously valuable experiences. But let's not forget, too, that the average youngster needs help and guidance in learning to care for the pet and attend to his needs at the right time. Too often parents express their own resistance to bringing animals into the home by rigidly demanding that the young child take complete charge from the start, and never miss a single cue after that. Actually, caring for another being is no simple matter for the child who is still learning to take care of himself. Therefore we, as parents, should resign ourselves to the fact that we will have to remind our youngsters to feed the goldfish or comb the collie, and find ways of inducing the older children to keep up their responsibility when they get tired of taking care of the pet. More than that, in most cases we ourselves will need instruction on many of the finer points of animal care. Gathering this information from books, breeders, and pet clubs might well become a family project—an opportunity for parents and children to learn together.

To take another direction, the child can be introduced to a good deal of information on health through the illnesses and accidents that befall his pets. He will learn that even a dog can catch a cold or have an earache, that a canary's broken leg requires a splint just as does a human being's, that carefully prescribed penicillin is good for animal as well as human infections. As a result of this contact with medical treatments the child will more readily accept medical care for himself, and feel more secure when he gets it. For one thing, the importance of taking medicine regularly and on time will be impressed upon him. Moreover, in caring for a sick pet he will learn how to nurse a living being, and realize that tenderness and reassurance are as vital as the medical treatment itself—for people as well as for animals.

Not the least value of pets is the large number of constructive projects to which they lead. Practically anything to be used for collecting or housing animals can be homemade, or at least home improved. A wire coat-hanger, a stick, and mosquito netting can be made into a butterfly net. A kitchen sieve attached to a bamboo pole makes a good river net. A Mason jar can be used for gathering eggs, and when the top is replaced with a wire screen, it becomes a collecting box for insects and small animals. For storing them, however, a larger screened box must be used. A discarded aquarium is ideal for this purpose.

There is no great expense in buying a cage for a hamster, but why not help the child make one himself? It will require not only the use of hammer and saw, but a good deal of ingenuity as well, since the little animal has sharp teeth that gnaw at any protruding edge. It is easy enough to buy a basket or crib for the new puppy, but there is lasting satisfaction in helping the youngster build one out of a few pieces of wood and the padding from an overstuffed chair. The goldfish bowl or aquarium can be left bare except for a few pebbles and a bit of seaweed—or it can be artistically decorated with shells and a homemade model of an ancient schooner that has sunk to the bottom of the sea.

Finally, the child who lives with pets—a process that can begin very early, as pointed out in chapter 4—will inevitably absorb many of the facts of life and death. Through observing the personality patterns and reactions of different animals, he will come to know not only their ways better but the ways of people, too. He will learn about the interdependence of animals, plants, and human beings in the order of nature, and come to understand the necessity for protecting and preserving wild life. He will learn something of the processes of birth, nutrition, and growth, and in general attain a greater appreciation of the wonder of existence. Sex and reproduction will become part of this larger story, accepted as a natural step in the perpetuation of life. Questions on the human level, of course, arise; but parents will generally find it easier and more comfortable to answer them when the children have the observation of animals as a background.

Solving Problems Through Pets

The experience of raising a pet can help to meet special needs and straighten out personality quirks. Little Anne, at four, was so shy and diffident that she rarely spoke a word to visitors; but, in the few months that she has had a parakeet, her whole manner has changed for the better. She now talks with almost anyone about her fascinating pet, and right away the ice is broken for conversation about other things as well. Stanley used to be even more disorderly than the average nine-year-old; but when his parents finally yielded to his pleading and let him have his pet hamster in his bedroom, he readily agreed not only to keep its cage but his whole room spotlessly clean. Hugh, an eight-year-old, is a rough and tumble lad who ordinarily teases his six-year-old brother to distraction. Lately, however, the two have teamed up happily to care for the puppy their uncle gave them. Ellen, now five, used to be afraid of practically any large animal. Her parents decided to try a suggestion made by a psychologist friend—to buy her a series of pets, beginning with the simplest and least fearsome. First it was a chameleon, then a turtle, then a white mouse, then a small puppy. Now, after a year, she seems to have no fear of living things of any kind, and is looking forward to the time when her puppy will be a full-grown dog. On the other hand, ten-year-old Arnold spends so much time alone with his cat that his parents suspect he is using it as a refuge from ordinary activities with other children. They have decided to have a talk with his teacher and with the guidance counselor at his school, to see why he withdraws from group sports.

Enriching Their Play with Pets

Alert parents will watch for every opportunity to help their children get the most out of their association with pets. For a child to tease an animal is unthinkable, of course. For a child to have a dog merely to pet and stroke is really too little. Children can enjoy their pets so much more if they are only shown how. As a child learns more, he will become more and more absorbed, and his development will be promoted in many ways. But he will need suggestions from others. Few children would think of raising their own rabbit food—lettuce, carrots, etc.—but once they get started, they will find this to be an exciting enterprise in itself. Most children are unaware how intimately the lives of dogs and cats have been tied up with different countries and great personages—but books can be found on this subject. Animal stories and animal lore also make excellent reading, and give added flavor to the hobby of raising a pet. There is no more stimulating introduction to biology than observation and study of the different animals and how they live.

Through the ownership of a pet, the growing child can experience the double satisfaction of working with special organizations and becoming an "expert." Pamphlets and bulletins can be obtained from humane societies such as the A.S.P.C.A., from the Department of Agriculture in Washington, the American Museum of Natural History in New York City, as well as from local zoos and natural history museums. The Boy's Clubs of America, the Junior Audubon Clubs, the 4-H clubs, the Scouts and the Campfire Girls—all these are sources not only of information but of exciting activities that grow out of an interest in animals. Pet shows or "circuses" and exhibits of the proper food for each species are two of the activities, as mentioned on page 217. Through these organizations the youngster's pet becomes a passport to wider social contacts, and casual play is transformed into an ever-expanding hobby.

A dog (or a cat as well) can lead to still another form of recreation. If he is purebred, and a good specimen, it is a good idea to register him with a national kennel club. (Sometimes one of the less popular breeds is preferable, since in this case the club is likely to be small and the members will get to know each other well.) The activities of the club will open up a whole new set of interests as well as a new group of friends, not only for the child but for the whole family. Conformation shows are a healthy incentive for caring for the dog and keeping him in top shape. The youngster will be eager to study the points that count in the judging and will spend many absorbing hours learning how to groom his pet to perfection and handle him in the competition. But even if the dog does not measure up for showing—or if he is not a thoroughbred at all—he can still be a candidate for obedience tests. Very simple animal training is within the reach of almost any child from ten up, and the pleasure, pride, and skill that result are well worth the effort. But not the least of the benefits is the fact that, in teaching an animal patience and self-control, the child is acquiring these qualities himself.

Older children, from ten to fifteen, frequently find in pets a source of work experience and income. A few obtain part-time jobs as helpers in pet shops, while others breed mice, hamsters, guinea pigs, parakeets, rabbits, or dogs for sale. Hospitals and university laboratories are constantly in need of small animals for experimentation and medical tests. In more than one city there is a "Pet Lending Library," where schools can rent small animals at nominal prices for classroom study and play. An organization of this kind might be stocked at least partially by teen-agers.

Though we have never come across it, we suggest that older children could organize a "pet service" for convalescing or handicapped children and adults. Time and again it has been found that the companionship of a pet gives shut-ins an interest outside themselves, and actually speeds their recovery or readjustment. However, we hasten to add that the animal should not be merely loaned, but given outright, since the sick and disabled are likely to become particularly attached to a pet and will find it hard to give it up.

Sometimes the people next door want to leave their dog or cat for a few days. This is a wonderful chance for your child. He may be given the opportunity to take care of the pet, with the special responsibility that this entails, *and* he will be *paid*.

Both features help him to grow up. So do let him take on the job, even if it is some nuisance for you.

When Are They Ready for Pets?

When might a child first have a pet? The answer is twofold: when he gets pleasure from it, and when he can give it at least a minimum of basic care. Put in another way, we can say that a child is ready for a pet when he is capable of treating it as a living thing and not merely as another toy. It may take a little time and the sacrifice of a few butterflies or snails before he recognizes the difference, but it is one of the elementary lessons that every child must learn.

You may notice one day that your youngster gets a great thrill from a pet belonging to someone else. He may show that he is not afraid of the animal. He may indicate in his treatment that he will not often be intentionally cruel and that he knows the animal has feelings. At this point it is likely that the child is ready to have a pet of his own. On the other hand if he is afraid of the creature or if he begins by teasing him, hold up. It is better not to force a pet upon a child, with the hope that he will later become "used" to it.

As for care, even a two-year-old can learn to shred paper for the canary's cage or feed a leaf of lettuce to a rabbit. In general, we should let him take over whenever he wants to, even though it may be quicker for us to do the job. He will feel important in doing his share, and will learn, too, that the animal's welfare is dependent on his ministrations. A little later —at three or four—the youngster can help mix food or clean the animal's living quarters. By the time he has reached five, he should be able to take charge of most of the pet's daily needs, but still with supervision and guidance. Now of course a good deal depends upon the size and temperament of the pet—as well as that of the child! A five-year-old might cope with a kitten or a quiet dog, but hardly with a Great Dane or a scrappy Scottie. Indeed, it is best to favor mild dogs for small children. The large ones can be too rough, albeit unintentionally, and the peppy ones can be too capricious. Parents, however, must realize that emergencies will occur time and again and must be ready to help meet them: the dog gets sick, the rabbit disappears, the kitten makes a mess. Such emergencies take time and energy, but they are a small price to pay for the many advantages of owning a pet.

Should every child have a pet? Here, as always, there is no fixed rule; but if a youngster has his heart set on owning an animal, parents should think twice before denying him this deep satisfaction. And if a mother's only hesitation lies in the extra work it will make, she'd better ask herself whether her standards of order and cleanliness are not too rigid. Many people, of course, hesitate to have a dog in an apartment, or object to the odor of rabbits. Why not use these problems as an opportunity to have the youngsters do some research—to find out the characteristics of different animals or different breeds, as well as their availability and the care they require? The very small boy or girl might cut animal pictures out of magazines, while older children can read up on them, or visit pet shops, breeders, or shows. The problem will in this way become a project—a family project—and any decision that is made will more likely be accepted by everyone involved.

How to Choose a Pet

The child's first contact with animals is generally a casual matter. A turtle or chameleon is brought home from the circus, a garter snake or a couple of snails are found in the grass. Frequently small children keep several such creatures in a "menagerie" of their own—the more the better since every experience with living things gives them a fuller appreciation for nature and increased opportunities for healthy play. Simple animals which require little care provide excellent preparation for the responsibilities of owning more advanced pets. They *may* also serve to break down parental hesitations and squeamishness about having animals in the home!

Many considerations are involved in choosing a regular pet. The age of the child is perhaps first. As pointed out above, even a two-year-old can help to feed animals that are cared for by other members of the family. Hamsters and white mice can be appreciated by three- or four-year-olds, while guinea pigs and rabbits are best suited to those a little older. At six or seven, children are usually ready for canaries, kittens, or puppies, although parents or older brothers and sisters will have to be ready with help, and take over fully at times.

Size is important when it comes to dogs in small apartments or small homes—and activity as well. It is inhuman to keep an energetic animal in close confinement (and hard on the family also). Regular pets must also be chosen for hardiness, since children are sometimes apt to forget their food or water. Moreover, they become deeply attached to their pets and, though they must learn that death is inevitable, we can spare some suffering by avoiding the delicate varieties that are likely to have particularly short lives. Although expense is no great consideration with many small animals, it is of real importance with purebred dogs, cats, and birds, as well as some tropical fish.

There is one more essential consideration: the personality needs of the child. For the inactive boy or girl, it might be better to have a romping dog than a caged bird. For the youngster who is scattered and disorganized, the care and feeding of a dozen fish might supply just the practice in concentration that is needed. But though we may help to guide the child's choice of a pet, his own preferences must be given the utmost respect, since there is no more consuming passion than that of a child for a pet of his *own* choosing. Moreover, the benefits of owning a pet can be realized to the fullest only if he is happy with the choice.

Brief Guide to Pets

The following guide is not meant to be a complete key to pets and their care. Rather, it is designed to show the enormous variety of available animals, so that an intelligent selection may be made. We have limited ourselves to household pets, however; ponies, chickens, bees, pigs, and farm animals have been omitted, although we realize that they can make excellent pets and lead to profitable hobbies.

The simplest creatures found in gardens, ponds, woods, and fields often make the most interesting pets for the young child, as we have noted earlier. They give him practice in caring for living creatures, and serve as an exciting introduction to natural history. Even the lowly earthworm becomes engrossing when the child learns the story of his life—how he "sees" without eyes, "hears" without ears, moves without legs, and "chews" without teeth; how he repairs himself in ways that human beings cannot; how he helps to air and fertilize the soil so that crops grow better.

The busy ant will make a much better pet when he and his fellow citizens are kept in a glass-front house, so that the well-ordered life of the colony can be closely observed. Children are endlessly intrigued by ant society, with its queens, males, and workers, each carrying out special functions.

A praying mantis can be kept in an ordinary insect box; in time he will take water from a spoon and even get to know his keeper. Butterflies and moths can hardly be classed as pets, but if the eggs are found, the child will be fascinated by the life cycle from egg to caterpillar to pupa to adult. Tadpoles can be kept alone or with goldfish. Like the frog, salamanders are amphibious, need rocks and moss as well as water, and eat small living things. Water snails can be found in almost any pond and can be kept in a Mason jar or an aquarium with fish and water plants. Land snails have four tentacles instead of two; their movements, feeding habits, and self-made "house," like that of water snails, make an absorbing study. The *anolis,* or chameleon—a lizard—makes an interesting pet; its changes in color (not for camouflage) are particularly amusing. For details and vivid pictures of all these creatures and more, we refer you to the charming and informative book *Odd Pets,* by Lilo Hess and Dorothy Childs Hogner.

Hamsters are small, easily handled creatures with soft, golden coats. They eat carrots, peanuts, lettuce, and dog food, storing the food in interesting muzzle pouches. They multiply rapidly, but females must be separated from males and young. Clean and odorless, they can be kept in an apartment, housed in a small wire cage with shredded paper for bedding.

White mice are more amusing than most hamsters. They will run up small stairs and play with spools. They need water and food frequently: oats, seed, lettuce, condensed milk. Mice are clean, easily bred, good for small homes. They need a cage of wood and wire with a hinged roof for cleaning and hay or sawdust for bedding.

Guinea pigs are friendly, appealing, inexpensive. They like to be picked up, need a mate for companionship. They need the same type of pen as mice and hamsters—off the ground or floor to avoid drafts and dampness, with an extra enclosure for exercise. Their diet is the same as for mice.

Rabbits are affectionate and devoted, but they will not survive rough handling. They eat clover, vegetable tops, hay, and carrots; and they like to gnaw on twigs and bark. One or two can be kept in a small hutch indoors, but outdoors is preferable, in an enclosed yard for protection from other animals. A larger hutch is necessary for breeding, with a nest box in a dark corner. Wild rabbits will not live long in captivity. A good rabbit breeder will have many types. The Angora (white) and Belgian hare (reddish tan) are most common and cheapest; the Dutch-marked (dark and white) is also gentle. Others are silver, gray, tan, and blue.

Many varieties of turtles are available at any pet shop. A small aquarium is better than a glass bowl. Brighten it with colored pebbles, and add a stone island. They eat any sort of raw meat, chopped in bits, or living worms and insects.

Even the cheapest goldfish thrive best in a carefully planned aquarium in which there is a balance between plant and animal life. The aquarium can be virtually self-sustaining, requiring only the addition of water and food. It should be rectangular to permit adequate air surface, with one gallon capacity for each inch of fish, and should contain sand, snails, tadpoles, the right amount of vegetation. Artificial lights are necessary for delicate varieties to keep the temperature between 65 and 80. Besides the common variety of goldfish, there are the jumping Comet, the fantails, webtails, and veiltails, the strange Lionheads, and the grotesque Telescope with its protruding eyes. Commercial preparations are the best food, with shrimp, beef, salmon, and crumbs for variety. The fish should be fed tiny quantities several times a day.

Tropical fish are almost unlimited in variety: over a hundred kinds are available. They require careful feeding, clean water, controlled temperature. This is an interest that naturally expands, becomes expensive, and takes up more and more room, as well as unlimited time and effort. Children should start with the hardier, less expensive varieties, such as guppies or rainbow fish, Paradise, swordtails, the gorgeously colored angelfish, the striped zebra, the platys or moon fish, which can be bred in all shades of gold, blue, yellow, and orange. Others, to be added later, are the Canchito, the black or blue mollies, the variegated pearl Danio, the magnificent Tetra with its vivid "neon" red and blue stripes, the mouthbreeders, barbus, killifish, and the brilliantly colored jewelfish.

The varieties of canaries are numerous: the Norwich, Yorkshire, yellow warbler, American roller and dozens of others. Feeding is relatively simple, since packages of seed are readily available and a bit of green can be added each day. Most children from seven or eight up can take over the care of the bird—keeping the cage clean, covering it with a cloth at night, and providing fresh water for drinking and bathing.

Birds of the parrot family make a colorful and entertaining hobby. In general, the care and feeding are the same as for canaries. Teaching the parrot to talk is particularly appealing to children though it requires some knowledge and much patience. Breeding brilliantly colored parakeets and love birds is well suited to young people in the later teens. Finches are also colorful and docile, and some have delightful voices. If they multiply, it will be necessary to build an outdoor aviary.

The selection of a dog should be particularly careful, since the whole family will have to live with him for a long period. Here again is a first-rate opportunity for practice in gathering information and making a decision. Visits to various kennels, pet stores, and dog shows can be the most satisfying kind of undertaking. The major decisions will revolve around these alternatives: small or large size, lively or calm temperament, purebred or mongrel, male or female, puppy or full grown.

In general, a dog for children should be gentle and affectionate, active but not excitable and nervous, protective but not pugnacious, alert and easily taught, capable of taking considerable playful mauling. Opinions differ as to the advisability of choosing a puppy or a full-grown dog, but our own preference is for a puppy over three months of age, to give the child a chance to participate in its training and to observe its growth step by step. Some experts feel that females are generally more affectionate than males; but the difference, if it exists, is not great enough to decide the choice. Moreover, the general disposition of the dog is not fully inborn, but depends primarily on the general atmosphere of the home and the way it is treated. The idea that mixed-breed dogs are usually healthier, smarter, and easier to get along with than purebreds is false—rather, they are unpredictable in every way. Like all other dogs taken into the home, they should be carefully examined by a veterinarian and given all the protective shots he recommends. Purebred dogs have been carefully developed for special characteristics of health and behavior. You know pretty well what you are getting. Therefore the safest way to select a dog is to go to a reputable breeder or a reliable, sanitary, well-stocked pet shop. Consult the owner, if you can, rather than a clerk.

The hundred recognized breeds of dogs are classified into six "variety groups." A word about each of them may help to narrow the choice. The sporting group, because of their long background in hunting, are healthy, adaptable, and easily trained. The larger breeds—setters, pointers, Weimaraner, and retrievers—enjoy the country or the suburbs where they can run freely. Spaniels, including the lively and popular cocker, are at home everywhere and are especially well liked by small children. For very little children, however, some male cockers are too aggressive.

The hound group as a whole are less popular as household pets, except the congenial beagle, which is among the first ten in popularity. Many of them make ideal companions for children. Among them, the intelligent and tolerant dachshund and the rarer Basenji are excellent housedogs, while the greyhound, borzoi, and deerhound are too large and expensive to be considered.

Many members of the working group (so-called because they were originally guardians of herds and homes) are better companions than playmates because of their large size. Also, most of them consume too much food to be supported by the average family. In the suburbs and the country, however, the boxer, as well as the collie and schnauzer, is well suited to children. The German shepherd (police dog), the mastiffs, and the Doberman pinscher often make better watchdogs than playmates.

All the terriers are small enough to serve as pets in any home, and most of them make ideal dogs for children. The Airedale is a favorite, though as large as several working dogs. It and the Welsh terrier are quieter than the lively fox terrier; but anyone considering terriers should not overlook the Irish, the Sealyham, and a number of lesser-known breeds. The cairn, though, is yappy, and often scrappy, and not good for children. The bullterrier and the Kerry blue are often unreliable.

The toy group is toy in size but not in intelligence, animation, and the ability to "take it." However, the Pekingese, Pomeranian, toy poodle, Maltese, and Chihuahua are apt to be expensive. They are also limited in their ability to play with children, and must usually be watched closely since they cannot hold their own with other dogs.

The last group, called nonsporting, are primarily pets, and adapted to either city or country living. The smooth-coated, lively Boston terrier is a fine companion for children, the clean and playful French bulldog fits into the smallest apartment, and the striking Dalmatian makes a better household pet than most people realize.

Most cats are clean, easy to train, adaptable, responsive to affection—and for these reasons make good pets even for small children. The care they require is well within the abilities of youngsters from five or six up: daily brushing, fresh water, regular feeding, airing. Older children can successfully train a cat to do simple tricks; they can also construct a box for it to sleep in, as well as a scratching-post to help save the furniture. For those who are looking for a hobby rather than merely a pet, there are a number of clubs which hold regular meetings and shows.

Generally speaking, children derive more pleasure and satisfaction from active, playful kittens and cats than from the reserved, dignified specimens. It is far better to obtain a cat from a friend, or from a good dealer or breeder, than to pick up a stray animal. The wide variations in the color of cats make the problem of selection an interesting one. Most families would be well-advised to choose our domestic, short-haired cats rather than the long-haired Persian (Angora), the tailless Manx, or the rarer varieties such as the Siamese, Abyssinian, or Peke-faced. Children will get as much fun or more out of the energetic and inexpensive domestic cats as out of the imported varieties. Moreover, the basic values of play and responsibility will not be obscured by emphasis on prestige and pride of ownership.

CHAPTER XV

Finding Room for Play

YOU MIGHT BEGIN to explore the play possibilities of your home with a questionnaire of the following sort.

Is the living room so formal that it is only used for entertaining guests? Could there be at least one informal corner for games and hobbies?

Which is preferable—to make at least part of the attic into a recreation room for the whole family, or to use it all for storage?

Could part of the front yard be used for play, or an outdoor living area?

If there is a paved driveway, is it being used for skating or games like shuffleboard?

Wouldn't it give teen-age sons and daughters a better chance to entertain their friends if parents had a hobby or games retreat in their own bedroom?

If there is a guest room, could it be made into a play room, with studio couch or fold-away bed for the occasional visitor?

Might not the porch be enclosed for use as a recreation room, music room, garden room?

Could a closet be freed for games and play equipment through ingenious use of other closets or built-ins?

Is it possible to turn part of a large hall, foyer, or stair landing into a play area?

Which is more important—keeping the car in a garage, or an ample play room? How about turning the garage into a recreation room, and building a car port beside it?

The Play Room or Play Corner

It is usually not feasible to set aside a special room for children's play, but half or three-quarters of the child's bedroom might be devoted to this purpose. More space for play can often be provided by using a bunk with drawers beneath, by building a wardrobe into the closet, by constructing a "space-divider" between the sleeping and play areas, with one side for storing clothes and the other for toys, books, phonograph, aquarium, plants, and so on.

A composition floor covering and washable walls are practically a necessity, although a skid-proof scatter rug can be used to dress up the sleeping corner. A large bulletin board or tackboard will provide space for exhibiting drawings and paintings. Shelf space should be ample since neatness and orderliness are encouraged when things are in full view. We again advise against toy chests, since they tend to become catch-alls and frequently lead to broken toys. Furniture should be strong and movable and without dangerously sharp corners. Wallpaper, curtains, and other decorations should be gay and colorful but not harsh and restless. Wooden lockers or cubbyholes can be built into a corner or in the space-divider, to be used as a storehouse for aprons and smocks, skates, bows and arrows, and other paraphernalia. A low, sturdy table covered with linoleum or other composition surface is most practical for finger painting, clay work, and hobbies of all sorts. Be sure it has a bright but not glaring light above it.

Equipment for special activities should be adapted to the needs of the individual child. Most of it can be homemade—an excellent recreational project in itself. Place a simple carpentry bench in a corner, or even folded down from a wall, and have the tools mounted handily. For large-muscle activity, consider installing a small jungle gym, slide, or doorway gym. Directions for making an easel have already been given (chapter 3), as well as suggestions for storing paints and brushes. Construct a train unit that folds flat against the wall when not in use. You might also build a small platform "stage" in a corner, with a movable screen as a backdrop. A painted crate makes a good prop or costume box. Keep it filled with a large assortment of old clothing, uniforms, ribbons, fans, broken jewelry, badges, and other odds and ends which your child will use for putting on a skit, dramatizing a story, or just plain "dressing up." (The use of these materials has been discussed on pages 74, 98, and 124.)

The Recreation Room

Building a recreation or rumpus room in the basement or on a porch or in the attic is a major undertaking for the whole family. Plan it with the interests of each member in mind: woodworking, model-building, painting, tropical fish, etc. It will be more attractive and creative if you adopt a motif for decoration, such as a ship's grill, a dude ranch, a Paris bistro—whatever suits the fancy of the family. This is one time you can let your imaginations run riot, without regard for "what goes with what."

A wealth of recently developed materials is available at local supply houses: wallboards, floor tiles, acoustical ceiling tile, damp-proof paint. A study of new materials and processes makes an absorbing interest in itself. Excellent designs can be found in magazines and books devoted to home building and decoration. Practically all the furnishings can be homemade—for example, built-in seats that double as storage bins, a soft-drink bar, a folding table for ping-pong, iron furniture. To save money, some of the chairs and tables might be made of light, waterproof materials so they can be used out of doors as well. To save space, make storage benches, corner cupboards, drop-leaf and fold-down tables, and a built-in under the stairs.

A spacious recreation room will lead to freer, more satisfying activities for the entire family. Dad and Mom will play charades with the kids and keep young in heart by learning new dance steps from the older children. The living room rug and furniture will be spared, and noise will be confined to the recreation room. Junior will have ample space for his electric trains or experiments, and an ideal spot for his gang or Cub Scout den to meet. Sis will be delighted to have a place to entertain her teen-age friends in relative privacy, while her parents will be glad to have them in their home, to get to know them better. Birthdays and holidays will be celebrated in a gay atmosphere; winter evenings and summer vacations will never seem long and dreary. In a word, the finished basement, attic, or porch can be the play center of the home.

The Backyard

The way to get the maximum use out of the backyard is to lay it out with the same care that is used in planning the house itself. Instead of the usual haphazard procedure, make a list of the outdoor play activities that each member of the family prefers, then make a scale drawing of the entire yard, including the trees. The problem will then be to find room for as many activities as possible without interference with each other. Where the children of the family differ rather widely in age, it is generally wise to have their play space as far apart as possible.

Most of the play equipment for small children can be built at home, and some of the most intriguing sources of fun, like dirt piles and barrels, need not be built at all. A sandbox, whose endless possibilities we have already described, might well be first on your construction list. It can be made of two- by ten-inch planks, measuring about four by six feet overall. A single plank of the same stock, but about ten feet long, can be balanced on a low sawhorse to make a seesaw; your child will doubtless use it as a bridge or gangplank as well. A wooden or automobile tire swing can be easily hung on the limb of a tree or on a framework made of heavy pipe. A homemade slide requires a good deal of care to make, since it should be made of hardwood and carefully finished to avoid splinters. If the slide is not feasible, a heavy climbing rope, a ladder, or a wooden jungle gym will satisfy the youngster's urge to climb. To complete the children's corner, a playhouse might be made of crude lumber or old packing cases, as recommended in chapter 3. If the child is encouraged to paint and decorate it himself, and care for it as he would a real house, it can be a major incentive for growth.

Even in a small backyard, games can be provided for older children and their parents. Some of these, however, will have to be tailored to fit the available space. Badminton, paddle tennis, deck tennis, volleyball, and croquet can all be played on small-scale courts. One basket is enough for basketball practice and simple games. With proper precautions, or rubber suction arrows, archery can be an excellent backyard game. Horseshoe pitching can be played with regulation equipment at distances ranging from 25 to 40 feet. Quoits can be made of circles of old rubber hose. Bounce-ball requires only a blank wall and a rubber ball; the same wall can be used for tennis practice. Clock golf requires a circle of smooth lawn twenty-four feet in diameter, with the hole in the center. Tetherball is somewhat more complicated, since a ten foot pole is needed, plus a tennis ball dangling from the top by a heavy cord, and wooden paddles to bat it. If you have a paved driveway or walk, or a concrete patio, you have a possible set-up for shuffleboard, hopscotch, or hand tennis.

Gardening is as important as games. Ideally, each child of the family should have a small plot of his own, if he wants one, with the freedom to select the things he wants to grow—and with this freedom, the responsibility of watering and weeding. As we indicated earlier, children as young as three can derive pleasure and benefit from growing their own vegetables and flowers. Naturally parents must realize that it takes time for youngsters to develop this sense of responsibility, and a "crop failure" or two has to be expected. Here again is a big chance for us to teach our children and to work along with them under the most enjoyable circumstances. The thrill of watching a garden grow should not be denied any child, and the excitement of being shown the first pansy or radish should not be denied any parent.

A swimming pool and a greenhouse may sound like the height of luxury to most of us. Yet modern materials and techniques have put both within reach of many average families today. Plans can be readily obtained for window greenhouses or the lean-to type that is attached to the side of the house. Both can be heated electrically or from the house heating system. Larger greenhouses, of course, require separate heating and ventilating systems as well as full foundations. For those who wish to begin in the easiest way, but one that can be quite gratifying, a tiny greenhouse measuring about one by three feet can be bought, or home built, and used for growing flowers or cooking herbs.

Water is one of the most versatile and satisfying play materials outside as well as inside the house. A tub of water or a hose spray will keep young children happy for hours. Even more fun is a plastic wading pool, and most fun of all is, of course, a swimming pool for the whole family. Although poured concrete and steel pools still run into thousands of dollars, it is now quite possible for the home handyman to build a pool (with help from the neighbors) for a few hundred or less. Hand digging should not be attempted for anything but a very small pool. A bulldozer or steamshovel can be rented by the day, and the shell can be made of concrete block with a plastic lining. (One homeowner has built a successful pool using heavy waterproof building paper for lining, but it has to be replaced every year or two.) These pools can be filled with a garden hose and drained with a small sump pump. However, while mechanical and financial difficulties are being rapidly overcome, there is still the problem of safety and the probability of being deluged with visitors. There must be adequate supervision whenever children use the pool, as well as a systematic way of regulating the flow of guests—if that is possible!

The Outdoor Living Room

The idea of an outdoor living room, so popular in Europe and South America, is beginning to come into its own all over the United States. Many of the newer homes have glass doors opening to flagstone patios, and some families are lucky enough to have a combination indoor fireplace and outdoor grill. But families whose homes are not so fully equipped to start with can have most of the benefits of outdoor recreation if they are prepared to provide the necessary effort, ingenuity, and expenditure.

A patio can be built out of concrete or brick at a cost far lower than flagstone, and a fireplace or grill can be constructed of ordinary rocks gathered by the whole family. The beauty and durability of redwood furniture can be captured in ordinary pine that has been painted with a preservative stain.

Everyone in the family can contribute something to the outdoor living room and the land around it. Here are a few suggestions: a vine arbor, plant boxes, bushes planted for privacy, a rock garden, a small pool for fish, a bird feeding station, lockers to keep cooking equipment and tools, an indoor-outdoor garden that unites the inside living room with the one outside.

Do You Have a Play Closet?

If you are fortunate enough to have plenty of closets, think about setting one aside for storing play materials of all kinds. We all spend so much time looking for skates, games, jumping ropes, ball gloves! You might consider building an extra closet for this purpose in the basement, the garage, or against the rear of the house—but be sure that it is readily accessible. A storage wall will also serve for this purpose, with shelves for books as well as play equipment—a gentle reminder about reading. It will help the children keep things in good order, and they will know where to find their play equipment without asking others. In planning a closet or wall of this kind, shelves, pigeonholes, and hooks should be provided for each individual article and labeled accordingly—otherwise it will become a catch-all and lead to chaos.

The Home Workshop

Whenever possible, a home workbench for family use should be placed where it can be used the year round. Though useful in a garage, there is generally too little space and it is too cold for work during the winter. A better location can usually be found in a utility room, attic, or basement. Workbenches can be bought in knock-down form; however, it takes little skill to build one to order.

Most people buy toy tools for their small children and cheap tools for themselves. This is a mistake, as we have already pointed out, since poor tools make for slovenly work and have to be replaced within a year or so. Moreover, it is wise to encourage children to respect good tools and handle them with care. Experience has shown that the following tools are almost invariably needed: claw and tack hammers, cross-cut and rip saws, coping saw, hack saw, keyhole saw, jack plane, block plane, draw knife, hand drill, brace and bits, large and small screw drivers, vise, adjustable wrench, tin shears, clamps, ordinary and long-nosed pliers, awl, files, rasp, chisels, square, metal tape measure, folding rule, level.

The most useful and versatile power tool is the quarter-inch drill. With its attachments, it will not only drill holes up to $2\frac{1}{2}''$ in diameter, but will grind, polish, sand, sharpen tools and utensils, remove paint, clean paint brushes, and trim hedges. In combination with more complex apparatus, it becomes a drill press, plane, saw, and even a lathe. (These are generally unsafe for children under high school age; an eleven- or twelve-year-old can handle the tool for standard uses.) For heavy work, single power tools are more satisfactory; of these, a circular saw is most useful, although combination outfits are available.

Important, too, is a convenient arrangement of shelves, hooks, and storage boxes, so that both tools and materials are within easy reach. A perforated pegboard can be used for hanging tools, and baby-food jars make good containers for nails and screws. Even younger children can help to plan and build a workshop; there is no better opportunity for father and son (or daughter) to work together and get better acquainted.

For Apartment Dwellers

Although the play facilities of apartment houses are bound to be more limited than those of private homes, they can be immensely expanded through thoughtful planning. With the co-operation of the owner, basement rooms can sometimes be turned over to recreation activities such as ping-pong and woodcraft. An active tenants' association may be instrumental in securing garden plots, an equipped playground, a cooperative nursery school, and, in some cases, hobby classes for young and old.

Within the apartment, the problem is generally to find enough space for varied play. Floor-to-ceiling built-ins placed in the living room, foyer, child's room, or parents' bedroom can be used for storing all types of equipment for games, books, music, outdoor activities, collections, arts and crafts. Its doors can serve as drop-leaf tables, and bridge and game tables can be stored in a space behind it. Throughout the apartment, doors make excellent places to hang tools, baskets for small toys, baseball gloves, fishing tackle. Wooden chests, hollow hassocks, and window seats serve doubly for sitting and storage. Expansible sectional units and room-dividers of metal and wood can be used for plants, an aquarium or terrarium, exhibit cases for crafts or collections, a radio or television set on a swivel. Additional space for play can also be obtained by clearing the rooms of unnecessary furniture. This can best be done through ingenious planning of closets to include, for example, built-in chests of drawers.

CHAPTER XVI

Play as You Go

If You Go by Train

As most of us know only too well, traveling by train with small children can be an ordeal for the entire family. Before leaving, everyone is caught in a last-minute rush, and no thought is given to keeping the young ones occupied. Perhaps it is taken for granted that, because the children are thrilled at the prospect of a trip and show a great interest in trains, they will surely find plenty to amuse them for hour after hour. Nothing could be further from the truth.

The excitement of being on a train wears off in a matter of minutes, and is often replaced by teasing, nagging, and every other expression of boredom and restlessness. However, if we recognize this fact in advance and make the children's need for "something to do" an integral part of our preparations, the hours spent en route can be reasonably pleasant for all concerned.

The prime preparation for a young child consists of assembling a "travel kit," containing a variety of playthings. The best way to pack the material is in a doll suitcase or train case which the youngster himself can carry (a covered basket or shopping bag would also do). This will give him an adult feeling and act as an incentive to behave in a more mature manner. Let the materials be largely of the child's own choosing, but slip in a few surprises that seem appropriate for the restricted space of the train. Here are a few samples that have been put to the test: a coloring book and crayons, small cars or trains, hand puppets, a kaleidoscope, story and picture books, a magnet, a pocket-size doll family.

Improvised playthings are just as appealing as those already prepared. The mother who has been wise enough to slip a pair of scissors into her bag will find good use for it. Flat paper cups, or any stiff paper folded double, can be cut into all sorts of interesting animal shapes. They can be colored by the child and made to stand up on a suitcase. Any number of other objects can be made, including soldier hats, boats, airplanes, fans, and boxes. A good trick is to make a variety of these objects, then arrange them in some kind of order and tell a story, using each one as an illustration.

Play can accomplish much on even a long trip. Children cannot sit still or idly look out of the window for long, unless they are either browbeaten or phlegmatic. But give them the right kind of activities, and they will drain off excess energy and not develop the kind of fatigue that makes them whine and wiggle.

The play materials we have just mentioned will ordinarily keep the four- and five-year-olds happy. But the Twos and Threes are quite a different story. Children of these ages are too old to spend most of their time sleeping, and too young to manage their own entertainment. Their interest in the passing scene is limited and their attention span is short. These are the youngsters who most easily become tired and irritable and make the trip a nightmare for everyone, including themselves.

The answer—if there is an answer—is twofold. First, as much as possible of their regular routine should be preserved while traveling: napping, toileting, moving about, hugging their favorite blanket or stuffed animal. And second, it is up to us to have a variety of amusements on tap, ready for the first signs of restlessness. A good deal can be done with nothing but a pair of hands and a couple of handkerchiefs. Fingerplay, that old stand-by, works wonders with small children. Practically everyone knows "This is the church and this is the steeple," and "Peter and Paul" not to mention "Pat-a-cake," "Pease Porridge Hot," and "Ten Little Indians." As for the handkerchiefs, most of us find it easy to knot them into a crude likeness of a mouse, a hammock, or a doll. The less we worry about close resemblance to things, the better. All we need is the idea and the child will supply the rest.

The major reason for our youngsters' restlessness aboard a train is the fact that they are confined to a small space and cannot release their energy freely. In most cases, too, they are further restricted by their parents' fear of disturbing other passengers. Nevertheless, we must give them an occasional chance to use their large muscles as well as their small ones. A tour of the train will help—done in two stages, if you like: through the forward cars at one time and through the rear cars at another. A child of four or five can usually be trusted to walk up and down the aisle of his own car, or bring us a cup of water from the cooler. If he stops to make friends with other passengers, so much the better, since it will encourage him to be more independent.

On a long trip it is also wise to make the most of the stops. A breath of fresh air and a chance to stretch his legs outside the train will give the child the relief he needs. After he has let off steam, he is likely to settle down again to quiet play.

Even on a train there are play activities that will further the growth of our children. One of these for eight and up is the game of Observation, as it might be called. Start by making up a list of things that may be found in the countryside as the train passes: a cow, a horse, a truck, a barn, a brook. Each person who plays must select one of these objects, and the one who spots examples most often within ten or fifteen minutes wins. The game can be repeated many times and in many variations before the child tires of it, and there is little doubt that it will sharpen his powers of observation.

A long train ride is an excellent opportunity for one of the most creative types of play: storytelling. The very young can be entertained for long periods with the parent's impromptu stories built around people and things that are seen on the train ride itself. Give the child a sense of participation by asking him to choose the subject for the story, and urge him from time to time to guess what is going to happen. (Many a sorely tried parent is helped out by the suggestions made by his audience!) Don't forget, too, that your child will get a special thrill out of turning the tables and entertaining you with a story of his own making. If he gets silly and nonsensical, just play along with him, since fun and laughter go a long way toward combating boredom and fatigue.

Singing is good, too, and other people won't mind if it is done softly. Folk songs, children's songs, and rounds are particularly appropriate. But don't neglect comedy songs that don't make much sense—for example, "Around the Corner." ("Around the corner, under a tree, a sergeant major once said to me, 'If I should have to look at your face, I'd want to go around the corner, under a tree,'" etc.)

When all else palls, bring out the hand puppet for a "surprise."

For the older children there are always the old favorites for travel: Ghost, Coffee Pot, checkers, puzzles of all sorts, and various pencil and paper games. But a train ride is the time for reading, too, and every older boy and girl should be reminded to slip a book or two into his pockets or luggage. Picture magazines or the better comic books may be easier on their eyes and more closely geared to the tempo of the train.

Most children have ridden on trains relatively little and particularly enjoy all the facilities. If you are in a Pullman, let the porter put up the table for you. Your youngster will enjoy seeing it done—and it makes spread-out games ever so much easier. Let your child use the plumbing to his heart's content. We once knew a little boy who washed his hands twenty-seven times between Boston and New Haven!

But the best game of all, and one that is too often neglected, is simply the game of conversation. A train ride is an ideal opportunity for parent and child to concentrate on each other and to develop the fine art of exchanging ideas and comments. Innumerable questions will arise in the mind of the youngster, stimulated by the people and things he observes on the trip. This is one time when attention can be undivided and unhurried. And as you let yourself become absorbed in your child's wide-eyed wonder, you will find that fatigue and restlessness are soon forgotten—both his and your own.

If You Go by Car

Summer has arrived and you are planning to take the family to Canada for a three weeks' vacation. The children are both young—two and seven—and it will be their first all-day trip in a car. You're looking forward to it with a mixture of pleasurable anticipation and, frankly, dread. A lot of questions are on your mind. If you put them in the back of the car, will they keep begging to be in front? Will they become irritable and restless? Will it be possible to make the entire trip in one day, as you hope?

All these questions can be answered as you want them to be—*if* you take into full consideration your childrens' normal needs and urges during a long motor trip. It goes without saying that they will be in a high pitch of excitement when the big day arrives. Their own feelings of anticipation will keep them busy for a while, but a reaction of fatigue is bound to set in later on. The constant jiggling of the car, plus the confinement to cramped quarters, will aggravate this reaction—and the risk of "missing something" will prevent them from resting or falling asleep. In consequence, what they most need is some means of (1) increasing their comfort, (2) draining off excess energy and excitement, and (3) combating the inevitable monotony of a day's motoring. Let's look at some concrete ideas for solving these problems.

The first goal is to provide the youngsters with a place for both play and relaxation. The ordinary back seat of the car is not built to keep children happy for a full day's drive, but it can be converted to a reasonably effective play-and-rest area by placing suitcases on the floor in such a way that they are level with the top of the seat, then spreading a cotton mattress or a couple of beach rolls over the whole extent. This will give the children a large, level space in which to play games, stretch their legs, and even curl up to take a nap in comfort. Some parents who like to get an early start to avoid traffic—an excellent idea—often find that the young ones complete their night's sleep in their back-seat nest. In fact, when parents spell each other in driving, they, too, can go back to the "children's quarter" for a nap. The children will not keep begging to be in the front seat (though an occasional switch is advisable), and they will be safer where they are, since some recent studies have shown that over twice as many front-seat as back-seat passengers are severely injured in automobile accidents.

Even with the greater freedom in the back seat, the children will inevitably become restless on a long trip. It is therefore best to stop briefly every hour or so and let them walk about and play catch or tag while the car is being refueled. This has the same effect as the regular five-minute "breaks" that have proved so helpful in factories. These are based on the observation that it is more efficient to forestall fatigue and boredom than to try to overcome them after they pile up. Moreover, the prospect of "time off" every hour prevents monotony and restlessness by giving us, and our children, a goal within reach. We like to see an end, or at least a break, in what we are doing, no matter what it is. The anticipation of a change accomplishes almost as much as the change itself.

There are many other ways of relieving the monotony of a long journey. The travel kit we mentioned above is as useful in the car as on the train, with a favorite toy or two and surprise packages to be opened every hundred miles. So are singing and storytelling games, as well as word games like Geography, number games like Buzz, and guessing games like Twenty Questions or Who Am I? Licenses are always fascinating, and if the children are old enough, they can compete in listing all out-of-state licenses, each taking one side of the road. Any number of variations on the Observation game can be invented; for example, a search for the most interesting or the most unusual thing within fifty miles. Another variation is Travel Bingo. Cards are prepared in advance, with the names of common objects written in the squares in place of the usual numbers. When these objects are observed along the road, they are checked off and the first to fill a line wins the round.

Less common, and more challenging, is the game of "helping Daddy (or Mommy) drive." Any child from seven or eight up can do it in some measure. To begin with, give the youngster a notebook and pencil so that he can keep a "log" of the entire trip. It might include not only the mileage readings at the beginning and end of the day, but also the number of miles covered each hour, the amount of gas and oil consumed, the cost of the fuel and any other expenditures for the car and the passengers. Consult him frequently, and let him feel he is doing an important job. He will not only be happily occupied, but will gain some excellent experience in keeping records and accounts—good preparation for the day he has a family of his own.

Another absorbing job for the older child is helping with the itinerary of the trip. You will have to show him how you select a route, and give him a lesson in map reading before the first long trip. But once he gets the hang of it, he can be of great help. He can list all route numbers and all towns and cities in his notebook, checking them off one by one as you drive along. He can also keep an eye on the map for you. Many a wrong turn has been avoided by an alert boy or girl who knows how to follow a map and interpret signs.

Fun on a Bus Ride

The close quarters of a bus are likely to restrict a child's play even more than travel by automobile or train. The bus does not stop on command to permit relaxation, and there is little or no chance to walk in the aisles. In most cases reading, coloring, and paper-cutting cannot be done, and the toys for a travel kit will have to be carefully chosen to avoid delicate work of any kind. Nevertheless, most of the word and observation games we suggested before can be played on a bus.

Buses have an advantage over trains on one score: the atmosphere is often more congenial. Passengers are more likely to talk with each other and engage the children in conversation or games. This may be due to the closer quarters or the fact that there are fewer ways to occupy one's self on a bus; at any rate the chance to meet people and hear stories about the towns and countryside may more than make up for the lack of free movement.

There is one aspect of bus transportation that is worth special consideration. More and more often our children are traveling in groups to activities of all sorts. School trips and day camps are two examples. Often, too, mothers are called on to go with the children for supervision, or to take small groups themselves.

In many communities keeping the children happy, safe, and reasonably orderly has become a real problem. But that problem has recently been studied in New York City, and the solution is once again in terms of planned play. The bus trip should be considered an integral part of the day's recreation program, and definite preparations should be made for it—with plenty of room for improvised fun and merely resting or "looking around." While the length of the trip and the make-up of the group have to be taken into consideration, it is generally advisable to have a more active program on the trip out than on the trip back, since on the way home the children have less energy and like to talk about what they have seen and done during the day.

Among the tried and tested activities are the following. Music brings the group together, inspires gaiety, and combats fatigue and crankiness. Songs with a definite rhythm and some action like swaying or handclapping are usually best. Such instruments as the banjo, ukulele, recorder, harmonica and accordion add to the fun. Often the seating positions in the bus can be turned to advantage, with the children on the left side of the aisle singing one strain and those on the right singing another.

Many group games can be played on a bus. Animal, Vegetable, Mineral is always attractive. Telephone is amusing and instructive: a sentence is whispered from ear to ear, and the last message compared to the first. Pack My Trunk challenges memory and keeps things lively: Says the first player, "I pack my trunk with airplanes and baseballs," and so on, with the forgetters dropping out one by one. Other sources of bus fun are rhyming games and simple charades, with one side of the bus pitted against the other.

CHAPTER XVII

The Doctor Prescribes Play

FOR THE BEDRIDDEN, the handicapped, and the convalescent child, play can be far more than merely a means of passing the time or easing the strain on the household. The boy or girl who keeps busy while confined does not become so tense and restless as the one with little to do. He has an outlet for pent-up feelings and is not likely to lapse into listlessness and apathy. With his attention focused on outward activities, he does not wonder and worry so much about himself. From guided, creative play he gets the kind of encouragement and sense of accomplishment that spur the will to get well. Even his bodily processes benefit, since mild activity improves circulation, stimulates the internal organs, and promotes healing. He is therefore likely to eat better and sleep better. The chances are that if he is sick, he will recover sooner; and if he is handicapped, he will reach a stable emotional adjustment earlier.

Keeping Them Busy in Bed

The close relation between recreation and recovery was demonstrated many times over during the past war. The Air Force and other branches of the service instituted elaborate reconditioning programs, aimed at bringing the sick or wounded back to duty as rapidly as possible. Recreational and occupational therapy reached a high point of development. Not only ambulatory but bedridden patients took part in the program under the guidance of trained directors. Arts and crafts, motion pictures, organized games, and correspondence courses were among the activities that helped bring the disabled back in record time. Even the major illnesses responded to treatment more quickly. In one Air Force study, a convalescent program was credited with cutting the length of the average hospital stay for virus pneumonia practically in half.

Parents can take many a cue from the programs in service and veterans hospitals. The recreation specialist does not haphazardly assign activities to patients. Rather, he works out an individual program for each man or woman with the supervising doctor. Similarly, we ourselves should pay close attention to our child's particular abilities and disabilities, his interests and his needs during the period of confinement. There is no point in making a "problem" of it when he is merely down with a cold, but in any case of serious, extended illness, we should not neglect to check with the doctor and plan with him the type of recreation that will be most beneficial. Play should be an essential part of the doctor's prescription.

Observations of sick children suggest some general guides. In most cases their attention span is shorter than usual; they tire too easily to be able to concentrate for long. The span is further reduced by the fact that the activities available to them are usually limited and must often be pursued alone, so that the interest and excitement of moving about and being with other people are largely lacking. During illness, too, most children turn the clock back to earlier stages of development, and parents should be prepared for the fact that simpler play, often the kind they have long since discarded, will be most appealing to them. It is best to yield to their preferences here, and not to make them feel (or feel ourselves) that they are permanently retrogressing. They will catch up when they feel better.

Convalescent and handicapped children are frequently creative and resourceful in their play; on the other hand, a child who is in the midst of an illness is seldom in condition to suggest new activities or make up games of his own. Almost invariably, sickness drains away initiative, and we must be prepared to take the lead. Actually there is another reason behind this lack of initiative. The ailing child wants the reassurance of his parents' presence, and repeated requests for new activities are a good excuse to get it.

Before we can expect any child to keep busy in bed, we must do whatever we can to make him physically comfortable. Place the bed as near a window as possible so he can look out. Prop him up with a couple of pillows behind his back—or better yet, with an adjustable back rest (a beach rest is good). Pillows placed beneath his knees will add to his comfort, and a rolled-up cushion makes a good foot rest to keep him from sliding down.

For most games and crafts, he will need a firm bed table. Good tables can, of course, be bought, but an old bridge table with sawed-off legs will do. You can also make one out of plain boards or plywood with hinged legs high enough to clear the child's knees. Simpler still is the improvised affair made by placing a dining-table leaf on the backs of two kitchen chairs, one on each side of the bed. It has the double advantage of being wide and not resting on the bed. Be sure there is plenty of light over the child's shoulder. Keep a plastic or oilcloth apron and bed cover handy for messy play. Finally, put a bridge table or low bookcase beside the bed to hold tools and materials, and pin paper bags or shoe bags to the mattress for odds and ends. If things are within easy reach, your child will keep occupied for longer stretches of time and won't keep calling for help.

If we recognize the child's short interest span and do some advance planning, the need for a frequent change of activities should not be too hard to meet. The very young have the greatest difficulty amusing themselves in bed—but fortunately the average household contains a virtually inexhaustible supply of the kind of play materials that appeal to them most. Several of the following suggestions have been described in detail at their appropriate age levels.

You might give your youngster a stack of old magazines, for example, and let him search for some particular illustrations—dogs, for instance—which he likes or which you "need." He can cut them out with scissors (the rounded-point kind!) and paste them in a scrapbook. Other pictures and old postcards can be pasted on heavy shirt cardboard, then cut into homemade jigsaw puzzles. Still others can be cut into tapering strips, rolled and glued, then strung together to form a necklace.

Everyday kitchen supplies take on new meaning for the child who is laid up. He will have a happy time with cookie cutters, using them as patterns for tracing and for making "cookies" out of clay. (Real cookies will thrill him even more, if you have time to mix the dough.) Short lengths of macaroni can be colored with crayons and strung on gaily-colored thread or yarn. Milk containers make lightweight building blocks or model trucks and railroad cars. A potato, a carrot, a few matches, and a bit of lettuce can be fashioned into an amusing likeness of a human being.

The sewing box is another rich mine for playthings: spools, colored and strung on yarn, make a necklace; buttons make good wheels for the milk-carton cars. Simply sorting these articles is itself an absorbing activity. Dad's or Mother's desk is another source: with a little instruction, four- or five-year-olds will make chains and airplanes out of typewriter paper. Onion skin paper is useful for tracing. Paper clips can be bent into intriguing shapes, and old letters can be used to start a stamp collection.

This is an excellent time to teach the young child to tell time. He will be fascinated, and learn more quickly, if you show him how to make a play clock. The face can be made out of heavy cardboard, folded at the bottom so that it will stand by itself. Let him cut the numbers out of an old calendar and paste them on the face. Mark the minutes with a crayon, and make hands out of cardboard or narrow pieces of wood (tongue-depressors do very well). Attach the hands with brass fasteners so they will move easily, and the clock is ready. Once you teach your child the rudiments of telling time, he can use his knowledge to watch for a favorite radio program or remind you when it is time for his sponge bath.

There is one good way to be prepared for those brief but rather frequent illnesses of childhood: make a "sick box." It is simply an old shoe box or basket that is used as a treasure trove for bed play, and perhaps for rainy days as well. Save it for these occasions only, and hold it out as a special attraction. With care and ingenuity, it can be made so intriguing that the child who does not feel very ill can be lured into bed with the promise that it will be taken out. Here are some typical contents, which you can amplify in your own way: small boxes, milk bottle tops, clothespins, pipe cleaners, string, toothpicks, spools, corks, buttons, bits of yarn, scraps of cloth, scissors, small mirrors, crayons, pieces of wire, old birthday cards, calendars, discarded playing cards, an old alarm clock. Ask Father to bring odds and ends from his work, such as labels, large paper clips, old staplers, and samples of any kind. Be sure to include some outgrown toys like plastic cars and blocks because of the tendency to go back to simpler play.

You can count on the sick box as a source of creative bed play up to the age of ten or eleven. To give it the element of surprise, you might hold some things out, and add to it from time to time. Invite relatives and friends to contribute, too. Young children will spend at least an hour simply exploring its contents. A few will concentrate on one type of item at a time, making a tower out of spools, fitting boxes into each other, building card houses. But most youngsters will need some help in finding interesting things to do, such as how to make clothespin people or how to build a box car, using milk bottle tops as wheels and toothpicks as axles. This is a golden opportunity to teach your child new forms of play.

One of the best incentives to the more creative kinds of bed play is to use the child's own handiwork in decorating his room. Let your three- or four-year-old cut pictures out of his coloring book and paste them on the wall. Place plasticene sculpture conspicuously on the night table. Hang his mobiles from the ceiling fixture; put his paintings, collages, and drawings on the wall. Brighten up the room with paper plates he has decorated with variegated designs in crayon. Or get him the materials for loop-weaving, and help him sew together the squares he weaves to make a table scarf or a throw for the bed.

The admiration your child receives for these accomplishments will raise his spirits and give him new courage. Inspired by recognition, he will find new things to create and new ways to express himself. He will be giving, not merely getting. As a result, his disposition and outlook will improve, and his chances for a quick recovery will be vastly increased.

If, however, the illness lingers on, there are three particularly effective ways to keep a child happy and at the same time keep him from becoming preoccupied with himself. One is to encourage him to make gifts for relatives and friends. However inconsequential these gifts may be, they will keep him in touch with other people and make him feel he has something to contribute to society. The most useful articles are usually suggested by the needs of the household: a decorated wastebasket, a raffia-bound pencil container, gaily colored potholders, ornamental boxes for stamps or string, kitchen aprons in appliqué. Help him wrap the gift in bright paper—and be sure that he is told in glowing terms how attractive and useful his handiwork is.

A second source of outgoing occupations can be found in the daily duties of the home. Let your child help you, and let him feel that you really need him. Bring him peas to be shelled, ask him to look up and record telephone numbers, let him sort clothes, polish silver, sew buttons, and even help you keep your accounts. It will doubtless take longer to get things done, since the work has to be brought to his bedside and he tires easily, but this is a small price to pay for one of the most salutary things that can be done for a sick child: to make him feel useful.

A third suggestion for managing a long illness is to plan and schedule fun and entertainment in advance. Let's say your youngster's play project is to make up a scrapbook of all the photos that have been accumulating for years. Why not have him do it as a "surprise" for his father, and work toward a specific date, such as his birthday? Why not set aside certain evenings or afternoons for special family events, when everyone gathers in the child's room to have a game party, a song fest, or a "picnic," with everything arranged exactly as it would be out of doors? And how about having father or an uncle make a date for some special activity such as anagrams or checkers or making a crystal radio? In a word, let's give our sick children something to look forward to; for anticipation is often the best medicine.

Creative Convalescence

When youngsters are confined for extended periods, a good part of their recreation should be of the long-term variety—the kind they can look forward to, not merely once but day after day.

One source of continued enjoyment is the window of their room, not merely for idly looking out, but for making friends with birds and observing the growth of plants. This is an ideal time to introduce some play ideas we recommended earlier. A bird-tray, made out of a small piece of plywood, can be tacked on the windowsill in view of the bed. If crumbs or suet are placed on it, birds are almost certain to be attracted, and the child will get a good deal of fun out of watching and naming his steady customers. If there is a second window, let him plant a wooden box with seeds and place it on the inside sill. He will be fascinated by their development and will keep a close eye on them to see which one wins the race of growth. Quicker results can be achieved by putting bird seed on a damp blotter or placing a sweet potato in a jar of water, but the opportunities for caring for such plants are limited.

Convalescence can lead to discovering new interests and starting new hobbies. Ordinary games and pastimes will hold the child's attention only briefly, and he will be eager to find more absorbing things to do. Since distractions are at a minimum there will be plenty of time to help him explore the ramifications of different activities. You will of course have to supply him with materials and directions and lend a willing and enthusiastic ear when he wants to talk about a new-found interest. Half the fun of a hobby lies in telling others about it.

Practically any interest can develop into a full-blown hobby. Let's go back to that window box for a moment. A child seems to have a special interest in nature and growth during convalescence—perhaps as a reflection of his own inner needs. If he is "middle-aged" or older, his indoor "garden" can become far more than a passing fancy. You have only to supply books and magazines on the subject of plants and their care, as well as the pennies he will need to send away for seeds. Let him experiment with different mixtures of soil and humus, and try some of the newer plant chemicals. He will soon have the whole house decorated with the flowers he raises, and you will probably find him giving you sound advice on your outdoor garden. If he is confined to a wheel chair for a long period, you might also look into the possibility of building a small window greenhouse where it will get the most sun. Plans can probably be obtained from your local lumber supply company.

Other nature hobbies are worth considering. A well-stocked aquarium is an absorbing diversion for the disabled child if he is old enough and interested. He will spend hours not only caring for the fish but reading about the many varieties. A terrarium, containing not only plants but lizards, turtles, and other small animals, can also be a constructive pastime. Those clean little animals we have already discussed—hamsters—are easy to manage and fun to watch. So are ants in a glass-walled ant-house. Even the observation of clouds through the window may develop into a lasting interest. If you get some library books on cloud formations and weather signs, and perhaps an instrument or two, you may start him on the way to the more advanced hobby (and science) of meteorology.

The weeks of convalescence can be used to widen your child's horizons in many ways. In his reading, don't limit him to stories —usual or unusual—but see that he is well supplied with books that open up new worlds of nature, invention and folklore. This is also an excellent opportunity for establishing "pen friendships" with youngsters in other countries. Sometimes this can be done by getting names and addresses from friends who know people abroad. Some children write "blind" to a school or a postmaster in a small town of their own choosing, but this often leads to disappointment. A far better plan for teenagers is membership in an organization that has been set up for the express purpose of getting young people of different countries in touch with each other. It is Youth of All Nations, Incorporated, located at 16 St. Luke's Place, New York 14, N. Y.

Collections of all kinds are another "natural" for convalescence. Stamps, post cards, or interesting buttons can be gathered through correspondence or through the cooperation of those who visit the child. Membership in a national stamp or button club gives him an opportunity to make new friends, and mounting the collection can be an artistic activity of the first order.

So far we have been suggesting some long-term varieties of convalescent play. It might be useful now to list a few specific activities which have been found to be particularly appropriate. Individually, most of them are well known and many have been described in earlier chapters, but when put down collectively they might suggest interests that have been overlooked or forgotten, and save some brain-searching when the plaintive cry "What shall I do now?" becomes frequent and insistent. As a general rule, games and other activities for convalescent children should be well within their ability, since they are often easily frustrated and upset. When they succeed in solving a puzzle or winning a game, give them an extra amount of praise. They need all the confidence they can muster.

Papercraft: masks, hats, chain decorations, bookmarks, dolls, boxes, place cards, baskets, stenciling, doilies, carton animals, carton trains, and doll houses.

Braiding: braid and weave long strips of twisted crepe paper or cloth into table mats or doll rugs; decorate tin cans or cardboard containers with braids, to be used as coin banks, knickknack boxes, etc.

Spool knitting (or "rake"): obtain spool and yarn at knitting or notion shop; make "beanie" hats, table mats, scarves.

Puppets: finger puppets, papier-mâché puppets, paper bag puppets, stick puppets; puppet and marionette stages of cardboard boxes.

Drawing and painting: finger painting, spatter painting, water coloring, oil painting, lettering, crayoning, chalk drawing, tracing, block printing, poster making; not merely representations of people and things, but patterns, designs, signs, decorations, and anything that expresses feelings or passing whims; occasionally the prepared paintings (drawings, with numbered segments for color) may be tried for amusement, but not to replace more creative forms.

Weaving: raffia baskets, loop weaving, string weaving, loom weaving.

Needlework: knitting, crocheting, embroidery; sewing doll clothes, repairing clothes, making neckerchiefs, aprons, etc.

Papier-mâché: dolls, puppets, animals, landscaped dioramas, masks, Christmas decorations.

Clay: bowls, animals, ash trays; interesting shapes that represent nothing—or just kneading, pounding, rolling, squeezing to heart's content. (Both physically and emotionally therapeutic!)

Whittling and carving: soap carving, potato carving, soapstone carving, plaster of Paris carving, wax carving—to make figurines, plaques, boxes, whistles.

Board and table games: checkers, Fox and Geese, Parcheesi, lotto, dominoes, baseball, Chinese checkers, various card games and proprietary games.

Puzzles and word games: wire puzzles, rebuses, crosswords, ghost, geography, anagrams, word derivation, quizzes, riddles.

Active games: ring toss, card toss, jacks, darts, grab-bag, "fishing."

Model-making: airplanes, trains, villages, boats, antique cars.

Play material: "sick box", magnet, kaleidoscope, microscope, construction sets; anything to take apart, such as an old clock or radio.

Music: comb and tissue paper, water glasses; simple instruments such as psaltery, ocarina, harmonica; records to suit the age and interest; construction of instruments such as tom-tom out of a wooden bowl.

Reading: stories, how-to books, books on games and hobbies, "series" books for a long convalescence.

Motion pictures: short pictures of all kinds: sports, travel, science. These can be rented at stores or by mail. Some state and local government agencies and a few libraries lend films without charge. Borrow some from the school also.

Television and radio: not only favorite programs, but exploring for new "finds"; keeping a schedule for himself and for the family.

Play for the Handicapped

Of all the wonders wrought by play, none is more striking than what it accomplishes for the handicapped. Through carefully chosen activities, practically any child or adult, no matter how severely disabled, can experience the thrill of personal achievement and the satisfaction of earning approval from others. By developing the resources that are within himself, he can counterbalance many of his limitations; and by exploring the world through books, films, and collections, he can capture much of the fullness of life.

A careful study must be made of the child, with emphasis on his abilities even more than on his disabilities—on what he has left rather than what he has lost. In most cases it is advisable to seek professional guidance from those who have specialized in the handicap in question. Because of the recent interest in occupational and recreational therapy, many hospitals and social agencies now have counselors on their staffs who will examine the child and suggest a program of activities to fill his special needs.

Since the play program for handicapped children must be individually planned, we shall only suggest goals that it might set out to reach and directions that it might take.

If your child has a handicap, be on the lookout for activities that *build*. Solitaire may be amusing for the time being, but it leads nowhere. Listening to radio dramas interests many older children, gives them an outlet for pent-up feelings, and vicarious satisfaction of their need for adventure and excitement. But too heavy a dose brings with it a sense of futility, a feeling of "so what?" On the other hand, think of the joy experienced by an eleven-year-old boy, confined to a wheel-chair existence, as he finally completes a four-masted schooner and adds it to his collection of great sailing vessels! And what satisfaction it gives the little girl with a rheumatic heart as she sews the last stitch of clothing on a Swiss Alpine doll! These are the kinds of play activities that give the handicapped youngster the most lasting rewards. They are not merely time-consuming, but productive; and the products are not cold and impersonal, but part and parcel of their maker. As they grow, so grows the child.

Creative hobbies have another advantage that is too often overlooked. Disabled children necessarily lead restricted lives. They are usually unable to get around and mingle with others on their own terms. Their handicap makes them feel different, sometimes even ashamed, and as a result they often do not make an effort to seek out the company of other children. In some instances, an unconscious feeling of guilt may lurk within them, and as a consequence they may become morose and withdraw completely into their shell. A few respond to the advances of others with anger and unfriendliness, claiming that their interest is based on pity alone. If, however, we help any of these children develop an absorbing hobby, we can be confident that these unfortunate reactions will soon begin to disappear.

To prove this point, just watch one of these youngsters as he shows his handiwork to the boy or girl next door, and excitedly explains its mysteries. He suddenly comes alive, answers questions like an expert, and forgets the protective wall he has erected around himself. The reason is clear: he has recaptured his own self-respect; he now feels that he has achieved something worthy of admiration, something that puts him on a plane with others who have skills and abilities he lacks because of his handicap. Actually, there is a good chance that he has "overcompensated," and has far outdistanced the accomplishments of his friends. At any rate, creative play has taken him a long way toward a stable and useful life.

The problem, then, is to help the handicapped youngster discover these special interests and abilities. He may not become an expert, but with the extra time that is at his disposal, and the lack of distractions, some area of proficiency can almost surely be developed. It may be music—the flute, the guitar, the harmonica. It may be wood-carving, for which more active children seldom have the time or patience. Or it may be making toy animals out of sheet plastic or chintz, stuffed with cotton batting. Any one of these activities may bring several benefits at once. They are a form of self-expression and enjoyment. They make the youngster socially interesting, helping him to attract the visitors he needs so much. And they provide physical exercise, for the doctor may suggest a wind instrument to strengthen weak lungs or wood-carving to keep muscles from going soft. This is "prescribed play"—occupational, physical, and recreational therapy all rolled into one effective whole.

Play-with-a-purpose does not end here. As we have already indicated, the handicapped child has a special need to prove himself. The older boy, particularly, may have a gnawing fear that he will remain dependent on others and never be able to earn his living. To relieve this anxiety, and perhaps to start him on the way toward a permanent vocation, we should encourage him to develop one or two of his interests along practical lines. The stuffed animals we mentioned are always in demand. An interest in magazines can grow into a subscription service. Tinkering with radio or electrical appliances can lead to correspondence courses and a license to open a home repair shop. Breeding tropical fish, reconditioning toys, mending clothes, making greeting cards or table decorations—each of these suggests an absorbing and profitable vocation. No handicapped person should be denied the chance to become as self-reliant as possible.

Within the past few years, still another approach has been made to the handicapped: the use of "adapted" sports for recreation, morale, and general health. We have outgrown the period when setting-up exercises alone were prescribed for the disabled. As George T. Stafford writes in his *Sports for the Handicapped,* "As long as physical education was concerned with the production of perspiration, calisthenic exercises answered the purpose." Today fun and fitness have been combined into a single goal, and the result is that the program of many schools and convalescent homes now centers around standard games and sports that have simply been modified for the particular handicaps. Doctors who care for the homebound handicapped are likewise prescribing these activities. For example, children confined to the wheel chair can often engage in dart-throwing, archery, and modified basketball; children who wear braces can usually play box hockey and clock golf, and derive great benefit as well as pleasure from swimming and boating. There is practically no child who is not capable of one sport or another. But again we would like to stress the fact that professional guidance is a "must" in these cases.

One more suggestion. If you or your teen-aged son or daughter is in the market for a hobby that will bring the utmost in satisfaction, consider the possibility of starting a recreation service for the handicapped in your community. Many disabled people lack the materials for play, many more lack the know-how for finding or developing a hobby, and still others lack the companionship they need. A recreation service center would mobilize and train volunteers to meet these needs. An excellent model for such an organization is already in existence: The Handicapped Children's Home Service, in New York City. Its members make weekly visits to children afflicted with polio, heart disease, cerebral palsy, muscular dystrophy, and other ailments. Their object is not simply to amuse them, but to teach them to play imaginatively and creatively on their own. Each child is studied individually to see what he can do within his particular limitations. Often it is possible to encourage a vocational interest, and articles made by the children are regularly sold through the service. Results, however, can rarely be measured by the dollars received, but rather in terms of delighted smiles and the anticipation of even better things to come.

With an estimated twenty-three million people in this country in need of rehabilitation of one kind or another, and with a large proportion of them leading restricted lives, every community, large and small, could benefit from such a service for the handicapped. Why not start one in *your* home town?

CHAPTER XVIII

Fun on the Town

ONE OF THE THEMES of this book is that the play life of children and adults cannot simply be left to take care of itself. True, the impulse to play does seem to come naturally; yet to get the maximum benefit from recreation, it has to be planned wisely, and geared to interests, abilities, and above all to growth. One way is to foster the creative use of leisure time in our family life. But the home cannot do the whole job. There are many forms of play, and many facilities, that can be provided only by the community at large. For a full life of play, there must be not only fun in the family but fun on the town. And don't think that play-planning is needed for the underprivileged only. It is needed for all!

Community recreation is not a mere supplement to play at home. It has merits of its own. A town- or city-wide program is the only way to make sure that everyone—young and old, rich and poor—gets a chance to play. Social gaps are bridged, unity and morale are enhanced. Supervision is provided where needed, and safety is stressed. Properly planned, and with carefully chosen leaders, it will almost certainly help to prevent delinquency. It is excellent insurance for both the emotional and the physical health of the community. Through instruction in arts and crafts, games and hobbies, education is extended to extracurricular pursuits and to every age. All these benefits together make the community a livelier and happier place in which to live.

Today some three thousand American communities have recognized the need for a recreation program. Thirty states have specific laws enabling municipalities to appropriate and administer funds for this purpose. But how are we to judge whether we, our children, and our neighbors, are getting a full measure of fun "on the town"? What is being done by localities other than our own, and what constitutes an ideal, or at any rate a substantial program? Fortunately, certain standards have been set up, largely by the National Recreation Association, and it is now possible for us to give our communities at least a rough and ready "recreation rating." The following questionnaire is offered for this purpose—with the ulterior aim of suggesting that if some major phases are missing, *you* may be the one to do something about them. It takes only one person to start the ball rolling, but the number who benefit can run into the hundreds.

What Is Your Town's Recreation Rating?

Let's start with leadership and organization since they are so essential to a community program. Then we'll outline the facilities that are needed. Finally, we'll follow the developmental pattern applied in most of this book, and enumerate the opportunities that should be open to each major age group, as well as to everyone together.

I. Leadership and Organization

1. Does your town have a Recreation Department or its equivalent?
2. Is there a Recreation Council, or its equivalent, made up of representative citizens and organizations, which offers recommendations and assistance to the Recreation Department?
3. Is there a full-time superintendent of recreation?
4. Are there professional leaders for playgrounds and other facilities? (Towns of five thousand and over should have paid leaders.)
5. Is there adequate provision for recruiting and training volunteers?
6. Is there adequate equipment and maintenance of facilities?
7. Is recreation planned on a year-round basis?
8. Are opportunities available for all groups and all ages?

9. Is there a long-range plan for recreation so that land will be available and natural features preserved? (For example, are real estate developers required to set aside recreation areas?)
10. Is adequate publicity given to the community's recreational opportunities?
11. Do organizations such as veterans groups, P.T.A.'s, lodges, etc., foster community recreation through gifts, contests, special events, etc.? (See section "What Can You Do about It?")

II. Facilities

12. Is there sufficient park area? (A large park occupies fifty acres or more.)
13. Do parks contain flower gardens, picnic areas, band shell, mall for dancing and skating, pond for model boats?
14. Is there a well-equipped and staffed neighborhood playground within half a mile of every home? (It should occupy four to seven acres, usually located at or near the elementary school, and contain special areas and materials for preschool children, school children, and the elderly, as well as a shelter house and landscape area.)
15. Is there a playing field within one mile of every home? (It should occupy at least ten acres, usually located at or near the high school, and contain a neighborhood playground plus facilities for baseball, tennis, field hockey, shuffleboard, horseshoes, track and field events, picnic area, lawn area for croquet, etc., and an outdoor swimming pool if possible.)
16. Are empty lots maintained and used as temporary playgrounds in crowded districts?
17. Is there a public golf course?
18. Are both outdoor and indoor swimming available to all?
19. Is there at least one tennis court for every two thousand people?
20. Is there at least one softball diamond for every three thousand people?
21. Is there a lighted playing field for evening sports?
22. Is there an auditorium with well-equipped stage for concerts and plays?

23. Is there a modern library with special attractions for children?
24. Is there a historical or natural history museum?
25. Is there space readily adapted to art exhibits, hobby shows, and other exhibitions?
26. Does the community make the most of natural endowments such as a waterfall, a hill for skiing and tobogganing, trail regions for hiking and riding, a lake for swimming, boating, and fishing?
27. Is there a recreation building that houses such facilities as club rooms, gymnasium, arts and crafts workshops, game room, reading room—as well as the exhibit space, auditorium, and swimming pool mentioned above? (If not, are the new schools designed for community recreation?)
28. Is there a Volunteer Service Bureau for those who wish to devote leisure time to community work?

III. *Opportunities for All Ages*

For the Very Young

29. Do the playgrounds have separate, safe areas for very young children, with special equipment such as slides and swings?
30. Are there wading pools or spray pools for them?
31. Does the community include preschool and kindergarten children in a supervised summer play program?
32. Are there day-care centers with good play facilities for young children of working mothers?

For School Children

33. Is there an adequate number of Scout and Campfire groups, using public meeting-places such as schools?
34. Does the library have a story hour?
35. Are there arts and crafts classes for young people?
36. Is there some form of organized community athletics such as a Little League?
37. Is there a supervised summer play program provided by the community?
38. Is swimming instruction available to all school children?
39. Are there free summer camps for underprivileged children?

For Teen-agers

40. Do schools or private organizations have "Friday Night Clubs"?
41. Is there a Teen Center or Teen Canteen operating under adequate supervision?
42. Is dramatics encouraged?
43. Is there a sufficient number of hobby groups and clubs?
44. Are teen-agers invited to do social service work?
45. Is free or inexpensive dancing instruction available, including folk as well as social dancing?

For Adults

46. Are school facilities available for adult use?
47. Are there regular lecture series or courses?
48. Are there community book clubs and discussion groups?
49. Is there an adequate number of garden, outing, arts and crafts, and hobby clubs?
50. Is there a little-theater group?
51. Is some form of music participation available to all adults?

For the Aging

52. Are there secluded quiet corners in the playgrounds, with tables and benches for their use?
53. Are there Golden Age clubs, or the equivalent, for all who want them?
54. Is there an opportunity for elderly people to exhibit their handicrafts?
55. Are they given a chance to contribute to community service?
56. Is there an outing or camping program for them?

For Everybody

57. Are there tennis tournaments and other contests for the community as a whole?
58. Is there a community music program: town band or orchestra, choral group, etc.?
59. Are there community celebrations on Independence Day or other holidays?
60. Are there enough events of the informal variety—neighbor-

hood, school, Scout, "Y" events, etc.—to which everyone is invited? Among these are pet shows, roller derbies, and field days.

What Can *You* Do about It?

The recreation program cannot be left entirely in the hands of public officials as they themselves will usually tell you. The effectiveness of their work depends in large part on the co-operation of individuals and organizations in making known the needs of different groups and recommending the facilities required to meet them. Moreover, few if any communities appropriate enough funds for a complete program—which means that the efforts of different groups and individuals must be enlisted if a thorough job is to be done. As a consequence, more people will have an interest in the community program and more will be stimulated to devote some of their own spare time to making it a success.

More specifically, what can the average citizen do to insure better recreation for the whole town? Volunteers are always needed to assist in playground supervision, to teach games, organize teams, and act as umpires. As we have noted in previous chapters, people are needed to play with children in hospitals and convalescent homes, to drive the handicapped to swimming pools, the circus, or the county fair. Every teen center or teen social affair requires the services of chaperones and other adults. Volunteers are constantly in demand for such jobs as the clerical work involved in organizing a concert or lecture series, building and maintaining a neighborhood skating rink, and teaching hobby groups. Anyone who wants to use some of his own recreation time to help others with *theirs* will find plenty of opportunities to be of service.

Most of us will find it more effective to work through organizations like clubs, church groups, neighborhood associations, and parents' groups than to work individually. When one of these groups takes responsibility for a project, or when several work together, it is almost certain to be carried through. However, it takes individuals to "sell" the project to the group. Among the successful undertakings of these organizations are the following: sponsoring a children's band, conducting a home-garden contest, organizing a winter sports school, starting hobby clubs, stocking lakes and streams with fish, arranging courses for volunteer leaders, promoting a summer playground program, and developing a recreation area as a war memorial. These are but samples of projects that contribute to health and welfare on a community scale. Any group of citizens in any town can find similar recreation jobs that need doing, and nothing will be more gratifying or more constructive than to see that they are done well.

CHAPTER XIX

Play That Develops Minds

Ask almost anyone what first comes to mind when you say "play," and the answer is almost certain to be "fun," "good time," "leisure activity" or the like. Seldom will you find play associated with intellect, intelligence or other mental qualities—in fact, the mind is far more likely to be associated with work than with play. Even those who claim that play can be a powerful instrument for "all-around development" tend to emphasize its influence on our children's physical, social, and emotional life much more than its effect on mental growth.

Play and Mental Development

Yet the fact is that a wide variety of absorbing and enjoyable activities exercise practically every mental faculty. Mental play can be found to suit all age levels. In many instances it generates deeper and more lasting satisfactions than activities that are purely entertainment.

Many of the activities suggested in previous chapters contribute to mental development in the broad sense of the term. All through this book we have described games and playthings that sharpen the senses, stimulate co-ordination, and cultivate concentration. And we have suggested that the systematic pursuit of almost any hobby will not only bring pleasure but will enrich the mind as well.

This chapter will focus on concrete examples of play that enhance specific uses of the mind—logic, memory, reading ability, and verbal skills—as recreation rather than formal education. The most intellectually challenging play can often be the most intriguing and satisfying.

Mental Play for Two Generations

Mental play can bridge generations. Children, parents, even grandparents are likely to find "brain games" equally exciting. It is important that old and young have a chance to share their recreational experience on a more advanced level. The children will feel flattered and perhaps inspired.

Most of the activities suggested in this chapter can interest both the older and the younger generation. But here are several examples that give parents special opportunities for stimulating their children's mental development.

Brainstorming Puzzles. The first is the kind of problem that calls for creative thinking. A simple match puzzle will illustrate: make four triangles out of six matches. Almost any eight- or nine-year-old will begin by putting the matches on a table and attempting to arrange them in different combinations. But he won't solve the problem that way, no matter how hard he tries. He can succeed only by making a pyramid out of the six matches. In other words, he has to think in three-dimensional terms.

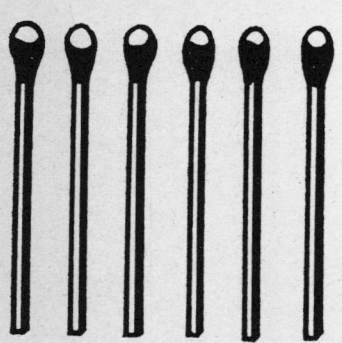
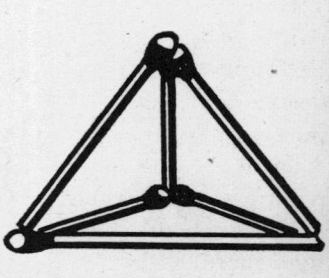

If your child fails to get the answer, you might point out that it does little good to try to solve a problem by random activity— by just "fooling around." This is all one can expect of a bear trying to get out of a trap, since the bear has little or no reasoning power. But human beings can use their imagination to perform "thought experiments." They can think of a possible solution and try it out internally instead of wasting time and effort by immediately putting it into action.

This type of puzzle suggests another useful point. Sometimes the solution to a problem is found only when a new and unusual approach is made. In the case of the match puzzle, one must think quite literally in a different dimension. The person who can break ordinary thought habits will not only solve more problems but is more likely to create new ideas.

In a recent study of the thinking process, one group of people was given a set of problems like the triangle puzzle and was simply instructed to find the answer as quickly as possible. A second group, of approximately equal intelligence, was instructed, "Try to get away from your 'natural' way of approaching the problem. Think of many other possibilities, no matter how absurd they may seem at first. Above all, don't stay in a rut." The second group scored twice as well as the first group!

Now try a little experiment yourself. After discussing the solution to the match problem and the necessity for a free and fresh approach, pose this puzzle: without lifting the pencil from the paper or folding the paper, trace out the following figure, going over every line once and only once.

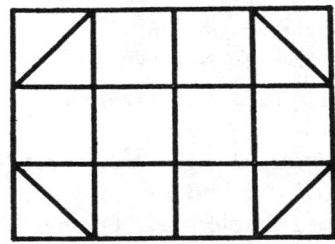

Notice whether your child now uses a simple trial-and-error approach or uses his mind in trying for the solution.[1] (The solution to this and other problems will be found on the last page of this chapter.)

Games of Chance. Many children's games are based on chance —for example, spinning an arrow to determine the next move.

One father and mother took a cue from this idea and now play roulette with their children. The parents had visited a gambling casino during a European trip and felt that roulette would be a stimulating and harmless form of family play. Actually they got more than they anticipated. The children took turns acting as croupier, and picked up some French expressions: "Faites vos jeux, mesdames et monsieurs," and "Rien ne va plus." They also learned how to calculate odds, and one of them enlisted the aid of her mathematics teacher in an effort to break the bank. Roulette is an excellent introduction to the mathematics of probability, which was originally invented to aid gambling but is now fundamental to much of modern science.

Limericks. Another mental game is suggested by a radio program that was on the air some time ago, "The Limerick Show." Four lines of a limerick were read to the guests, and they were given one minute in which to devise a concluding line. Many of these lines were extremely clever. Here is a sample from the program itself:

> As Marie, the blushing bride
> Gazed at the groom at her side,
> She cried out in dismay,
> "Stop this wedding, I pray—"

The first member of the panel supplied this concluding line:
> "There's a hat sale at Gimbels I spied."

The next said:
> "This man isn't fit to be tied."

But the third won the prize with:
> " 'Cause he said he was rich and he lied."

The limerick game makes an excellent party activity as well as a family pastime. It is first-rate mental exercise, since it requires creativity within a rigid framework. It also helps to cultivate a sense of rhythm and a feeling for rhyme. Even a child of eight may suggest suitable lines. Older children might themselves supply the first four lines for others to finish. If you want to try out the idea, use the lines already suggested, or these:

> There was a young fellow named Wier,
> Who hadn't an atom of fear,
> He indulged a desire,
> To touch a live wire,
> *(Supply last line.)*

Logical Reasoning. Brain teasers can stimulate the habit of logical thinking. Well-chosen puzzles can give children practice in seeing relationships, drawing inferences, and using syllogisms long before they know what these terms mean. Some of the older problems are still the best, and of course they are all likely to be new to your child. Here is one that requires a fairly logical approach:

"A tall Indian and a short Indian were standing under a tree. The short Indian was the son of the tall Indian, but the tall Indian was not the father of the short Indian. How come?"[2]

If the child has already heard that one, try this: "Dr. Harry Jones is Dr. Leslie Jones' father. Mrs. Harry Jones is Dr. Leslie Jones' mother. Dr. Leslie Jones is not Dr. Harry Jones' son. How come?"[3]

It is probably best to avoid problems that are too tricky. The following is a borderline case: "Johnny and Jimmy were born on the same day of the same year. They had the same father and mother, but they were not twins. Can you explain this?"[4]

Another type of "brain-buster" hinges on logic alone: "Stephen, Andrew, and Daniel are all married. The names of their wives are Jane, Alice, and Laura. The couples all have one child each: Joe, Ronald, and Helen. These, however, are not necessarily in the right order. But you can find which wife and child go with each man from the following facts: Two of the children, Alice's and Daniel's, are on the school football team. Stephen's son is not Joe. Andrew's wife is not Laura."[5]

Problems of this kind can be found in some of the older game books, or in paperback reprints of these books. Through them you can teach your child some valuable lessons: the importance of using a chart or diagram, how to draw inferences from a hypothesis, and how to use the process of elimination. You might mention in passing that most scientists use these methods in arriving at their conclusions.

You can even make a game of the more formal kind of logic, in which a conclusion is drawn from two given premises. If Scotsmen tend to be thrifty and Andy is a Scotsman, does it follow that Andy is thrifty? No, a conclusion must *necessarily* follow from the premises, and we only said that Scotsmen *tend* to be thrifty. How about: All Harvard men are tall, Richard is a

Harvard man, therefore Richard is tall. Here the conclusion follows quite logically—but you might explain that there is sometimes a difference between logic and truth, for obviously it is quite untrue that all Harvard men are tall.

If your older child is intrigued with these problems, he might try constructing some of these arguments (syllogisms) himself. You might also show him that he can test them by drawing circles that represent the subject and predicate of the statements. In the first argument, a circle representing Scotsmen and another circle representing thrifty people would overlap:

And Andy may or may not be found in that part of the Scotsmen circle that coincides with the thrifty circle. In the second argument, the circle representing the Harvard men would be entirely inside the circle representing tall men, and Richard would have to be tall since he is inside the Harvard circle:

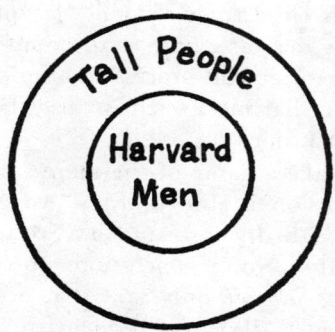

In the Early Years

It is a mistake to think that very young children are merely playful kittens who enjoy nothing but physical activity. They want to stretch their minds as well as their muscles—and, above all, they want to *learn*. They watch older brothers and sisters make change, tell time, and figure distances—and they want to learn about numbers. They see and hear others read, and they want to do it themselves.

There is much they can do to satisfy this drive to know and understand. We can encourage them to talk with the postman and the plumber, listen in on adult conversations, watch a highway or building under construction. And we can help them to develop their ability to express themselves through making up their own rhymes, retelling stories they hear, and giving accounts of their experiences. Such activities are an enjoyable form of play, but they also help to stockpile words and ideas.

Too often the "readiness" period is overextended and the child who is eager for more specific learning becomes bored and frustrated. The author (R. M. G.) will never forget the plaintive question of one of his sons after he had spent almost three years in nursery school and kindergarten: "But Daddy, when do we stop playing and begin to learn something?" He really wanted to learn how to *read*.

Children can and should be introduced to reading before kindergarten or first grade. Most four- and five-year-olds try to read signs, labels, and titles on the TV screen. Learning to recognize them can be one of their most enjoyable activities. With parental help they can also learn to recognize and even print their own names. A little later they will be able to pick out the same letters in the headlines of a newspaper or the title of a book. From that point it is a natural step to "sounding out" the letters and deciphering a few easy words on their own. Here are some reading games:

Word Blocks. One useful device is to paste simple words on blocks. One or two blocks should contain nouns only: book, cat, table, Jim, etc. Another should show verbs: put, hit, went, etc.

Prepositions should be pasted on one block and articles on another. In playing the game the child mixes them up and rolls them on the table like dice. He then tries to make sentences out of the words that appear on top.

Word Bingo. Standard Bingo cards may be used, with simple words pasted over the numbers. The same words are then printed on small cards. In playing the game, the cards are shuffled, and a word is drawn and called out. The children look for this word on their cards, and if it is there they cover it with a counter. The game continues until a full line is covered, as in regular Bingo.

Word Fishing. Print about fifty simple words on slips of paper and attach a paper clip to each slip. Then make a fishing line out of long thin wood and a piece of string, and attach a magnet at the end of the line in place of the usual hook. Mix up the slips of paper and put them in a pail. The child then fishes them out one at a time and reads the printed words. This can be turned into an activity game by printing short instructions on the slips. The child not only reads them but carries them out: "Stand up," "Open the door," etc.

Here are a few other activities that may be used to exercise memory, reasoning, and imagination during the pre-school and early school years:

What to Do? Write down a number of simple situations that pose problems, and ask your child what he would do about them. Example: You are in the bathtub and the water is running. Suddenly you find that the faucet is stuck and you can't turn it off. The water is rising higher and higher. What would you do?

Following Directions. Make up sets of directions to give your child. Example: "Stand up, turn around twice, then put this book on the table." Use no more than three instructions at first, and repeat them before he carries them out. If varied and amusing actions are used, this can make an enjoyable party contest. Half the group might compete against the other half, with an adult keeping score.

What Happens Next? This game can be played with one adult and one or more children. Start a story, and have each child in turn tell "what happened next" until the story is finished. Example: "One day we went out for a walk, and on the side of the road we found a tiny brown puppy. Suddenly . . . what happened?"

The Store Game. This activity can also act as a mental stimulus. In building the store out of boxes or shelving, the child can be taught how to use a ruler, and its divisions into feet, inches, and fractions of inches can be explained. We can help, too, to cultivate a sense of order and design through the arrangement of boxes and cans on the shelves. Making change will provide practice in arithmetic—some children will actually learn mental addition and subtraction. A "Store-wide Sale" can introduce the child to percentages: "50% off." Some children will be able to grasp the concept of "cost per ounce" or "cost per pound." All these ideas can be put in practice during an actual shopping tour—particularly if you ask your child's advice as to which is the better buy, the "large economy size" or the "giant size."

Some Card Games. Children generally approach cards as a simple and undemanding form of fun. But if we go to the trouble of explaining some of the finer points, card games can be a genuine challenge to mental activity. The game of Concentration will be more than a bare exercise in memory if the child learns the denominations in the pack and develops his own method of systematically locating the cards that have been turned up. Go Fish is as simple a game as you can find, yet it does require keeping track of the 4 cards of the same rank that make a book. Rummy expands this idea into the various kinds of sequences, and stimulates the child not merely to remember the cards he has given to his opponent but to try to figure out the chance that another four or another Jack will show up. A further advantage of Rummy is the fact that it is good preparation for the most advanced of all card games, Bridge.

In the Middle Years

For these youngsters a varied panorama of intellectual play opens up.

The popularity of quiz contests continues today even though the big quiz shows have gone off the air. Almost any game book contains quizzes, and the toy stores offer many varieties. Most of these have the limitation of stressing isolated facts, sometimes of a trivial character. But some of them will arouse curiosity or link up with school work.

It is more challenging for parents and children to make up their own quizzes to give to each other. One intriguing variety is the Picture Quiz. Pictures of trees, animals, birds, or artifacts of different civilizations are cut out of *Life, Natural History, National Geographic* or other magazines, and the contestant is asked to identify them. Here are some examples:

What is the right name for this canoe?[6]

What is this baby called?[7]

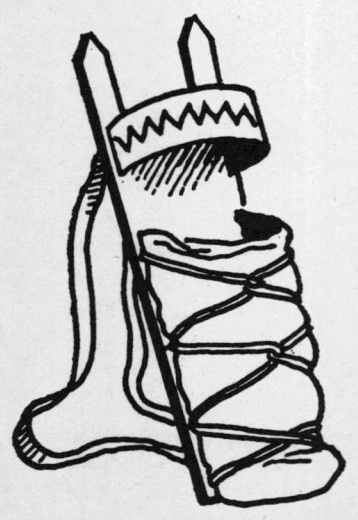

This necklace is used by Hawaiian women.[8]

Question and Answer Games. Children of 10 to 12 find another quiz game particularly intriguing—the kind in which teams or individuals attempt to find a correct answer to a problem by asking revealing questions. There are many varieties: Twenty Questions, Who Am I, and the television games, "I've Got A Secret" and "What's My Line." The game of Murder adds another dimension: the technique of cross-examination. In this game, the lights are put out for a minute and a mock murder is staged by a previously informed murderer and victim. The host then appoints a District Attorney who must try to discover the murderer by asking questions of the guests. Everyone must answer truthfully except the murderer.

You might point out to your child that the most successful contestant in all these games generally uses a system in questioning, instead of haphazardly asking anything that comes to mind. This point can be proved by watching and analyzing the television panel shows with your child.

Verbal skills are an endless source of productive play for "middle-aged" children. Scrabble, crosswords, and anagrams have been mentioned elsewhere—but here is a handful of games that can be played without special materials. Names are suggested for them, since this puts them in the category of games rather than schoolwork.

Misprint (or Typo) makes an excellent party activity. Select paragraphs from a book or article, and make a number of typed copies, each containing two to four misprints. Choose up sides and distribute the paragraphs face down. At a given signal the contestants turn the paper over and the one who finds the misprints first wins the round. The scores are then totaled to see which side wins.

Who Can Spell? Prepare large drawings—no matter how crude —showing scenes in which there are signs and advertisements, but deliberately misspell three or four words in each drawing. Contestants are required to look at a drawing for two minutes, and write down correct spellings for all the misspelled words they can find. Examples: FORIEGN CARS . . . IRRESISTABLE PERFUME . . . REVEALLING FACTS ABOUT HEADACHES.

What's Wrong? Pick out a number of sentences or short paragraphs from books or articles, and in each one alter a word or phrase in such a way that the whole meaning is destroyed. Show them, one at a time, to your child and see if he can discover the errors. Example: "The unchanging clouds took on many different shapes as they drifted by."

How Many Words? Any number of children can play this game. Pass out pads and pencils, and give them four or five minutes to find as many words as possible for one general idea. Example: How many ways can a person get from one place to another by himself? He can walk, run, creep, jump, etc., etc. A variation: How many words can you think of that begin with com- (or end with -ject)?

Other Word Games. The traditional word games are as good as ever. Ghost, Scrambled Words, and Derivations (deriving little words from one big word) have been mentioned in other chapters. The television game Password makes an excellent group game that requires quick thinking. In Word Chain (Word Dominoes) the first player selects a word of a certain category, such as carnation. The next player must name another flower that begins with the last letter of this word—nasturtium, for example.

This continues around the room, and players who cannot supply a suitable word drop out.

In Categories (Guggenheim), a master word is selected, and each player is required to write down words that begin with each of its letters. These words, however, must be in certain categories: animal, country, author, etc. A time limit of 15 minutes is set, and the number of correct entries is then counted to see who wins. Example, BREAD is a master word, and a contestant might write: buffalo, rat, elk, armadillo, and duck in the animal category; and Bolivia, Rumania, England, Armenia, and Denmark in the country category.

Logic. Games and problems that require reasoning are likely to interest most "tween-agers"—provided they are not too abstract. One example is the old Cannibal and Missionary problem: There are three missionaries and three cannibals on one side of a river. The only rowboat available seats three people and no more, and only the missionaries can row. The missionaries must never be outnumbered by the cannibals. How can they all get across alive?[9]

Mathematical reasoning is another source of constructive fun. The Bookworm Problem is one example: A three-volume set of books stands on a table in the usual order. Each of the covers of each book is one-eighth of an inch thick, and the pages in each book measure one inch. If a bookworm eats his way from Page 1 of Volume I to the last page of Volume III, how far does he travel?[10]

Here is another type of mathematical problem: I have three jars and an unlimited supply of water. One jar holds 11 ounces, the second 45 ounces, the third 7 ounces. How can I measure out exactly 20 ounces in five moves or less?[11]

Puzzles can also be created from material that is reminiscent of intelligence-test items. Here are a few examples:

A box always has: (a) hinges, (b) lid, (c) sides, (d) money, (e) wood.[12]

My father is the brother of your sister. What relative am I of yours: (a) cousin, (b) uncle, (c) nephew, (d) son-in-law, (e) son?[13]

The next number in the series 2, 4, 6, 8, is 10. What is the next number in the series 12, 11, 9, 6?[14]

If east and west are reversed, and north and south are reversed, what direction will be on your right if you are then facing south?[15]

Count the number of Z's that are immediately followed by F if the F is not followed immediately by S: ZFZSEYZFSYF ZFFZAYSZFEZFSFZYFZFY.[16]

The boy or girl who finds problems of this kind too much like school can sometimes be lured into mathematics through an interest in sports. A good deal of practice in multiplication and division can be gained through calculating batting averages of individual players or a whole team. One father taught his son the entire multiplication table and introduced him to fractions as well, by asking questions of this kind: "What does it mean to be in the top third of the league?" "What is meant by odds of 9 to 5 that the champion will retain his heavy-weight title?"

Strategy. Syllogistic thinking is beyond the ken of most youngsters in middle childhood. But a practical kind of logic can be taught through certain board games. Checkers can be played and enjoyed without much effort. But to get the maximum out of the game, our children should be gradually introduced to the various strategies of play and the logic behind them. They might also be encouraged to devise their own tactics and to explain why they make each move. A similar approach can be used with some of the copyright games of strategy, such as Gettysburg, in which the player studies the deployment of troops as a means of winning a battle.

Outdoor games which children in the middle and teen years watch and play also provide many opportunities for studying strategy. Baseball and football have many fine points which the casual spectator is likely to miss. People can argue endlessly over the virtues of one system of play or one football formation over another. The many decisions required in a game also raise interesting questions: If there are men on first and second, with two out, should a weak hitter wait for a walk or try for a hit? If the ball is on your one-yard line on a fourth down, and your team is behind, should you kick, run, or pass? Tennis, too, is a game of strategy, and a good teacher can often get his point across by drawing a picture of a court and indicating the positions of the players. Too often young people are so eager to use their muscles that they fail to see that all these games must be played with the head as well.

Hobbies. Many hobbies and transient interests can become a means of stimulating mental activity—particularly if parents make suggestions at the right time and in the right way. Most boys and girls fly kites at one time or another, but how many children explore the many facets of this interest? Yet material can readily be found on such topics as the history of kites, their uses in wartime, the huge variety of shapes and materials found in different cultures, the aerodynamic principles that govern heavier-than-air objects in flight, the use of kites in meteorology and the exploration of space. The youngster who pursues any of these questions will soon find that the physical thrill of flying kites may be matched by intellectual satisfaction.

An interest in gathering and pressing flowers can also lead in many directions. The girl who adopts this hobby can learn to identify different species, and begin to make a serious study of botany. She can investigate the many techniques for drying and preserving flowers, and discover ways of keeping them looking fresh for long periods of time. She can experiment with different ways of mounting and displaying them. The arrangement of flowers is an art in itself, and this may lead to reading books and manuals, visiting exhibits, and taking special courses. And if she develops her interest and her skill to a high degree, she will probably find many practical applications of flower pressing—home decoration, party favors, birthday presents, and the like.

Amateur ("ham") radio is still another stimulating hobby. Most boys (girls, too) start by constructing small receiving sets of their own, perhaps using factory-made kits. Others—and this of course is better—wind their own coils and make their own mountings. They soon learn to follow a wiring diagram and discover that there are different kinds of circuits.

If the interest in amateur radio develops, they will soon be shopping around for their own equipment. At this point they should be told to get in touch with the Amateur Radio Relay League, West Hartford, Connecticut, to obtain booklets and instructions to be used in preparing for a novice license. No one can study for the government tests without learning a good deal about the physics of wave transmission, the functions of the various components of senders and receivers, and the strict regulations that must be followed at all times. Those who pass the novice test (usually administered by an experienced operator in the neighborhood) will begin to participate in the unique camaraderie that exists among hams all over the globe. A whole new world of communciation and scientific information will be open to them for years to come.

A neighborhood newspaper is another interest that has intellectual ramifications. It may be a one-page bulletin reporting events on a single street, or it may be, or become, the "voice" of a neighborhood association or other community organization. In going to the sources of information, a child will learn how to ask revealing questions, how to take notes, and how to sift out the most interesting items. He will then get practice in writing, make-up, and printing or mimeographing the paper. Parents can further this activity by helping him make appointments with editors and reporters of local newspapers to find out how they do their jobs, or by taking him to visit a printing plant. Some children will want to study typing, and may even learn one of the simpler ABC shorthand systems that are now available in home-study form.

In the Teen Years

Even the most socially-minded party givers and party goers may be induced to prepare original songs and skits, or perhaps a 15-minute "musical comedy" for special occasions. If they meet several times beforehand to work out their presentation, they will probably get as much enjoyment from "producing" a birthday or graduation party as they do in attending it. This is a painless way to learn that racking one's brain can be fun.

As we have pointed out in another chapter, Charades (also called The Game) is one of the most stimulating party games for teen-agers as well as adults. But here let us add that some groups meet regularly for a whole evening of Charades. In this way they develop their proficiency to a high and satisfying degree. Some groups even form fixed teams to challenge all comers.

The two games that most require the use of the mind are probably Chess and Bridge, and the teen years are the ideal time to develop some expertise in them. Both are games of logic and strategy, and in both, practice and study can pay dividends of enjoyment that can last a lifetime. Charles H. Goren's comments are particularly apt. He remarks that "the millions that play Contract Bridge treat it more as a hobby and as a science than as a pastime, and its wide-spread use as a medium of intellectual competition is one of the most outstanding sociological phenomena of the 20th Century." And speaking of Chess he says, "There is no other game so esteemed, so profound and so venerable as Chess; in the realm of play it stands alone in dignity. . . . The ultimate science of the game is unfathomable, which, no doubt, explains its inexhaustible appeal even to its best-informed students, and its infinite vitality."

Card games of all kinds are a painless introduction to probability theory, which many high schools now teach as a formal course. Expert card playing benefits from sophisticated knowledge of this branch of mathematics.

Specialty periodicals can be a source of considerable mental stimulation for teen-agers. Some of them contain a great deal of technical information: for example, magazines on cars, ham radio, and model airplanes. Others, such as sports magazines, contain stories and articles that stir imagination and ambition. Many newsdealers and libraries also stock a variety of arts-and-crafts pamphlets and periodicals that contain information on dress design, needlework, and metalcraft. Although these are not ordinarily classed as intellectual hobbies, they can nevertheless help to develop such mental qualities as accurate observation, sequential thinking, ability to follow directions, and precision.

The teen period is the time par excellence to carry learning beyond the classroom. Extracurricular study is often initiated by the school itself through such activities as language and science clubs, the school paper or literary magazine. But if our sons and daughters are to get into the habit of spending part of their free time in intellectual pursuits, the home must provide as much impetus as the school.

Today there is no limit to the potential of the home. An endless amount of stimulating material is available in every conceivable form. Since our chapter on the "easy media" was written, there has been a considerable increase in the number of television public-affairs programs on the arts and sciences, and on historical and contemporary events.

Few individuals can afford a 16mm. motion-picture projector, but families can get together to borrow school or library apparatus. Literally thousands of educational films are available on a free-loan or rental basis, and local film councils have been formed throughout the country. Slide and film-strip projectors are far less expensive than motion-picture projectors, and many young people build their own libraries or rent slides from local camera stores.

Another rewarding intellectual pastime is learning to speak a foreign language. Many first-rate phrase books are available at paperback bookstores. Self-teaching language records provide an even better way to learn how to get around in another country. They are also a valuable supplement to courses given in school. When these records are used in conjunction with a tape recorder, the student can compare his own pronunciation with that of the expert and repeat the material until substantial improvement is achieved. If a group of teen-agers meet regularly for conversation and practice, this activity can become an especially enjoyable form of recreation.

Finally, the new field of programmed learning and teaching machines offers opportunities for developing special interests at home. Home study courses are already available on a wide variety of topics, such as bridge, rocks and minerals, and the solar system. Other subjects are in process of development: for example, art, music, space science, chess, and nature study.

In programming these subjects, the content is broken up into clear, simple, and systematic steps. Here are three "frames" from a program on football. The answers, in parentheses, are covered. The student fills in his own answer, then uncovers the correct answer to see if he is right.

In a *running* play a back runs (forward/backward) and the offense tries to block out the defense's _____ so the back can get through with the ball.

(forward; line)

The quarterback's and end's movements are clues, but NOT GUARANTEES, that the offense is going to try a _____ play.

(passing)

What makes football challenging to watch is the element of deception. The offense tries to confuse the defense by pretending a passing play and suddenly switching to a r_____ play.*

(running)

A program has the air of a quiz because each step or "frame" contains not only an explanation but a question on which the student tests himself. Since the answer is given in the next frame—instead of at the back of a textbook—he knows how well he is doing at every moment. Even more important, he can proceed at his own pace and under his own steam, since the material is self-instructional.

Setting the Stage for Mental Play

There is bound to be considerable variation among children in their appreciation of the activities discussed in this chapter. Some will prefer intellectual pursuits to any other type of pastime. A few will consider them "too much work." But most children will stand somewhere between these two extremes. They will readily respond to some, though not all, of the activities, and we can attract them to new forms of mental play if we make a special effort. Here are a few ways this can be done.

1. Mental play generally requires some degree of peace, quiet, and privacy. Let us see that our children have several hours each week by themselves, or with one or two companions at most. This means that they will need a place they can call their own, apart from the intrusion of brothers, sisters, or television. It should also be a haven where they can keep the equipment for these activities, for if it is ready at hand, they will use it more frequently.

* From *How to Watch a Football Game*, Learning Incorporated, 1962. By permission.

2. As parents, we should be on the lookout for materials that will encourage new activities and excite new interests. But materials are not enough. Our own enthusiasm and participation will be needed, but with full regard for our children's level of ability and patterns of interest.

3. As always, attitudes are a crucial ingredient. If our children are to seek out and enjoy mental play, we must do what we can to help them appreciate the basic values that derive from intellectual activity: the excitement of discovery, the satisfaction of curiosity, the thrill of getting the right answer, and above all the gratification of feeling their minds stretch and grow.

Answers to Problems

1. Start at the mid-point of the top or bottom:

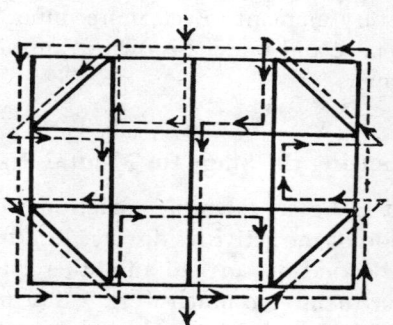

2. The tall Indian was the mother.
3. Dr. Leslie Jones is a woman and therefore the daughter.
4. They are two of triplets.
5. The three families are: Stephen, Alice, Ronald
    Andrew, Jane, Helen
    Daniel, Laura, Joe
6. Kayak
7. Papoose
8. Lei
9. Missionary takes one cannibal across, and returns. Three missionaries cross, two return. Two missionaries, one cannibal cross, one missionary returns. Missionary and remaining cannibal cross.

10. 1½ inches
11. Fill largest jar. Fill each of the other jars from this jar. Pour out smallest jar and fill it again from largest jar, leaving 20 ounces.
12. (c)
13. (c)
14. 2
15. West
16. Four

Appendix

Appendix

HOUSEHOLD ITEMS TO SAVE AND USE IN PLAY

From Kitchen, Laundry, and Mending Equipment

Elastic (3 months–12 years)—dangle toys, headdresses, doll clothes, wrist bells

Plastic salt shakers (4–7 months)—rattles

Plastic napkin rings (4–12 months)—dangle toys, teething rings

Pea beans (5 months–4 years)—rattles, bean bags

Plastic measuring spoons (6 months–8 years)—toys for handling, sand play, domestic play

Plastic tumblers (6–18 months)—nesting toys, sand play, domestic play

Plastic bowls (6 months–6 years)—nesting toys, water play, sand play, domestic play

Plastic cups (6–18 months, 2–8 years)—nesting toys, water play, domestic play, sand play

Foam rubber sponges (6 months–10 years)—bath toys, water play, stuffing soft animals

Plastic sponges (6 months–10 years)—bath toys, water play

Pieces of cotton cloth (7 months–12 years)—doll clothes, doll covers, baby books, dressing up

Small wooden bowls (8 months–5 years)—nesting toys, tom-toms, sand play

Small metal pie tins (8 months–10 years)—nesting toys, doll dishes, doll dishpan, sand play

Small metal ring molds (8 months–10 years)—nesting toys, doll dishes, sand play

Wooden spoons (10–18 months)—banging toys

Milk cartons (1–10 years)—rattles, storage, trains, blocks; tops slitted, to drop in small objects

Milk-bottle tops (1–10 years)—paper doll faces, game counters, to drop through slits

Round refrigerator boxes of plastic, with covers (1–10 years)—baby toys, storing small objects

Jars with screw tops (1–12 years)—storage for small items

Round plastic cheese-boxes (1–12 years)—manipulation play, storage

Cereal cartons (15 months–3 years)—tops slitted, to drop in small objects; table blocks; drums

Pieces of silk, velvet, bright colors (18 months–12 years)—touching, sorting, play clothes

Clothespins (2–7 years)—manipulation play, small dolls
Wrapping paper (2–10 years)—drawing, painting, hats, masks
Salt and flour (3–5 years)—nonsticky dough
Cooking pans (3–6 years)—water play, sand play
Flour sifters (3–6 years)—sand play
Funnels (3–6 years)—water and sand play
Muffin tins (3–6 years)—sand play
Sieves (3–6 years)—water and sand play
Spoons, metal (3–6 years)—water and sand play, dipping out finger paints
Tea strainers (3–6 years)—sand and water play
Small dessert molds (3–8 years)—mud and sand play
Dish mops (3–10 years)—domestic play
Metal washtub (3–10 years)—water play, sailing boats
Soap flakes, soap powder (3–10 years)—water play, soap bubbles
Flour (3–12 years)—paste, stiff dough, papier-mâché
Paper bags (3–12 years)—hats, masks, puppets
Cookie-cutters (4–6 years)—sand play, clay play, dough play
Large darning needles (4–6 years)—sewing, stringing beads, weaving
Chairs (4–7 years)—train play
Buttons (4–10 years)—sewing, stringing, pasting, making "jewelry"
Dishpan (3–10 years)—water play, domestic play
Eggbeaters (4–10 years)—water play, domestic play
Food coloring (4–10 years)—water play, dough for play, finger paint, dyeing spaghetti "beads"
Food mixes for cakes, puddings (4–10 years)—domestic play
Large spaghetti (4–10 years)—stringing, necklaces, bracelets, sewing on cards
Large wooden bowls (4–10 years)—tom-toms
Paper plates (4–10 years)—pictures, merry-go-rounds, doll hats, tambourines
Corks (4–12 years)—making animals, birds, pipe-cleaner dolls; stands for paper dolls; tiny boats to float; party favors
Squat pint jars (4–12 years)—to hold finger paints, poster paints, nails and screws, "collections"
Starch (4–12 years)—homemade finger paint, "chemistry" experiments, modeling materials
Clothesline (5–10 years)—jump rope, domestic play, horse reins
Colored straws (5–10 years)—stringing, Christmas ornaments, pasting in designs
Lima beans (5–10 years)—growing experiments
Paper picnic spoons (5–10 years)—doll heads
Scraps of cloth (5–6 years, 10–12 years)—sewing, doll clothes, bean bags
Paper candy cups (5–12 years)—doll parasols, parts of party favors, doll hats
Potatoes (5–12 years)—finger puppets, making prints

HOUSEHOLD ITEMS TO SAVE AND USE IN PLAY 395

Sweet potatoes (5–12 years)—growing experiments
Tape measures (5–12 years)—playing house, making doll clothes, constructions
Nuts, any kind, unshelled (6–12 years)—heads of small dolls, animals, birds
Paper doilies (6–12 years)—holiday cards, doll skirts, fancy headdresses, coloring designs, fans
String, wool, carpet yarn (6–12 years)—string games, knitting, spool knitting, weaving, doll and puppet hair
Toothpicks (6–12 years)—birds, animals, small dolls, parasols, party favors, masts on tiny sailboats
Walnut shell halves (6–12 years)—tiny cradles, Christmas ornaments, "magic" games, tiny sailboats, fantasy animals
Small paring knife (10–12 years)—soap carving, clay work, whittling, mumblety-peg
Soap bars (10–12 years)—soap carving, "boats" to float

From Bedroom, Clothes Closets, and Linen Chest

Plastic bracelets (3 months–6 years)—dangle toys, toys for handling, mouthing, dressing up
Cotton socks and stockings (6 months–10 years)—balls, dolls, strips for braiding and weaving, doll clothes
Shoelaces (2–4 years)—stringing beads, practicing lacing shoes
Pieces of fur (2–10 years)—animals, doll rugs, doll hats, muffs
Old gloves (2–12 years)—puppet heads, dress-up, balls, doll clothes
Cold cream (3–6 years)—messy play
Costume jewelry (3–12 years)—dressing up, doll jewelry, Christmas ornaments
Men's clothing: shoes, gloves, shirts, jackets, pants, caps, work aprons, work jackets, uniform parts, mufflers (3–12 years)—making large dolls, dress-up games
Women's clothing: shoes, gloves, dresses, skirts, blouses, capes, coats, artificial flowers, aprons, handkerchiefs, scarves (3–12 years)—dress-up games, playing house, giving "concerts" and "plays," making large dolls
Felt hats, men's and women's (3–12 years)—dress-up, doll clothes, felt flowers, felt belts, millinery play
Feathers (3–12 years)—Indian headdress, playing milliner, making party favors, doll clothes, doll hats, funny animals
Leather handbags (3–12 years)—doll shoes, doll bags, doll hats, costume flowers, belts, dress-up
Nylon stockings (4–12 years)—wigs, doll hair, puppet bodies, weaving, braiding
Tablecloths, sheets, bed covers (4–12 years)—houses, caves, capes, skirts, ghost costumes
Bead necklaces (5–10 years)—dress-up, Indian headdresses

Rouge and lipstick (5–12 years)—playing grownup, circus, doctor
Mirrors from handbags (6–12 years)—doll house mirror, miniature scenes
Nail polish (7–12 years)—playing manicure, playing grownup, making Christmas cards
Hairpins (10 years)—lace making

From the Writing Desk

Paper clips (3–12 years)—necklaces, bracelets, manipulation toys
Paper fasteners (3–12 years)—paper dolls, scrapbooks
Tissue paper (1 year up)—to tear, to twist and braid, to make puppet hair, to stuff paper-bag faces
Poker chips (15 months–2 years)—manipulation, with slitted boxes
Scotch tape (3 years up)—hats, pictures, scrapbooks, paper constructions
Playing cards (3 years up)—toss games, "building," card house, card games
Paper, medium weight (4–11 years)—airplanes, parachutes, darts, drinking cups, baskets, woven mats, hats, boats, coloring, paper dolls, tearing
Glue, paste (4–12 years)—modeling material, pasting
Ink (6–12 years)—ink-blot pictures
Pipe cleaners (6–12 years)—fantastic animals, dolls, party favors, "pictures," mobiles
Rulers (6–12 years)—drawing, construction

From Cellar, Workshop, Medicine Chest, and General Discard

Boxes from gifts (all ages)—storage, doll beds, doll houses, creating tiny scenes
Strips of patterned oilcloth (2–6 months)—crib or wall decorations
Small Christmas bells (3 months–8 years)—dangle toys, rhythm instruments, bracelets, necklaces
Wooden spools (3 months–10 years)—dangle toys, pull toys, parts of doll furniture, necklaces, stringing, spool knitting
Worn towels (6 months–10 years)—cuddly toys, doll towels, doll bathrobes
Pieces of oilcloth with simple designs (7–12 months)—baby books
Round wooden boxes with covers (1–10 years)—baby toys, storage
Cardboard grocery cartons (2–10 years)—doll houses, blocks, seats, for climbing
Large pieces of plastic material, old plastic pads, tablecloths (2–10 years)—protection for floors, tables, during messy play
Christmas cards (2–10 years)—cutting, pasting, scrapbooks, small puzzles, illustrating stories
Old magazines (2–12 years)—cutting, pasting, scrapbooks, beads
Cotton batting (2–12 years)—dolls, puppets, doll pillows, mattresses, Christmas decorations

HOUSEHOLD ITEMS TO SAVE AND USE IN PLAY

Film spools and reels (2–12 years)—wheels for small trains, keep string and yarn tidy, making pulleys

Rectangular wooden cheese boxes (2–12 years)—trains, blocks, storage

Planks (3–8 years)—seesaws, jouncing board, slide, rocking board

Wallpaper samples (3–10 years)—cutting and pasting, making beads, papering dollhouse

Wooden packing cases (3–8 years)—outdoor play

Orange crates (3–10 years)—shelves, small-size furniture

Small brushes (3–10 years)—water play, domestic play

Sandpaper (3–12 years)—sensory play, collages, construction

Watering can (4–7 years)—sand play, water play

Crates, large (4–14 years)—outdoor play, huts

Magnet (4–14 years)—play with nails and pins, experiments

Barrel hoops (4–10 years)—outdoor play

Cardboard rolls from paper or towels (4–10 years)—telescopes, talking tubes, smokestacks

Hose (4–10 years)—water play

Kegs, barrels (4–10 years)—outdoor play

Old mattresses (4–10 years)—jumping, tumbling

Package handles (4–10 years)—shades for doll houses, free-form constructions

Ping-pong balls (4–10 years)—dolls, puppets

Small garden tools (4–10 years)—sand play, digging

Typewriter ribbon spools (2–12 years)—wheels, pulleys, tops

Wooden dowel, $1/4''$ (4–10 years)—constructing wagons with spool wheels, merry-go-round with paper plates, small totem poles, drumsticks, rhythm sticks

Wood, short pieces of 2 x 4, $1/4''$ rounds, thin blocks (4–10 years)—doll house furniture, cabins in village scenes, small constructions, castanets

Cardboard from shirts and pads (4–12 years)—drawing, painting, pasting, constructions, jigsaw puzzles, clock face

Composition board (4–12 years)—bulletin board, dartboard, nailing, constructions

Glycerin (4–12 years)—soap bubbles

Small tools (4–12 years)—dramatic play, construction

Bolts and nuts (5–6 years)—manipulation toys

Bottle tops (5–10 years)—game counters, doll dishes, bases for fantasy dolls and animals

Matchsticks (5–10 years)—making toys, doll furniture, miniature trees

Toilet-paper tube (5–10 years)—body of a doll or animal, "looking" tube, barn silo, part of steam roller

Cigar boxes (5–12 years)—doll beds, wagons, hobby collections, doll furniture, musical instruments, weaving frame

Match boxes (5–12 years)—doll's suitcases, hobby storage (stamp, coins, etc.)

Shoe boxes (5–12 years)—doll beds, doll houses, string and yarn holder, storage for small objects, shadow boxes
Wire (5–12 years)—mobiles, constructions
Heavy rope (6–7 years)—with knots, for climbing
Calendars (6–10 years)—number games, playing school, clock faces, numbers on playhouses
Berry boxes (6–12 years)—doll beds, storage
Corrugated cardboard (6–12 years)—building small houses, fences, animals, pencil and brush holder
Sawdust (6–12 years)—stuffing doll mattresses, modeling material (mixed with paste)
Tinsel from Christmas trees (6–12 years)—doll clothes, special occasion cards, "pictures," party favors
Old clocks (8–10 years)—mechanical experimentation
Manila rope (8–12 years)—doll hair, animal tails, braiding and knot-tying
Electric wiring (9–11 years)—electrical "gadgets," buzzers, light signals
Flashlight batteries (9–11 years)—making electrical signal sets
Iodine (10–12 years)—chemistry experiments
Litmus paper (10–12 years)—chemistry experiments

Items from Out-of-doors

Small stones (4–10 years)—playing Duck on the Rock, collections, collages
Berries (such as cranberries, bittersweet, etc.) (6–10 years)—Christmas decorations, beads, doll ornaments
Sea shells (6–12 years)—fantastic animals, birds, place-card holder, jewelry, ash trays
Pine cones (8–10 years)—fantasy animals, Christmas ornaments, artificial flowers
Acorns (8–12 years)—string, make animals, birds, tiny dolls, doll's beret, play pipe

PLAY MATERIALS TO BUY FOR DIFFERENT AGES

The following list is meant to be suggestive only. Each year manufacturers offer many new items that we cannot include in detail. Our list, however, includes all the *types* of toys that are appropriate at the ages mentioned for them. It can be used as a guide in buying new toys that come on the market by comparing these with the old established favorites. If they have similar kinds of appeal, are constructed as well, and can be handled as easily as those we mention for a certain age group, they are probably just as appropriate.

We have arranged our list so that a toy is first mentioned at the age when its usefulness usually begins. Some toys, of course, continue to be useful for several years, and a few seem never to outlive their appeal. To avoid repeating the same names under each age heading, we have put a number at the right of most items to indicate the age at which interest usually begins to fade. Items that are apt to remain indefinitely useful have no numbers after them.

To use this list for any age after the first year, it is a good idea to look at the items under several years preceding the specific one wanted, as well as that one. Thus, if one were trying to get ideas for toys for a three-year-old, he would look at each list coming before 3–4 years, starting at the first year. Under *6 months* we find "Floating bath toys" with (4 years) after it, showing that interest in this item continues through that age; therefore, it should be considered for the three-year-old. Continuing, under *1–2 years, 18 months,* and *2–3 years* we find at least two dozen items appropriate for a three-year-old. The same method should be used with all the other age groups.

The First Year

3–5 Months
Dangle toys for crib or carriage (8 months)
High-chair toys with suction cup base (9 months)
Crib and play-pen "gyms" (1 year)
Interlocking plastic rings (1 year)
Plastic disks on chain (1 year)
Rubber, bone, or plastic teething rings (1 year)
Ring or dumbbell-shaped rattles (1 year)
Wind harps to hang by window (1 year)
Large, bright, simple pictures (5 years)

6 Months
Hard rubber bones or rings from pet shops (1 year)
Roly-poly (1 year)
Rubber beads on string (1 year)
Soft rubber squeeze-toys (1 year)
Pull and push toys without handles (18 months)
Bright-colored, medium-sized balls (2 years)
Cloth or heavy cardboard books (2 years)
Rubber blocks that rattle or tinkle (2 years)
Soft, washable animals and dolls (2 years)
Floating bath toys (4 years)

1–2 Years

12 Months
Color cones (2)
Low rocking horse (2)
Nesting bowls or tumblers (2)
Pegboard with a few large pegs (2)
Bean bags (4)

18 Months

Low slide (2)
Low swing with arms and back (2)
Nesting blocks (2)
Toys with openings of different shapes to receive blocks of different shapes (2)
Hammer boards (3)
Large "ride-'em" toys (locomotive, tractor, etc., for straddling) (3)
Simple wooden train (3)
Large hollow wooden blocks (4)
Nursery-size table and chairs (5)
Rocking chair (5)
Sand toys (pail, shovels, sieve, molds) (5)
Wading pool (6)
Wrist bells (6)
Stuffed toys (Teddy bear, slumber-pup, cloth doll)

2–3 Years

Interlocking block trains (3)
Braided strings with rigid tips (4)
Cards with holes punched in them (4)
Cloth books with pages for lacing (4)
Large beads to string (4)
Large hexagonal crayons (4)
Washable rubber 12-inch doll (4)
Wooden or rubber vehicles (auto, truck, ambulance, fire engine) (4)
Wooden shoe for lacing (4)
Blunt scissors (5)
Unpainted, hardwood "kindergarten" blocks (half unit, unit, double unit, small triangle) (6)
Wooden puzzles graded according to age (6)
Carriage, doll bed, doll's high chair (8)
Housekeeping toys (carpet sweeper, broom, dust mop) (8)
Toy telephone (8)
Sand box (9–10)
Colored construction paper

3–4 Years

Hammer with short handle and heavy head (7)
Box ladder (out of doors) (5)
Doorway gym (5)
Full-sized rocking horse (5)
Vehicles to ride in (fire engine, Irish mail-car, etc.) (5)
Musical and rhythmic toys (drums, maracas, tambourines) (6)
Tricycle (6)
Wheelbarrow size graded to age

Flannel-surfaced board and pieces of flannel and felt in different shapes and colors (8)
Flexible plastic sheet, and colored cut-out pieces (8)
Pregummed dots, strips, squares, triangles of colored paper (8)
Adjustable easel (10)
Doll bathinette (10)
Horizontal bars to be raised as child grows (10)
Ironing board and iron (10)
Large brushes for poster paint (10)
Laundry equipment for doll clothes (10)
Newsprint for painting (10)
Wagon to haul things in (10)
Poster-paint powder to be mixed as needed (12)
Roller skates speed-graded to skill
Sled size-graded to age (12)
Finger paints
Phonograph, records

4-5 Years

Three-, four-, sixpenny nails (5)
Medium-height slide (6)
Picture lotto games (6)
Plastic mosaic blocks (6)
Play pony with horse reins (6)
Realistic wooden trains with wheels (6)
Wooden short pillar, large triangle, quarter-circle, small half-circle, small bridge, quadruple block unit (8)
Small cars and trucks (6)
Cowboy and cowgirl costumes, completé (7)
Parts of costumes (policeman's badge and handcuffs, nurse's cap, cowboy hat, etc.) (7)
Barnyard set (8)
Blackboard and colored and white chalk (8)
Cash register (8)
Doll bed and bedding (8)
Dump truck (8)
Small wooden people for use with blocks (8)
Snowplow (8)
Steam shovel (8)
Tractor (8)
Wooden and plastic construction sets (Tinker Toy type) (8)
Workbench and vise
Additional phonograph records
Adjustable swing (10)
Child-size playhouse (10)
Doctor and nurse kit (10)

Doll dishes (10)
Large play stove and sink (10)
Sailboat (10)
Seesaw (10)
Small sturdy crosscut saw
Swing and bar set (10)
Color-paddles (12)
Xylophone (12)

5–6 Years

Bow and arrows with suction heads (8)
Dishwashing set (8)
Doll clothes with simple fastenings (8)
Doll feeding sets (sterilizer, etc.) (8)
Animals and vehicles (10)
Cosmetic kit (10)
Doll furniture (10)
Jump-rope (10)
Looms (looper-loom, very simple heddle loom) (10)
Miniature-life dolls (10)
Pastry and cooking set (10)
Play and camping tent, size according to age
Realistic toy refrigerator and storage cabinets (10)
Scooter (10)
Small scale-model machinery and vehicles (10)
Stockade, fort, and frontier sets (10)
Toy soldiers (10)
Walkie-talkie (10)
Ice skates
Jigsaw puzzles varying in difficulty (12)
Magnet
Magnifying glass
Mechanical boats and ships (12)
Metallic-surfaced and shiny-coated paper
Pick-up sticks (12)
Realistic mechanical cars and army vehicles (12)
Ring toss
Scrapbooks
Shuffleboard
Simple wind instruments for experimentation (harmonica, song flute, ocarina, etc.)
Skis

6–7 Years

Bead jewelry set (8)
Small bicycle (8)
Coloring books (10)

Lightweight bat and softball (10)
Paper dolls (10)
Tops (10)
Mechanical trains (11)
Baseball catcher's mitt
Boxing gloves
Cooking sets with real dessert and cakes mixes
Fishing tackle (very simple) (10–12)
Horseshoe pitching set (10–12)
Jacks and marbles (10–12)
Larger working models of road-building, hauling, and agricultural machinery (10–12)
Make-up and disguise kits (10–12)
Ordinary round crayons (10–12)
Rhythm instruments (triangle) (10–12)
Self-hardening clay (10–12)
Sketch pads and drawing paper (10–12)
Tenpins (10–12)
Punching bag (on stand) (10–12)
Two- and sevenpenny nails (10–12)
Wooden trains with tracks (10–12)
Workable toy sewing machine (10–12)
Equipment for playing store (10)

7–8 Years

Doll house (10)
Dominoes (10)
Pogo stick (10)
Yo-yo (fly-back top) (10)
Checkers
Chinese checkers
Flying planes and helicopters
Football equipment
Gliders
Kite
Larger heddle loom
More elaborate costumes (spaceman, ballerina, circus queen, ringmaster, etc.)
More elaborate disguise and make-up kits
Quiz, puzzle, and things-to-do books
Simple erector sets
Specialized building sets (Bill Ding Clowns, etc.) (12–14)

8 Years

Type-setting printing sets with large type (10)
Badminton

Basketball hoop and ball
Bingo
Coin folders (for collectors)
Cut-out towns, foreign communities, forts (12)
Field glasses
Hand puppets
Hockey equipment
Interlocking small wooden or plastic brick building sets (12)
Leather and plastic braiding (12)
Leathercraft materials
Magnetic dart set (12)
Medium-sized bicycle (12)
Model airplane kits graded in difficulty (12)
Pastels
Special water-color crayons or pencils
Ping-pong set
Recorder (wind instrument)
Tennis racket and balls
Toy typewriter (12)
Underwater equipment (goggles, flippers) for good swimmers
Water colors and small brushes

9 Years

Bent-wire puzzles
Costume-dolls (for collectors)
Electric trains
Electrical signaling set
Mannequin sewing set
Metalcraft set
Practical jokes and tricks (exploding cigars, dribbling glasses, etc.)
Puppet theater
Small remote-control vehicles
Steam engine with real steam
Table and card games that depend on simple numerical combinations
Walking, little-girl dolls
Wood-burning set

10 Years

Adult-type card games of simpler sort
Advanced tools (screw driver, brace, pliers, auger bit, tri-square, coarse file, plane)
Carom board
Dart set (used under supervision)
Educational table games
Electrical assembly kits

Erector set with engines
Marionettes and stage
Microscope
Mineralogy set
Real typewriter
Stamp album
Tools for carving wood, soap, and sculpstone

11–12 Years

Additional aids for serious collectors of butterflies, stamps, minerals, etc.
Additions to electric train sets (lights, signals, over-and-under roadbed and tracks, etc.)
Chemistry set
Detective table games (Clue, etc.)
Full-sized bicycle
Liquid plastic flower-making sets
Magnetic and electrical table games
Miniature attachments for steam engine (fan, grindstone, power press, etc.)
Mix-your-own perfume sets
Model cars and planes with real engines
Printing press (circular drum type)
Put-together kits (electric clock, historical models of cars and trains)
Real archery sets
Real-brick building set
Shell jewelry sets
Soldering iron
Tailless kites
Wire cutter
Word-building games

BUILDING PLAY EQUIPMENT

Outdoor Equipment [1]

The designs shown here are for sturdy, long-time outdoor equipment. Lumber that is well seasoned, comparatively straight grained, and free from cracks or splits should be selected. All lumber used for playground apparatus should be surfaced on four sides and the corners planed. If lumber is difficult to obtain, pipe may be used for frames. Galvanized iron pipe, 2 to 3 inches in diameter, is best for play apparatus. Pipe

[1] This section on outdoor play equipment is from *Home Play and Play Equipment for the Preschool Child*, U. S. Children's Bureau Publication No. 238.

and pipe fittings may be bought from hardware stores or plumbing firms.

Special fittings for swings and rings are sold by manufacturers of playground equipment and by dealers in hardware or in barn and hayloft equipment. A hooked bolt, galvanized thimble, or black enameled clamp costs only a few cents apiece. Although chain is more durable than rope, swings made of rope are strong enough for small children in the home playground. If chain is used, it should not be too heavy.

Outdoor play apparatus must be constructed so that it is firm and secure. Uprights and cross beams must be set straight and level. Frames for swings and bars need not be braced if they are set 3 feet deep in concrete.

Wooden apparatus should be given a coat of linseed oil and painted with waterproof paint as a protection from the weather. All parts of apparatus that are to be placed underground should be treated with a preservative to a point at least 6 inches above the ground. Friction points on metal should be greased frequently. Bolts should be used to fasten wooden parts together wherever it is possible; they fasten the parts more securely than nails and are less likely to split the wood or to work loose. Where wooden parts are bolted together, washers should be used to protect the wood, and the bolts should be tightened frequently. Bolt holes treated with a preservative will prolong the life of the joint. Playground apparatus should be inspected often, as ropes fray and bolts loosen. Sharp corners of swing boards and sand boxes should be cut off, and rough edges of boards should be smoothed to prevent splinters. The swing should be placed close to and parallel with a fence or a wall; or a fence should be built around the frame to keep children from running into the swing while it is in motion.

In the following descriptions of equipment all dimensions specified for lumber represent the "nominal" dimensions according to which lumber is usually described. The actual dimensions of the surfaced lumber are slightly smaller; for instance, a 2-inch board is about $1\frac{5}{8}$ inches.

Douglas fir and southern yellow pine are suitable woods for most of the equipment described.

Sand Box
Material Needed

(All lumber surfaced on four sides)
SIDES: 2 pieces of lumber, 2 in. thick, 10 in. wide, and 6 ft. long.
ENDS: 2 pieces of lumber, 2 in. thick, 10 in. wide, and 4 ft. long.
SHELVES: 2 pieces of lumber, 2 in. thick, 8 in. wide, and 4 ft. 4 in. long.
NAILS: 1 pound 16-penny common.
SAND: 1 wagonload (to fill the box to a depth of 8 in., approximately $\frac{1}{2}$ cu. yd. or 16 cu. ft. of sand will be required).

BUILDING PLAY EQUIPMENT

Construction

Nail the side boards to the ends. Center the boards for the shelves on the end boards and nail them firmly to both end and side boards, so that they are half inside and half outside the box and will not need to be braced. Cut off the sharp corners of the shelves. Brace the corners of the box with iron or wood. A wooden bottom in the sand box will keep the children from digging into the soil underneath and mixing it with the sand.

The sand box should have a cover to protect the sand from stray cats and dogs. Canvas weighted at the corners with stones may be used, or wallboard nailed on two strips of wood may be laid over the sand box at night. Another type of cover is a light wooden frame covered with 1-inch galvanized-wire mesh, which permits the sun and air to reach the sand. To keep the sand dry in wet weather, however, a permanent cover, hinged to the box, is best. It may be made of waterproof canvas or other fabric stretched and nailed to a frame, or of wood, or of wallboard and wood. Both wood and wallboard should be painted with waterproof paint.

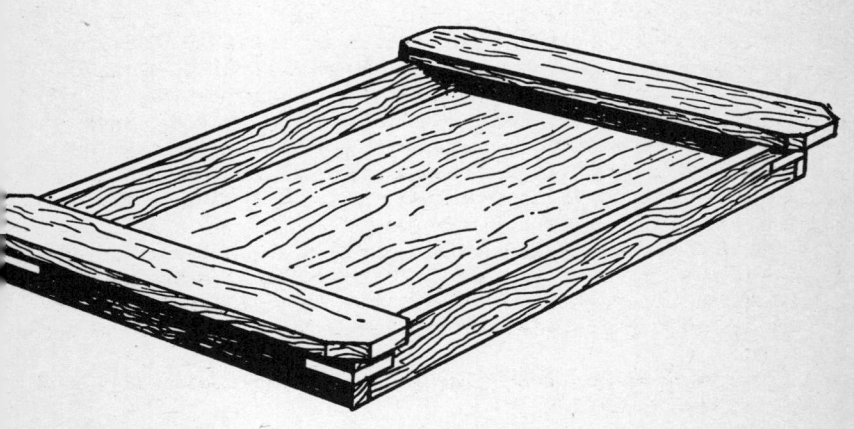

Unless the sand is moistened occasionally, it will get dusty. Little stools or boxes, large enough for children to sit on but small enough for them to carry around, will help to keep children from sitting in the sand when it is too damp. The shelves on the ends of the sand box give them work tables or seats and help to keep the sand in the box.

This sand box is large enough for two or three children to play in. It should be placed where it will get the direct sun at some time during the day but where there is shade also. The sun helps to keep the sand clean. The shade adds to its comfort as a play spot.

Play Plank and Sawhorse

Material Needed for Play Plank

(All lumber surfaced on four sides)

PLANK: 1 piece of vertical grained Douglas fir or southern yellow pine, 2 in. thick, 10 in. wide, and 12 ft. long. (Maple or birch, 1¼ in. thick, in clear or select grade, may be used.)

CLEATS: 2 pieces of lumber, 2 in. thick, 4 in. wide, and 10 in. long.

Construction of Play Plank

Bolt a cleat to the bottom of the plank 6 inches from each end. This is to keep the plank from slipping when it is placed on boxes or on the sawhorse.

It is especially important that a plank that is to be used as a slide be free from splinters. Select a smooth, vertical-grained piece of lumber and give it the following treatment: A thorough sandpapering, a coat of linseed oil to protect it from the weather, a coat of white shellac or varnish, and a heavy coat of floor wax. The children should not be permitted to slide against the grain of the wood. A cleat at only one end of the plank that is to be used as a slide will help to prevent its being placed in the wrong position.

Planks that are not to be used as slides should be smoothed with a plane or a wood rasp, given a coat of linseed oil, and painted with waterproof paint.

The play plank may be placed across the sawhorse to make a seesaw. It may be used also on large blocks of wood or on the sawhorse as a slide board or on two boxes as a walking board for the smallest children to practice balancing.

There should be plenty of wooden boxes of different sizes to use with the play planks, from closed boxes 5 inches by 5 inches by 8 inches to large packing boxes. The nails should be removed from the open end of the packing boxes.

Material Needed for Sawhorse

(All lumber surfaced on four sides)

TOP AND LEGS: 1 piece of No. 1 common grade Douglas fir or southern yellow pine, 2 in. thick, 4 in. wide, and 9 ft. long.

BRACES: 1 piece of lumber, 1 in. thick, 4 in. wide, and 6½ ft. long.

NAILS: 1 pound 16-penny common nails or carriage bolts.

Construction of Sawhorse

Saw the long piece of lumber as follows: top, 24 inches long, and 4 legs, each 20 inches long. At a distance of 6 inches from each end of the top, bolt two small blocks of wood or saw out a section ¾ inch deep to keep the play plank from slipping off the sawhorse. Saw the shorter piece of lumber into four pieces to be used as braces, as follows: two 24 inches, two 15 inches.

To assemble the sawhorse, cut off the upper ends of the legs at about a 30 degree angle, to fit against the sides of the top piece. Fasten them to the top at its extremities with nails or bolts. Nail the braces horizontally, spanning the legs about a quarter of the length of the leg from the ground.

Swing and Climbing Bars

Material Needed for Frame

(All lumber surfaced on four sides)

UPRIGHTS FOR SWING: 2 pieces of No. 1 common grade Douglas fir or southern yellow pine, 4 in. thick, 4 in. wide, and 14 ft. long.

CROSS BEAM FOR SWING: 1 piece of No. 1 common grade Douglas fir or southern yellow pine, 4 in. thick, 4 in. wide, and 6 ft. long.

UPRIGHT FOR CLIMBING BARS: 1 piece of No. 1 common grade Douglas fir or southern yellow pine, 4 in. thick, 4 in. wide, and 10 ft. long.

BRACES: 4 pieces of No. 1 common grade Douglas fir or southern yellow pine, 2 in. thick, 4 in. wide, and 8 ft. long (not required if uprights are set 3 ft. in concrete).

NAILS: 1 pound 20-penny common nails and 1 pound 7-in. heavy nails or bolts.

(NOTE.—The frame may be made of 3-in. pipe of approximately the same lengths as the lumber.)

Construction of Frame

Unless specially treated lumber is bought for the uprights, the parts that are to be placed underground should be treated to a point 6 inches above the ground to prevent decay or damage from insects.

Fasten the cross beam to the tops of the uprights for the swing with heavy bolts or nails as shown in the illustration. Square the beam and posts with a carpenter's level or a wide board that has been cut square. Brace the angles (joints) of the cross beam and uprights securely with wood or iron. Dig three post holes for the uprights 3 feet deep. Center the two post holes for the swing uprights 6 feet apart. The post hole for the other upright, to support the climbing bars, should be 4 feet from the upright for the swing. Make square forms for the holes. Set the uprights on pieces of wood so that they will be level. Rough, ready-made wooden boxes to fit the holes may be used as forms for the concrete. The uprights will not need permanent braces if they are set 3 feet deep in concrete. They must be braced temporarily, however, until the concrete is set.

Exact proportions for a concrete mixture cannot be specified, as the proportions depend upon the size and nature of the sand and gravel (aggregate) that is used. A proportion of water to cement that would give adequate strength in concrete foundations for playground equipment is 6 gallons of water to 1 sack of Portland cement. If the maximum screening size of the gravel is 1 inch, the proportions may be 1 part of cement, 2 parts of sand, and 3 parts of gravel. If the maximum size of the gravel is 2 inches, the proportions may be 1 part of cement, 2 parts of sand, and 3½ parts of gravel. The exact amount of sand and gravel necessary to make the mixture workable may be determined by mixing trial batches. Spread the sand out evenly on a wooden floor and spread the dry cement evenly over it. Turn the cement and sand thoroughly with a shovel until they are well mixed. Then spread the gravel in an even layer on the cement-sand mixture and continue mixing and turning with a shovel. Add water, and mix until the cement, sand, and

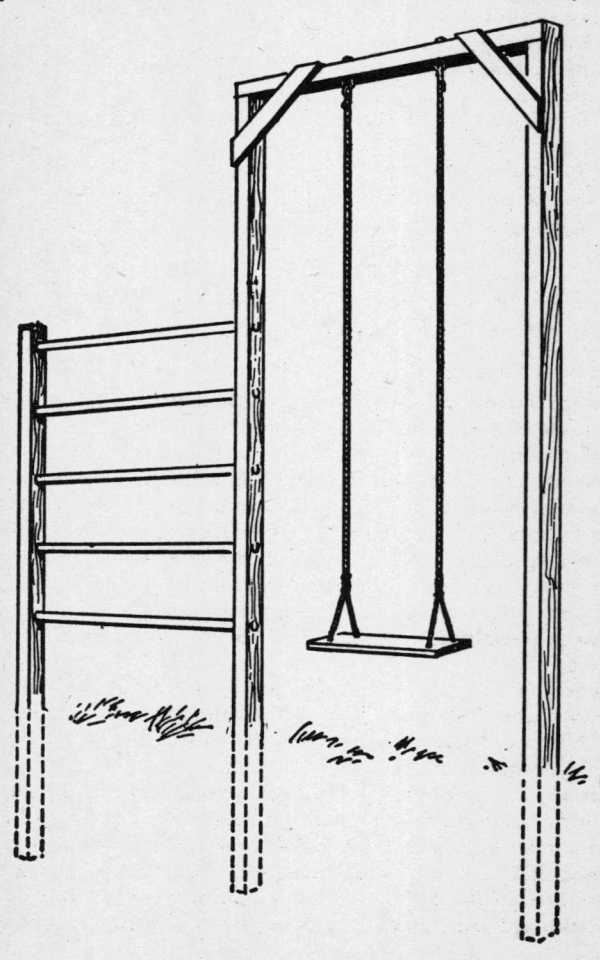

BUILDING PLAY EQUIPMENT 411

pebbles have been thoroughly and uniformly combined. Pour the concrete mixture into the form around the upright and tamp it thoroughly. Smooth the top surface with the trowel and slope it so that water will run off instead of seeping in and around the upright. The forms may be removed after 24 hours. Concrete should be protected from the sun and kept damp for several days, and the equipment should not be used until the concrete has hardened.

Material Needed for Swing

ROPE: Waterproof manila rope, 3/4 in. in diameter and about 25 ft. long (length depending upon height of child and kind of swing).

SWING SEAT: 1 piece of maple or birch, 1¼ in. thick, 8 in. wide, and 24 in. long. Other kinds of swings shown require the following material:

    1 pair of galvanized steel or aluminum rings 1 in. thick and 8 in. in diameter.
    1 automobile tire.
    1 pair of rings made of rubber hose or bicycle tires.
    1 piece of log 21 in. long and 5 in. in diameter, and balancing rung of oak, ash, or hickory, 21 in. long and 1¼ in. in diameter, for standing-log swing.

Rope for climbing, 2 in. in diameter and approximately 14 ft. long.

Construction of Swing

The safest method of constructing the swing is to use special metal fittings, such as a 6-inch hooked bolt to attach the rope to the cross beam; a galvanized thimble through the hook to prevent wear on the rope; and a clamp to fasten the rope. If a bolt cannot be bought already hooked, have a blacksmith bend a heavy, threaded bolt into a J-shaped hook, and put the thimble through the hooked end of the bolt. Bore a hole through the cross beam. Put the threaded end of the bolt up through the hole in the cross beam and fasten the nut with a wrench, using a washer against the wood. As the bolt is screwed into the cross beam, the hooked end will be forced into the wood so that it cannot pull loose.

Pull one end of the rope through the hook so that the rope rests on the thimble, and fasten the end of the rope with the black enameled clamp. A bowline knot may be used, but the clamp is a more permanent means of fastening the rope to the cross beam.

The swing seat should be low enough for the small child to touch the ground with his whole foot, about 12 inches from the ground. For older children, 20 or 22 inches is the usual height. For the small child it is better to drill four holes in the swing seat, one in each corner, and run the rope through the holes. Cut off the corners of the swing seat. Put the rope through the holes in the swing seat and fasten by wrapping the ends tightly to the rope with marline (a cord that can be bought at a hardware store or a marine supply house). Galvanized wire is often used to wrap rope, but the ends must be fastened carefully and inspected often to prevent the child's getting scratched. The kind of clamp that is used to fasten the rope to the cross beam cannot be used here, because children might get hurt on the metal end.

An effective way of fastening the rope to the hook in the cross beam and to the swing seat is to splice the rope. Usually the company that sells the rope will do the splicing. If this method is used, however, the swing cannot be adjusted to different heights.

The swing may be a standing-log swing, designed to develop the arches of the feet, or a pair of flying rings for strengthening arm and shoulder muscles. For the small child, rings made of rubber hose or bicycle tires slipped over the rope and fastened tightly will serve very well, but the older, more active child will need metal rings as the hands will not slip on rubber easily enough for a comfortable change of grip.

An automobile tire swing is popular and can be used in many ways. A casing from which the inner tube and valve have been removed is firmly fastened to a single rope. A used tire is satisfactory, if it is not worn through and the fabric is not thin.

The climbing rope is a heavy single rope in which knots are tied 9 to 14 inches apart, the distance depending upon the size of the child who is to use the rope.

Material Needed for Climbing Bars

BARS: 5 straight-grained maple, hickory, or birch bars, $1\frac{1}{4}$ in. in diameter, 4 ft. long.

Construction of Climbing Bars

The bars can be bought, finished, from a lumber company or a planing mill. Bore holes $1\frac{1}{4}$ inches in diameter, 12 inches apart, in both uprights of the frame. Sandpaper the holes enough to permit the bars to enter. Drive the bars through the holes with a heavy block of wood and a hammer. The bars should fit in the holes so tightly that they cannot slip out or turn in the child's hands.

The climbing bars will be enjoyed by children under five. One end of the play plank may be placed on one of the lower bars and the other end on the ground or on a box for a walking or bouncing plank. One end of the plank may be placed on a higher bar to make a slide. The cleat on the sliding plank will prevent its slipping.

When the child is older, the wooden bars may be removed by sawing them off close to the upright, and a piece of 1-inch pipe placed through the upright for a horizontal bar. This bar should be 1 or 2 inches higher than the child's extended finger tips and should be bolted to the uprights. This may be done by having holes $\frac{7}{16}$ inch in diameter bored through the pipe 2 inches from each end. Bore a $1\frac{1}{2}$-inch hole in each upright through which to place the pipe; then at right angles to the first hole in each upright bore another hole $7/16$ inch in diameter, exactly intersecting the first hole at the center. Put the bar in place and bolt it with $3/8$-inch carriage bolts and washers through upright and bar.

Swing, Rings, Trapeze, and Bar

Material Needed for Frame

UPRIGHTS FOR SWING: 2 pieces of No. 1 common Douglas fir or southern yellow pine, 4 in. thick, 6 in. wide, and 14 ft. long.

CROSS BEAM FOR SWING: 1 piece of No. 1 common Douglas fir or southern yellow pine, 4 in. thick, 6 in. wide, and 14 ft. long.

UPRIGHT FOR HORIZONTAL BAR: 1 piece of No. 1 common Douglas fir or southern yellow pine, 4 in. thick, 6 in. wide, and 9 ft. long.

BRACES: 4 pieces of No. 1 common Douglas fir or southern yellow pine, 2 in. thick, 4 in. wide, and 10 ft. long (not required if uprights are set 3 ft. in concrete).

NAILS: 1 pound of 20-penny common nails or carriage bolts.

(NOTE.—The frame may be made of 3-in. pipe of approximately the same lengths as the lumber.)

Material Needed for Swing, Rings, and Trapeze

ROPE: Waterproof manila rope, $3/4$ in. in diameter (length depending upon height of child; approximately 25 ft. will be needed for swing, 15 ft. for rings, and 15 ft. for trapeze).

SWING SEAT: 1 piece of maple or birch, $1\frac{1}{4}$ in. thick, 8 in. wide, and 24 in. long.

RINGS: 2 galvanized steel or aluminum rings, 1 in. thick, 8 in. in diameter.

TRAPEZE: 1 straight-grained maple, birch, or hickory bar, $1\frac{1}{4}$ in. in diameter, 24 in. long.

Construction of Swing, Rings, and Trapeze

See directions for constructing swing, pages 385-388.

Material Needed for Horizontal Bar

BAR: 1 piece of pipe, 1 in. in diameter, 6 ft. long.

BOLTS: 2 carriage bolts, $3/8$ in. in diameter.

Construction of Horizontal Bar

See directions for attaching climbing bars to uprights, page 388.

It is especially important that this combination of swing, rings, trapeze, and bar be well constructed. Inspect it frequently. The combination is a good piece of apparatus for a large yard. It may be placed across the end of a yard where it will cover a space about 20 feet long and 18 feet wide. If several children of about the same age use the equipment, three swings may be preferred. The attachments may be varied to suit the children's ages and interests.

Horizontal Ladder

In this piece of equipment the horizontal ladder is supported by two perpendicular ladders. The easiest way to construct it is to buy a 30-foot ladder, either single or extension, and cut it into three sections. Set two of the sections in concrete (see directions on page 385) for the perpendicular ladders, and place the other section across the top for the horizontal ladder. For older children, the horizontal ladder should be firmly bolted to the uprights at both ends. For children under five, the horizontal ladder can be made adjustable. Cut a groove in the frame at each end of the horizontal ladder so that the ladder will not slip when one end is placed on a rung of one of the perpendicular ladders and the other end on the ground. Younger children will like to climb on the ladder and swing from the rungs when it is in this position. A play plank for walking or bouncing may be laid on the lower rungs of the perpendicular ladders or placed at an angle from an upper rung and used as a slide.

A 10-foot ladder may be bought and used as a horizontal ladder, and the perpendicular ladders may be constructed according to the following specifications:

Material Needed for Perpendicular Ladders

UPRIGHTS: 4 pieces of No. 1 common Douglas fir or southern yellow pine, 2 in. thick, 4 in. wide, and 9 ft. long.

BRACES: 4 pieces of No. 1 common Douglas fir or southern yellow pine, 2 in. thick, 4 in. wide, and 10 ft. long (not required if uprights are set 3 ft. in concrete).

RUNGS FOR UPRIGHTS: 10 pieces of maple or birch, $3/4$ in. thick, 3 in. wide, 20 in. long.

NAILS: 1 pound 16-penny common nails.

BOLTS: Carriage bolts, $3/8$ in. in diameter, 5 in. long.

Construction of Perpendicular Ladders

Set uprights in concrete (see directions on pages 385-387). Bolt the rungs tightly to the uprights about 10 inches apart.

Indoor Equipment [2]

Work Bench as Play Table and Storage Chest

To meet children's desire for the largest possible work bench—play table, a bench 6 feet long and 2 feet wide slides under a larger bench

[2] This section is adapted from *How to Make Room for Play* and *Make More Room for Play*, courtesy of The American Toy Institute, New York. The illustrations are redrawn from drawings by Joseph Aronson for the Institute.

against the wall when not in use. This work bench is designed to do double duty as a toy storage cabinet.

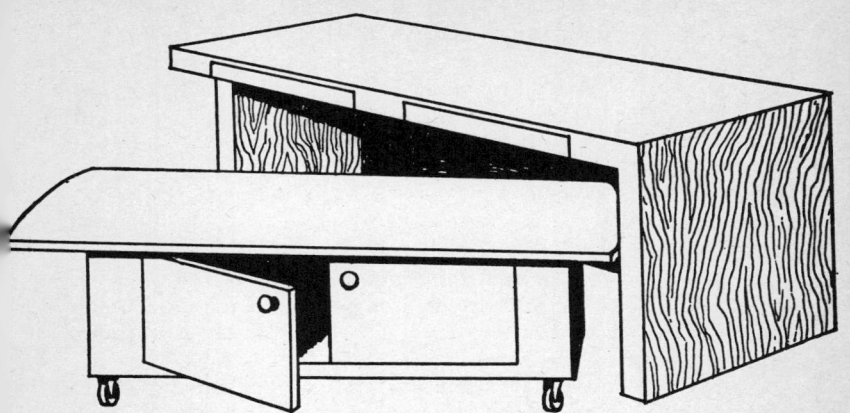

Above it is a work space surfaced with durable material, such as Masonite on 3/4-inch fir plywood. This upper unit includes drawers large enough to accommodate large sheets of drawing paper.

The lower bench can be hinged at one of the near corners to allow it to swing from the side of the upper bench. If this is done, make the upper bench 2 feet longer than the lower one. However, if the children who use it are likely to be rough on their equipment, the hinge may be pulled loose.

Suggested height for the lower bench is 17 inches; for the upper one, 27 inches. All dimensions, of course, may be varied to fit individual needs.

Lock-Blocks Provide Flexible Storage Units

Your children's favorite toys, at any age level, are likely to be irregular in shape. Yet, to provide maximum play value, each toy should be stored away in easy reach of the youngster who will use it.

To solve the problem, Joseph Aronson designed Lock-Blocks, open-faced storage units fastened together with dowel pegs and rubber bands, which can be adjusted easily and quickly to fit the space requirements of new toys.

By combining Lock-Blocks with lengths of ordinary board, a great variety of storage units can be developed to fit whatever space the family has available and to store each child's toys.

Illustrated is an arrangement of the Lock-Blocks which makes provision for storing large games, such as dart boards, and also makes convenient storage units for dolls, trucks, or juvenile housekeeping equipment.

Lock-Blocks also can be used as the base for a large board table top, which will serve for trains or hobbies.

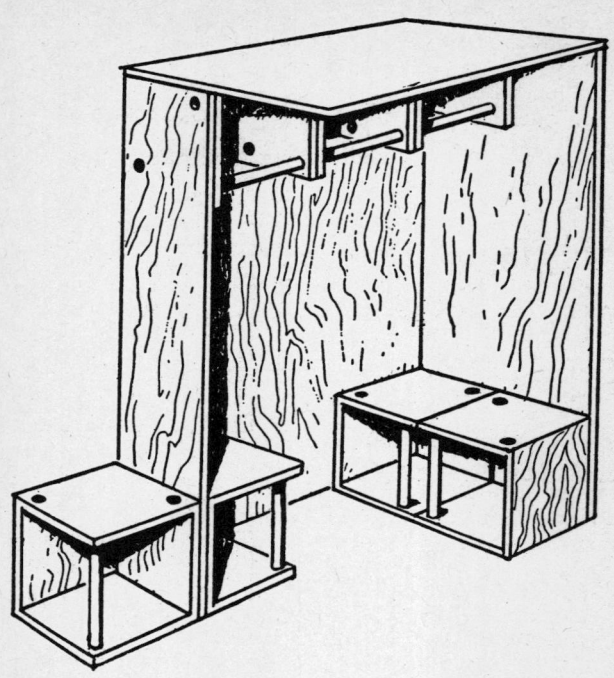

The illustration shows the open-faced cube assembled from 4 pieces of ½-inch-thick fir plywood, plus a 1⅛-inch round post at the open corner and a quarter-round molding for bracing at the inside corner. The sizes and material indicated are based on standard sizes of plywood and poles available in every lumber yard. A satisfactory construction is to nail and glue along all joints. Hold in clamps until the glue sets; and, if your butting surfaces are cleanly made, the blocks will be very strong.

Bore the holes in the top and bottom after the glue has completely set and be sure that the holes are uniformly spaced to make the blocks interchangeable. As a guide, cut a piece of light cardboard the shape of the top and punch a small hole to mark the center of each hole to be bored. Place this on the outside of the top and bottom when marking for the holes.

The block peg shown can very easily be turned down to ¾-inch diameter from ⅞-inch doweling by a man with a lathe. The groove near

BUILDING PLAY EQUIPMENT 417

the far end can be any kind of sinkage or fillet to receive a stout rubber band. At the other end is the head which may be any mushroom shape. The solid shank of the turning should be scant two thicknesses of the plywood used. Join the blocks together by means of these turned pegs and rubber bands which keep the pegs from slipping out of the holes.

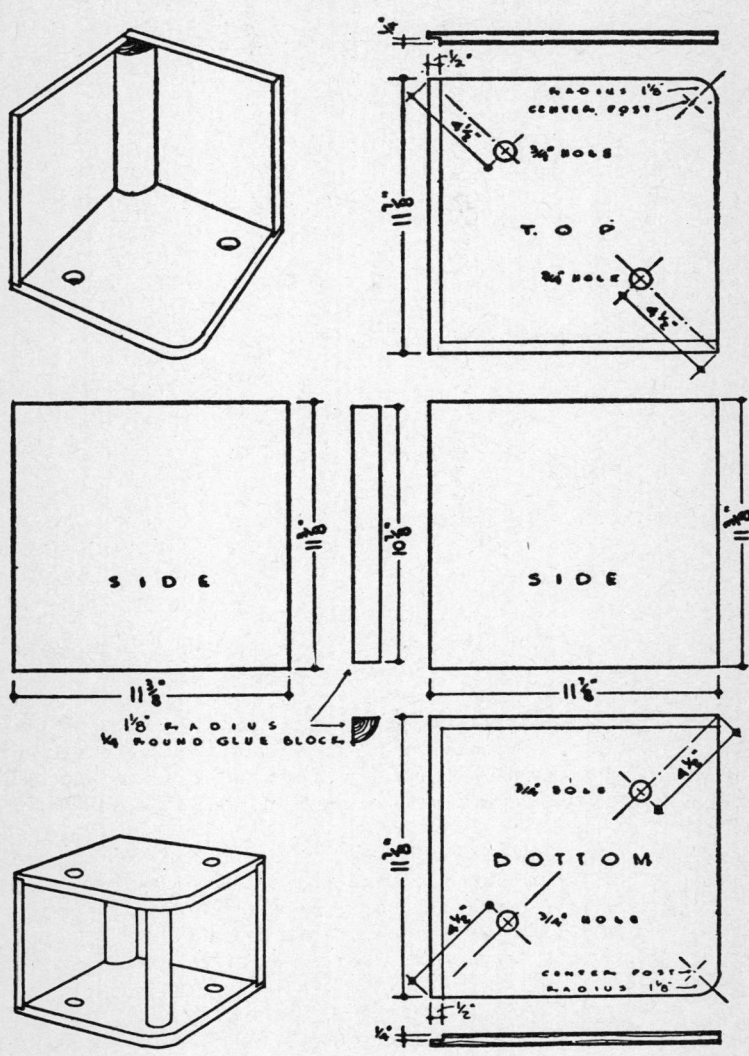

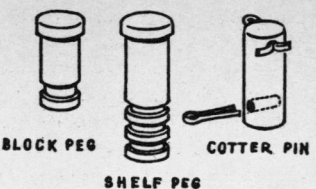

BLOCK PEG   **SHELF PEG**   **COTTER PIN**

The shelf peg is the same peg but made enough longer to accommodate a 3/4-inch shelf between the blocks.

The cotter-pin peg is for the man who has no lathe. He can take ordinary 3/4-inch dowels and drill 1/8-inch holes through them at a distance equal to two thicknesses of the plywood. Use ordinary cotter pins (or even matchsticks) to hold the pegs in place.

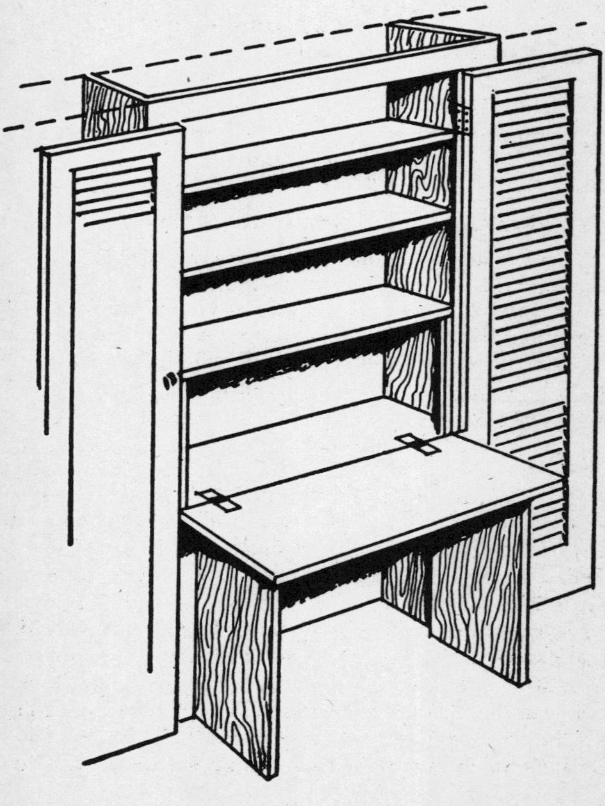

Lock-Blocks can be joined in any combination, limited only by the number of blocks and one's imagination. They can be stood two or three on top of each other and side by side to make cubbyholes; they can be built up two or three high as legs and a board can be run between them for a shelf. Bore holes in the board to join it to the blocks with shelf pegs. Or they can be made up into a semipermanent arrangement for clothes hanging and toy storage such as shown in the first illustration.

Hobby Closet That Does Double Duty as Play Area

When young builders and hobbyists get to work, there is inevitable disorder. As camouflage, Mr. Aronson suggests a pair of jalousie blinds. The work table, of hardboard or hardwood, folds up against the shelves of this unit when not in use, and the supporting doors close beneath. Shelves above and below permit storage of a variety of play materials. This unit makes the greatest use of narrow vertical space.

Three-quarter-inch plywood is used for sides and 1-inch for shelves. The dimensions can vary, of course, according to the space available; and the shelves can be made adjustable.

RECORDS

Primarily Vocal, for Younger Children

The records listed below are only a sampling of all that are available for children today. The ages suggested should be considered as general guides only. Some children will respond to a few of the records at a younger age than suggested; others may need more experience before they are ready for them. All the records will have some appeal for several years beyond the earliest age mentioned. All records are 33⅓ rpm unless otherwise noted.

Starting at Two

Birds, Beasts, Bugs and Little Fishes, Pete Seeger, Folkways 7010
The Carrot Seed, Children's Record Guild 1003 (45 and 78 rpm)
Follow the Sunset, Charity Bailey, Folkways FC 7406
Golden Treasury of Mother Goose and Nursery Songs, Golden LP 12
The Little Brass Band, Young People's Records 703 (45 and 78 rpm)
Mother Goose Songs, Frank Luther, Decca DL 8357
Look at Michie Banjo, Young People's Records 729 (45 and 78 rpm)
Skittery Skattery, Children's Record Guild 1005 (45 and 78 rpm)
Frank Luther Sings Songs of Lois Lenski, Walck WA 1a-1b
Songs to Grow On for Mother and Child, Folkways FC 7015

Train to the Zoo, Children's Record Guild 1001 (45 and 78 rpm)

A Walk in the Forest, Young People's Records 805 (45 and 78 rpm)

Starting at Three

Animal Folk Songs for Children, Peggy Seeger, Folkways 7051

A Child's First Record, Frank Luther, Decca VL 3625

Circus Comes to Town, Young People's Records 713 (45 and 78 rpm)

Eensie Beensie Spider, Children's Record Guild 1002 (45 and 78 rpm)

The Elephant Alphabet, Stanley Holloway, Riverside 1415

Golden Treasury of Train Songs, Golden LP 33

Lullabies for Sleepyheads, Dorothy Olson, Victor CAL 1003

Me, Myself & I, Burl Ives, Children's Record Guild 1007 (78 rpm only)

Men Who Come to Our House, Young People's Records 737 (78 rpm only)

Miss Frances Presents Ding Dong School, Golden LP 49

My Playful Scarf, Norman Rose, Children's Record Guild 1019 (45 and 78 rpm)

Noah's Ark, Oscar Brand and others, Children's Record Guild 1035 (45 and 78 rpm)

Peter Rabbit and Other Great Tales for Growing Boys and Girls, Paul Wing and Glenn Riggs, Victor CAL 1001

Rainy Day, Young People's Records 712 (45 and 78 rpm)

Songs to Grown On, Volume I—Nursery Days, Woody Guthrie, Folkways, FC 7005 or FC 7501

Where Do Songs Begin, Children's Record Guild 5026 (78 rpm only)

Starting at Four

Birds, Beasts, Bugs, and Bigger Fishes, Pete Seeger, Folkways FC 7011

Black Beauty and Other Great Stories, Victor CAL 1007

Children's Concert, Alex Templeton, Riverside 1403

A Child's Introduction to the Alphabet and Numbers, Ireene Wicker, Riverside 1448

Do This, Do That—Activity Record, Children's Record Guild 1040 (45 and 78 rpm)

Everybody Sings, Volume I, Leo Israel, Riverside 1418

Folk Songs for Young Folks, Volumes I and II, Folkways 7021, 7022

Forty-five Songs Children Love, Victor CAL 1038

Frere Jacques, Young People's Records 3402 (78 rpm only)

Great American and Indian Legends, Ireene Wicker, Riverside 1428

Johnny Crow's Garden and Other Stories, Owen Johnson, Weston Woods PBP 106

Let's Help Mommy, Children's Record Guild 1032 (45 or 78 rpm)
Let's Play Together, Young People's Records 4503 (45 or 78 rpm)
Little Indian Drum, David Brooks, Young People's Records 619 (45 or 78 rpm)
Marais and Miranda Revisit the South African Veldt, Decca DL 8811
Music for Children, Carl Orff, Angel 3582 B
My Playmate the Wind, Young People's Records 450 (45 and 78 rpm)
Peter, Tubby, and Pan, Basil Rathbone and Victor Jory, Columbia CL 671
Silly Liesl, Four Nonsense Songs, Children's Record Guild 5011 (45 and 78 rpm)
Sing Along, Burl Ives, Young People's Records 722 (45 and 78 rpm)
Songs for Little Cowboys, Famous Folk Singers, Riverside 1423
Songs for Little Sailors, Famous Folk Singers, Riverside 1424
Songs from the Children's Zoo, Famous Folk Singers, Riverside 1425
Songs of Safety, Frank Luther, Decca VL 3683
When I Grow Up, Burl Ives, Young People's Records 725 (45 and 78 rpm)
When I Was Very Young, Children's Record Guild 1031 (78 rpm only)
Winnie the Pooh Stories, James Stewart, Victor CAL 1008
Yankee Doodle: Let's All Join In, Pete Seeger, Young People's Records 9008 (45 and 78 rpm)

Starting at Five

Adventures in Rhythm, Folkways FL 8273
Bible Stories for Children, Sholem Asch, Folkways FC 7106
Build Me a House, Children's Record Guild 5018 (45 and 78 rpm)
Call and Response: Rhythmic Group Singing, Folkways 7308
Children's Concert, Oscar Brand, Riverside 1438
Child's Introduction to Folk Music, Ed McCurdy, Riverside 1436
Come to the Party: Songs for Special Days, Oscar Brand and others, Children's Record Guild 5032
Danny Kaye for Children, Decca DL 8726
Everyday We Grow-I-O, Young People's Records 8001–2 (45 and 78 rpm)
Favorite Songs from Walt Disney Motion Picture Hits, Golden LP 48
First Songs for Children, Marjorie Bennett, Riverside 1413
Golden Treasury of Christmas Carols and Stories, Golden LP 00004
Hot Cross Buns, Children's Record Guild 5005 (45 and 78 rpm)
Lentil and Three Other Stories, Owen Johnson, Weston Woods PBP 103
Little Pedro, Children's Record Guild 5025 (45 and 78 rpm)

Little Red Wagon, Children's Record Guild 1004 (45 and 78 rpm)
More Songs to Grow On, Alan Mills, Folkways FC 7009
The Mouse and the Frog, Children's Record Guild 5020 (45 and 78 rpm)
Peter and the Wolf, Boris Karloff, Mercury Childcraft CLP 1201
Pete Seeger Children's Concert at Town Hall, Columbia CL 1947
Ride 'Em Cowboy, Children's Record Guild 5001 (45 and 78 rpm)
Rhythms of the World, Folkways FC 7340
Ship Ahoy, Children's Record Guild 5003 (45 and 78 rpm)
Singing in the Kitchen, Young People's Records 730 (78 rpm only)
Songs from Walt Disney's Lady and the Tramp, Decca DL 8462
Strike Up the Band, Children's Record Guild 5027 (45 and 78 rpm)
Wait 'Till the Moon Is Full, Young People's Records 4504 (45 and 78 rpm)
Working on the Railroad, Young People's Records 427 (45 and 78 rpm)

Starting at Six

The Bear That Wasn't, Keenan Wynn, MGM 113
Captain Burl Ives Ark, Decca DL 8587
Chanticleer and the Fox and Other Stories, Owen Johnson, Weston Woods PBP 107
Cinderella, Pinocchio and Other Great Stories for Boys and Girls, Victor CAL 1000
Eagle and Thrush, Children's Record Guild 5024 (45 and 78 rpm)
Everybody Sings, Volume II, Riverside 1419
Folk Songs for Singing and Dancing, Tom Glazer, Young People's Records 8005-6 (45 and 78 rpm)
Grimm's Fairy Tales, Hanky Pank Players, Victor CAL 1037
Happy Wanderer, Obernkircken Children's Choir, Angel 65038
Little Pedro in Brazil, Children's Record Guild 5034 (45 and 78 rpm)
Major Classics for Minors, Whittemore and Lowe, Victor CAL 1016
Mozart Country Dances, Young People's Records (78 rpm only)
Now We Know, Songs to Learn By, Columbia CL 670
The Orchestra, Mitch Miller and others, Golden LP 1
Paul Bunyan and Other Tales, Will Rogers, Jr. and Tom Scott, Riverside 1414
Pedro and the Street Singers, Children's Record Guild 5028 (45 and 78 rpm)
RCA Victor Educational Library: Singing Program, Primary Grades, Victor E 83 (45 and 78 rpm)
Riddle Me This, Children's Record Guild 5015 (45 and 78 rpm)
Songs to Grow On, Volume II—School Days, many artists, Folkways FC 7020
Swing Your Partner, Young People's Records 9002 (45 and 78 rpm)

Starting at Seven

Burl Ives Sings for Fun, Decca DL 8248
Concerto for Toys and Orchestra, Young People's Records 432 (45 and 78 rpm)
Hunters of the Sea: There She Blows, Burl Ives, Young People's Records 9006 (78 rpm only)
Learn Square Dancing, Ed Gilmore, Decca DL 9051
Let's Square Dance (series of five albums), Victor LE 3000–3004
The Little Hero, Young People's Records 9010 (78 rpm only)
Marches in Hi Fi, Fiedler and Boston Pops, Victor LM 2229
Marching Down Broadway, Coldstream Guards, Victor LPM 1944
Pedro in Argentina, Children's Record Guild 5035 (45 and 78 rpm)
Square Dancing Made Easy, Epic LN 3607
Stephen Foster Favorites, Robert Shaw Chorale, Victor LPM 2295
Toy Symphony, Young People's Records 1001 (78 rpm only)

Primarily Vocal, for Younger Children

Story Records

Alice in Wonderland (Selections), Cyril Ritchard, Riverside 2406
Arabian Nights Entertainment, Riverside 1405
Columbus, California Gold Rush, Pony Express, Enrichment Records 102
Daniel Boone, Young People's Records 425 (45 and 78 rpm)
I Can Hear It Now: Volumes I, II, III, and Winston Churchill, Columbia ML 4095, ML 4260, ML 4340, KL 5066
Just So Stories, Boris Karloff, Caedmon 1038 and 1088
Little Match Girl and Other Tales, Boris Karloff, Caedmon 1117
Moby Dick and Treasure Island, Charles Laughton and Thomas Mitchell, Decca DL 9071
The Reluctant Dragon, Boris Karloff, Caedmon 1074
Tales of Hans Christian Andersen, Michael Redgrave, Caedmon 1073
There's Gold in California, Young People's Records 9009 (78 rpm only)
Ugly Duckling and Other Tales, Boris Karloff, Caedmon 1109
Who Built America: American History Through Song, Folkways FC 7402
Young Person's Guide to the Orchestra, Leonard Bernstein, Columbia ML 5768

Folk Music and Tales

American Folk Songs for Children, Pete Seeger, Folkways 7001
Coronation Concert, Burl Ives, Decca DL 8080
Flat Rock Ballads, Carl Sandburg, Columbia ML 5339
Folk Music of Haiti, Folkways FE 4407

Folk Songs of Brazil, Columbia ML 5231
Folk Tales of Indonesia, Folkways FC 7102
Folk Tales of West Africa, Folkways FC 7103
International Songs and Anthems, Norman Luboff, Epic LN 3320
Johnny Horton Makes History, Columbia CL 1478
Music of the Sioux and Navajo, Folkways FE 4401
Pete Seeger Story Songs, Columbia CL 1668
Return of the Wayfaring Stranger, Burl Ives, Columbia CL 1459
Songs of the Auvergne, Susan Reed, Columbia ML 4368
Songs of the Sea, Norman Luboff. Columbia CL 948
Songs of the West, Norman Luboff, Columbia CL 657
Songs of the World, Norman Luboff, Columbia C2L13
Songs to Grow On, Volume III: This Is My Land, Folkways FC 7027
The Wayfaring Stranger, Burl Ives, Columbia CL 628

Instrumental Selections

This list is not presented as a "standard record library"—there is no such thing—but as suggestions for trial. The selections listed have wide appeal for children, especially when accompanied by movement and other kinds of participation.

To supplement your home record collection, look into the possibility of a collection at your local library, or an exchange service at schools, clubs, or community center.

Inasmuch as most of these are standard works, available in numerous recordings, we have in most cases omitted manufacturers' identifications.

Anderson . . .	*Jazz Legato*
	Jazz Pizzicato
Bach	*Air on the G String*
	Little Preludes
Beethoven . .	*Minuet*
	Moonlight Sonata
	Fifth Symphony
	Sixth Symphony (*Pastoral*)
Bizet	*Petite Suite:* "March and Impromptu"
Borodin . . .	*In the Steppes of Central Asia*
	Polovetsian Dances
Brahms	*Little Sandman* (Children's Folk Songs, No. 4)
	Lullaby (Op. 49, No. 4)
	Hungarian Dances (Nos. 5 and 6)
	Waltzes (Nos. 1, 2, and 9)
Chabrier . . .	*España*
Chopin	*Concerto No. 1*
	Minute Waltz
	Polonaises

Copland	. . .	*Rodeo*
Debussy	. . .	*Afternoon of a Faun*
		Children's Corner
Delibes	. . . .	*Coppelia* Ballet Suite
Dukas	. . . .	*The Sorcerer's Apprentice*
Dvorák	. . . .	*New World Symphony*
Foster	. . . .	*De Camptown Races*
		Oh, Susanna
Gershwin	. . .	*American in Paris*
		Porgy and Bess
		Rhapsody in Blue
Gillis	. . . .	*Symphony 5½* (London)
Granger	. . .	*Country Gardens*
Grieg	. . . .	*Concerto in A Minor*
		March of the Dwarfs
		Peer Gynt Suite
Grofé	. . . .	*Grand Canyon* Suite: "On the Trail"
Handel	. . . .	*Hallelujah Chorus*
Haydn	. . . .	*Clock Symphony*
		Surprise Symphony
Herbert	. . .	*Babes in Toyland:* "March of the Toys"
Humperdinck	.	*Hansel and Gretel,* selections
Leoncavallo	. .	*Pagliacci*
Liszt	. . . . .	*Concerto No. 1*
McDonald	. .	*Children's Symphony*
		Wonderful One Hoss Shay (Capitol)
MacDowell	. .	*Visit of the Bear Marionettes* (Op. 38, Nos. 4, 5, 6—"Witch," "Clown," "Villain")
		Woodland Sketches
Mendelssohn	. .	*Bergamask Dance*
		Fairies' March
		Scherzo
		Wedding March
Mozart	. . . .	*Country Dances*
		Don Giovanni, excerpts
		Eine Kleine Nachtmusik
Moussorgsky	. .	*Pictures at an Exhibition*
Orth	. . . .	*In a Clock Store*
Quilter	. . . .	*Children's Overture*
Pierné	. . . .	*March of the Little Lead Soldiers*
Purcell	. . . .	*The Fairy Queen*
Ravel	. . . .	*Bolero*
		Mother Goose Suite
Rébikov	. . .	*The Christmas Tree:* "Dance of the Chinese Dolls," "March of the Gnomes"

Rimsky-Korsakov	*Capriccio Espagnol*
	Le Coq d'Or, selections
	The Flight of the Bumble Bee
Rossini	*William Tell* Overture
Schubert . . .	*Cradlesong*
	Marches Militaires (Op. 51)
	Moments Musicaux (Op. 94)
	Rosamunde Ballet
	Unfinished Symphony
Schumann . . .	*Album for the Young* (Op. 18): "The Wild Horseman" (No. 8), "The Rider's Story" (No. 23)
	Scenes from Childhood (Op. 15): "Traumerei" (No. 7), "Knight of the Hobby Horse" (No. 9)
Sibelius	*Valse Triste*
Sousa	*El Capitan*
	Semper Fidelis
	Stars and Stripes Forever
Strauss	*Artist's Life*
	Blue Danube
	Tales from the Vienna Woods
Stravinsky . . .	*Firebird* Suite
Tchaikovsky . .	*The Nutcracker* Suite
	Piano Concerto, B Flat Minor
	Sleeping Beauty
Von Suppé . . .	*Poet and Peasant* Overture
Wagner . . .	*Die Walküre* (Magic Fire Music)
Weber	*Invitation to the Dance*
Weinberger . .	*Schwanda*, Polka and Fugue

Selected Guides to Children's Records

Recordings for Children: A Selected List, New York Library Association, available through Office of Children's Services, New York Public Library, 20 West 53rd St., New York 19, N. Y.

Records for Your Children and You, Emma Dickson Sheehy, *Parent's Magazine* (monthly feature)

Selected Sources for Children's Records

(Catalogues and lists may be obtained by writing to these companies)

Affiliated Publishers (Golden Library Division), 630 Fifth Ave., New York 20, N. Y.

Children's Record Guild, 100 Avenue of the Americas, New York 13, N. Y.

Columbia Children's Records, catalogue available at local stores

Decca Records, 445 Park Avenue, New York 22, N. Y.

SONG BOOKS 427

Folkways Records, 121 West 47th St., New York 36, N. Y.
Picture Book Parade Records, Weston Woods Studio, Weston, Conn.
R C A Victor, catalogue available at local stores
Young People's Records, Inc., 100 Avenue of the Americas, New York 13, N. Y.

SONG BOOKS

The ages mentioned below are suggested as the earliest at which the books listed after them might be useful. All continue to have appeal for several years, many up to adulthood. Therefore, many books mentioned earlier are also appropriate for Sixes and Sevens.

Starting about Two

A Pre-School Music Book, Angela Dillen and K. S Page, G. Schirmer
Complete Nursery Song Book, Inez Bertail, Lothrop, Lee and Shepard
Music Time: Songs for Children from Two to Seven, Evelyn Hunt, Viking
Songs for the Nursery School, Laura MacCarteney, Willis
The Little Singing Time, Satis N. Coleman and A. Thorn, John Day

Starting about Three

Another Singing Time, Satis N. Coleman and A. Thorn, John Day
At Our House, Lois Lenski and Clyde Robert Bulla, Henry Z. Walck
Favorite Nursery Songs, Phyllis Brown Ohanian, Random House
Golden Song Book, Katherine Wessells, Golden Press
I Went for a Walk, Lois Lenski and Clyde Robert Bulla, Henry Z. Walck
Let's Sing and Play, Dorothy Wiltrout, Children's Press
More Songs to Grow On, Beatrice Landeck, William Sloane Associates—Mark Music Corp.
Sing, Swing, Play, Martha Stockton Russell, Viking
Singing Time, Satis N. Coleman and A. Thorn, John Day
Songs to Grow On, Beatrice Landeck, William Sloane Associates—Mark Music Corp.
Stories That Sing, Ethel Crowinshield, E. C. Schirmer, Boston
The New Singing Time, Satis N. Coleman, John Day
When I Grow Up, Lois Lenski and Clyde Robert Bulla, Henry Z. Walck

Starting about Four

A Cat Came Fiddling, Paul Kapp, Harcourt, Brace & World
Folk Songs of the Four Seasons, Susanna Myers, G. Schirmer

Follow the Music, Lottie E. Coit and Ruth Bampton, Summy-Birchard
Lollipop Songs, Rene G. Varlay, Holt, Rinehart & Winston
Singing America, Augustus Zanzig, Summy-Birchard
Sing It Yourself, Dorothy Gordon, E. P. Dutton
Sing Mother Goose, Opal Wheeler, E. P. Dutton
Songs of Peter Rabbit, Beatrix Potter, Warne
The Best Singing Games for Children of All Ages, Edgar S. Bley, Sterling
The Pooh Song Book, H. Fraser-Simon, E. P. Dutton

Starting about Five

American Folk Songs for Children, Ruth Crawford Seeger, Doubleday
Animal Folk Songs for Children, Ruth Crawford Seeger, Doubleday
Fireside Book of Favorite American Songs, Margaret B. Boni, Simon and Schuster
Singing Games for Children, Alice T. Hamlin, Willis
Singing Time Growing Up, Satis N. Coleman, John Day
Time for Music, Walter Ehret, Prentice-Hall

Starting about Six

Gilbert and Sullivan Song Book, Walter C. Fabell and Malcolm Hyatt, Random House
Sing and Strum, Alice M. Snyder, Mills
Sing in Praise, Opal Wheeler, E. P. Dutton
Sing Together, Girl Scouts of the U. S. A.

SOME REPRODUCTIONS OF PICTURES FOR CHILDREN'S ROOMS

The following list, meant to be suggestive rather than comprehensive, includes reproductions that appeal to a wide range of tastes. Many of them are available in various sizes, from post card up to 30 by 22 inches. Although we list a few sources for convenience, the reader would do well to explore his local art dealers, galleries, museums, and bookshops for additional possibilities. All such sources offer the prints in different sizes and quote different prices. Art dealers and museums usually respond cordially to inquiries concerning price and availability.

The Marboro Bookshops, 131 Varick St., New York 13, N. Y., offer excellent buys on items they have on hand, but they do not maintain a steady stock of prints. They will mail catalogues on request.

The numbers in the right-hand column of our list indicate sure sources for the prints that we list. See end of list for identifications.

Artist	Subject	Source
American Primitive	"American Indian Chieftains"	3
American Primitive	"Baby in the High Chair"	1
Audubon	"Mallard Ducks"	3
Babylonian	"Bull"	3
Babylonian	"Dragon"	3
Bellows	"Dempsey and Firpo"	1
Bellows	"Lady Jean"	3
Bingham	"Fur Traders Descending the Mississippi"	3
Bombois	"Before Entering the (Circus) Ring"	2
Botticelli	"Madonna and Child with Young St. John"	3
Breughel	"The Harvesters"	1
Breughel	"The Peasant Wedding"	3
Breughel	"The Wedding Dance"	3
Breughel	"Winter"	3
Cézanne	"The Blue Vase"	3
Cézanne	"The Card Players"	3
Cézanne	"Pines and Rocks"	3
Chagall	"The Green Violinist"	3
Chagall	"I and the Village"	3
Chardin	"The Young Governess"	3
Chinese	"Magpie on a Flowering Branch"	1
Cobelle	"Paris Street"	3
Currier and Ives	"The Lightning Express Trains"	3
Currier and Ives	"The American National Game of Baseball"	3
Currier and Ives	"Central Park Winter"	3
Currier and Ives	"Clipper Ship Sweepstakes"	3
Curros	"San Francisco Cable Cars" (6 prints)	3
Curros	"American Locomotives" (6 prints)	3
Da Vinci	"Mona Lisa"	3
Davis	"Summer Landscape"	2
De Chirico	"Horses on the Shore"	3
De Chirico	"Wild Horses"	3
Degas	"Dancer on the Stage"	1
Desnoyer	"Winding Wool"	5
Desnoyer	"Devil's Bridge"	5
Dürer	"Rabbit"	3
Dufy	"Chateau and Horses"	3
Dufy	"Flower Picture"	3
Dufy	"Race at Epsom"	3
Dufy	"The Sea at Le Havre"	1
Egyptian	"Owls and Ibis"	1
Fragonard	"The Love Letter"	3
Gauguin	"Landscape of Arles"	5
Gauguin	"Nafea"	3
Gauguin	"Ta Matete"	3

Artist	Subject	Source
Goya	"Don Manuel"	1
Grosz	"Manhattan"	3
Hals	"Laughing Cavalier"	3
Hicks	"The Peaceable Kingdom"	4
Holbein	"Edward VI as Prince of Wales"	4
Homer	"Gulf Stream"	3
Houghtelling	"Alice in Wonderland"	4
Jones	"Fair Ground"	4
Jules	"The Barnyard"	4
Jules	"The Circus"	4
Jules	"Noah's Ark"	4
Jules	"Pandas"	4
Jules	"Penguins"	4
Jules	"Seal and Penguins"	4
Jules	"Three Men in a Tub"	4
King	"Ten P.M."	4
Klee	"Blue Night"	3
Klee	"Propagation for Comics"	3
Klee	"Rocky Landscape"	3
Klee	"Decanter"	3
La Mare	"Children Flying Kites"	4
La Mare	"The Farm"	4
La Mare	"The Cow Jumped over the Moon"	4
Lawrence	"The Calmady Children"	4
Lawrence	"Lord Seaham as a Boy"	4
Lawrence	"Pinkie"	4
Manet	"The Balcony"	3
Manet	"The Fifer"	1
Marc	"The Gazelle"	4
Marc	"The Red Horses"	4
Marin	"Circus Elephants"	4
Matisse	"L'Odalisque"	3
Matisse	"Bouquet"	5
Matisse	"Young Girl in Peasant Blouse"	3
Millet	"The Gleaners"	3
Miro	"Dog Barking at the Moon"	4
Miro	"The Sun"	3
Modigliani	"Girl in Pink"	3
Monet	"Sunflowers"	3
Moses	"Sugaring Off"	5
Opper	"Fire Engine"	3
Orozco	"Zapatistas"	3
Perkins	"Simple Simon"	4
Perkins	"Tom, Tom the Piper's Son"	4
Perkins	"Jack and Jill"	4

REPRODUCTIONS OF PICTURES 431

Artist	Subject	Source
Perkins	"Jack Be Nimble"	4
Perkins	"There Was a Crooked Man"	4
Perkins	"There Was an Old Woman"	4
Persian	"Prince Riding on an Elephant"	1
Picasso	"Boy in Harlequin Jacket"	3
Picasso	"Harlequin à Cheval"	3
Picasso	"Le Gourmet"	4
Picasso	"Child with Dove"	3
Picasso	"Three Musicians"	2
Picasso	"Woman in White"	3
Pickett	"Manchester Valley"	2
Pissarro	"Red Roofs"	3
Pissarro	"Street at Rouen"	3
Portinari	"The Coffee Bearers"	3
Reeve	"Circus"	4
Remington	"The Emigrants"	3
Rembrandt	"The Elephants" (black and white)	3
Renoir	"A Girl with a Watering Can"	4
Renoir	"The Charpentier Children"	4
Renoir	"Child in White"	4
Renoir	"Child in White" (detail, head)	4
Renoir	"Jean Renoir"	4
Renoir	"Margot Berard"	4
Renoir	"Mlle. Lacaux"	4
Renoir	"On the Terrace"	4
Renoir	"Portrait of a Young Girl"	4
Renoir	"Roses"	3
Renoir	"The Small Painter"	4
Renoir	"Woman with a Cat"	4
Renoir	"Woman in a Field"	3
Renoir	"Girl Reading"	3
Reynolds	"The Age of Innocence"	4
Reynolds	"Miss Bowles"	4
Reynolds	"The Infant Samuel"	4
Reynolds	"Lady Betty Hamilton"	4
Reynolds	"Lady Caroline Howard"	4
Rivera	"Flower Seller"	3
Roualt	"Pierrot"	3
Rousseau	"Summer"	3
Rousseau	"The Sleeping Gypsy"	2
Sasseta	"Journey of the Magi"	1
Seurat	"Sunday on the Grande Jatte"	3
Seurat	"Fishing Fleets at Port-En-Bessin"	3
Sisley	"Street at Louveciennes"	3
Sisley	"A Street in Marly"	3

Artist	Subject	Source
Utrillo	"Mont-Cenis Street"	3
Van Gogh	"Bridge at Arles"	1
Van Gogh	"Fields at La Crau"	5
Van Gogh	"Gypsy Camp"	3
Van Gogh	"Regatta at Havre"	5
Van Gogh	"The Starry Night"	3
Van Gogh	"Sunflowers"	3
Velasquez	"Infanta Margarita Teresa"	3
Vlaminck	"Boat Wash-Houses"	5
Vlaminck	"Tugboat"	5
Vlaminck	"Winter Landscape"	3

Identification of Sources

1. Metropolitan Museum of Art, Fifth Ave. and 82 St., New York 28, N. Y.
2. Museum of Modert Art, 11 W. 53 St., New York 19, N. Y.
3. Oestreicher's Prints, Inc., 43 W. 46th St., New York 36, N. Y.
4. Raymond and Raymond, 54 E. 53 St., New York 22, N. Y.
5. Art-Full Picture Frame Co., 856 Cliff St., Pacific Palisades, Calif.

BOOKS FOR YOUNGER CHILDREN

These lists are given to show the kinds of books likely to appeal to a wide range of interests at each of the ages mentioned. There are many good books on the market that, because of space, could not be included here. A list of recommended booklists published by various organizations and books about children's books will be found on page 470. Additional help in selecting books may be found in the folder *Aids to Choosing Books for Your Children* revised annually by The Children's Book Council, Inc., 175 Fifth Ave., New York 10.

The age-grouping is not meant to be restrictive. Many books have appeal for a wide range of ages, and children differ considerably in their rate of readiness for specific books. This accounts for the overlap in the age estimates under which the lists appear. Some ages appear twice, others three times in the age headings. *For a specific child, it is wise to look at all the lists appearing under headings which include the child's age.* For example, if one were looking for books for a five-year-old, some suggestions could be found in the list headed *Three, Four, and Five* and *Four, Five, and Six,* as well as under *Five, Six, and Seven.*

The numbers in parentheses after the titles of some books indicate the latest ages at which they are likely to have strong appeal. Such numbers are used to mark books which hold interest for a wider age-range than is indicated by the heading under which they are listed.

One and Two

Baby Animals, Garth Williams, Golden Press
Baby Farm Animals, Garth Williams, Golden Press
Baby's Friends, Charlotte Steiner, Peggy Cloth Books (Platt and Munk)
Baby's Toys, Platt and Munk
First Things, George B. Adams, Platt and Munk
Kittens, Art Seiden, Grosset and Dunlap
Pat the Bunny, Dorothy Kunhardt, Golden Press
Puppies, Art Seiden, Grosset and Dunlap
"Quack-Quack" Said the Duck, Charlotte Steiner, Peggy Cloth Books, Platt and Munk

Two and Three

Words and Pictures

ABC, Bruno Munari, World Publishing Co.
ABC of Cars and Trucks, Anne Alexander, Doubleday
A Child's Goodnight Book (4), Margaret Wise Brown, William R. Scott
A House for Everyone, Betty Miles, Alfred A. Knopf
A Kiss Is Round, Blossom Budney, Lothrop, Lee & Shepard
Angus and the Cat, Marjorie Flack, Doubleday
Angus and the Ducks, Marjorie Flack, Doubleday
Angus Lost, Marjorie Flack, Doubleday
Animal Friends, Jane Werner, Golden Press
Animals Everywhere (5), Ingri and Edgar Parin d'Aulaire, Doubleday
Another Day, Marie Hall Ets, Viking
Ask Mr. Bear, Marjorie Flack, Macmillan
Baby Animal Friends, Phoebe Erickson, Grosset and Dunlap
Chicken Little Count to Ten (4), Margaret Friskey, Children's Press
Daddies, Lonnie C. Carton, Random House
Davy's Day, Lois Lenski, Henry Z. Walck
Everybody Eats (4), Mary McBurney Green, William R. Scott
Everybody Has a House, Mary McBurney Green, William R. Scott
Goodnight Moon, Margaret Wise Brown, Harper and Row
Green Eyes, A. Birnbaum, Golden Press
I Know a Lot of Things, Ann and Paul Rand, Harcourt, Brace and World
It Is Night, Phyllis Rowand, Harper and Row
Jerry and Ami (5), Anna Kopczynski, Charles Scribner's Sons

My Baby Brother, Patsy Scarry, Golden Press
My Teddy Bear, Patsy Scarry, Golden Press
Off to Bed, Maud and Miska Petersham, Macmillan
Old Mother Hubbard and Her Dog (5), Paul Galdone, Whittlesey House
Papa Small, Lois Lenski, Henry Z. Walck
Plink Plink!, Ethel and Leonard Kessler, Doubleday
Red Light, Green Light (4) Golden McDonald, Doubleday
Sleepy ABC, Margaret Wise Brown, Lothrop, Lee & Shepard
Sleepy Book, Charlotte Zolotow, Lothrop, Lee & Shepard
The Animals of Farmer Jones (4), Rudolph Freund, Golden Press
The Bundle Book (4), Ruth Krauss, Harper and Row
The Friendly Animals (4), Louis Slobodkin, Vanguard
The House That Jack Built (4), Paul Galdone, Whittlesey House
The Little Auto (4), Lois Lenski, Henry Z. Walck
The Little Family, Lois Lenski, Doubleday
The Little Sailboat (4), Lois Lenski, Henry Z. Walck
The Night When Mother Went Away, Charlotte Zolotow, Lothrop, Lee & Shepard
The Old Woman and Her Pig, Paul Galdone, Whittlesey House
The Thank-You Book, Françoise, Charles Scribner's Sons
Three Little Kittens, Masha, Golden Press
Time for Bed, Inez Bertail, Doubleday
Two Little Trains, Margaret Wise Brown, William R. Scott
Wait for William, Marjorie Flack, Houghton Mifflin
What Do They Say?, Grace Skaar, William R. Scott
Where's Andy?, Jane Thayer, William Morrow
Where's My Baby?, H. A. Rey, Houghton Mifflin
Where's the Bunny?, Ruth Carroll, Henry Z. Walck
Wide-Awake Owl, Louis Slobodkin, Macmillan

Rhymes and Verses

Book of Nursery and Mother Goose Rhymes (5), Marguerite De Angeli, ed. and illust., Doubleday
Hey Diddle Diddle, Randolph Caldecott, Frederick Warne
In a Pumpkin Shell (5), Joan Walsh Anglund, Harcourt, Brace and World
Lavender's Blue (5), Katleen Lines, compiler, Franklin Watts
Mother Goose (5), Hilary Knight, Golden Press
Mother Goose (5), Pelagie Doane, Random House
Sung Under the Silver Umbrella (6), Association for Childhood Education, Macmillan
The Tall Book of Mother Goose (4), Feodor Rojankovsky, Harper and Row
The Tenggren Mother Goose, Gustav Tenggren, Little, Brown
Very Young Verses (6), B. P. Geisiner and A. B. Suter, Houghton Mifflin

Collections

Favorite Stories Old and New (6), Sidonie Gruenberg, Doubleday
Here and Now Story Book (6), Lucy Sprague Mitchell, E. P. Dutton
Another Here and Now Story Book (6), Lucy Sprague Mitchell, E. P. Dutton
Let's Read a Story (6), Sidonie Gruenberg, Doubleday
Read-to-Me Storybook (6), Child Study Association, compiler, Thomas Y. Crowell
Read Me Another Story (6), Child Study Association, compiler, Thomas Y. Crowell
Read Me More Stories (6), Child Study Association, compiler Thomas Y. Crowell
Told Under the Blue Umbrella (6), Association for Childhood Education, Macmillan

Three, Four, and Five

Pictures and Stories, Imaginative and Factual

A Hole Is to Dig, Ruth Krauss, Harper & Row
A Is for Annabelle, Tasha Tudor, Henry Z. Walck
A Little House of Your Own, Beatrice S. de Regniers, Harcourt, Brace and World
Baby Elephant's Trunk, Sesyle Joslin, Harcourt, Brace and World
Bedtime for Frances, Russell Hoban, Harper and Row
Brave Baby Elephant, Sesyle Joslin, Harcourt, Brace and World
Caps for Sale (6), Esphyr Slobodkina, William R. Scott
Cathy Is Company, Joan Lexau, Dial
Choo-Choo (6), Virginia Lee Burton, Houghton Mifflin
Come for a Walk With Me, Mary Chalmers, Harper and Row
Cowboy Small, Lois Lenski, Henry Z. Walck
Do You Want to Hear a Secret? Sylvia Berger Redman, Lothrop, Lee & Shepard
Herbert the Lion (6), Clare Turlay Newberry, Harper and Row
Hundreds and Hundreds of Pancakes, Audrey Chalmers, Viking
I Like Winter, Lois Lenski, Henry Z. Walck
I'm Tired of Lions, Zhenya Gay, Viking
Karen's Opposites, Alice and Martin Provensen, Golden Press
Kiki Goes to Camp, Charlotte Steiner, Doubleday
Kiki Loves Music, Charlotte Steiner, Doubleday
Kiki's Playhouse, Charlotte Steiner, Doubleday
Kim and Me, Ethel and Leonard Kessler, Doubleday
Let's Be Enemies, Janice May Udry, Harper and Row
Little Frightened Tiger, Phyllis Krasilovsky, Doubleday
Little Lamb, Dahris Martin, Harper and Row
Lost and Found (6), Kathryn Hitte, Abingdon
Marshmallow (6), Clare Turlay Newberry, Harper and Row
Mrs. Tiggy Winkle (6), Beatrix Potter, Frederick Warne

My Red Umbrella, Robert Bright, William Morrow
On a Summer Day, Lois Lenski, Henry Z. Walck
Papa Small, Lois Lenski, Henry Z. Walck
Picture Book of Animal Babies (6), W. W. and Irene Robinson, Macmillan
Play With Me, Marie Hall Ets, Viking
SHHhhh . . . bang, Margaret Wise Brown, Harper and Row
Sing Sang Sung and Willie, Peggy Gulick, Alfred A. Knopf
Snipp, Snapp, Snurr, and the Gingerbread (6), Maj Lindman, Whitman
Snipp, Snapp, Snurr, and the Red Shoes (6), Maj Lindman, Whitman
Thank You—You're Welcome (7), Louis Slobodkin, Vanguard
The ABC Bunny, Wanda Gág, Coward-McCann
The Baby House, Norma Simon, J. B. Lippincott
The Boats on the River (6), Marjorie Flack, Viking
The Box With Red Wheels, Maud and Miska Petersham, Macmillan
The Dragon in the Clock Box, M. Jean Craig, W. W. Norton
The Four Riders, Charlotte Krum, Follett Publishing Co.
The Great Big Animal Book, Feodor Rojankovsky, Golden Press
The Little Airplane (6), Lois Lenski, Henry Z. Walck
The Little Farm (6), Lois Lenski, Henry Z. Walck
The Little Fire Engine (6), Lois Lenski, Henry Z. Walck
The Little Fireman, Margaret Wise Brown, William R. Scott
The Little Fisherman (6), Margaret Wise Brown, William R. Scott
The Little Train (6), Lois Lenski, Henry Z. Walck
The Quiet Noisy Book, Margaret Wise Brown, Harper and Row
The Runaway Bunny, Margaret Wise Brown, Harper and Row
The Seashore Noisy Book, Margaret Wise Brown, Harper and Row
The Smart Little Boy and His Smart Little Kitty, Louise Woodcock, William R. Scott
The Snowy Day, Ezra Jack Keats, Viking
The Story About Ping, Kurt Wiese, Viking
The Summer Noisy Book, Margaret Wise Brown, Harper and Row
The Tale of Jemima Puddleduck (6), Beatrix Potter, Frederick Warne
The Tale of Peter Rabbit (6), Beatrix Potter, Frederick Warne
The Tale of Squirrel Nutkin (6), Beatrix Potter, Frederick Warne
The Very Little Girl (6), Phyllis Krasilovsky, Doubleday
The Wet World, Norma Simon, J. B. Lippincott
The Winter Noisy Book, Margaret Wise Brown, Harper and Row
Timid Timothy, Gweneira Williams, William R. Scott
Twin Kids, Inez Hogan, E. P. Dutton
Umbrella, Taro Yashima, Viking
Willie's Adventures, Margaret Wise Brown, William R. Scott

Rhymes and Verses

Johnny Crow's Garden (6), Leslie Brooke, Frederick Warne
Johnny Crow's New Garden, Leslie Brooke, Frederick Warne
Johnny Crow's Party, Leslie Brooke, Frederick Warne
Poems to Read to the Very Young, selected by Josette Frank, Random House
Real Mother Goose (5), Blanche Fisher Wright, Rand McNally
Ring O' Roses, Leslie Brooke, Frederick Warne
Silver Pennies (6), Blanche Thompson, Macmillan
Sing Song (6), Christina Rossetti, Macmillan
Sparkle and Spin, Ann and Paul Rand, Harcourt, Brace and World
The Golden Flute (6), A. Hubbard and A. Babbitt, John Day
The Night Before Christmas (all ages), Clement C. Moore, Golden Press

Mostly Information—Science and Nature

Animal Babies, Ylla, Harper and Row
Barnyard Family, Dorothy Hogner, Henry Z. Walck
Fast Is a Ladybug, Miriam Schlein, William R. Scott
How Do You Travel?, Miriam Schlein, Abingdon
Over in the Meadow, John Langstaff and Feodor Rojankovsky, Harcourt, Brace & World
The Day We Saw the Sun Come Up (6), Alice E. Goudey, Charles Scribner's Sons
The Growing Story, Ruth Krauss, Harper and Row
The Listening Walk (7), Paul Showers and Aliki, Thomas Y. Crowell
The Sun—Our Nearest Star (7), Franklyn M. Branley, Thomas Y. Crowell
The Whirley Bird, Dimitri Varley, Alfred A. Knopf
Where Does Everyone Go?, Aileen Fisher, Thomas Y. Crowell

People and Their Works

Airplanes, Ruth M. Lachman, Golden Press
Daddies: What They Do All Day, Helen Walker Puner, Lothrop, Lee & Shepard
Davy Goes Places, Lois Lenski, Henry Z. Walck
I Like Animals, Dahlov Ipcar, Alfred A. Knopf
Policeman Small, Lois Lenski, Henry Z. Walck

Four, Five, and Six

Pictures and Stories

Anatole, Eve Titus, Whittlesey House
All About Dogs, Dogs, Dogs, Grace Skaar, William R. Scott
Another Day, Marie Hall Ets, Viking
April's Kittens, Clare Turlay Newberry, Harper and Row

Blueberries for Sal, Robert McCloskey, Viking
Bluebonnets for Lucinda, Frances Clarke Sayers, Viking
Brown Cow Farm, Dahlov Ipcar, Doubleday
Brownie's Hush, Gladys C. Adshead, Henry Z. Walck
Cheerful, Pamela Brown, Harper and Row
Curious George Rides a Bike, H. A. Rey, Houghton Mifflin
Down, Down the Mountain, Ellis Credle, Thomas Nelson
Father Bear Comes Home, Else Minerik, Harper and Row
Georgie's Pets, Marion Conger, Abingdon
Going Barefoot, Aileen Fisher, Thomas Y. Crowell
Grandmother and I, Helen E. Buckley, Lothrop, Lee & Shepard
Gwendolyn, the Miracle Hen, Nancy Sherman, Golden Press
Harold and the Purple Crayon, Crockett Johnson, Harper and Row
Harry, the Dirty Dog, Gene Zion and Margaret Bloy Graham, Harper and Row
Hide and Seek Day, Gene Zion, Harper and Row
Hurry! Hurry!, Edith Thacker Hurd, Harper and Row
I Had a Penny, Audrey Chalmers, Viking
"I Can't Said the Ant," Polly Cameron, Coward-McCann
In the Forest, Marie Hall Ets, Viking
Inch by Inch (7), Leo Lionni, Obolensky
Jeanne-Marie Counts Her Sheep, Françoise, Charles Scribner's Sons
Katy and the Big Snow, Virginia Lee Burton, Houghton Mifflin
Little Angela and Her Puppy, Dorothy Marino, J. B. Lippincott
Little Boy Brown, Isabel Harris, J. B. Lippincott
Little Bear (7), Else Minerik, Harper and Row
Little Bear's Friend (7), Else Minerik, Harper and Row
Little Bear's Visit, Else Minerik, Harper and Row
Little Lost Lamb, Golden MacDonald, Doubleday
Little Tim and the Brave Sea Captain, Edward Ardizzone, Henry Z. Walck
Little Toot, Hardy Gramatky, G. P. Putnam
Little Wild Horse, Hetty B. Beatty, Houghton Mifflin
Love Is a Special Way of Feeling, Joan Walsh Anglund, Harcourt, Brace and World
Lucky Pierre, Lorraine and Jerrold Beim, Harcourt, Brace and World
Magic Michael, Louis Slobodkin, Doubleday
Mike Mulligan and His Steam Shovel (7), Virginia Lee Burton, Houghton Mifflin
Millions of Cats, Wanda Gág, Coward-McCann
Mr. Rabbit and the Lovely Present, Charlotte Zolotow, Harper and Row
Moy Moy, Leo Politi, Charles Scribner's Sons
900 Buckets of Paint, Edna Becker, Abingdon
Nothing But Cats, Cats, Cats, Grace Skaar, William R. Scott

One Is the Engine, Esther K. Meeks, Follett Publishing Co.
One Snail and Me: A Book of Numbers and Animals and a Bathtub, Emilie McLeod, Little, Brown
Peter Churchmouse (8), Margot Austin, E. P. Dutton
Peter Goes to School, Wanda Rogers, Wonder Books
Peter's Long Walk, Lee Kingsman, Doubleday
Pumpkin Moonshine, Tasha Tudor, Henry Z. Walck
Snippy and Snappy, Wanda Gág, Coward-McCann
Song of the Swallows (7), Leo Politi, Charles Scribner's Sons
Speedy, the Hook and Ladder Truck, Edith Thacker Hurd, William R. Scott
Springtime for Jeanne-Marie, Françoise, Charles Scribner's Sons
Stephen's Train, Margaret G. Otto, Holt, Rinehart and Winston
T-Bone the Baby Sitter, Clare Turlay Newberry, Harper & Row
Ted and Nina Go to the Grocery Store, Marguerite De Angeli, Doubleday
The Backward Day, Ruth Krauss, Harper and Row
The Baron's Booty, Virginia Kahl, Charles Scribner's Sons
The Big Snow, Berta and Elmer Hader, Macmillan
The Birthday, Hans Fisher, Harcourt, Brace and World
The Buttons Go Walking, Edward W. Mammen, Harper and Row
The Camel Who Took a Walk, Jack Tworkov, E. P. Dutton
The Country Bunny, DuBose Heyward, Houghton Mifflin
The Cow Who Fell in the Canal, Phyllis Krasilovsky, Doubleday
The Duchess Bakes a Cake, Virginia Kahl, Charles Scribner's Sons
The Fox Went Out on a Chilly Night, Peter Spier, Doubleday
The Funny Thing, Wanda Gág, Coward-McCann
The Great Big Wild Animal Book, Feodor Rojankovsky, Golden Press
The King's Procession, James and Ruth McCrea, Atheneum
The Little Engine That Could, Mabel Bragg, Platt and Munk
The Little Fir Tree (8), Margaret Wise Brown, Thomas Y. Crowell
The Little Island, Golden MacDonald, Doubleday
The Little Stone House, Berta and Elmer Hader, Macmillan
The Little Town, Berta and Elmer Hader, Macmillan
The Real Hole, Beverly Cleary, William Morrow
The School Bus Picnic, Aaron Fine, Holt, Rinehart & Winston
The Secret Hiding Place, Rainey Bennett, World Publishing Co.
The Story of Ferdinand (10), Munro Leaf, Viking
The Three Pigs, William Pène du Bois, Viking
Thistly B, Tasha Tudor, Henry Z. Walck
Three Little Horses, Piet Worm, Random House
Timothy Turtle, Al Graham, Viking
Tobias and His Red Satchel, Sunny B. Warner, Alfred A. Knopf
When It Rained Cats and Dogs, Nancy Byrd Turner, J. B. Lippincott

Mostly Information

> *Do You Hear What I Hear?*, Helen Borten, Abelard-Schuman
> *How Big Is Big?*, Herman and Nina Schneider, William R. Scott
> *Let's Go Outdoors*, Harriet E. Huntington, Doubleday
> *Manners for Moppets*, Betty Betz, Grosset and Dunlap
> *The Shadow Book*, Beatrice S. de Regniers, Harcourt, Brace and World
> *Telltime the Rabbit*, William Hall, Thomas Y. Crowell
> *What Do You Do, Dear?* (8), Seslye Joslin, William R. Scott
> *What Do You Say, Dear?* (8), Seslye Joslin, William R. Scott
> *We Like Bugs*, Gladys Conklin, Holiday House
> *Wild Folk in the Woods* (10), Carroll Lane Fenton, John Day
> *Will Spring Be Early? Or Will Spring Be Late?*, Crockett Johnson, Thomas Y. Crowell

Poetry and Rhymes

> *A Child's Garden of Verses*, Robert Louis Stevenson, Henry Z. Walck
> *A Rocket in My Pocket*, Carl Withers, Holt, Rinehart and Winston
> *All Around the Town*, Phyllis McGinley, J. B. Lippincott
> *Counting Out*, Carl Withers, Henry Z. Walck
> *Hailstones and Halibut Bones* (8), Mary O'Neill, Doubleday
> *The Owl and the Pussy-Cat* (7), Edward Lear, Doubleday
> *When We Were Very Young*, A. A. Milne, E. P. Dutton

Collections and Short Stories

> *My Brimful Book*, Dana Bruce, Platt and Munk
> *Old, Old Tales Retold* (8), Frederick Richardson, M. A. Donohue
> *Read Me More Stories*, Child Study Association, etc., Thomas Y. Crowell
> *Story and Verse for Children*, Miriam Blanton Huber, Macmillan
> *Tall Book of Nursery Tales* (7), Feodor Rojankovsky, Harper and Row
> *The Poppy Seed Cakes*, Margery Clark, Doubleday
> *Told under the Green Umbrella* (8), Association for Childhood Education, Macmillan

Fun and Riddles

> *Book of Riddles*, Bennett Cerf, Random House
> *How to Make an Earthquake*, Ruth Krauss, Harper and Row

Five, Six, and Seven

Stories and Entertainment

> *A for the Ark*, Roger Duvoisin, Lothrop, Lee & Shepard
> *A Pair of Red Clogs*, Masako Matsuno, World Publishing Co.
> *All Ready for Winter*, Leone Adelson, David McKay

BOOKS FOR YOUNGER CHILDREN

Animal Babies, Alice Day Pratt, The Beacon Press
Apple Pie for Lewis, Helen Kay, E. P. Dutton
Circus Surprise, Winifred Bromhall, Alfred A. Knopf
Dear Garbage Man, Gene Zion, Harper and Row
Don't Frighten the Lion, Margaret Wise Brown, Harper and Row
Droopy (8), Hetty B. Beatty, Houghton Mifflin
Easter Treat, Roger Duvoisin, Alfred A. Knopf
Emmett's Pig, Mary Stolz, Harper and Row
Finders Keepers, Will and Nicolas, Harcourt, Brace and World
Follow the Road, Alvin Tresselt, Lothrop, Lee & Shepard
Frog Went A'Courtin', John Langstaff and Feodor Rojankovsky, Harcourt, Brace and World
"Hi, Mister Robin," Alvin Tresselt, Lothrop, Lee & Shepard
Horton Hears a Who!, Dr. Seuss, Random House
How to Read a Rabbit, Jean Fritz, Coward-McCann
Hurray for Bobo, Joan Savage, Children's Press
I Can Fly, Ruth Krauss, Golden Press
If I Ran the Zoo, Dr. Seuss, Random House
Journey Cake Ho!, Ruth Sawyer, Viking
Katy and the Big Snow, Virginia Lee Burton, Houghton Mifflin
Little Black Ant (8), Alice Gall and Fleming Crew, Henry Z. Walck
Little Pig Robinson, Beatrix Potter, Frederick Warne
Madeleine, Ludwig Bemelmans, Viking
Madeleine's Rescue, Ludwig Bemelmans, Viking
Middle Matilda, Winifred Bromhall, Alfred A. Knopf
Mike's House, Julia L. Sauer, Viking
Miss Flora McFlimsey and the Little Red Schoolhouse, Mariana, Lothrop, Lee & Shepard
Monkey See, Monkey Do, Inez Hogan, E. P. Dutton
My Dog Is Lost, Ezra Jack Keats and Pat Cherr, Thomas Y. Crowell
Nappy Has a New Friend, Inez Hogan, E. P. Dutton
Nibble, Nibble Mouseskin: A Tale of Hansel and Gretel, Joan Walsh Anglund, Harcourt, Brace and World
Noel for Jeanne-Marie, Françoise, Charles Scribner's Sons
Nine Days to Christmas, Marie Hall Ets, Viking
One Horse Farm, Dahlov Ipcar, Doubleday
One Kitten Too Many, Bianca Bradbury, Houghton Mifflin
One Morning in Maine, Robert McClosky, Viking
Olaf Reads, Joan Lexau, Dial
Otto at Sea, William Pène du Bois, Viking
Otto in Africa, William Pène du Bois, Viking
Otto in Texas, William Pène du Bois, Viking
Piccolo, Bettina, Harper & Row
Rabbitt Hill (10), Robert Lawson, Viking
Ringtail, Alice Gall and Fleming Crew, Henry Z. Walck
Ronnie's Wish, Jeannette P. Brown, Friendship Press

Rosa-Too-Little, Sue Felt, Doubleday
Sam's First Fish, Leonard Shortall, William Morrow
Saturday Walk, Ethel Wright, William R. Scott
Smallest Boy in the Class, Jerrold Beim, William Morrow
Squirrely of Willow Hill, Berta and Elmer Hader, Macmillan
Stone Soup, Marcia Brown, Charles Scribner's Sons
Ten Big Farms, Dahlov Ipcar, Alfred A. Knopf
The Animal Train, Catherine Wooley, William Morrow
The Bear on the Motorcycle, Reiner Zimnik, Atheneum
The Biggest Bear, Lynd Ward, Houghton Mifflin
The Christmas Bunny, Will and Nicolas, Harcourt, Brace and World
The Color Kittens, Margaret Wise Brown, Golden Press
The Five Chinese Brothers, Claire H. Bishop and Kurt Wiese, Coward-McCann
The Good Rain, Alice E. Goudey, E. P. Dutton
The Happy Lion, Louise Fatio, Whittlesey House
The Little House (10), Virginia Lee Burton, Houghton Mifflin
The Little Red Lighthouse and the Great Grey Bridge, Hildegarde H. Swift, Harcourt, Brace and World
The Lollypop Factory, Mary Elting, Doubleday
The Loudest Noise in the World, Benjamin Elkin, Viking
The Plant Sitter, Gene Zion, Harper and Row
The Shoemaker and the Elves, Adrienne Adams, Charles Scribner's Sons
The Story of Babar, Jean de Brunhoff, Random House
The Twelve O'Clock Whistle, Jerrold Beim, William Morrow
Three Little Horses, Piet Worm, Random House
Tommy and Dee-Dee, Yen Liang, Henry Z. Walck
Too Many Bozos, Lilian Moore, Golden Press
Tough Enough, Ruth and Latrobe Carroll, Henry Z. Walck
Two Is a Team, Lorraine and Jerrold Beim, Harcourt, Brace and World
Two Little Bears, Ylla, Harper and Row
Wagtail (8), Alice Gall and Fleming Crew, Henry Z. Walck
Wheel on the Chimney, Margaret Wise Brown, Lippincott
While Susie Sleeps, Nina Schneider, William R. Scott
White Snow, Bright Snow (9), Alvin Tresselt, Lothrop, Lee & Shephard
William's Shadow, Margot Austin, E. P. Dutton
Willie's Adventures, Margaret Wise Brown, William R. Scott

Mainly Information
Animals

Odd Pets (9), Lilo Hess and Dorothy Hognar, Thomas Y. Crowell
The Big Book of Animals Every Child Should Know (8), Dena Humphreys, Grosset & Dunlap

BOOKS FOR YOUNGER CHILDREN

The First Book of Cats, Gladys Taber, Franklin Watts
The First Book of Dogs, Gladys Taber, Franklin Watts
The More the Merrier, Fleming Crew, Henry Z. Walck
The True Book of Farm Animals, John Lewellen, Children's Press
The True Book of Pets, Illa Podendorf, Children's Press

Science and Nature

A Book of Moon Rockets for You, Franklyn Branley, Thomas Y. Crowell
A Book of Satellites for You, Franklyn Branley, Thomas Y. Crowell
A Tree Is a Plant, Clyde Robert Bulla, Thomas Y. Crowell
All Around You, Jeanne Bendick, Whittlesey House
All Kinds of Time, Harry Behn, Harcourt, Brace and World
Catch a Cricket, Carla Stevens, William R. Scott
Farther and Faster (8), John G. McCullough and Leonard Kessler, Thomas Y. Crowell
Follow the Wind (9), Alvin Tresselt, Lothrop, Lee & Shepard
Houses from the Sea, Alice E. Goudey, Charles Scribner's Sons
How a Seed Grows, Helene J. Jordan, Thomas Y. Crowell
I Know a Magic House, Julius Schwartz, Whittlesey House
Let's Go to the Seashore, Harriet E. Huntington, Doubleday
Plenty of Fish, Millicent Selsam, Harper and Row
Rain Drop Splash (8), Alvin Tresselt, Lothrop, Lee & Shepard
Seeds by Wind and Water, Helene J. Jordan, Thomas Y. Crowell
Sun Up (9), Alvin Tresselt, Lothrop, Lee & Shepard
The Storm Book, Charlotte Zolotow, Harper and Row
The True Book of Air Around Us (8), Margaret Friskey, Children's Press
The True Book of Pebbles and Shells, Illa Podendorf, Children's Press
The Wonderful Egg, G. Warren Schloat, Charles Scribner's Sons
The Wonderful Story of How You Were Born (8), Sidonie Master Gruenberg, Doubleday
Up Above and Down Below, Irma E. Webster, William R. Scott
What's Inside of Plants (10), Herbert S. Zim, William Morrow
When I Go to the Moon, Claudia Lewis, Macmillan

People and Their Work

Cowboy on the Ranch, Louise L. Floethe, Charles Scribner's Sons
The True Book of Little Eskimos, Donalda Copeland, Children's Press
Wake Up City!, Alvin Tresselt, Lothrop, Lee & Shepard
We Are a Family (8), Inez Hogan, E. P. Dutton

Poetry and Rhymes

All Together, Dorothy Aldis, G. P. Putnam
I Went to the Animal Fair, William Cole, World Publishing Co.

Nibble, Nibble, Margaret Wise Brown, William R. Scott
Now We Are Six, A. A. Milne, E. P. Dutton
The House at Pooh Corner, A. A. Milne, E. P. Dutton
The Rooster Crows, Maud and Misha Peterson, Macmillan
Very Young Verses, Barbara Geismer and Antoinette Brown Suter, eds., Houghton Mifflin
Winnie the Pooh, A. A. Milne, E. P. Dutton

Collections and Fairy Tales

Just So Stories (8), Rudyard Kipling, Garden City
Tales from Grimm, Wanda Gág, Coward-McCann

Things to Do

Kitchen Table Fun: Things to Make from the Kitchen Cupboard (9), Avery Nagle and Joseph Lemming, J. B. Lippincott

Six, Seven, and Eight

Stories and Entertainment

A Bear Called Paddington, Michael Bond, Houghton Mifflin
A Bell for Ursli, Selina Chönz, Henry Z. Walck
A Boat for Pepe, Leo Politi, Charles Scribner's Sons
Andy and the Lion, James Dougherty, Viking
Bouncing Betsy, Dorothy P. Lothrop, Macmillan
Boy at Bat, Marion Renick, Charles Scribner's Sons
Chanticleer and the Fox, Barbara Cooney, Thomas Y. Crowell
Cinderella (12), Marcia Brown, Charles Scribner's Sons
Circus Ruckus, Will and Nicolas, Harcourt, Brace and World
Crackerjack Halfback (9), Matt Christopher, Little, Brown
Crow Boy, Taro Yashima, Viking
Dusty and His Friends, Irma Simonton Black, Holiday House
Elephant Herd, Miriam Schlein, William R. Scott
Five Hundred Hats of Bartholomew Cubbins, Dr. Seuss, Vanguard
Flat Tail, Alice Gall and Fleming Crew, Henry Z. Walck
Florina and the Wild Bird, Alois Carigiet, Henry Z. Walck
Ginger Pye, Eleanor Estes, Harcourt, Brace and World
Golden Goose Book, L. Leslie Brooke, Frederick Warne
Grandpa's Farm, Helen and Melvin Martinson, Children's Press
Great-Grandfather and the Honey Tree, Sam and Zoa Swayne, Viking
Gypsy, Kate Seredy, Viking
Honeybee (9), Mary Adrian, Holiday House
Honker Visits the Island, Doris V. Foster, Lothrop, Lee & Shepard
Jenny's Adopted Brothers, Esther Averill, Harper and Row
Little Pear, the Story of a Little Chinese Boy, Eleanor Lattimore, Harcourt, Brace and World
Little Wild Horse, Hetty B. Beatty, Houghton Mifflin

BOOKS FOR YOUNGER CHILDREN

Looking-for-Something, Ann Nolan Clark, Viking
Make Way for Ducklings, Robert McCloskey, Viking
Maybelle, the Cable Car, Virginia Lee Burton, Houghton Mifflin
Mei Li, Thomas Handforth, Doubleday
Mr. Penny, Marie Hall Ets, Viking
Mr. Popper's Penguins, Richard and Florence Atwater, Little, Brown
Mrs. Cockle's Cat, Philippa Pearce, J. B. Lippincott
Mouse House, Rumer Godden, Viking
Nezbah's Lamb, Edith J. Agnew, Friendship Press
Nobody Listens to Andrew, Elizabeth Guilfoile, Follett Publishing Co.
Once a Mouse . . . , Marcia Brown, Charles Scribner's Sons
Over the Hills to Ballybog, Mabel Watts, E. P. Dutton
Patrick and the Golden Slippers, Katherine Milhous, Charles Scribner's Sons
Pelle's New Suit, Elsa Beskow, Harper and Row
Peter Pan (all ages), J. M. Barrie, Charles Scribner's Sons
Peter Pan and Wendy (all ages), James M. Barrie, Charles Scribner's Sons
Pumpkin, Ginger and Spice, Margaret G. Otto, Holt, Rinehart and Winston
Ruby Throat: The Story of a Humming Bird (9), Robert M. McClung, William Morrow
Skipper John's Cook, Marcia Brown, Charles Scribner's Sons
Spike (9), Robert M. McClung, William Morrow
Tale of the Terrible Tiger, Marion Renick, Charles Scribner's Sons
Taro and Tofu, Masako Matsuno, World Publishing Co.
The Bears on Hemlock Mountain, Alice Dalgliesh, Charles Scribner's Sons
The Best-Loved Doll, Rebecca Caudill, Holt, Rinehart and Winston
The Blind Men and the Elephant, Lillian Quigley, Charles Scribner's Sons
The Blue-Eyed Pussy, Egan Mathieson, Doubleday
The Cat Club, Esther Averill, Harper and Row
The Cat in the Hat, Dr. Seuss, Random House
The Crooked Colt, C. W. Anderson, Macmillan
The Doll's House, Rumer Godden, Viking
The Golden Touch (9), Nathaniel Hawthorne, Whittlesey House
The Restless Robin, Marjorie Flack, Houghton Mifflin
The Story of Serapina, Anne H. White, Viking
The Taming of Toby, Jerrold Beim, William Morrow
The Tin Fiddle, Edward Tripp, Henry Z. Walck
The Velveteen Rabbit, Margarie Bianco, Doubleday
The Wild Little Honker, Dorothy Hogner, Henry Z. Walck
The Willow in the Attic, Dana Faralla, J. B. Lippincott

The Wizard of Oz (10), L. Frank Baum, Reilly and Lee
The Wonderful Farm, Marcel Aymé, Harper and Row
Three Boys and Space, Nan H. Agle and Ellen Wilson, Charles Scribner's Sons
Thumbelina, Hans Christian Andersen, Charles Scribner's Sons
Tim in Danger, Edward Ardizzone, Henry Z. Walck
Tobe (10), Stella Gantry Sharpe, University of North Carolina Press
Toby: A Curious Cat, Irma Simonton Black, Holiday House
Walter, the Lazy Mouse, Marjorie Flack, Doubleday
When Jenny Lost Her Scarf, Esther Averill, Harper and Row
Who Goes There?, Dorothy P. Lothrop, Macmillan
Wish on the Moon, Berta and Elmer Hader, Macmillan
Wonderful Things (9), Zhenya Gay, Viking

Information

Science and Nature

Bits That Grow Big (10), Irma F. Webster, William R. Scott
Come to the Farm, Ruth M. Tensen, Reilly and Lee
Discovering Dinosaurs, Glenn O. Blough, Whittlesey House
Egg to Chick, Millicent E. Selsam, International Publishers
I Saw the Sea Come In, Alvin Tresselt, Lothrop, Lee & Shepard
Let's Go to the Brook (9), Harriet E. Huntington, Doubleday
Milk for You, G. Warren Schloat, Jr., Charles Scribner's Sons
The Green Thumb Story, Jean Fiedler, Holiday House
The Tall Grass Zoo, Winifred and Cecil Lubell, Rand McNally
Wait for the Sunshine (9), Glenn D. Blough, Whittlesey House
What's Inside of Me? (10), Herbert S. Zim, William Morrow
What's Inside the Earth? (9), Herbert S. Zim, William Morrow
Your Wonderful Teeth (9), G. Warren Schloat, Jr., Charles Scribner's Sons

Animals

Come to the Zoo, Ruth M. Tensen, Reilly and Lee
Goldfish (9), Herbert S. Zim, William Morrow
Owls, Herbert S. Zim, William Morrow
The First Book of Horses, Isabel McLennan McMeekin, Franklin Watts

People and Their Works

Getting to Know Korea, Regina Tor, Coward-McCann
In My Mother's House, Ann Nolan Clark, Viking
Let's Look Under the City, Herman and Nina Schneider, William R. Scott
Plenty to Watch, Mitsu and Taro Yashima, Viking
The Big Book of the Wild West (10), Sydney E. Fletcher, Grosset & Dunlap

The Big Treasure Book of Clowns (all ages), Felix Sutton, Grosset & Dunlap
Things Around the House (10), Herbert S. Zim, William Morrow
Your Breakfast and the People Who Made It (9), Benjamin C. Gruenberg and Leone Adelson, Doubleday
Paul Revere's Ride, Henry Longfellow, Thomas Y. Crowell
Song of the Seasons (9), Addison Webb, William Morrow
Taxis and Toadstools, Rachel Field, Doubleday
The Pied Piper of Hamelin (all ages), Robert Browning, Frederick Warne
Under the Tent of the Sky, John E. Brewton, Macmillan
Under the Tree, Elizabeth M. Roberts, Viking

Collections and Short Stories

Chimney Corner Stories, Veronica Hutchinson, G. P. Putnam's Sons
East o' the Sun and West o' the Moon, Asbjornsen, Macmillan
Favorite Stories Old and New, Sidonie M. Gruenberg, Doubleday
Holiday Storybook (9), Child Study Association, compilers, Thomas Y. Crowell
Once upon a Time (9), Rose Dobbs, ed., Random House
The Jack Tales, Richard Chase, ed., Houghton Mifflin
The Long-Tailed Bear and Other Indian Legends, Natalia Belting, Holt, Rinehart and Winston
The Tall Book of Christmas (10), Dorothy H. Smith, ed., Harper and Row

Seven, Eight, and Nine

Stories and Entertainment

A Cap for Mul Chand, Julie F. Batchelor, Harcourt, Brace and World
A Dog on Barkham Street, Mary S. Stolz, Harper and Row
Alice's Family, Lorraine Beim, Harcourt, Brace and World
A Pony Called Lightning, Miriam E. Mason, Macmillan
Annie Pat and Eddie, Carolyn Haywood, William Morrow
At the Palace Gates, Helen R. Parish, Viking
Baker's Man, Rosalys Hall, Lippincott
Beanie, Ruth and Latrobe Carroll, Henry Z. Walck
Betsy and the Circus, Carolyn Haywood, William Morrow
Big Black Horse, Walter Farley, Random House
Blaze Finds the Trail, C. W. Anderson, Macmillan
Buffalo Bill, Ingri and Edgar Parin d'Aulaire, Doubleday
Cats for Kansas (10), Le Grand, Abingdon
Cave Twins, Lucy Fitch Perkins, Houghton Mifflin
Circus April First, Louis Slobodkin, Macmillan
Dan and the Miranda, Wilson Gage, World Publishing Co.

Dick Whittington and His Cat, Marcia Brown, illust., Charles Scribner's Sons
Eagle Feather, Clyde Robert Bulla, Thomas Y. Crowell
Eddie's Pay Dirt, Carolyn Haywood, William Morrow
Elmer and the Dragon (10), Ruth Stiles Gannett and Ruth C. Gannett, Random House
Emil and the Detectives, Erick Kastner, Doubleday
Fish Head, Jean Fritz, Coward-McCann
Five Little Peppers, Margaret Sidney, World Publishing Co.
Freddy and the Men from Mars, Walter R. Brooks, Alfred A. Knopf
Frédou, Mary Stolz, Harper and Row
Garden Spider, Mary Adrian, Holiday House
Henry Huggins, Beverly Cleary, William Morrow
Holiday Hill, Edith M. Patch, Macmillan
Holiday Meadow, Edith M. Patch, Macmillan
Holiday on Wheels, Catherine Woolley, William Morrow
How Baseball Began in Brooklyn, Le Grand Henderson, Abingdon
Ice Cream for Two, Clare Turlay Newberry, Harper and Row
Impunity Jane, Rumer Godden, Viking
Jane's Father (10), Dorothy Aldis, G. P. Putnam's Sons
Judy Jo's Magic Island, Mabel Betsy Hill, Lippincott
Kodru the Monkey (10), E. Cadwallader Smith, Alfred A. Knopf
Kongo the Elephant (10), E. Cadwallader Smith, Alfred A. Knopf
Little Navajo Bluebird (10), Ann Nolan Clark, Viking
Little Wu and the Watermelons, Beatrice Liu, Follett Publishing Co.
Lucky Blacky, Eunice Lackey, Franklin Watts
Magic Maize, Mary and Conrad Buff, Houghton Mifflin
Mine for Keeps, Jean Little, Little, Brown
Mr. Mysterious & Company, Sid Fleishman, Little, Brown
Mr. Petersand's Cats, Louis Slobodkin, Macmillan
My Father's Dragon (10), Ruth Stiles Gannett and Ruth C. Gannett, Random House
Nkwala, Edith Lamber Sharp, Little, Brown
Nobody Plays with a Cabbage, Meindert De Jong, Harper and Row
Mary Poppins (10), P. L. Travers, Harcourt, Brace and World
Mary Poppins Comes Back (10), P. L. Travers, Harcourt, Brace and World
Old Rosie, the Horse Nobody Understood (10), L. Adelson and L. Moore, Random House
Pepper, Barbara L. Reynolds, Charles Scribner's Sons
Pete the Parakeet, Irma Simonton Black, Holiday House
Pete's Home Run, Marion Renick, Charles Scribner's Sons
Pipkin Sees the World, Rosalie K. Foy, E. P. Dutton
Pippi Longstocking, Astrid Lindgren, Viking

BOOKS FOR YOUNGER CHILDREN

Pogo's Farm Adventure: A Story of Soil, Jo and Ernest Norling, Holt, Rinehart and Winston
Pogo's Fishing Trip: A Story of Salmon, Jo and Ernest Norling, Holt, Rinehart and Winston
Pogo's Lamb: A Story of Wool, Jo and Ernest Norling, Holt, Rinehart and Winston
Pogo's Mining Trip: A Story of Gold, Jo and Ernest Norling, Holt, Rinehart and Winston
Pogo's Truck Ride, Jo and Ernest Norling, Holt, Rinehart and Winston
Project: Genius, William Hayes, Atheneum
Rainbow Round the World (11), Elizabeth Yates, Bobbs-Merrill
Robinson Crusoe (all ages), Daniel Defoe, World Publishing Co.
Rocket Away! (10), Frances Frost, Whittlesey House
Sal Fisher, Brownie Scout, L. S. Gardner, Franklin Watts
Scrambled Eggs Super, Dr. Seuss, Random House
Shadrach, Meindert DeJong, Harper and Row
Star of Wild Horse Canyon, Clyde R. Bulla, Thomas Y. Crowell
Stripe, Robert M. McClung, William Morrow
That Summer on Catalpa Street, Louise Pliss, Reilly and Lee
The Adventures of Robin Hood (11), World Publishing Co.
The Beatinest Boy, Jesse Stuart, Whittlesey House
The Best Birthday, Quail Hawkins, Doubleday
The Big World and the Little House, Ruth Krauss, Harper and Row
The Courage of Sarah Noble, Alice Dalgliesh, Charles Scribner's Sons
The Cricket in Times Square, George Selden, Farrar, Strauss
The Enormous Egg, Oliver Butterworth, Little, Brown
The Gray-Nosed Kitten, Miriam E. Mason, Houghton Mifflin
The Griffin and the Minor Canon, Frank Stockton, Holt, Rinehart and Winston
The Happy Orpheline, Natalie Savage Carlson, Harper and Row
The Heart for Baseball, Marion Renick, Charles Scribner's Sons
The Hundred Dresses (10), Eleanor Estes, Harcourt, Brace and World
The Juggler of Notre Dame (10), Mary F. Todd, Whittlesey House
The Lone Hunt, William O. Steele, Harcourt, Brace and World
The Magic Ball from Mars, Carl L. Biemiller, William Morrow
The Magic Fishbone, Charles Dickens, Vanguard
The Most Wonderful Doll in the World, Phyllis McGinley, Lippincott
The Secret Language, Ursula Nordstrom, Harper and Row
The Sugarbush Family, Miriam E. Mason, Macmillan
The Talking Cat, Natalie S. Carlson, Harper and Row

The Terrible Mr. Twitmeyer, L. Adelson and L. Moore, Random House
The Thanksgiving Story (10), Alice Dalgliesh, Charles Scribner's Sons
The Twirly Skirt, Martha Goldberg, Holiday House
The Wonderful Fashion Doll, Laura Bannon, Houghton Mifflin
Three Boys and a Tugboat, Nan H. Agle and Ellen Wilson, Charles Scribner's Sons
Time of Wonder, Robert McCloskey, Viking
Tom Benn and Blackbeard the Pirate, Le Grand Henderson, Abingdon
Waterless Mountain (12), Laura A. Armer, McKay
We Live in the City, Lois Lenski, Lippincott
Wu the Gatekeeper's Son, Eleanor F. Lattimore, William Morrow

Information

Animals

Alligators and Crocodiles (11), Herbert S. Zim, William Morrow
All Kinds of Cats, Walter Chandoha, Alfred A. Knopf
Animal Homes (11), George F. Mason, William Morrow
Animal Sounds (11), George F. Mason, William Morrow
Animal Tools (11), George F. Mason, William Morrow
Animal Tracks (11), George F. Mason, William Morrow
Animal Weapons (11), George F. Mason, William Morrow
Birds in Their Homes (11), Addison Webb (Garden City), Doubleday
Elephants (10), Herbert S. Zim, William Morrow
Exploring the Animal Kingdom, Millicent Selsam, Doubleday
Frogs and Toads (10), Herbert S. Zim, William Morrow
Pet Book for Boys and Girls, Alfred P. Morgan, Charles Scribner's Sons
Rabbits (10), Herbert S. Zim, William Morrow
Rabbits in the Meadow, Lilo Hess, Thomas Y. Crowell
Snakes (10), Herbert S. Zim, William Morrow
The First Book of Bugs (10), Margaret Williamson, Franklin Watts
The First Book of Snakes (10), John Hoke, Franklin Watts
The Great Whales (12), Herbert S. Zim, William Morrow
Starlings (10), Wilfred S. Bronson, Harcourt, Brace and World

People and Their Works

A Garden We Planted Together, U.N. Department of Public Information, Whittlesey House
Big Book of Real Boats and Ships, George Zaffo, Grosset & Dunlap
Big Book of Real Fire Engines, George Zaffo, Grosset & Dunlap
Big Book of Real Trucks, George Zaffo, Grosset & Dunlap
New Ways in Math, Arthur Jonas, Prentice-Hall

Manners Can Be Fun, Munro Leaf, J. B. Lippincott

Pumpers, Boilers, Hooks and Ladders: A Book of Fire Engines, Leonard Everell Fisher, Dial

The Big Book of Cowboys (12), Sydney E. Fletcher, Grosset & Dunlap

The Big Book of Indians (12), Sydney E. Fletcher, Grosset & Dunlap

The First Book of Airplanes (11), Jeanne Bendick, Franklin Watts

The First Book of America (11), Edith Heal, Franklin Watts

The First Book of Cowboys (12), Benjamin Brewster, Franklin Watts

The First Book of Eskimos (11), Benjamin Brewster, Franklin Watts

The First Book of Indians (12), Benjamin Brewster, Franklin Watts

The First Book of Negroes (11), Langston Hughes, Franklin Watts

The First Book of Presidents (11), Harold Coy, Franklin Watts

The First Book of Supermarkets (10), Jeanne Bendick, Franklin Watts

The First Book of Trains, Russel Hamilton, Franklin Watts

The Wonderful World of Food, John Boyd-Orr, Doubleday

What's Inside of Engines? (11), Herbert S. Zim, William Morrow

Who Built the Highway?, Norman Bate, Charles Scribner's Sons

Science and Nature

A Baby Is Born (10), Milton Levine, M.D., and Jean Seligman, Golden Press

All About the Human Mind, Robert M. Goldenson, Random House

All Around You, Jeanne Bendick, McGraw-Hill

Everyday Weather and How It Works (10), Herman Schneider and Jeanne Bendick, McGraw-Hill

How Your Body Works (11), Herman and Nina Schneider, William R. Scott

I'll Show You How It Happens (10), Marie Neurath, Chanticleer

Let's Find Out, Herman and Nina Schneider, William R. Scott

Let's Look Inside Your House, Herman and Nina Schneider, William R. Scott

My Body and How It Works, Dorothy W. Baruch and Oscar Reiss, M.D., Harper and Row

Now Try This, Herman and Nina Schneider, William R. Scott

Picture Book of the Earth, Jerome S. Meyer, Lothrop, Lee & Shepard

Picture Book of the Weather, Jerome S. Meyer, Lothrop, Lee & Shepard

The Adventure of Light, Frank Jupo, Prentice-Hall

The First Book of Space Travel, Jeanne Bendick, Franklin Watts

The First Book of Stones (12), M. B. Cormack, Franklin Watts
The First Book of Trees (10), M. B. Cormack, Franklin Watts
The First Book of Weeds (12), Barbara L. Beck, Franklin Watts
The Rainbow Book of Nature, Donald Culross Peattie, World Publishing Co.
The Sun, The Moon, and the Stars, Mae and Ira Freeman, Random House
Young Scientist Takes a Walk, George Barr, Whittlesey House

Arts and Crafts

Cooking Fun: A Cook Book for Beginning Readers, Barbara C. McDonald, Henry Z. Walck
Famous Paintings: An Introduction to Art (12), Alice E. Chase, Platt and Munk
Fun with Next to Nothing: Handicraft Projects for Boys and Girls, Wesley F. Arnold and Wayne C. Cardy, Harper and Row
Leathercraft (10), Roger Lewis, Alfred A. Knopf
Let's Be Indians, Peggy Parish, Harper and Row
Indian Games and Crafts, Robert Hofsinde, William Morrow
Let's Make Presents: 100 Gifts for Less than $1.00, Esther Hautzig, Thomas Y. Crowell

Collections and Short Stories

Aesop's Fables (all ages), Laura Harris, ed., (Garden City) Doubleday
Bible Stories (11), Mary A. Jones, Rand McNally
The Big Book of Animal Stories, Margaret Green, Franklin Watts
Small Rain: Selections from the Bible, Jessie D. Jones, Viking
Tales of Faraway Folk, Babette Deutsch and Avrahm Yarmolinsky, Harper and Row
The Rainbow Book of American Folk Tales and Legends, Maria Leach, World Publishing Co.
The Train That Never Came Back and Other Railroad Stories, Freeman H. Hubbard, Whittlesey House

Poetry and Rhymes

The First Book of Poetry (10), Isabel J. Peterson, ed., Franklin Watts
This Way, Delight, Herbert Read, Pantheon

Fun and Riddles

Fun for One and Two (10), Bernice W. Carlson, Abingdon
Fun With Pencil and Paper, Joseph Leeming, J. B. Lippincott
Fun With Puzzles, Joseph Leeming, J. B. Lippincott
Fun With Magic, Joseph Leeming, J. B. Lippincott
Mother Goose Riddle Rhymes (10), Joseph Low, Harcourt, Brace and World

HOBBY AND INFORMATIONAL BOOKS AND PAMPHLETS, AND SOURCES OF INFORMATION FOR OLDER CHILDREN

The following selected list of books and pamphlets should help you develop almost any leisure-time interest. A further source of titles is *A Guide to Recreation Books,* published at regular intervals by the National Recreation Association or *How-to-Do-It-Books, a Selected Guide* by Robert E. Kingery (R. R. Bowker Company).

The first list below are the hobby books that come in series, then are the books listed by subject, approximately as in chapter XII. At the end of the lists we have given the addresses of some additional sources of general information.

The "Magazines for Creative Play" list, though arranged somewhat differently, carries on the suggestions of the present lists.

Hobby Books in Series

(Many of these are excellent introductory books.)

Abelard-Schuman Ltd., 6 W. 57th St., New York 19, N.Y.
   "How to Draw" Series: birds, fish, reptiles, animals, bridges, people, ships, trains, cars, etc.

Arco Publishing Company Inc., 480 Lexington Ave., New York 17, N.Y.
   "Do-It-Yourself" Series: astronomy, ceramics, cooking, needlecrafts, old cars, home improvement and repairs, interior decorating, flower arranging, gardening, house plants, landscaping, archery, bowling, hunting, skin-diving, horses, tropical fish, birds.

Thomas Y. Crowell Company, 201 Park Ave. South, New York 3, N.Y.
   "Science Experiments" Series: chemistry, optical illusion, sky watching, sound, airplane instruments, microscope, atomics, electricity, light.

Golden Press, Inc., 850 Third Avenue, New York 22, N.Y.
   "Golden Nature Guides": weather, fossils, fish, mammals, trees, reptiles, amphibians, etc.

Harper and Row (Eastern Division of El-hi), Sawmill River Road, Elmsford, New York.
   "Basic Science Education" Series: eighty or more books on science fundamentals.

Alfred A. Knopf, Inc., 501 Madison Ave., New York 22, N.Y.
   Books by Harry Zarchy: boating, camping, fishing, ceramics, crafts and hobbies, model railroading, stamp collecting.

J. B. Lippincott, East Washington Square, Philadelphia 5, Penna.
   Books by Joseph Leeming: Fun with beads, boxes, clay, fabrics, leather, magic, paper, plastics etc.
   "Sports Illustrated Library": baseball, diving, driving, dog train-

ing, basketball, tennis, fencing, football, riding, fishing, skiing, boating, etc.

David McKay Company, Inc., 119 W. 40th St., New York 18, N.Y.
Beginner's handbooks on various hobbies: cards, checkers, chess, enameling, jewelry-making, magic, toymaking.

Thomas Nelson & Sons, 18 E. 41st St., New York 17, N.Y.
"The Young Sportsman's Guides": fishing, skin diving, sailing, golf, riding, hunting, water skiing, skiing, tennis, etc.

G. P. Putnam's Sons, 200 Madison Ave., New York 16, N.Y.
"Here Is Your Hobby" Series: art, ceramics, fishing, archery, stamp collecting, etc.

"Nature Field Book" Series: trees, flowers, rocks, insects, mammals, ponds and streams, seashore, skies, nature activities, and conservation.

Random House, Inc., 457 Madison Ave., New York 22, N.Y.
"All About Books" Series: mountains and mountaineering, science, animals, weather, etc.

The Ronald Press Company, 15 E. 26th St., New York 10, N.Y.
"The Ronald Sports Library": basic and advanced books on a wide variety of sports (formerly The Barnes Sports Library).

Sterling Publishing Company, Inc., 419 Park Ave. South, New York, N.Y.
"How to Raise and Train" Series: books on individual breeds of dogs, as well as cats, and birds.

The Viking Press, Inc., 625 Madison Ave., New York 22, N.Y.
Studio "How to Do It" Series: drawing, etching, photography, metalwork, pottery making, weaving, woodcarving, interior decorating.

Franklin Watts, Inc., 575 Lexington Ave., New York 22, N.Y.
"First Book" Series (for young children): ballet, baseball, bees, birds, boats, bugs, cats, caves, chess, dogs, dolls, fishing, horses, magic, music, photography, plants, puppets, sailing, snakes, science experiments, etc.

Science Hobbies

Adventuring in Nature, Betty Price, Association
A First Electrical Book for Boys, Alfred Morgan, Charles Scribner's Sons
After-Dinner Science, Kenneth M. Swezey, McGraw-Hill
All About the Weather, I. R. Tannehill, Random House
Atoms Today and Tomorrow, Margaret O. Hyde, McGraw-Hill
Building With Electronics, Harry Zarchy, Thomas Y. Crowell
Engines and How They Work, Geoffrey Boumphrey, Franklin Watts
Everyday Machines and How They Work, Herman Schneider, Whittlesey House
Fun With Astronomy, Mae and Ira Freeman, Random House
Fun With Chemistry, Mae and Ira Freeman, Random House
Fun With Science, Mae and Ira Freeman, Random House

Fun With the Sun, D. S. Halacy, Macmillan
It's Fun to Know Why, Julius Schwartz, Whittlesey House
Model Rockets for Beginners, H. H. Gilmore, Harper and Row
More Research Ideas for Young Scientists, George Barr, Whittlesey House
Point to the Stars, Joseph Maron Joseph and Sarah Lee Lippincott, Whittlesey House
Science Magic, Kenneth M. Swezey, McGraw-Hill
Sea Shells, Ruth H. Dudley, Thomas Y. Crowell
Stars, Herbert S. Zim and Robert H. Baker, Golden Press
Stars, Men, and Atoms, Heinz Haber, Golden Press
Strange Worlds Under a Microscope, Margaret Cosgrove, Dodd, Mead
The Amateur Naturalist's Handbook, Vinson Brown, Little, Brown
The Crazy Cantilever and Other Experiments, Robert R. Kadesch, Harper and Row
The World We Live In, Lincoln Barnett, Golden Press
Through the Magnifying Glass, Julius Schwartz, Whittlesey House
Using Electronics, Harry Zarchy, Thomas Y. Crowell
Young People's Book of Atomic Energy, R. D. Potter, Dodd, Mead
Young Scientist and Sports, George Barr, Whittlesey House

Amusement Hobbies

Act It Out, Bernice Wells Carlson, Abingdon
Active Games and Contests, B. X. Mason and E. D. Mitchell, Ronald Press
Best Short Plays (annual), Margaret Mayorga (ed.), Beacon Press
Book of Games—for Home, School, Playground, William Forbush and Harry R. Allen, Holt, Rinehart and Winston
Chess for Young People, Fred Reinfeld, Holt, Rinehart and Winston
Children's Games from Many Lands, Nina Millen, Friendship Press
Children's Theatre and Creative Dramatics, Geraldine Siks and Hazel B. Dunnington, University of Washington
Christmas Plays and Programs, Aileen Fisher, Plays Inc.
Clown Act Omnibus, Wes McVicar, Association
Creative Dramatics, Association for Childhood Education International
Creative Dramatics for Children, Frances C. Durland, Antioch
Creative Dramatics: An Art for Children, Geraldine B. Siks, Harper and Row
Creative Play Acting: Learning Through Drama, Isabel B. Burger, Ronald Press
Easy Puppets, Gertrude Pels, Thomas Y. Crowell
Family Fun Book, H. and L. Eisenberg, Association
Finger Puppets, pamphlet, National Recreation Association
Folding Paper Puppets, Shari Lewis and Lillian Oppenheimer, Stein and Day
Fun with Brand-New Games, Allan and Paulette MacFarlan, Association

Games for Children, Marguerite Kohl and Frederica Young, Hill and Wang
Games for Grownups, Marguerite Kohl and Frederica Young, Hill and Wang
Handbook of Fist Puppets, Bessie A. Ficklen, J. B. Lippincott
High Times: 100 Suggestions for Social Activities, N. Z. Thompson, E. P. Dutton
Holiday Programs for Boys and Girls, Aileen Fisher, Plays Inc.
How to Have a Show, Barbara Berk and Jeanne Bendick, Franklin Watts
Houdini's Fabulous Magic, Walter B. Gibson and M. N. Young, eds., Chilton
Inexpensive Puppets, Frank A. Staples, National Recreation Association
Let's Give a Show, Bill and Sue Severn, Alfred A. Knopf
Magic and Magicians, Bill Severn, David McKay
Magic As a Hobby, Bruce Elliott, Harper and Row
Marionettes: Easy to Make! Fun to Use!, Edith Ackley, J. B. Lippincott
Modern Comedies for Teen-Agers, Paul S. McCoy, Plays, Inc.
Modern One-Act Plays, Griffith and Mersand, Harcourt, Brace and World
New Games for Tween-Agers, A. A. Macfarlan, Association
Omnibus of Fun, Helen and Larry Eisenberg, Association
On Stage, Everyone, Grace Barnes and M. J. Sutcliffe, Macmillan
One-Act Plays for Young Actors, John Murray, T. S. Denison
101 Best Card Games for Children, Alfred Sheinwold, Sterling
Party Game Book, Margaret E. Mulac and Marian S. Holmes, Harper and Row
Plays and How to Put Them On, Moyne Rice Smith, Henry Z. Walck
Puppet and Pantomime Plays, Vernon Howard, Sterling
Puppet Theatre Handbook, Marjorie H. Batchelder, Harper and Row
Remo Bufano's Book of Puppetry, Arthur Richmond, ed., Macmillan
Shadow Magic, Bill Severn, David McKay
Shadow Puppets: Their Construction, Operation and Stage, National Recreation Association
Six More Dramatic Stunts, National Recreation Association
Stagecraft and Scene Design (for little theaters), Herbert Philippe, Houghton Mifflin
The ABC's of Play Producing: A Handbook for the Non-Professional, Howard Bailey, David McKay
The Amateur Magician's Handbook, Henry Hay, Thomas Y. Crowell
The Book of Games, G. S. Ripley, Brown Book
The Book of Games for Boys and Girls: How to Lead and Play Them, Evelyne Borst, Ronald Press
The Cokesbury Party Book, A. M. Depew, Abingdon
The First Book of Chess, Joseph Leeming, Franklin Watts
The First Book of Magic, Edward Stoddard, Franklin Watts

The First Book of Stage Costume and Make-up, Barbara Beck, Franklin Watts
The Fun Encyclopedia, E. O. Harbin, Abingdon
Twenty-five Modern Plays, S. M. Tucker, Harper and Row
Ventriloquism for Fun and Profit, Paul Winchell, Ottenheimer

Information on Plays

Index to One-Act Plays, Hannah Logasa, Faxon
Index to Plays in Collections, John Ottemiller, Scarecrow Press, New Brunswick, N.J.
Play Index, H. W. Wilson Co.

Play Sources

American Theatre Wing (mental health, child guidance plays), 161 W. 93 St., New York 25, N.Y.
Denison and Co., Minneapolis, Minn.
Dramatists Play Service, 14 E. 38 St., New York, N.Y.
Northwestern Press, Minneapolis, Minn.
Plays, Inc., 8 Arlington St., Boston 16, Mass.
Samuel French Co., 25 W. 45 St., New York, N.Y.

Manual Hobbies

General

Book of Hobby Craft, Glenn A. Wagner, Dodd, Mead
Crafts for Fun, Evadna Kraus Perry, William Morrow
Creating With Materials for Work and Play, Association for Childhood Education, International
Creative Crafts for Everyone, G. Alan Turner, Viking
Creative Hands, Doris Cox and Barbara Warren, Wiley
Creative Hobbies, Harry Zarchy, Alfred A. Knopf
Easy Crafts, Ellsworth Jaeger, Macmillan
Fun With Next to Nothing, Wesley F. Arnold and Wayne C. Cardy, Harper and Row
Here's Your Hobby, Harry Zarchy, Alfred A. Knopf
It's Fun to Make Things, Martha Parkhill and Dorothy Spaeth, Ronald Press
Let's Make a Lot of Things, Harry Zarchy, Alfred A. Knopf
101 Funny Things to Make and Do, Paul Castle, Sterling
The Book of Arts and Crafts, Marguerite Ickis and Reba Selden Esh, Association
The Golden Book of Crafts and Hobbies, W. B. Hunt, Golden Press
The Home Crafts Handbook, Ray E. Haines, ed., Van Nostrand
Things to Make from Odds and Ends, Jessie Robinson, Meredith

Specific

Art Metalwork, a Manual for Amateurs, Emil K. Kronquist, McGraw-Hill

Betty White's Teenage Dancebook, Betty White, Grosset & Dunlap
Block and Silk Screen Printing, G. Ahlberg and O. Jarneryd, Sterling
Block Printing on Fabrics, Florence H. Pettit, Hastings House
Boats, Airplanes, and Kites, A. J. LaBerge, Bennett
Bookbinding Made Easy, L. M. Klinefelter, Bruce
Braiding and Knotting for Amateurs, C. A. Belash, Branford
Building and Flying Scale-Model Aircraft, W. A. Musciano, Rolton
Carpentry for Children, Jerome Leavill, Sterling
Clay Modeling, National Recreation Association
Creative Claywork, Harold Isenstein, Sterling
Everyone Can Paint Fabrics, Pearl F. Ashton (Studio), Viking
Fun With Artificial Flowers, Joseph Leeming, J. B. Lippincott
Fun With Leather, Joseph Leeming, J. B. Lippincott
Fun With Paper, Joseph Leeming, J. B. Lippincott
Fun With Shapes in Space, Toni Hughes, E. P. Dutton
Fun With Shells, Joseph Leeming, J. B. Lippincott
Fun With String, Joseph Leeming, J. B. Lippincott
Fun With Tools, William Moore and Robert Cynar, Random House
General Leathercraft, Raymond Cherry (McKnight), Taplinger
General Plastics: Projects and Procedures, Raymond Cherry (McKnight), Taplinger
Gifts and Gadgets Made from Paper, National Recreation Association
Gliders, Larry Kettelkamp, William Morrow
Glovemaking for Beginners, Natalie S. Woolf, Taplinger
Handbook of Knots, Raoul Graumont, Cornell Maritime Press
Historic Models of Early America: And How to Make Them, C. J. Maginley, Harcourt, Brace and World
Holiday Craft and Fun, Joseph Leeming, J. B. Lippincott
How to Dance, Thomas E. Parson, Barnes and Noble
How to Improve Your Model Railroad, Raymond F. Yates, Harper and Row
How to Make Modern Jewelry, Charles J. Martin and Victor D'Amico, Doubleday
How You Look and Dress, Byrta Carson, Whittlesey House
Indian Beadwork, Robert Hofsinde, William Morrow
Jewelry Making and Enameling, Harry Zarchy, Alfred A. Knopf
Jewelry Making: As an Art Expression, D. Kenneth Winebrenner, International Textbook
Kites, How to Make and Fly Them, Marion Downer, Lothrop, Lee & Shepard
Leathercraft for Amateurs, Eleanore E. Bang, Branford
Make Your Own Christmas Tree Ornaments, National Recreation Association
Masks, National Recreation Association
Masks and Mask Makers, Kari Hunt and Bernice Wells Carlson, Abingdon

Model Planes for Beginners, H. H. Gilmore, Harper and Row
Model Railroading, Harry Zarchy, Alfred A. Knopf
Mosaics: Hobby and Art, Edwin Hendrickson, Hill and Wang
Paper Bag Masks, National Recreation Association
Paper, Ink, and Roller: Print-Making for Beginners, Harvey Weiss, William R. Scott
Papercraft, Joseph Leeming, J. B. Lippincott
Papier-Mache, Lillian Johnson, David McKay
Plastics for the Beginner, Frank A. Staples, National Recreation Association
Print Making With a Spoon, Norman Gorbaty, Reinhold
Printing for Fun, Koshi Ota and others, Obolensky
Rope Roundup, Bill Severn, David McKay
Sand Sculpturing, Mickey Klar Marks, Dial
Scrapwood Fun for Kids, Robert F. Endicott, Association Press
Sewing, Jeannette Zarchy, Alfred A. Knopf
Silk Screen Printing, James Eisenberg (McKnight), Taplinger
Spatter Prints, National Recreation Association
The Art and Craft of Hand-Weaving: Including Fabric Design, Lili Blumenau, Crown
The Art of Knotting and Splicing, Cyrus Lawrence Day, U.S. Naval Institute
The Art of Origami, Samuel Randlett, E. P. Dutton
The Art of Wood Carving, John Upton, Van Nostrand
The Boys' Book of Model Railroading, Raymond F. Yates, Harper and Row
The Boys' Book of Tools, Raymond F. Yates, Harper and Row
The Complete Book of Furniture Repair and Refinishing, Ralph Kinney, Charles Scribner's Sons
The Complete Book of Knitting, Elizabeth L. Mathieson, World Publishing Co.
The Fannie Farmer Junior Cook Book, Wilma L. Perkins, Little, Brown
The Golden Book of Indian Crafts and Lore, W. B. Hunt, Golden Press
The Good Housekeeping Needlecraft Encyclopedia, Alice Carroll, Holt, Rinehart and Winston
The Hand Decoration of Fabrics, Francis J. Kafka (McKnight), Taplinger
The Model Aircraft Handbook, William Winter, Thomas Y. Crowell
The Radio Amateur's Handbook, A. Frederick Collins, Thomas Y. Crowell
The Seventeen Book of Decorating, David McKay
This Is Crocheting, Ethel Evans, Macmillan
Tin Can Crafting, Sylvia Howard, Sterling
Toys to Sew, Charlotte Davis and Jessie Robinson, J. B. Lippincott
Wide World Cookbook, Rebecca Shapiro, Little, Brown
With Scissors and Paste, Leila Wilhelm, Macmillan

Wood Carving and Whittling Made Easy, Franklin H. Gottshall, Bruce
Young America's Cookbook, New York Herald Tribune Home Institute, Charles Scribner's Sons

Art Hobbies

Anyone Can Draw, Arthur Zaidenberg, Doubleday
Anyone Can Paint, Arthur Zaidenberg, Crown
Anyone Can Sculpt, Arthur Zaidenberg, Harper and Row
Ballet for Beginners, Margaret F. Atkinson and Nancy Draper, Alfred A. Knopf
Better Homes and Gardens Flower Arranging, Meredith
Ceramics and Pottery Making for Everyone, Carol Janeway, Tudor
Ceramics Handbook, Richard Hyman, Arco
Clay, Wood, and Wire, Harvey Weiss, William R. Scott
Decorating on a Budget, Elizabeth Ogg, Barrows
Decorating With Seed Mosaics, Chipped Glass, and Plant Materials, Eleanor Van Rensselaer, Van Nostrand
Flower Arrangement Workbook, Myra J. Brooks, Barrows
Flower Arranging, Loret Swift, Arco
Flower Arranging for Juniors, Virginia Stone Marshall, Little, Brown
Folk Dances for All, Michael Herman, Barnes and Noble
Get in There and Paint, Joseph Alger, Thomas Y. Crowell
How to Make Good Home Movies, Eastman Kodak Co., Random House
How to Make Good Pictures, Eastman Kodak Co., Random House
How to Make Mobiles, John Lynch (Studio), Viking
Hunting With the Camera, Allan D. Cruickshank, ed., Harper and Row
Interior Decorating for You, Florence B. Terhune, Barrows
Japanese Flower Arrangement for Beginners, Nina Clark Powell, Charles Scribner's Sons
Oil Painting Is Fun, Alois Fabry (Studio), Viking
Photography for Everyone, Fritz Henle and H. M. Zinzer, Viking
Photography for Teen-Agers, Lucile Marshall, Prentice-Hall
Photograph With Basic Cameras, William Gottlieb, Alfred A. Knopf
Recreation Through Music, Charles Leonhard, Ronald Press
Say It With Your Camera, Jacob Deschin, A. S. Barnes
Secrets of Taking Good Pictures, Aaron Knopf, Doubleday
The Amateur Photographer's Handbook, Aaron Sussman, Thomas Y. Crowell
The Art of Driftwood and Dried Arrangements, Tatsuo Ishmoto, Crown
The Art of Readable Writing, Rudolph Flesch, Harper and Row
The Beginner's Book of Oil Painting, Adrian Hill, Emerson Books
The Beginner's Book of Watercolour Painting, Adrian Hill, Emerson Books
The Book of Ballet, James Audsley, Warne
The Burl Ives Song Book, Ballantine

The Complete Book of Interior Decorating, Mary Derieux and Isabelle Stevenson (Greystone), Hawthorn
The Fireside Book of Folk Songs, Mary B. Boni, ed., Simon and Schuster
The First Book of Drawing, Louis Slobodkin, Franklin Watts
The First Book of Music, Gertrude Norman, Franklin Watts
The Whole World Singing, Edith Lovell Thomas, Friendship Press
What Shall We Draw? The Beginner's Book of Drawing, Adrian Hill, Emerson Books

Animal Hobbies

An Aquarium Book for Boys and Girls, Alfred Morgan, Charles Scribner's Sons
An Introduction to Birds, John Kieran, Garden City
A Pet Book for Boys and Girls, Alfred Morgan, Charles Scribner's Sons
Beginner's Guide to Fresh-Water Life, Leon Hausman, G. P. Putnam's Sons
Beginner's Guide to Seashore Life, Leon Hausman, G. P. Putnam's Sons
Book of Nature Hobbies, Ted Pettit, Didier
Cage Birds in Color, Mandahl-Barth, M. Barrows
Collecting Cocoons, Lois J. Hussey and Catharine Pessino, Thomas Y. Crowell
Dog Training for Boys and Girls, Blanche Saunders, Howell Book House
Earthworms, Dorothy Childs Hogner, Thomas Y. Crowell
Field Book of Nature Activities, William Hillcourt, G. P. Putnam
Frogs and Polliwogs, Dorothy Childs Hogner, Thomas Y. Crowell
Fun-Time Terrariums and Aquariums, Jerome Leavitt and John Huntsberger, Children's Press
Golden Hamsters, Herbert S. Zim, William Morrow
Home-Made Zoo, Sylvia S. Greenberg and Edith L. Raskin, David McKay
How to Know the Birds, Roger Tory Peterson, Houghton Mifflin
Insects and the Homes They Build, Dorothy Sterling, Doubleday
Nature Crafts, Ellsworth Jaeger, Macmillan
Odd Pets, Lilo Hess and Dorothy Hogner, Thomas Y. Crowell
Pets, Frances N. Chrystie, Little, Brown
Pets From the Pond, Margaret Waring Buck, Abingdon
Small Pets From Woods and Fields, Margaret Waring Buck, Abingdon
Spiders, Dorothy Childs Hogner, Thomas Y. Crowell
Starting an Aquarium, Miriam Gilbert, Hammond
Starting a Terrarium, Miriam Gilbert, Hammond
The Bird Watcher's Guide, Henry Hill Collins, Golden Press
The Care of Water Pets, Gertrude Pels, Thomas Y. Crowell
The Horse Book, John Rendel, Arco
Tropical Fish, Lucile Quarry Mann, Sentinel Books
Tropical Fish As a Hobby, H. R. Axelrod, McGraw-Hill

Tropical Fish As Pets, C. W. Coates, Liveright
Underwater Zoos, Millicent Selsam, William Morrow
Wild Animals of the World, William Bridges, Garden City
Wonders of the Seashore, Jacquelyn Berrill, Dodd, Mead

Gardening and Plants

How to Grow House Plants, Millicent E. Selsam, William Morrow
Plants in the City, Herman and Nina Schneider, John Day
Play With Plants, Millicent E. Selsam, William Morrow
Play With Trees, Millicent E. Selsam, William Morrow
The Beginning Gardener, Katherine N. Cutler, M. Barrows
The Complete Guide to Garden Flowers, Herbert Askwith, ed., A. S. Barnes
The Golden Book of Gardening, Frances Giannoni and Seymour Reit, Golden Press
Young America's Garden Book, Louise Bush-Brown, Charles Scribner's Sons

Collecting Hobbies

Autographs, A Key to Collecting, Mary A. Benjamin, Kinney's Bookshop
Coin Collector's Handbook, Fred Reinfeld, Sterling
Coinometry, Robert V. Masters and Fred Reinfeld, Sterling
Complete Book of Coin Collecting, Joseph Coffin, Coward-McCann
Fun for Young Collectors, Joseph Leeming, J. B. Lippincott
How to Build A Coin Collection, Fred Reinfeld, Sterling
How to Know American Antiques, Alice Winchester, Dodd, Mead
Old Things for Young People, A Guide for Young People, Ann Kilborn Cole, David McKay
Sea Treasure: A Guide to Shell Collecting, Kathleen K. Johnstone, Houghton Mifflin
Stamp Collecting, Roger Lewis, Alfred A. Knopf
Stamp Collector's Guide, Harry Zarchy, Alfred A. Knopf
Stamps, A Guide to Your Collection, Jim Turner, J. B. Lippincott
Standard Handbook of Stamp Collecting, Richard McP. Cabeen, Thomas Y. Crowell
Starting A Rock and Mineral Collection, Miriam Gilbert, Hammond
Starting A Shell Collection, Miriam Gilbert, Hammond
The Art of Drying Plants and Flowers, Mabel Squires, M. Barrows
The Complete Book of Collecting Hobbies, W. P. Bricker, Sheridan
The Complete Book of Gun Collecting, Charles Edward Chapel, Coward-McCann
The Encyclopedia of Furniture, Joseph Aronson, Crown
The Practical Book of Chinaware, Harold D. Eberlain and Roger W. Ramsdell, J. B. Lippincott

The Rock-Hunter's Range Guide, Jay Ellis Ransom, Harper and Row
Treasury of Early American Automobiles, 1877–1925, Floyd Clymer, McGraw-Hill

Sports Hobbies

A Complete Guide to Fishing, Vlad Evanoff, Thomas Y. Crowell
Anyone Can Live off the Land, James R. Johnson, David McKay
Baseball for Young Champions, R. J. Antonacci and Jean Barr, Whittlesey House
Basketball for Young Champions, Robert Antonacci and Jean Barr, Whittlesey House
Basketball Fundamentals and Techniques, Clair Bee and Ken Norton, Ronald Press
Beginner's Guide to Golf, Bob Toski, Grosset & Dunlap
Beginning With Boats, David Klein, Thomas Y. Crowell
Bowling to Win, Buzz Fazio, Grosset & Dunlap
Boxing for Boys, Donald K. Silks, Alfred A. Knopf
Boys' Book of Outboard Boating, Tom Parsons, Macmillan
Bucks and Bows (hunting with bow and arrow), Walter Perry, Stackpole
Camping and Woodcraft, Horace Kephart, Macmillan
Canoe Camping, Carle W. Handel, Ronald Press
Canoeing, Carle W. Handel, Ronald Press
Fencing, Joseph Vince, Ronald Press
Field, Skeet, and Trap Shooting, Charles E. Chapel, A. S. Barnes
Fishing Is Fun, Arthur H. Carhart, Macmillan
Football for Young Champions, Robert Antonacci and Jean Barr, Whittlesey House
Fun in the Water, T. K. Cureton, Association Press
Games the World Around, Sarah Hunt and Ethel Cain, Ronald Press
Golf for Boys and Girls, Chick Evans (Popular Mechanics), Hawthorn
Guide for Young Campers, Mauno Lindholm, Hart
Heads Up—Heels Down, C. W. Anderson, Macmillan
Hiking, Camping, and Mountaineering, Roland C. Geist, Harper and Row
Horsemanship for Beginners, Jean Slaughter, Alfred A. Knopf
How to Play Better Tennis, William T. Tilden, Cornerstone
Ju-Jitsu, Self-Defense for Teen-Agers, Robert Lichello, Messner
Midget Motoring and Karting, Kenton D. McFarland and James C. Sparks, Jr., E. P. Dutton
Let's Go Camping, Harry Zarchy, Alfred A. Knopf
Race Your Boat Right, Arthur Knapp, Van Nostrand
Sailing, Bill Wallace, Golden Press
Skating for Beginners, Barbara Ann Scott and Michael Kirby, Alfred A. Knopf
Skiing for Beginners, Conrad Brown, Charles Scribner's Sons
Sports and Games, Harold Keith, Thomas Y. Crowell

Sportsman's Digest of Fishing, Hal Sharp, Sterling
The Book of Games, G. S. Ripley, Brown Book
The Boy's Book of Physical Fitness, Hal G. Vermes, Association Press
The Complete Book of Karting, Dick Day, Prentice-Hall
The Encyclopedia of Sports, A. S. Barnes
The Girl's Book of Physical Fitness, Hal G. Vermes, Association Press
The Golden Guide to Power Boats, Bill Wallace, Golden Press
The Junior Book of Camping and Woodcraft, Bernard S. Mason, Ronald Press
Underwater Sports, Albert Vander Kogel with Rex Lardner, Holt, Rinehart and Winston
Your Own Book of Campcraft, Catherine Hammett, Pocket Books

Profitable Hobbies

Dolls to Make for Fun and Profit, Edith F. Ackley, Lippincott
Enameling for Fun and Profit, Mary Larom, David McKay
Hand-Weaving for Pleasure and Profit, Harriette J. Brown, Harper and Row
Homemade Toys for Fun and Profit, Arthur Lawson, David McKay
How to Write for Pleasure and Profit, Warren Bower (ed.), Lippincott
Jewelry Making for Fun and Profit, Helen Clegg and Mary Larom, David McKay
Raising Small Animals for Pleasure and Profit, F. G. Ashrook, Van Nostrand
Stamps for Fun and Profit, Henry Ellis, Funk and Wagnalls
Wood Carving for Fun and Profit, Al Ball, Exposition Press

Recreation for the Sick and Handicapped
(see Chapter XVII)

A Doctor Looks at Toys, Elizabeth Lodge Rees, Charles C Thomas
How to Choose Toys for Convalescent Children, Grace Langdon, American Toy Institute, 200 Fifth Ave., New York 10, N.Y.
How to Help the Shut-In Child, Margery D. McMullin, E. P. Dutton
Play for Convalescent Children in Hospitals and at Home, Anne Marie Smith, A. S. Barnes
Play Activities for the Retarded Child, Bernice Carlson and David R. Ginglend, Abingdon
Recreation for the Handicapped, Valerie V. Hunt, Prentice-Hall
Recreational Activities for Crippled Children, Lois Perrin, University of Iowa
Recreation Is Fun—A Handbook on Hospital Recreation and Entertainment, Esther M. Hawley, The American Theatre Wing
Sports for the Handicapped, George T. Stafford, Prentice-Hall
Working With the Handicapped, Joan L. Carter, Girl Scouts of U.S.A.

Community Recreation and Service (see Chapter XVIII)

Community Organization for Recreation, Gerald B. Fitzgerald, Ronald Press
Community Planning for Human Services, Bradley Buell and Associates, Columbia University Press
Community Recreation, Harold D. Meyer and Charles K. Brightbill, D. C. Heath
Introduction to Community Recreation, George D. Butler, McGraw-Hill
Recreation Leadership, H. Don Corbin, Prentice-Hall

Pamphlet Source

Superintendent of Documents, U. S. Government Printing Office, Washington 25, D. C. (Free pamphlet *Hobby Publications* lists and describes about a hundred inexpensive government pamphlets on a wide variety of subjects).

Organizations Publishing Material Helpful in Recreation Projects

American Clay Co., Indianapolis 24, Ind. (free folders on clay, papier-mâché, etc.)
American Crayon Co., Sandusky, Ohio
Association for Childhood Education, International, 3615 Wisconsin Avenue, N. W., Washington 16, D. C.
Chicago Park District, Division of Recreation, 425 E. 14 Blvd., Chicago 5, Ill. (crafts of many kinds)
Child Study Association of America, Inc., 9 East 89th St., New York 28, N. Y.
Committee on Art Education, Museum of Modern Art, 11 W. 53 St., New York 19, N. Y.
Dennison Manufacturing Co., Framingham, Mass. (party favors, handicrafts with paper)
Federal Security Agency, Children's Bureau, Washington, D. C.
Girls Friendly Society of the U. S. A., 345 East 46th St., New York 17, N. Y. (Pamphlets on dancing, marionettes, lending libraries, hobby shows, musical instruments)
Girls Scouts of the U. S. A., 830 Third Avenue, New York 22, N. Y. (dramatics, outdoor cooking, arts and crafts with inexpensive materials, songbook, hiking, etc)
National Recreation Association, 8 W. 8 St., New York, N. Y. (hobby shows, puppetry, dramatics, parties, crafts, singing games, nature study, recreation for older people, etc.)
Play Schools Association, 120 West 57 St., New York 19, N. Y. (puppets, play groups, trips)

Sixty-Nine Bank Street Publications, 69 Bank Street, New York 14, N. Y.
Stanley Tools, Educational Department, New Britain, Conn. (workshop
  patterns for toys, etc.)

Organizations Publishing Informative Catalogues of Hobby and Play Equipment

American Handicrafts Co., Inc., 4 East 16 St., New York 3, N. Y.
America's Hobby Center, Inc., 146 West 22 St., New York 11, N. Y.
Arthur Brown and Brothers, 2 W. 46 St., New York, N. Y.
Binney and Smith Co., 380 Madison Ave., New York 17, N. Y. (leaflet
  on arts and crafts)
Childcraft Equipment Co., Inc., 155 East 23 St., New York 10, N. Y.
Cleveland Crafts Co., 4707 Euclid, Cleveland, Ohio
Creative Playthings, Inc., Edinburg Road, Cranbury, N. J.
The Arts Cooperative Service, 312 East 23 St., New York 3, N. Y.
The Playskool Manufacturing Co., Merchandise Mart, Chicago, Ill.

MAGAZINES FOR CREATIVE PLAY

There is a magazine to feed practically every leisure-time interest, and most of the specialty periodicals give the reader a chance to contribute his own ideas and experiences to others. The following list includes magazines published by national organizations, as well as independent publications. Addresses can be obtained from the reference room of your local library, or from your newsdealer. Send for a sample issue if you haven't seen the magazine. In addition to the hobby magazines, the hobby books (in a separate list) will be helpful. In selecting magazines for children, a helpful folder, *Guide to Children's Magazines, Newspapers, Reference Books,* is available from the Association for Childhood Education International.

Humpty Dumpty (ages 4 to 6); *Children's Playmate* (5 to 9); *Jack and Jill* (5–9); *Child Life* (6–10); *Children's Digest* (8–12); *Boys' Life* (11 up); *The American Girl* (11–14); *Seventeen* (14 up).

Scientific Interests

Audubon Magazine; Junior Natural History; National Geographic; Natural History; Popular Science Monthly; Science Digest; Science News Letter; Scientific American; Science World.

Hobbies

Craft Horizons; Handweaver and Craftsman; Yankee (hobbies); *Family Handyman; Homecraftsman; American Home; House Beautiful; House and Garden; Better Homes and Gardens; Popular Ceramics; Model Airplane News; Popular Mechanics; Mechanix Illustrated; Popular Science; Model Railroader; Interiors; Dramatics; Plays; Farm Journal; Amateur Photographer; Popular Photography; Modern Photography; Travel and Camera; Photography Magazine; Popular Boating; Car and Driver; Popular Electronics; CQ; QST* (amateur radio magazines); *Gourmet; Musical America; Dance Magazine; Art News; Design.*

Animals, Gardening

All-Pets; Cats Magazine; Dog World; Your Dog; Pure-Bred Dogs; American Cage-Bird Magazine; Riding, the Horselover's Magazine; Small Stock Magazine; Tropical Fish Hobbyist; Aquarium; American Pigeon Journal; American Bee Journal; Flower Grower; Popular Gardening; Flower and Garden Magazine; Better Homes and Gardens; House and Garden; American Home; House Beautiful; Horticulture; Camping Magazine.

Collecting

American Philatelist; Stamps; Numismatist; Coin World; Antiques Journal; Antiques; The Antique Trader; Spinning Wheel; Antique Automobile; American Book Collector; Toy Trader (dolls); *Doll Talk; Gems and Minerals; Hobbies, The Magazine of Collectors; Lapidary Journal; Rocks and Minerals; Postcard Collectors Magazine; National Button Bulletin.*

Sports and Entertainment

Chess Correspondent; Chess Review; Bridge World; Genii (conjurors' magazine); *Holiday; Sports Illustrated; Sports Afield; Archers Magazine; Baseball Monthly; Baseball Magazine; Bowling; National Bowler's Journal; Judo Journal; Skin Diver Magazine; Junior Swimmer; American Field; American Motorcycling; Motorcyclist; Field and Stream; Fishing World; Fur-Fish-Game; Bowhunting; Golfing; Golf World; Guns Magazine; Camping Magazine; Better Camping; Motor Boating; Outdoor Life; Scouting Magazine; Ski Magazine; Skiing; Speed Age; Flying; Soaring; Aviation Age Illustrated; Yachting.*

REFERENCES FOR PARENTS AND RECREATION AND HOBBY LEADERS

The books, pamphlets, and magazines listed here will give leads to the information, skills, and that special sense of what's "right" that the modern recreation leader needs. Although some of the books have been written for children, parents and recreation leaders will find them useful. Additional help will be found in our list entitled "Hobby Books and Pamphlets, and Sources of Information."

Animals and Nature Study

Adventuring in Nature, Betty Price, Camp Fire Girls Publications
A First Book of Tree Identification, Matilda Rogers, Random House
Gardening: A New World for Children, Sally Wright, Macmillan
Let's Go Outdoors, Harriet E. Huntington, Doubleday
Let's Go to the Brook, Harriet E. Huntington, Doubleday
Let's Go to the Desert, Harriet E. Huntington, Doubleday
Let's Go to the Seashore, Harriet E. Huntington, Doubleday
Out of Doors in Autumn, Clarence J. Hylander, Macmillan
Out of Doors in Spring, Clarence J. Hylander, Macmillan
Out of Doors in Summer, Clarence J. Hylander, Macmillan
Out of Doors in Winter, Clarence J. Hylander, Macmillan
The Young Child Learns about Nature, Rhoda Bacmeister, Arts Co-operative Service

Science and the Young

Growing Up With Science, Marianne Besser, McGraw-Hill
Science for Children and Teachers, Association for Childhood Education International
Teaching Elementary Science, Bulletin No. 5, Federal Security Agency, Washington, D. C.
Young Scientists Takes a Ride, George Barr, Whittlesey House
Young Scientist Takes a Walk: Guide to Outdoor Observations, George Barr, Whittlesey House

Music

Children and Music: An Informal Guide for Parents and Teachers, Beatrice Landeck, William Sloane Associates
Children Discover Music and Dance, Emma D. Sheehy, Holt, Rinehart and Winston
How to Bring Up Your Child to Enjoy Music, Howard Taubman, Doubleday
How to Make and Play a Shepherd Pipe, Augustus D. Zanzig, National Recreation Association

Music for Family Fun, Harriet Buxton Barbour, E. P. Dutton
There's Music in Children, Emma D. Sheehy, Holt, Rinehart and Winston
The Young Child and His Music, Margaret Thorne, Arts Cooperative Service
Time for Music, Beatrice Landeck, Public Affairs Pamphlets

Art, and Arts and Crafts

Art Activities for the Very Young, Francis Louis Hoover, Davis Publications
Arts and Crafts for Primary Grade Children, Arthur S. Green, Denison
Arts and Crafts Series (manuals for recreation leaders), Frank Staples, National Recreation Association
Art for Children's Growing, Association for Childhood Education International
Children's Art, Miriam Lindstrom, University of California Press
Creative Activities, Rebecca Rice, Pilgrim
Creative Arts and Crafts Activities, Arthur S. Green, T. S. Denison
Creative Crafts for Children, Kenneth R. Benson, Prentice-Hall
Handcrafts Simplified, Martha Ruth Amon and Ruth Rawson (McKnight), Taplinger
The Young Child Uses Clay, Eileen S. Nelson, Arts Cooperative Service
Tools for Woodworking in the Elementary Schools, Sara L. Patrick, Arts Cooperative Service
Your Child and His Art: A Guide for Parents, Viktor Lowenfeld, Macmillan

Use of Waste Materials

Art from Scrap, Carl Reed and Joseph Orze, Davis Publications
10¢ Crafts for Kids, Jane Wardwell, Association Press

Do-It-Yourself Projects in Play Equipment

Home and Play Equipment for the Preschool Child, Publication No. 238, Federal Security Agency, Social Security Administration, Children's Bureau
Make Your Own Games, National Recreation Association

Games and Group Play

A Pocket Guide of Games and Rhythms for the Elementary School, Marjorie Latchaw, Prentice-Hall
All in Play: Adventures in Learning, Play School Association
Children's Games from Many Lands, Nina Millen, Friendship Press
Enjoy Your Children, Lucille E. Hein, Abingdon Press
Fun and Games, Margaret E. Mulac, Harper and Row
Games for All Ages and How to Use Them, Marjorie Wackerbarth and Lillian S. Graham, T. S. Denison

Play—Children's Business, Association for Childhood Education International

Trips and Camping

Activities for Summer Camps, Arts Cooperative Service
Better Homes and Gardens Family Camping Book, Meredith Publishing Co.
Summer Programs for Children Who Stay at Home, Play School Association
Trips for Children, Play School Association
You Can Take Them With You: A Guide to Traveling with Children in Europe, Viola Weingarten, E. P. Dutton
Your Family Goes Camping, Doris T. Patterson, Abingdon

To Help Insure a Good Start in the World of Books

A Parent's Guide to Children's Reading, Nancy Larrick, Doubleday and Co.
Adventuring With Books (a list for elementary grades), National Council of Teachers of English, 508 South 6th St., Champaign, Ill.
An Ample Field: Books and Young People, Amelia Munson, American Library Association, 50 East Huron St., Chicago 11, Ill.
Best Books for Children (revised annually), R. R. Bowker Co., 1180 Avenue of the Americas, New York 36
Bibliography of Books for Children, Association for Childhood Education International, 3615 Wisconsin Ave., N.W. Washington 16, D. C.
Books, Children and Men, Paul Hazard, The Horn Book, Inc., 585 Boylston St., Boston, Mass.
Books for Beginning Readers, Elizabeth Guilfoile, National Council of Teachers of English, 508 South 6th St., Champaign, Ill.
Books for the Teen Age (revised annually), The New York Public Library, Public Relations Office, Fifth Ave. at 42 St., New York 18
Books for You (senior high school), National Council of Teachers of English, 508 South 6th St., Champaign, Ill.
Books of the Year for Children and About Children, Parents and Family Life (issued annually), Child Study Association of America, 9 East 89 St., New York 28
Children and Books, May Hill Arbuthnot, Scott Foresman
Children's Books for $1.25 or Less, Association for Childhood Education International, 3615 Wisconsin Ave., N.W. Washington 16, D. C.
Children's Books Too Good to Miss, The Press of Western Reserve University, 2029 Adelbert Road, Cleveland 6, Ohio
Growing Up with Books (revised annually), R. R. Bowker, Co., 1180 Avenue of the Americas, New York 36

Growing Up With Science Books, R. R. Bowker Co., 1180 Avenue of the Americas, New York 36

Helping Your Child to Read Better, Robert M. Goldenson, Thomas Y. Crowell

Let's Read Together: Books for Family Enjoyment, National Congress of Parents and Teachers, 700 North Rush Street, Chicago 11, Ill.

Stories: A List of Stories to Tell and to Read Aloud, Augusta Baker, The New York Public Library, Public Relations Office, Fifth Avenue at 42 St., New York 18

The AAAS Science Book List for Children, American Association for the Advancement of Science, 1515 Massachusetts Avenue, N.W., Washington 5, D. C.

The Children's Bookshelf: A Parents' Guide to Good Books for Boys and Girls, prepared by The Child Study Association of America, Bantam Books

The Proof of the Pudding: What Children Read, Phyllis Fenner, John Day Co.

The Unreluctant Years: A Critical Approach to Children's Literature, Lillian H. Smith, American Library Association, 50 East Huron St., Chicago 11, Ill.

Treasury of Books for the Primary Grades, Mildred A. Dawson and Louise Pfeiffer, Chandler Publishing Co., 604 Mission St., San Francisco, California

Your Child's Reading Today, Josette Frank, Doubleday and Co.

Your Reading (junior high school) National Council of Teachers of English, 508 South 6th St., Champaign, Ill.

Helpful Magazines

Parents' Magazine (articles on photography, games, party ideas, home improvement, cooking, sewing, play, crafts, camps; reviews of records, movies, books)

Recreation (directed primarily to professionals, but contains useful articles for the layman)

The Horn Book Magazine (about children's books and reading, with articles by or about authors and illustrators in the field and book reviews)

ORGANIZATIONS PROMOTING LEISURE-TIME INTERESTS

(Write for descriptions of services, membership information, pamphlets.)

General Interests

Adult Education Association of the U.S.A., 743 N. Wabash Ave., Chicago 11, Ill.

Amateur Athletic Union of the United States, 233 Broadway, New York 7, N. Y.

American Automobile Association, 1712 G St., N.W., Washington 6, D. C.
American Women's Voluntary Services, 125 E. 65 St., New York 21, N. Y.
Association of the Junior Leagues of America, Waldorf-Astoria Hotel, Park Ave. and 50 St., New York 22, N. Y.
Boy Scouts of America, New Brunswick, N. J.
Camp Fire Girls, Inc., 65 Worth St., New York 13, N. Y.
Child Study Association of America, 9 East 89 St., New York 28, N. Y.
Community Chests and Councils of America, 345 E. 46 St., New York 17, N. Y.
Girl Scouts of America, 830 Third Avenue, New York 22, N. Y.
Hobby Guild of America, 550 Fifth Ave., New York 19, N. Y.
National Recreation Association, 8 W. 8 St., New York 11, N. Y.
Play Schools Association, Inc., 122 W. 57 St., New York 19, N. Y.
United Service Organization, 237 W. 52 St., New York 19, N. Y.
Young Men's Christian Association, 291 Broadway, New York 7, N. Y.
Young Women's Christian Association, 600 Lexington Ave., New York 22, N. Y.

Specific Interests

Academy of Model Aeronautics, 1025 Connecticut Ave., N.W., Washington 6, D. C.
Amateur Chamber Music Players, 15 W. 67 St., New York 23, N. Y.
American Camping Association, Bradford Woods, Martinsville, Ind.
American Contract Bridge League, 33 W. 60 St., New York 23, N. Y.
American Cryptogram Association, Apt. 2C, Oakwood Manor, Woodbury, N. J.
American Federation of Arts, 41 East 65 St., New York 21, N. Y.
American Federation of Film Societies, c/o Mrs. Carolyn Henig, 110-42 69 Ave., Forest Hills, N. Y.
American Forestry Association, 919 17 St., N.W., Washington 6, D. C.
American Kennel Club, 221 Park Avenue South, New York 16, N. Y.
American Library Association, 50 E. Huron St., Chicago 11, Ill.
American Museum of Natural History, Central Park West and 79 St., New York 24, N. Y.
American Nature Association, 1214 16 St., N.W., Washington 6, D. C.
American Numismatic Association, Box 577, Wichita, Kansas
American Numismatic Society, Broadway and 156 St., New York 32, N. Y.
American Philatelic Society, Box 800, State College, Penna.
American Press Association, 1102 W. Mesa Ave., Pueblo, Colo.
American Radio Relay League, 38 La Salle Road, West Hartford, Conn.
American Rose Society, 4048 Roselea Place, Columbus 14, Ohio
American Symphony Orchestra League, Box 164, Charleston, W. Va.
American Youth Hostels, 14 W. 8 St., New York 11, N. Y.

ORGANIZATIONS PROMOTING LEISURE-TIME INTERESTS 473

Antique Automobile Club of America, Post Box 98, Hyattsville, Md.; or c/o Fiscal Agent, Tradesmen's Bank & Trust Co., Broad and Chestnut Sts., Philadelphia 10, Penna.

Civitan International, 1525 Comer Bldg., Birmingham 3, Ala.

Educational Film Library Association, Inc., 250 W. 57 St., New York 19, N. Y.

Folk Arts Center, Inc., 11 Middagh St., Brooklyn 2, N. Y.

International Federation of Homing Pigeon Fanciers, Inc., 51 Carson Ave., Metuchen, N. J.

Limited Editions Club, 595 Madison Ave., New York 22, N. Y.

Model Yacht Racing Association of America, 11 Tunitas Lane, So. San Francisco, Calif.

Motion Picture Association of America, Inc., 522 Fifth Avenue, New York 22, N. Y. (35-mm. [theater size] films)

National Audubon Society, 1130 Fifth Ave., New York 28, N. Y.

National Federation of Music Clubs, Suite 1215, 600 South Michigan Avenue, Chicago 5, Ill.

National Federation of Stamp Clubs, 153 Waverly Place, New York, N. Y.

National Hot Rod Association, 5959 Hollywood Blvd., Hollywood, Calif.

National Model Railroad Association, Inc., Dept. D., Box 1238, Station C, Canton 8, Ohio

National Philatelic Society, 55 Harmon Ave., Painesville, Ohio

National Sculpture Society, 1083 Fifth Ave, New York 28, N. Y.

National Speleological Society, 125 Tapawingo Road, S.W., Vienna, Va.

Photographic Society of America, 2005 Walnut St., Philadelphia 3, Penna.

Science Clubs of America, 1719 N St. N.W., Washington 6, D. C.

Society for the Preservation and Encouragement of Barbershop Quartet Singing in America, 20619 Fenkel Ave., Detroit 23, Mich.

The Society of American Magicians, 93 Central St., Forestville, Conn.

Sports Car Club of America, P. O. Box 791, Westport, Conn.

National Sports Associations

Amateur Bicycle League of America, 4 Pauline Place, Middlesex, N. J.

Amateur Fencers League of America, 9 Sixty-Second St., West New York, N. J.

Amateur Hockey Association of the U. S., 2309 Boardwalk, Atlantic City, N. J.

Amateur Softball Association of the U. S., 11 Hill St., Room 201, Newark 2, N. J.

Amateur Trapshooting Association, Vandalia, Ohio

The American Alpine Club, 113 E. 90 St., New York 28, N. Y.

American Amateur Baseball Congress, P. O. Box 44, Battle Creek, Mich.

American Badminton Association, 905 South Los Robles Ave., Pasadena, Calif.
American Bowling Congress, 1572 E. Capitol Drive, Milwaukee 11, Wis.
American Camping Association, Bradford Woods, Martinsville, Ind.
American Horse Shows Association, 40 E. 54 St., New York 22, N. Y.
American Motorcycle Association, 106 Butis Ave., Columbus 8, Ohio
American Power Boat Association, 700 Canton Ave., Detroit 7, Mich.
American Shuffleboard Leagues, 533 Third St., Union City, N. J.
American Snowshoe Union, 198 Lisbon St., Lewiston, Maine
American Water Ski Association, 307 N. Michigan Ave., Chicago 1, Ill.
Bicycle Institute of America, 122 E. 42 St., New York 17, N. Y.
Field Hockey Association of America, 30 Wall St., New York 5, N. Y.
Horseshoe Pitchers Association of America, 15316 Cabell Ave., Bellflower, Calif.
International Game Fish Association, American Museum of Natural History, 79 St. and Central Park West, New York 24, N. Y.
Izaak Walton League of America, 31 N. State St., Chicago 2, Ill.
National Field Archery Association, Box 388, Redlands, Calif.
National Baseball Congress, Box 1420, Wichita, Kansas
National Bowling Council, 1420 New York Ave. N.W., Washington 5, D. C.
National Boxing Association, 1601 Cadillac Square Bldg., Detroit 26, Mich.
National Duck Pin Congress, 1420 New York Ave. N.W., Washington 5, D. C.
National Golf Foundation, 407 S. Dearborn St., Chicago 5, Ill.
National Rifle Association of America, 1600 Rhode Island Ave. N.W., Washington 6, D. C.
National Shuffleboard Association, Box 1371, St. Petersburg, Fla.
National Skeet Shooting Association, 3409 Oaklawn Ave., Suite 208, Dallas 19, Texas
National Ski Association of America, 1130 Sixteenth St., Denver 2, Colo.
National Softball-Basketball Congress, Box 2708, Phoenix, Ariz.
Outboard Boating Club of America, 307 N. Michigan Ave., Chicago 1, Ill.
Soaring Society of America, Box 71, Elmira, N. Y.
U. S. Amateur Roller Skating Association, 120 W. 42 St., New York 18, N. Y.
U. S. Figure Skating Association, 30 Huntington Ave., Boston 16, Mass.
U. S. Golf Association, 40 E. 38 St., New York 16, N. Y.
U. S. Handball Association, 505 N. Michigan Ave., Chicago 11, Ill.
U. S. Lawn Tennis Association, 120 Broadway, New York 5, N. Y.
U. S. Paddle Tennis Association, 301 E. 29 St., New York 16, N. Y.
U. S. Revolver Association, 59 Alvin St., Springfield, Mass.
U. S. Soccer Football Association, 320 Fifth Ave., New York 1, N. Y.
Woman's International Bowling Congress, 694 S. High St., Columbus, Ohio

GUIDE TO COMMUNITY SERVICE

A great many social services are dependent on volunteers, wholly or in part. Brief training courses—educational and enjoyable in themselves—are often required. To find jobs and projects that are needed and at the same time suited to your own interests and abilities, call your local Community Chests and Councils, Volunteer Bureau, Council of Social Agencies (or individual agencies), Junior League, Girl or Boy Scouts, P. T. A., hospital, Camp Fire, Red Cross. The following suggestions may start imaginations working.

Pre-Teens

Scrapbooks for shut-ins; favors for hospital trays; caroling at Christmas; packaging supplies for campaigns; clothing, book, magazine, eyeglass collections; pen pals; beautifying school grounds; poster-making for Fire Prevention Week, etc.; toy reconditioning; companionship for handicapped children; junior museum.

Teen-Agers

Library aide; museum aide; occupational therapy aide; child care aide (at day care center and day camps); ranger aide (forests); office aide in clinics, social agencies; Scout program aide; town clean-up; games leader at playground; physical therapy aide; recreation work at home for aged, convalescent home, home for handicapped children; toy workshop; home nursing aide; hospital assistant (help nurses, read aloud, deliver supplies, entertain children); clerical assistant (address envelopes, filing, etc.); campaign volunteer (poster work, deliver supplies, etc.).

Older Teen-Agers and Young Adults

Social service aides (assist medical social workers, group workers, occupational therapists, etc.); friendly visitors (visiting shut-ins, taking patients for treatment); hospital recreation; blood donor program; conducting children's theater; hospital library and gift shop; counselor at free camp; teaching arts and crafts to handicapped; Scout Den mother or father; home sewing for the needy; assisting in music therapy, recreation; beauty shop at mental hospital; coaching junior teams; Senior Canteen aide; nurse's aide; gray lady or gray man; tutoring shut-in children; receptionist at clinics, agencies; community music program; day care center assistant; P. T. A. committees; Lodge service work; work for improved sanitation, safety, summer play camp, library, etc.; excursions for the handicapped or aged; repairing, redecorating meeting places, recreation rooms etc.; homemaker service for the needy or sick; recording textbooks for blind; assistant in mental health clinic; servicemen's center aide; classes for aliens or new citizens; raising money for campaigns or social service through bazaars, auctions, theater parties, dances, fashion shows, rummage sales, thrift shops, concerts, concession booths at fairs, Christmas card sale, art exhibits, revues and plays; civil defense and disaster work.

Index

abilities of Fives, 129–130
activities:
  for boys and girls together, 183–184
  for Fives, 130–131
  for Fives not in school, 140–141
animal hobbies, books for (*see also* pets), 461–462
animals:
  books on, 433, 437 ff, 442–443, 446, 450
  magazines on, 467
art:
  books on, 460, 469
  reproductions for children's rooms, 428–432
arts and crafts (*see also* specific hobby), 385
  books on, 452–469
  magazines on, 467
"average" child, 2–3

babies:
  interest in, 121–122
  interest in origin of, 164
ballet, *see* dancing

baseball, 147, 180–181, 382
  books on, 453, 454, 463
  magazines on, 467
basketry, 244
bath play, 21, 31
battles, *see* fighting
behavior:
  with adults, Six's, 173
  characteristics:
    of Eights and Nines, 213
    of Fours, 89–90, 92
    of girls (Sevens), 182–183
    of Sevens, 175–180
    of Sixes, 144, 172–173
    of teen-agers, 256–257
    of Threes, 68–69
    of Twos, 39–40
  preadolescent, 230–231
bicycles, 148–149
birds, 166, 167–168
birth, interest in, 164
birthday parties, 65–66
block building, 74, 100–101, 134–135
blocks:
  for building, 32, 60
  for climbing, 30
  word, 375–376

block toys, 61
bookbinding, 244
  books on, 458
books, first-year, 21–22
books and stories:
  for Eights and Nines, 222, 444–452
  fairy tales (*see also* specific group), 137–138
  for Fives, 137–138, 435–444
  for Fours, 107–109, 435–437
  lists of, 432–464
  for Ones, 433
  for pre-teens, 252, 453–464
  for Sevens, 193–195, 440–452
  for Sixes, 158, 437–447
  for teen-agers, 267–270, 453–464
  for Threes, 80, 433–437
  for Twos, 35, 63–64, 433–435
brainstorming, 370–371
"buffets," 69–70
button play, 84–85

camping trips, 222, 274
  books on, 470
camps, summer, 189–190, 272–274
canteens (social centers), 258–261
cardboard craft, 244
card games, *see* games
carpentry, *see* woodworking
charades, 384
cheating, 149
chess, 385, 386
Christmas, 66, 86, 112
clay-modeling, 47–48, 77
  behavior during, 101–102
  technical details, 46, 119–120, 169, 200, 242
  value of, 50
climbing activities:
  of Fives, 128, 129

climbing activities (*Cont.*)
  of Fours, 91
climbing equipment, 30, 53
cliques, *see* group formations
clocks, 131
clothing, young child's attitude toward, 38
collages, 200, 201, 249
collections (*see also* hobbies), 163, 205–206, 216
comic books, 139, 160–161, 195–196, 224, 225, 252, 304–307
community recreation, 362
  books on, 465
  citizens' contributions to, 367–368
  facilities and programs, 363–367
community services, 276–278, 289–290
  books on, 465
  guide to, 475–476
concertgoing, 248
constructions (constructs), 200, 201
cooking:
  books on, 452, 459, 460
  by Fives, 142–143
  by teen-agers, 270–272
costumes, 74, 98, 124, 226, 332–333
counting, *see* numbers
cowboy and Indian play, 122–123
cradle gym, 12
crafts (*see also* hobbies; *also* various crafts by name), 129–131, 219–220, 226, 239–245
  books and pamphlets on, 452, 457–461, 469
criticism of others, by Sixes, 156–157
cutting-out play, 60, 85, 110

dancing:
  ballet and modern, 246–247

dancing (*Cont.*)
    books on, 460
    of Eights and Nines, 228–229
    of Fives, 136–137
    folk, 247
        books on, 460
    lessons, 107, 193
    of Sevens, 192–193
    for teen-agers, 265–266
death, interest in, 164
diary-keeping, 159–160
dioramas, 249–250
disorder of home surroundings, 123–124
doll houses, 125–127
dolls and doll play, 32, 43, 121, 123, 153–154
    boys' interest in, 121–122
dramatic play, *see* play, imaginative
dramatics, 226
    books on, 455–457
drawing, 34–35, 198–199, 226
    books on, 460–461
drumming, *see* music

Easter, 66, 86
emotions, managing children's, 68–69
entertainments, formal, 197
"exercises," 9–10
exploration trips, 93–95
extracurricular activities, 385–387
eye play, 11

fairy tales, *see* books and stories
family activities:
    with Fives, 141–142
    with Fours, 111–112
    with pre-teens, 377–384

family activities (*Cont.*)
    with Sevens, 211–212
    with Sixes, 174
    with teen-agers, 275, 384–386
father, children's relationships with, 210–211
Father's Day, 209
fears:
    of failure, 185–186
    of Sixes, 158–159
    stories to counter children's, 158–159
flowers:
    arranging, books on, 462
    growing, books on, 462, 468
    teen-age hobby, 383

games, 235–238, 369–389
    books on, 469–470
    card, 163, 206, 377, 389
    of chance, 371–372
    for Eights, 370 ff
    family, 142, 369–389
    for Fours and Fives, 375–377
    group:
        for Sevens, 186–189
        for Sixes, 150
    letter, 163
    logic, 373–374, 381–382
    mathematical, 381–382
    mental development and, 369–389
    for Nines, 370 ff
    noncompetitive, 129
    number, 163
    outdoor, 382–383
    for pre-teens, 377–384
    quiz, 378–379
    with rules, 169–170
    for Sevens, 206–207
    singing, 263

games (*Cont.*)
  for Sixes, 147, 162–163
  sources of information on, 469
  for teen-agers, 261–263, 384–386
  word, 375–376, 379–381
gang warfare, 176, 177
gardening, 83, 165, 335
  books on, 462, 468
  magazines on, 467
group formations:
  of Eights and Nines, 213–215
  management by parents, 75, 214–215
  rules of, 178–179
  of Sevens, 175–177
  of Sixes, 145, 146–148
  of Threes, 75
group play:
  management of:
    Fours', 89
    Twos', 37, 56–57
  of Sevens, 184–185
  sources of information on, 465–466, 469–470
  of Twos, 38, 54–57

Halloween, 86, 113
hammer and nails, *see* woodworking
handicapped, play activities for, 357–361
  books dealing with, 464
handicrafts, *see* crafts
handwork (general), 201–202
hearing, experiments with, 95
help by parents, *see* play
hobbies, 281–298, 383–384
  amusement, 294
  books on, 453–464
  check list of, 285–288
  collections, 295–296

hobbies (*Cont.*)
  crafts, 291–293, 383
  fishing, 297–298
  hiking, 296–297
  home repair, 296
  magazines on, 466–467
  newspaper, 384
  organizations promoting, 471–474
  pamphlets on, 453, 465
  photography, 294–295
  radio, 383–384
  sailing, 297
  science, 293, 383
  sources of information, 465–466
  study, 298, 386–387
home study courses, 386–387
housekeeping play, 36, 154

imaginative play, *see* play
insects and aquarium animals, 93, 165–167
intolerance, 176–177
invalids:
  play activities for, 349–357
    books dealing with, 464
  value of play for, 348–349

ladder-box, 53
language studies, 386
leather work, 244
leisure-time activities, organizations promoting, 471–474
letters, interest in, 132
limericks, 372
lipstick, 124

magazines:
  for children, 466–467

magazines (*Cont.*)
  helpful to parents and recreation leaders, 471
  for teens, 385, 466–467

magic:
  books on, 452, 456
  interest in, 203

make-up and manicure kits, 124, 155

management of play, *see* play

mass entertainments (*see also* motion pictures; radio; television):
  influence of, 299–300
  management of, by parents, 313–314

mathematics learned through play, 372, 377, 381–382, 385

meeting place, home as, 170–171

mental development, play and, 369–389

messy play, 34, 45–46, 52

metalwork, 243

mobiles, 11, 249, 292

model-making, 243

Mother's Day, 209

motion pictures, 196, 307–310

museum visiting, 250

music (*see also* records; singing):
  books and pamphlets on, 426, 461, 468–469
  drumming, 106, 191
  experiences in, 191, 245
  instruments for, 80–81, 106, 135–136, 161–162, 245
  making of, 80–82, 135–136, 161–162
  movements to, 64–65, 106, 107

musical toys, 35

music lessons, 192, 227–228

nail polish, 124

nature materials, for handicrafts, 205

nature study, 165–168, 221–222
  books and pamphlets on, 437, 440, 443, 446, 451–452, 461–462, 468

numbers, interest in, 131–132

nursery school:
  choosing a, 78–79
  value of, 77

outdoor equipment, *see* play-yard equipment

outings, 18, 29, 67, 142

painting:
  behavior during, 104–105
  books on, 460–461
  developments in, 133–134
  and drawing of:
    Eights and Nines, 226
    Sevens, 198 199
  equipment for, 50–51
  significance of, 51–52, 103
  of Sixes, 168–169
  value of, 76–77

paintings, display space for, 103

papier-mâché, 242–243

parents:
  dependence on, 174
  mental play shared, 370 ff

parties:
  for Sevens, 207–209
  for Sixes, 172–173
  for teen-agers, 264–265, 384

party clothes, 5

peg boards, 17, 25

pets, 83–84
  activities with, 320

pets (*Cont.*)
  books on, 461–462
  cats, 329–330
  choice of, 323–324
  dogs, 27–28, 327–329
  guide to, 324–330
  magazines on, 467
  value of, 315–319
photography, 294–295
  books and pamphlets on, 460, 467
pictures (reproductions) for children's rooms, 428–432
plants (*see also* gardening), 82–83
plastic, pieces for pictures, 60
plastic craft, 243
plasticene, 46
play (*see also* group formations; group plays):
  benefits to teen-agers of, 256–258, 384
  connected with arrival of new baby, 42–43
  imaginative, 40–43, 69–74, 114, 150–152, 184
  imitating life, 115–116
  mental development and, 369–389
  outdoor:
    for Fives, 128–129
    for pre-teens and teens, 382–383
  parental help in, 25, 37, 92, 147–148, 370 ff, 387
  parental management of Sixes, 170, 171–172
  personal problems worked out through, 96–98
  planning for, 4–5
  as preparation for feared visit, 74

play (*Cont.*)
  setting stage for mental, 387–388
  sex differentiation in, 95–96
  social, 14, 15, 18, 19–20, 27, 72–73
  useful, 119
  value of, 1–2, 3, 369 ff
play equipment, information on building, 405–419, 466, 469
play materials:
  home-found, 369–389, 393, 398, 469
  purchased in stores, 399–405
  sources of information on, 465–466
play space, 331–334
play-yard equipment, 33–34, 53–54, 91, 128–129, 334–336
  directions for building, 405–418, 466, 469
pottery, 200
prejudice, *see* intolerance
printing, 384
  books on, 457–459
privacy, child's need of, 85, 387
pull-toys, 32
puppets, 110–111, 155, 204, 244
  books on, 455–456
puzzles, 57, 58, 110, 206
  mental development and, 369–389
  for middle years, 377–382
  for young children, 370–374

quiet play, for Fives, 130–131

radio, 140–141, 160–161, 196, 224–225
  as hobby, 383–384

reading (*see also* books and stories):
  books, pamphlets, bulletins, and lists on, 470–471
  games, 375–376
  parental encouragement of, 223–224, 375
  of pre-teens, 251–252
reasoning stimulated by brain-teasers, 373–374, 376, 381 ff
reassurance, need for, 156
record-player, 64–65
records, phonograph, 35, 64–65, 81, 107, 136, 162, 227, 247–248, 310–312
  guides to, 426
  lists of, 419–426
  sources of, 426–427
recreation projects, sources of information on, 465–466
recreation room, *see* play space
reproductions, *see* pictures
responsibilities, rejection of, 152
rhythm bands, *see* music
riddles, books on (*see also* puzzles), 440, 452

safety measures, 20, 25, 30–31
salt dough (clay substitute), 102
sandbox play, 34, 77
science, experiments in, 82, 118–119, 218–219
scientific interests:
  books on, 454–455
  magazines for, 466
  pamphlets for, 468
Scouts, Boy, Girl, 216
screen, portable, 44
sewing, 130, 244–245
sex differences, curiosity about, 102

singing, 105, 191, 136, 226–227, 246
small-muscle play, 62, 84–85
smelling, experiments with, 94
social centers, *see* canteens
solitude, interest in, 145–146
song books, 81
  lists of, 427–428
sound sensations, 9
sports, 182, 220, 231–235
  books on, 463–464
  magazines on, 467
  national sports associations, 473–474
storage:
  directions for building units, 414–419
  of play materials, 337, 338–339
  of toys, 33, 44
stories (*see also* books and stories):
  improvised by Fives, 138–139
  improvised by parents to allay children's fears, 158–159
  improvised by Sevens, 195
stunts, 217–218

talk-sessions, teen-age, 266–267
tastes, preadolescent, 251
tasting, experiments with, 94
tattling, 149–150
teen-agers:
  community work by, 276–278, 475–476
  independent activities of, 275–276
  leisure activities of, 279–280, 384–387
television, 140–141, 160–161, 196–197, 224–225, 300–304
Thanksgiving, 66, 86, 113

theatricals (see also play, imaginative), books on, 455–457
time, parental managment of preteens', 253–255
toilet talk, 102
tools, see woodworking
touching, experiments with, 94
toys (see also play materials), 44, 62
   for bath, 21
   child's feeling for, 37
   group purchase of, 75
   household, 98–99
   household objects as, 16, 19, 22–23
   for infants, 10–11, 12–13, 14–15, 17, 19, 32
   for interest in letters, 133
   for interest in numbers, 131–132
   purchased in stores, 5–8, 398–405
   for quiet play, 109–110
   scale-model, 127–128
   for Sixes, 153
   storage of, 33, 44, 414–419
trading, 186

trains, 69, 99, 153
travel:
   by bus, 346–347
   by car, 344–346
   by train, 340–343
trips, 115–117
   follow-up activities, 117–118
   sources of information on, 470

Valentine's Day, 86, 113, 209

water play, 34, 45–46, 119
weaving, 130, 204, 243
   books on, 457 ff
wood-carving, 244
woodworking, 85, 120–121, 157–158
   books on, 457 ff
   tools for, 120, 156, 202–203
word games, 375–376
word play, 37–38
words, interest in, 79, 375–376
workshop, home, 337–338